Economic Reform in Developing Countries

GLOBAL DEVELOPMENT NETWORK

Series editor: George Mavrotas, *Chief Economist, Global Development Network*

Meeting the challenge of development in the contemporary age of globalization demands greater empirical knowledge. While most research emanates from the developed world, the Global Development Network series is designed to give voice to researchers from the developing and transition world – those experiencing first-hand the promises and pitfalls of development. This series presents the best examples of innovative and policy-relevant research from such diverse countries as Nigeria and China, India and Argentina, Russia and Egypt. It encompasses all major development topics ranging from the details of privatization and social safety nets to broad strategies to realize the Millennium Development Goals and achieve the greatest possible progress in developing countries.
  Titles in the series include:

Testing Global Interdependence
Issues on Trade, Aid, Migration and Development
Ernest Aryeetey and Natalia Dinello

Political Institutions and Development
Failed Expectations and Renewed Hopes
Edited by Natalia Dinello and Vladimir Popov

Economic Reform in Developing Countries
Reach, Range, Reason
Edited by José María Fanelli and Lyn Squire

Economic Reform in Developing Countries
Reach, Range, Reason

Edited by

José María Fanelli

Senior Professor of Macroeconomics, University of Buenos Aires, Argentina

Lyn Squire

Past President, Global Development Network, New Delhi, India

GLOBAL DEVELOPMENT NETWORK

Edward Elgar
Cheltenham, UK • Northampton, MA, USA

© José María Fanelli and Lyn Squire 2008

All rights reserved. No part of this publication may be reproduced, stored in a retrieval system or transmitted in any form or by any means, electronic, mechanical or photocopying, recording, or otherwise without the prior permission of the publisher.

Published by
Edward Elgar Publishing Limited
Glensanda House
Montpellier Parade
Cheltenham
Glos GL50 1UA
UK

Edward Elgar Publishing, Inc.
William Pratt House
9 Dewey Court
Northampton
Massachusetts 01060
USA

A catalogue record for this book
is available from the British Library

Library of Congress Control Number: 2008926567

ISBN 978 1 84720 248 2

Printed and bound in Great Britain by MPG Books Ltd, Bodmin, Cornwall

Contents

Notes on the Contributors	vii
Foreword: The Three Rs of Reform by Amartya Sen	xi
Introduction by José María Fanelli and Lyn Squire	xix
Acknowledgements	xxxv

	PART ONE: REACH: PERSON-CENTERED, EVENHANDED	1
1.	Economic Transition and Income Distribution in Hungary, 1987–2001 István György Tóth	3
2.	Socioeconomic Vulnerability and Trade Liberalization: Cross-Country Evidence in Central and Eastern Europe Pierluigi Montalbano, Alessandro Federici, Carlo Pietrobelli and Umberto Triulzi	35
3.	Market Failures in Human Development: The Intergenerational Poverty Trap in Mexico David Mayer-Foulkes	77
	PART TWO: RANGE: INSTITUTIONAL REFORM, POLICY CHANGE	115
4.	Government Policies and FDI Inflows of Asian Developing Countries: Empirical Evidence Rashmi Banga	117
5.	The Effect of Free-Trade Agreements on Foreign Direct Investment and Property Rights Protection Lorenza Martínez Trigueros and Roberto Romero Hidalgo	147

v

| 6. | Attending School, Reading, Writing and Child Work in Rural Ethiopia
Assefa Admassie and Arjun Singh Bedi | 185 |

PART THREE: REASON: STRATEGIES, NOT SLOGANS 227

7.	Declining Primary School Enrollment in Kenya *Arjun Singh Bedi, Paul K. Kimalu, Damiano Kulundu Manda and Nancy Nafula*	229
8.	Shock Therapy versus Gradualism Reconsidered: Lessons from Transition Economies *Vladimir Popov*	270
9.	Enhancing Income Opportunities for the Rural Poor: The Benefits of Rural Roads *Javier Escobal and Carmen Ponce*	307
10.	The Performance of State-Owned Enterprises and Newly Privatized Firms: Does Privatization Really Matter? *Mohammed Omran*	337

Index 365

Notes on the Contributors

ASSEFA ADMASSIE was an Associate Professor at the Addis Ababa University before he moved to his current position in 2004 as the Director of the Ethiopian Economic Policy Research Institute. He has also worked in various capacities at the Alemaya University and as a Senior Research Fellow at the Center for Development Research at the University of Bonn. Dr. Assefa Admassie received his Ph.D. degree from the University of Hohenhaim in Stuttgart-Germany. Together with his colleague Professor Arjun Bedi, Admassie won the Global Medal for Outstanding Research on Development in 2004.

RASHMI BANGA is currently an economist with the United Nations Conference on Trade and Development (UNCTAD-India Programme). She received her doctorate and Masters degrees from the Delhi School of Economics, India. She was an Associate Professor in the School of International Studies, Jawaharlal Nehru University (JNU), India. She has taught at Delhi University, Jesus and Mary College, for 15 years. She has also been a consultant for the Indian Council for Research in International Economic Relations (ICRIER) and has worked extensively on various trade and investment-related issues.

ARJUN SINGH BEDI is a Professor in the Economics of Development Group at the Institute of Social Studies in the Netherlands. He earned graduate degrees in Economics from Tulane University and has previously held appointments at the University of Bonn, National University of Ukraine and Columbia University. His research focuses on human capital and labor market issues in developing countries and more recently the link between economic reforms and socio-cultural practices in India.

JAVIER ESCOBAL is Research Director and Senior Researcher with the Group of Analysis for Development (GRADE) in Lima, Peru. His research focuses on rural development, poverty and equity issues, particularly the impact of the macroeconomic adjustment and structural reforms in the farming sector. He holds a doctorate in development economics from Wageningen University, the Netherlands.

JOSÉ MARÍA FANELLI is a Senior Researcher at the Center for the Study of the State and Society (CEDES) in Argentina. He holds a Ph.D. in economics from the University of Buenos Aires. He specializes in the analysis of macroeconomic and financial problems in developing countries and has been actively involved in the establishment of permanent research networks in the Latin American region.

ALESSANDRO FEDERICI received a Ph.D. in economics at the University of Rome 'La Sapienza' in Italy with a thesis on socioeconomic vulnerability. His research interests are econometrics, environmental economics and socioeconomic development and vulnerability. He is a Research Fellow at ENEA (Italian National Agency for New Technologies, Energy and the Environment) specializing on the topic of environmental and economic data analysis for sustainable energy planning and management.

DAVID MAYER-FOULKES has been a researcher in economics at the Centro de Investigación y Docencia Económicas in Mexico since 1991, and a visiting fellow at the Kiel Institute for the World Economy, Brown University and the University of California – Los Angeles. He has directed a series of research projects on the impact of health on economic growth for the Pan American Health Organization. Professor Mayer-Foulkes has won two Global Development Medals for Research on Development.

ROBERTO ROMERO HIDALGO works at the Research Department of Banco de México.

PAUL K. KIMALU is a researcher at the Kenya Institute for Public Policy Research and Analysis (KIPPRA), Nairobi, Kenya.

DAMIANO KULUNDU MANDA is a senior lecturer at the University of Nairobi School of Economics and a research associate at the Kenya Institute for Public Policy Research and Analysis (KIPPRA). He has an M.A. in Economics from the University of Nairobi, Kenya, and a doctorate from Gothnburg University, Sweden, where he studied development economics and specialized in labor economics.

PIERLUIGI MONTALBANO is Director of the International Economics and Political Economy program at the University of Cassino. He has doctorate in international economics from Sapienza University in Rome and the Graduate Institute of International Studies in Geneva. His research addresses international commerce, European integration, economic vulnerability and the macroeconomic relations among countries of various levels of development.

NANCY NAFULA holds B.A. and M.A. degrees in economics. She is currently working as a policy analyst at the Kenya Institute for Public Policy Research and Analysis (KIPPRA). She is also serving as a member of the governing council at the Kenya Institute for Education (K.I.E). Ms. Nafula, along with Paul Kimalu, Arjun Bedi and Damiano K. Manda, won second prize in the 2003 Global Development Network Research Medals competition.

MOHAMMED OMRAN is the Vice Chairman of the Cairo and Alexandria Stock Exchanges and Professor of Finance at the Arab Academy for Science and Technology. Professor Omran has been a visiting professor at the University of Plymouth, the University of Oklahoma, the World Bank, University of Laval and Vaasa University. He has served as an economist at both the Arab Monetary Fund in Abu Dhabi and the International Monetary Fund in Washington DC. He has received several research grants and prizes, a Fulbright fellowship, and he is a Research Fellow at the Economic Research Forum. He specializes in financial markets, corporate governance, corporate finance and privatization concentrating on the MENA region.

CARLO PIETROBELLI is Professor of Economics at the University of Roma Tre, where he directs the Center for Research on the Economics of Institutions (CREI). He has served as consultant and policy advisor to major international organizations such as the European Commission, the World Bank, the Inter-American Development Bank, and various UN agencies. His last book, *Upgrading to Compete: Global Value Chains, Clusters and SMEs in Latin America*, was published by Harvard University Press in 2007.

CARMEN PONCE teaches at Pontificia Universidad Católica del Perú and at the University of Texas at Austin. She earned an M.S. in economics from the University of Texas at Austin. Her areas of interest are poverty and equity, rural economics and development, and employment and labor markets.

VLADIMIR POPOV is a Professor at the New Economic School in Moscow, a sector head at the Academy of the National Economy in Moscow and Visiting Professor at Carleton University in Ottawa. In 1996–98 he was a Senior Research Fellow at the World Institute for Development Economics Research of the United Nations University (WIDER/UNU) in Helsinki, Finland, co-directing a project 'Transition Strategies, Alternatives and Outcomes'.

AMARTYA SEN is currently the Lamont University Professor at Harvard University and previously was Master of Trinity College of Cambridge University. Sen's work has focused on poverty, welfare economics and social choice theory. He was awarded the Nobel Prize for economics in 1998.

LYN SQUIRE was the first president of the Global Development Network. After gaining his Ph.D. from Cambridge University, he has spent his professional career at the World Bank. He has served as Chief Economist of the Middle East and North Africa Vice-Presidency, Director of the Research Department, and Director of the 1990 World Development Report on Poverty.

ISTVÁN GYÖRGY TÓTH is director of the Budapest-based TÁRKI Social Research Institute Inc., an independent applied social research company. He received his Ph.D. in Sociology in 2003 at Budapest Corvinus University, where he is also an adjunct professor. He has headed the Hungarian Household Panel Study and a number of other projects on income distribution and social policies. He has been consultant to various international organizations like the OECD and World Bank.

LORENZA MARTÍNEZ TRIGUEROS is a Senior Economist in the Research Department of Banco de México. Before joining the Central Bank of Mexico she worked at McKinsey and Co., and at the Ministry of Finance in Mexico. She holds a Ph.D. in economics from the Massachusetts Institute of Technology. Her research topics include monetary policy in Mexico, financial markets and property rights, financial crises, wage differentials and international trade and the costs of inflation.

UMBERTO TRIULZI is Professor of Political Economy at Sapienza University in Rome, and Scientific Director of the Institute for Relations between Italy and the Countries of Africa, Latin America and the Middle East (IPALMO). He is an advisor to the Italian Ministry of Foreign Affairs and a member of the Advisory Board of the Center for Economic and Law of the Markets, at Sapienza University.

Foreword: The Three Rs of Reform

Amartya Sen

The basic issue underlying any reform is simple enough. Some existing arrangements appear to us to be not right, and we want to put them right. When dealing with public institutions or policies, the central question, then, must be: How can we improve the institutions and policies which exist and make sure that they work better?

If there is a foundational issue to address here, it surely is the elementary fact that we cannot understand the requirements of reform without sorting out what social objectives and values should be promoted by public policy. It would be a great mistake to take reform to be some means-centered, goal-independent institutional requirement which 'must be' pursued (like the imperative to privatize or to balance the budget or to make users pay for the social services they receive) without asking any questions about how that institutional demand would influence the lives of the people involved. There may or may not be any payment-free lunch, but it would certainly be extremely odd to pursue ethics-free reform.

Let me illustrate the point by addressing a question which has been put to me by my friend, Lyn Squire, the president of the Global Development Network: 'What three factors would concern you most if you were charged with the task of initiating and implementing a major reform?' Let me start by trying to answer this question with telegraphic brevity. The three factors I would emphasize are: reach, range and reason – or more elaborately: (1) the reach of the results to be achieved, (2) the range of the ways and means to be used and (3) the reason for choosing the priorities we pursue. Let me elaborate the 'three Rs' one by one.

REACH: PERSON-CENTERED, EVENHANDED

Since there is no ethics-free reform, a central question to be addressed is: What kind of ethics should we have? Given the objectives of development, it is easy to see that the ethics involved must be person-centered as well as evenhanded.

It has to be 'person-centered' in the sense that it must not be divorced from the lives which people can lead and the real freedoms which they can enjoy. Development cannot be seen merely in terms of the enhancement of inanimate objects of convenience, such as merely raising the GNP (or even personal incomes). High economic growth would, of course, tend to be valuable – often crucially important – accomplishments. But its value must depend on what the size, composition and nature of that growth do to the lives and freedoms of the people involved. So the basic issue is not so much whether we end up having a high rate of economic growth (important as it undoubtedly is – through its causal connections), but what that growth – along with everything else happening in the economy – does for the people involved.

Further, the assessment has to be evenhanded, in the sense that it must not overlook the interests and freedoms of any group of people, particularly of those who are disadvantaged and downtrodden. The question which has to be persistently asked, while planning and implementing an economic reform, is what it is doing – directly or indirectly – to those who are at the bottom of the pyramid.[1]

It might be thought that all this is so obvious that it barely needs to be stated. But, I fear, that is not so. Indeed, the neglect of this basic understanding can be seen across the world. Let me illustrate the need for this person-centered, evenhanded perspective with an example from the experience of China – in many ways the most successful economic reformer in the world. One of the generally agreed understandings in applied development economics is China's remarkable success in introducing and cultivating markets and in making good use of the trading opportunities of the globalizing world. China's success has indeed been spectacular, and there is a tremendous amount that countries like India can learn from the open-minded way China has moved from being imprisoned in dogmas and red tape to become the fastest growing pragmatic economy in the world with massive economic expansion each year. If China was only a little ahead of India in terms of price-adjusted GNP or GDP per capita at the time of its economic reforms in 1979, it is immensely ahead now, despite the fact that India has also grown reasonably fast, on average, over these 25 years.

But what about the quality of life, represented, for example, by life expectancy at birth? There is quite an interesting story here. When, in the late 1940s, China had its revolution and India became independent, China and India had about the same life expectancy at birth, well below 40 years. But post-revolution China, with its egalitarian politics and continued public commitment to improve health care and education (a commitment which was carried over from its days of revolutionary struggle), brought a level of dedication to radically enhance schooling and health care which the more moderate Indian administration could not match. To be sure, China had the largest famine in history during 1958–61 (with close to 30 million deaths), when the so-called Great Leap Forward failed miserably. But China pulled out of that crisis soon enough. Also, the Chinese health care system, extensive and free as it was, had many problems, including a lack of quality care and much inefficiency. But there was still a general entitlement for all to some basic medical attention, irrespective of the ability to pay. As a consequence by 1979, when the economic reforms were introduced, China had a lead of about 14 years over India in longevity. Chinese life expectancy then was about 68 years, compared with India's 54 years – almost 15 years less.

Then came the economic reforms of 1979, with the Chinese economy surging ahead and growing much faster than India's more modest performance. However, despite China's much faster rate of economic growth, life expectancy in India has been growing three times as fast, on average, as that in China since 1979. China's life expectancy, which is now just about 71 years, compares with India's figure of 64 years, so that the life-expectancy gap in favor of China has been halved to seven years, over the last 25 years.

Of course, note must be taken of the fact that it gets increasingly harder to expand life expectancy further as the absolute level rises, and it could be argued that perhaps China might have now reached a level where further expansion would be exceptionally difficult. But this explanation does not work, since China's life expectancy of 71 years is still very far below the figures for many countries in the world, where the numbers stretch well into the 80s. Indeed, China's longevity is lower than some parts of India.

At the time of economic reforms, the Indian state of Kerala had a life expectancy similar to China's – about 67 years. By now, however, Kerala's life expectancy, which had already reached 74 years by 1995–99, is considerably above China's (the latest firm figure for China's life expectancy is 71 years for 2000). Even though Beijing and Shanghai, as city-provinces, outmatch the state of Kerala (with its 30 million rural and urban inhabitants), most provinces of China have life expectancy figures far lower than Kerala's.

Going further, if we look at specific points of vulnerability, the infant mortality rate in China has declined very slowly since the economic reforms, whereas it has continued to fall quite sharply in Kerala. While Kerala had roughly the same infant mortality rate as China – 37 per thousand – at the time of the Chinese reforms in 1979, Kerala's present rate, ten per thousand, reached by 2002, is one-third of China's 30 per thousand (where it has stagnated over the last decade).

There is clearly some problem with the 'reach' of the benefits of economic reform in China, despite its astounding rate of economic growth. There are three distinct problems of 'reach' here, to which any scrutinizing reformer must pay attention. First, even within the economic field, the poverty-removing character of Chinese economic expansion was much sharper in the early post-reform period than it is today. While the early reforms caused an astonishing jump in rural production and incomes, since the late 1980s the focus of growth has been much more urban, largely related to increasing global integration of China's industrial economy. It cannot, of course, be doubted that this global integration and the related expansion of urban incomes have brought a great many rewards to the Chinese people. And yet the poverty-reducing character of Chinese economic growth, while still quite firm, has relatively slackened. Furthermore, there has been a big surge in Chinese economic inequality, that is brought out by many empirical studies, including those by Ravi Kanbur and Xiaobo Zhang and by Azizur Rahman Khan and Carl Riskin.[2]

However, China's slow growth in life expectancy and stagnation in infant mortality are not the result only of the worsening reach of economic growth in particular. It also relates to the social and political reach of the reforms. So, the second factor to note is that along with the political change that ushered in the economic reforms came a slackened social commitment to public health care. It led, in particular, to the eschewal of free and universal health coverage which existed prior to the reforms, provided by the state or by the collectives or cooperatives, that also poured resources directly into public health care. Now individuals needed to buy private health insurance at their own cost (except in the small minority of cases where it is provided by the employer). Interestingly, this very retrograde movement in the coverage of health care received little public resistance – as it undoubtedly would have met in any multi-party democracy like India. Indeed, it is very hard to imagine that an established public facility of great value to people could be dispensed with so easily in a country where the opposition has a strong voice. The denial of that social facility certainly had a role in the slowing down of the progress of longevity in China.

Democracy also makes a direct contribution to health care by bringing social failures into public scrutiny. India's health services are quite terrible, as Jean Drèze and I discussed in some detail in our book, *India: Development and Participation*.[3] In December 2003, I had the dubious privilege of presenting in a news interview in Kolkata the depressing findings, related to parts of east India, of the first Health Report of the Pratichi Trust.[4] But the possibility of such intense criticism is, of course, also a social opportunity to make amends. Indeed, open and persistent reporting of the dreadful state of Indian health services is, ultimately, a source of India's dynamic strength.

The informational and incentive roles of democracy, working mainly through open public discussion, can be pivotally important for the reach of public policy. Even the Chinese famines of 1958–61 were directly fed by the absence of democratic elections and opposition parties and the nature of the censored media. But more recently, the fact that the sudden abandonment of free public health coverage and its replacement by privately purchasable insurance could be carried through with such meager discussion and debates, and with so little opposition, points to another glaring gap. There is also the comparative immunity from political criticism which Chinese health services tend to enjoy, that, too, can be linked to the lack of a multiparty system.

This limitation came sharply to attention in the context of the SARS (Severe Acute Respiratory Syndrome) epidemic in 2003. Although SARS cases first appeared in Southern China in November 2002 and caused many fatalities, information about this new deadly disease was kept strictly under a lid until April 2003. Indeed, it was only when that highly infectious disease started spreading to Hong Kong and Beijing that the news had to be released. By then the epidemic had already gone beyond the possibility of isolation and local elimination. The lack of open public discussion evidently played a critical role in the spread of the SARS epidemic. This is a small example, but the general penalty of the lack of transparency and public scrutiny can be very pervasive indeed.[5]

We have to be concerned with 'reach' in all its diverse forms, including economic reach, social reach and political reach. They are individually important and jointly momentous.

RANGE: INSTITUTIONAL REFORM AND POLICY CHANGE

I come now to range – the range of the ways and means we use. Here I can free ride to some extent on what has already been discussed in the context of reach. It is not only important to remember that the ends of institutional reform and policy change have to be 'person centered' and 'evenhanded', but also to recognize that the means to pursue those ends involve a variety of institutions – not just the invoking of a few magic bullets.

Consider the admiration for China which is a characteristic of many Indian discussions and for which there are excellent reasons in general. This, by the way, is not a new phenomenon. In the seventh century, when Yi Jing, the Chinese scholar, returned to China after spending ten years in India (studying in the Buddhist university in Nalanda but also traveling widely across the country), he asked the rhetorical question (with some evident satisfaction): 'Is there anyone in any of the five parts of India who does not admire China?'

The more recent admiration for China has tended to come in India in discrete lumps. There are those who greatly admire China's post-1979 use of reformed markets at home and abroad and link the lesson to be learned from China to the possibility of making intelligent use of markets. And there are others who greatly admire what China did in its pre-1979 period through radically expanding health care, basic education and social infrastructure, the benefits of which came in the form of enhanced living standards and human capabilities, including economic skills.

Which group is right? I would argue that they both are right in what they assert, and rather negligent in what they respectively ignore. India needs to learn from both parts of the momentous Chinese experience. The range of instruments has to cover, on the one hand, education, health care, building of infrastructure and land reforms and, on the other, intelligent use of domestic and global markets (rather than treating globalization as some kind of gigantic 'Jaws' which would gobble up the world). And, no less importantly, the range of instruments has to go well beyond the ground covered by the two lessons taken together. There is, in particular, the important contribution of democracy and the need to strengthen further our democratic practice.

The need for a wide 'range' relates to the fact that social changes are not only diverse, they also interrelate with each other in many different ways. To consider just one illustration, women's school education tends to have the most far-reaching effects on the lives and freedoms of all – women, men and children. There is much empirical evidence that women's literacy and schooling tend to (1) enhance the quality of women's lives, (2) reduce gender disparity in family decisions, (3) help the process of economic expansion, (4) reduce child mortality, (5) reduce gender bias in the mortality of children, (6) diminish fertility rates, (7) augment the education of all children through the influence of their mothers and (8) contribute to expanding the range and effectiveness of public debates. Similar interdependences can be seen in other areas of social change.

REASON: STRATEGIES, NOT SLOGANS

I come finally to the last of my three Rs – reason. Nothing, ultimately, is as important for reformers as the constant willingness to ask *why* exactly they are doing what they are doing. This is easier said than done. Recommendations for reform tend to come, alas, in the form of neat little slogans: 'open up the markets', 'get rid of the 'license Raj', 'education is the way forward', 'food first, then other things', 'fight corruption before anything else can happen', and so on. There often is considerable wisdom, not to mention energizing inspiration, in each of these mottos, but they are really battle *cries*, rather than battle *strategies*. An adequate program of reforms demands much more than aphorisms and epigrams. While we must aim at reach and must understand the need for range, the drawing up of policy packets requires detailed reasoning rather than being guided by piercing slogans.

Consider schooling. We certainly need more schools, including more elementary schools. But the problem of basic education is not only one of having enough schools. It is also a matter – just to give some examples – of the facilities which the schools have, the way the teachers work (whether they show up regularly, engage in teaching all children with needed care – rather than only the richer kids, preferably through private tuition), whether the parents – particularly poorer ones – have a voice in the functioning of the schools, whether the schools are safe and secure enough (especially for young girls), how the related problem of child under-nourishment affects learning and how the serving of cooked mid-day meals can be efficiently used for advancing both elementary education and basic nutrition of children. We also have to see what private schools can do and what happens to families who cannot afford such schools, and whether the private schools themselves would have adequate incentives to deliver education to the underdogs of society, even with a voucher system. There are a lot of details there, but the performance of the society and of the economy would depend, to a great extent, on reasoned assessment of precisely those details. The need to reason our way through them cannot be evaded by relying on some grand slogans or general-purpose maxims.

In his famous poem, Alfred Tennyson expressed much admiration for the 'light brigade' for following the noble principle of charging ahead without reason: 'Their's not to reason why, / Their's but to do and die'. That, I fear, won't do at all for economic or social change. Good reform is the charge of the heavy brigade. The 'reason why' is altogether central to the task.

NOTES

This is a slightly amended text of a talk given in January 2004 at the inaugural meeting of the Global Development Network in New Delhi.

1. This talk was given before the Indian general elections in May 2004, in which this issue proved to be especially critical in the downfall of the ruling Indian government. The rulers had to learn the hard way that a shining bellybutton did not a 'shining India' make.
2. See Ravi Kanbur and Xiaobo Zhang, 'Fifty Years of Regional Inequality in China: A Journey through Revolution, Reform and Openness'. Paper presented at the United Nations University World Institute for Development Economics (WIDER) conference 'Spatial Inequality in Asia', 28–29 March 2003; Azizur Rahman Khan and Carl Riskin, *Inequality and Poverty in China in the Age of Globalization*, New York: Oxford University Press, 2001.
3. Jean Drèze and Amartya Sen, *India: Development and Participation*, New York: Oxford University Press, 2002.
4. I established the Pratichi Trust with the Nobel Prize money that came my way some years ago.

5. To avoid any uncalled for smugness about the vigor of public discussion in India, I should mention that the attention paid to health care in debates and deliberations in the Indian media, although much greater than in China, is still far from adequate (see Drèze and Sen, *India: Development and Participation*). The special neglect of the rising epidemic of AIDS is a particular case in point. Much more can be done in India through the use of public reasoning on such issues, especially since we are unusually fortunate in having a very long argumentative tradition and in enjoying the great opportunities provided by a multiparty democracy and a comparatively free press. See Amartya Sen, *The Argumentative Indian: Writings on Indian History, Culture and Identity*, New York: Farrar, Straus and Giroux, 2005.

Introduction

José María Fanelli and Lyn Squire

Imagine that you have recently assumed the position in your government which has full responsibility for the implementation of your country's ambitious program of reform. Imagine further that at your very first press conference you are asked to list the three most crucial points that must be kept in mind when managing reform. What would you say?

This is not an easy question to handle at any time, and it is especially awkward at an initial press conference and when posed in such a precise form. On the other hand, we have all probably pondered at least some aspects of this question and can draw on experience of one kind or another to fashion a reply. Thus, the economists among us may well stress the importance of macroeconomic stability as their first and foremost point, followed by liberalization of key markets including trade and then by more complex reforms, including privatization, to improve incentives in key executing agencies. The economist, therefore, may worry about the key elements of policy and also about their appropriate sequencing. Of course, for every economist there may well be a different set of policies and a different sequence, but the focus will be very much on measures.

A political scientist confronted by the same question will take a different route. He may well give pride of place to forging a consensus within society prior to reform. His second point may be the importance of managing the distribution of costs and benefits of reform in relation to the distribution of political voice. And his third point may have to do with efforts to lock-in reform and prevent reversals. In other words, the points appearing in the political scientist's reply may be more process-oriented. If we next consult an institutional expert, we may learn that the first point to keep in mind is the fundamental importance of the rule of law, closely followed by the effectiveness and transparency of the agencies of central government and then their local and sectoral counterparts which will have much of the responsibility for implementing reform. In short, the emphasis would now be on, predictably, institutions in their various manifestations.

We could continue in this vein and garner more views from other disciplines and perspectives. All of the points emerging in this fashion are important in some sense and at some level, and yet none easily emerges as one of the three most crucial. The identification of three such points which would command a broad consensus is not to be found by sifting through the many plausible responses generated in this way. Instead, they must be sought at a more fundamental level, one that cuts across the different perspectives and identifies more basic points which should command the attention of the would-be reformer without question. In a speech to open the Fifth Annual Global Development Conference held in New Delhi in January 2004, Nobel Laureate Amartya Sen probed this question at such a deeper level. The three points emerging from his analysis are the subject of this volume.

Denoted the 'Three Rs', Sen identified Reach, Range and Reason as the key dimensions of reform. As its name suggests, *Reach* refers to the requirement that reform be inclusive. Sen emphasized two dimensions of inclusiveness: across all facets of society – not just economic, but political and social as well – and across all individuals in society, especially those at the 'bottom of the pyramid'. *Range* is to instruments as Reach is to ends. Consequently, the means to pursue the ends of reform inevitably involve many institutions and policies. Finally, *Reason*, which Sen considers to be the most important of the Three Rs, captures the absolute necessity of systematically and continuously asking why a particular reform has been selected or why a particular reform is being implemented.

While the Three Rs have been introduced separately (and will be treated separately in this volume for presentational reasons), they should be considered in unison to fully appreciate Sen's contribution. Thus, when illustrating how to use the Three Rs as criteria to assess reforms in the 'battlefield', Sen underlines two points: social changes create *interdependencies* among different political, economic and social dimensions, and the performance of the economy and society largely depend on the reasoned assessment of *details*. These points have two consequences: One, the reach and range of reforms cannot be defined independently of the context; and two, the constant scrutiny of the reason for reform must take into account the precise way in which specific reforms influence living standards and human capabilities. Therefore it is important to flesh out Sen's principles with empirical evidence concerning particular reform experiences. This volume undertakes that task.

Each chapter addresses particular aspects of the Three Rs in specific reform contexts. We have used Sen's construct as the organizing principle to group the chapters under three headings: Reach, Range and Reason. The ten chapters include cross-country studies of developing countries, as well as country-specific studies for Egypt, Ethiopia, Hungary, Kenya, Mexico and Peru. They also cover a diverse range of reforms including broad reforms, such as trade liberalization, privatization and even the transition process itself, in addition to far more narrowly defined ones dealing with rural roads, primary school enrolment, child labor, property rights and poverty traps. An important and distinctive characteristic of this volume, and indeed of all activities sponsored by the Global Development Network, is that the chapters are written primarily by researchers from the developing and transition worlds, yielding two advantages. First, the research is the work of those with genuine local knowledge of reform. Second, the research provides a perspective on reform from the developing and transition world. Their contributions are organized under the three headings as follows.

REACH: PERSON-CENTERED, EVENHANDED

Sen's notion of reach stresses the importance of the ethical foundations of any reform program. Reach refers to the coverage or breadth of the goals of reform and has two distinct but related elements. First, reform must be 'person-related' or people-centered. His basic example draws and builds on much of his previous work (Sen 1999). He notes that it is not sufficient to focus on economic growth, important though that may be. Other aspects of life – health, educational attainment, political rights and social inclusion – are also important both in their own right and, in many cases, as significant contributors to future growth in incomes (Stern, Dethier and Rogers 2005). Second, if reform is concerned with improving the lives and well-being of people, then it is only natural that the scope of reform should encompass all people: reform must also be inclusive. Inclusiveness obviously extends to all people, but it implies a particular emphasis on the poor since their needs are the greatest and often the most neglected. Reforms must, therefore, be designed and implemented in a manner that explicitly accounts for the poor.

Part One of the volume uses specific examples to explore Sen's two elements of reach. The chapters in this part establish two key points. First, reforms do indeed touch the lives of all people and do so in diverse and varied ways. This broad scope is patently obvious when the reform involves a major restructuring of society as has occurred in the transition economies and as illustrated in Chapter 1. This chapter, however, also reveals the many channels through which reform affects people's lives and in particular, the way in which human capital and demographic characteristics combine to influence outcomes. Furthermore, more specific reforms also have wide influence as the examples of trade liberalization (Chapter 2) and education (Chapter 3) reveal.

The chapters of Part One also reinforce Sen's concern with the poor in the context of reform. The poor may suffer disproportionately during systemic reform and may face barriers to their full participation in more specific reforms. Thus, during the course of major restructurings, societies may become more unequal (Chapter 1). Similarly, the major changes in relative prices and labor-market conditions which trade liberalization usually induces can have disproportionately negative effects on the well-being of the more vulnerable groups. The research findings presented in Chapter 2 suggest that this can create path-dependence to the extent that the harmful effects of trade liberalization can hinder the lower-income groups' ability to accumulate human capital. In other cases, poverty traps may prevent the poor from participating fully in programs designed to build human capital, thereby compromising their future prospects relative to those of richer members of society and limiting the success of reform (Chapter 3).

THE CASES

Sen uses relatively long periods of history, drawing on Chinese and Indian experiences to illustrate why it is important to be clear about the ethical foundations of reform. The point is simple: reforms inevitably have implications for many if not all members of society.

Inequality

In Chapter 1 István György Tóth continues in a similar vein, exploring the changes in inequality during the 'Great Transformation' in Hungary. He uses a decomposition analysis to examine the impact of three phases of transition (1987–92, 1992–96 and 1996–2001) on inequality. The analysis reveals that inequality increased especially during the first period; incomes became more dispersed at the top of the distribution mostly at the expense of a shrinking middle class and in contrast to a relatively stagnant position for the poorest. It also reveals the main factors influencing individual outcomes: labor market participation, location and human capital. Thus, a young individual with a higher education degree enjoyed many new opportunities in the labor market; but his older colleague, long-employed in one of the now-declining heavy industries, faced prolonged unemployment. Similarly, prospects for younger workers with low levels of education deteriorated. The chapter not only illustrates that reform affects all members of society, but also identifies the main channels, especially the important role of human capital, through which that effect is manifested.

Uncertainty

Chapter 2 introduces a factor which may have a significant influence on the reach of reform: uncertainty. The authors, Pierluigi Montalbano, Alessandro Federici, Carlo Pietrobelli and Umberto Triulzi focus on trade liberalization and underline that the economy has a very limited ability to cope with trade shocks, particularly 'extreme' shocks when financial markets are incomplete and institutions weak. Relying on an analysis of the experiences of Central and Eastern European countries with trade reform, the authors demonstrate that shocks arising from changes in the terms of trade and trade openness (proxied by their 'extreme volatility') reduce the resources which are available for private investment and consumption and disproportionately affect the poor. They argue that one important factor explaining this is the lack of appropriate policy tools to cope with or at least mitigate trade shocks and their repercussions on the domestic economy. The poor are particularly vulnerable, because they cannot access instruments to cope adequately with shocks. Vulnerability thus emerges as an important ingredient or dimension of Sen's concept of reach.

Their analysis also illustrates the importance of interdependencies in the reform process and has the following implications for the range of policies, a topic discussed in more detail in Part Two. First, trade reforms should be accompanied by policies which can cope with or mitigate any resulting negative impacts. Second, the 'coping mechanisms' which are available to the population should be improved. In particular, explicit or implicit insurance should be considered an important form of pro-poor expenditure. Third, the institutions which govern globalization should consider the need to limit the size and frequency of macroeconomic shocks. In this regard, the authors call for a new 'culture of prevention' at the international level.

Poverty Trap

Chapter 3, by David Mayer-Foulkes, provides one of the few empirical demonstrations available in the literature of the existence of a poverty trap which limits the accumulation of human capital by the poor. It then shows that the consequent low level of human capital among the poor has diminished the success of Mexico's reforms, including trade liberalization. The chapter demonstrates that increasing returns to education go untapped by many children in the population whose human capital decisions depend on their family situation and parental assets. As a result, the population classifies itself by educational status into two groups: one with completed lower secondary school or less; and one with 15 or more years of schooling. Since only the latter group realizes the benefits of increasing returns, the evidence supports the existence of a poverty trap in Mexico. The bulk of the population is unable to invest enough in nutrition and early schooling to benefit from the higher returns to higher education. While Sen's emphasis on reach tells us that reforms must embrace all, especially the poor, Mayer-Foulkes shows that this has not happened in an important sphere of person-centered development in Mexico. Indeed, he argues that past reforms have not had the range (see also Part Two) necessary to achieve the desired level of reach and that future reforms, if they are to reach the lower-income groups, will probably have to rely on public funds to break the poverty trap.

In sum, the chapters in Part One show that when reforms are assessed using Sen's criteria of being person-centered and inclusive, both the details of the context and the interdependence associated with social change matter. Pervasive financial market failures and policy-induced worsening in income distribution and in macroeconomic volatility can severely affect the reach of reform. They can perpetuate rather than weaken poverty traps and social vulnerability. The same interdependencies also become important when considering the range of reforms, the second of his Three Rs.

RANGE: INSTITUTIONAL REFORM, POLICY CHANGE

Range refers to the ways and means which are used to implement reform. Sen's approach to this issue has two distinctive features. First, reform should not be means-centered. Rather, reformers must take into account the way in which policies influence the lives of the people involved. This implies that, as with ends, means must also be people-related and evenhanded. Second, means are complex. They typically involve policy bundles and a cluster of institutions. This is a direct consequence of the fact that social changes are diverse and interrelate with each other in many different ways. From these two features it follows that interdependency and details will play a critical role not only in the design and selection of the range of instruments but also in their implementation. The three chapters in Part Two discuss a number of issues which must be considered when deciding the appropriate range of policies and show how failure to do so can lead to problems during implementation which can be critical in determining whether or not the expected results materialize.

All three chapters illustrate the central point that the range of reform almost always involves a combination of policies to deal with the interdependencies. Each chapter, however, illustrates a different aspect of this basic point. Thus, the range of policies may have to be different depending on the groups whose behavior the policy is meant to influence. One illustration of this is provided in

Chapter 4, that shows that there must be an appropriate combination of policies in order to influence the behavior of foreign investors (the basic point) but that the package must be tailored to meet the needs of different agents (in this case investors from developed countries and investors from developing ones). The appropriate combination of policies will also depend on the presence or absence of other policies or institutions as shown in Chapter 5. Also dealing with foreign direct investment, it illustrates the way in which trade agreements can offset the absence of secure property rights. The final chapter in this part illustrates how the interdependence between two different social spheres has important implications for the range of reform. In this case, the interaction between the social spheres of work and education jointly determines the outcome of reform designed to increase the participation of children in school: reforms are required in both spheres.

Foreign Investment

In Chapter 4, Rashmi Banga analyzes the range of policies that host governments in Asia are adopting to attract investors, as well as the role of regional investment agreements. The chapter addresses first the question of the effectiveness of selective government policies and investment agreements in attracting FDI into developing countries of Asia. It then explores whether investors from developed countries and developing ones respond similarly to the host governments' policies. Drawing on data on FDI inflows into 15 developing countries of Asia for between 1980–81 and 1999–2000, separate analyses are undertaken for FDI from developed countries and from developing ones.

The results highlight the importance of ensuring the mutual consistency of the policies implemented and of considering agents' diversity in order to ensure successful implementation. With regard to policy consistency, the authors show that to attract foreign investors, initiatives which improve economic fundamentals must be complemented with those which facilitate the operations of foreign firms. And with regard to the tailoring of policies to take into account investors' heterogeneity, the study finds that policies with respect to cost factors, e.g., lower tariff rates, tax concessions and tax holidays play an important role in attracting FDI from the developing countries, but these same policies may not attract FDI from developed ones. What matters more to FDI coming from developed countries are the policies which facilitate the business of foreign firms in the host country.

Trade Agreements

Lorenza Martínez Trigueros and Roberto Romero Hidalgo investigate how the appropriate range of policy has to be adjusted to fit the presence or absence of key institutions. In Chapter 5 they tackle this issue in the specific context of the interactions between secure property rights and investment, investigating the hypothesis that, beyond the effects on trade, the signing of a multilateral trade agreement can enhance FDI when property rights are not adequately protected. The study examines treaties which include the option of going through an international panel to resolve disputes under the hypothesis that this provides protection which might otherwise be missing or inadequate. After analyzing a 38-country panel, the authors conclude that signing a treaty has a positive overall effect on FDI flows and that the effect is greater in countries with weak property rights. The authors show how this has unfolded in the specific case of NAFTA, where the study finds that foreign investors make considerable use of the mechanism for dispute resolution and frequently win. They also note the possibility of positive spillover effects on domestic institutions.

Multiple Interventions

In Chapter 6 Admassie and Bedi argue that more than one intervention in different social spheres may be required to realize a particular goal. In their case, the goal is to encourage school participation by children, but the authors show that an exclusive focus on reforms relating to school cost and quality, the obvious and most direct points of intervention, may not be sufficient for the task at hand. They identify other policies, especially agricultural modernization, which exert an indirect effect on school participation by influencing the returns to child labor.

Using household data from Ethiopia, Admassie and Bedi provide fascinating insight into the beneficial and the harmful effects of child labor in the field and in the home. They show that beyond a certain threshold, 16 to 22 hours a week, child participation in the labor force, especially for herding, reduces school participation. They note that 60 per cent of the children in their sample work more than 16 hours a week. Policy changes with respect to school cost and quality do indeed affect school participation but do not influence child participation in the labor force. Other policies, however, particularly different types of agricultural modernization and the availability of agricultural machinery, do reduce the use of child labor. The authors conclude that efforts to improve educational outcomes must embrace not only educational reforms but also the effect of agricultural modernization, since the latter exerts a powerful influence on child labor force participation.

This chapter also illustrates a point to be developed further in Part Three. Sen emphasized the importance of reason, the need to constantly analyze and thoroughly assess what is being done. The Ethiopian example demonstrates this point. Admassie and Bedi show that a superficial examination of school participation and child labor suggests no trade-off. A more thorough analysis which specifically incorporates a non-linear relationship, however, demonstrates the presence of a trade-off after a certain threshold of hours worked. Had the analysis not been so thorough, this point would not have emerged and the negative consequence of labor force participation beyond the threshold on 60 per cent of Ethiopian children would have been missed. The importance of questioning the reason for reform systematically, as this example reveals, is examined further in Part Three.

REASON: STRATEGIES, NOT SLOGANS

Reason is Sen's most important dimension of reform and justifiably so. It refers to the need to constantly analyze and assess what is being done and what needs to be done. This involves understanding the intended reach or aim of reform, and it involves evaluating the range of instruments and policies. This evaluation, nonetheless, is not a task which a reform team can do in isolation. Evaluation must be conceived of as a complex process of social learning and the process must consider political factors. Complexity, in turn, requires – as Sen puts it – detailed reasoning about policy packages rather than slogans. The chapters in the last part of the volume address these dimensions of reason.

The reason for reform can be considered in both an ex-ante and an ex-post sense. Research can play a key role in the design of reform programs in several ways. It can provide a theoretical rationale for reform. It can provide important factual information which grounds the reform in the realities of local circumstances. And it can offer more sophisticated empirical analysis to establish the likely impact of reform in a statistically rigorous manner. Arguably, reform has the most convincing reason for its implementation when all three – appropriate theory, local information and empirical analysis – are brought to bear on the issue and point to the same conclusion.

In principle, assessing the impact of a reform involves comparing the well-being of individuals or households following the reform with their well-being had the reform not been implemented. Since the latter circumstance is never observed, any attempt to justify the reform is fraught with difficulty. In the physical sciences researchers identify two randomly selected groups – the control group and the treatment group. The latter is exposed to the new medicine, or whatever the experiment involves, while the control group is not.

A comparison between the two groups after the treatment provides an estimate of the impact of the treatment, because all other factors which could possibly affect the outcome have been held constant through the random selection of the members of each group. Conducting such experiments in the social sciences is rarely possible for both practical and ethical reasons. Social scientists, therefore, are obliged to develop innovative ways to 'construct' a control group that hopefully matches the target group in all respects other than impact of the treatment or reform.

None of the chapters in Part Three deals with the 'ex-ante' concept of reason in a strict sense, since all of them examine reforms which have already been implemented. Nevertheless, Chapter 7 illustrates the combined use of appropriate theory, local knowledge and empirical analysis – the principle of triangulation – in the context of ongoing educational reform in Kenya. Chapter 8 focuses on the experience of transition economies and sheds light on key initial conditions and the quality of institutions which should have been at the forefront of reform design. The final two chapters demonstrate the use of control groups to assess the reason for reform ex post. Thus, Chapter 9 provides an excellent example of such an effort applied to the evaluation of reforms in the rehabilitation of rural roads in Peru and Chapter 10, in an original analysis of privatization in Egypt, constructs a control group of state-owned enterprises (SOEs) against which to assess the performance of privatized firms.

In Chapter 7, Bedi, Kimalu, Manda and Nafula explore the reasoning behind recent educational reforms in Kenya. The chapter illustrates well the three key ingredients of a thorough assessment of the reason for reform: it provides a theoretical framework for analyzing the issue, it is grounded in local knowledge and it conducts a careful empirical investigation. In particular, it shows that the use of cross-section data suggests that school costs, a key element of the reforms, do not play a large role in determining enrollment. Had the analysts stopped here, the policymaker would conclude that the reforms had been well designed and that there was indeed good reason to continue them. But the authors extend the analysis in two important respects.

First, they switch to panel data (or more accurately pseudo-panel data comprising repeated cross-section data) which enables them to control for unobserved fixed effects. This adjustment reveals that school costs are in fact a significant deterrent to enrollment. Second, they extend the analysis to look at the effect of school costs for five per capita expenditure groups. Now it is evident that school costs have no impact on the richest quintile but affect enrollment in the other quintiles and especially the poorest. On the basis of this evidence, the Kenyan educational authorities may well be persuaded to reconsider the level of school costs, especially for the poor, or else devise ways of offsetting their negative impact on the ability of the poor to enroll their children in school. Education is one of the central elements of people-related reform but, to realize Sen's notion of reach, it also has to be inclusive. Extending the analysis to embrace the distributional effects of reform, as shown in this chapter, is essential for a thorough assessment of the reason for continuing a particular program or policy.

Looking at the outcome of reform in the transition economies, Popov (Chapter 8) calls attention to the fact that, following the collapse of the Berlin Wall in 1989 and the initiation of market reforms, economic performance in the post-communist states was disappointing. In Eastern Europe and the former Soviet Union output collapsed, inequality and the crime rate increased and life expectancy fell. He argues that it is not surprising that the question of the 'reason' to reform has been at center stage in the policy discussions in the post-reform period. His chapter tries to clarify why institutional and policy reforms in transition countries were unable to achieve their goals and provides a fresh perspective on the shock-versus-therapy dimension of the debate.

The chapter makes three contributions to the debate. First, differences in performance during the initial stage of transition (transformational recession) depend strongly on initial conditions – pre-transition levels of GDP per capita and distortions in industrial structure and external trade patterns. Second, the institutional capability of the state is a key determinant of post-reform performance. Market liberalization alone, when it is not complemented with strong institutions and macroeconomic stability, cannot ensure good performance. Hence, the evidence indicates that the conventional wisdom's emphasis on macroeconomic stability is justified, but its insistence on rapid liberalization is not. It follows that the debate about the speed of liberalization (shock therapy versus gradualism) was to a large extent misfocused, whereas the crucial importance of initial conditions and strong institutions for good performance was overlooked.

The third contribution relates to the interactions between institution building and the political regime. According to Popov's findings, institutional capability depends to a large extent on the combination of the rule of law and democracy. While the optimal combination is liberal democracy and firm rule of law, the illiberal democracies which appeared in a number of transition countries created an environment which was not conducive to building institutional capabilities and to enforcing government regulations. These conclusions are in line with Sen's view of the role of democracy in the process of reform. A multiparty democracy and a free press are central to guaranteeing transparency and public scrutiny. In this sense, democracy and political participation have become instrumental to the process of social learning, a process which is essential for the proper assessment of the reasons and outcomes of reform and, therefore, for ensuring that policymakers take into account the provisions that reforms must be people-related and evenhanded. That said, the chapter shows that democratization without a strong rule of law more often than not undermines institutions and contributes to disorder and poor economic performance.

Chapter 9, by Javier Escobal and Carmen Ponce, addresses directly the difficult question of 'constructing' a control group as a means of isolating the impact of a public intervention from other factors. This is a key instrument for analyzing the 'reason' for a particular intervention. Such careful evaluation can also be used to broadcast the benefits of particular programs to garner public support. Escobal and Ponce examine the benefits of a reform program intended to rehabilitate motorized and non-motorized rural roads in Peru. They use a technique known as propensity score matching in order to construct an appropriate control group of households.

The main result is that the rehabilitation of motorized roads increases household income but not consumption, because the increased income is invested in livestock. The results are smaller and not statistically significant for the rehabilitation of non-motorized roads. For those living near motorized roads, there was an increase in non-agricultural and agricultural wage income whereas the increase in non-agricultural wage income for those living by non-motorized roads was offset by a decline in non-agricultural self-employment (handicrafts, commerce). The difference may reflect the greater ownership of assets (education, land, public services) of households living near motorized roads. The chapter demonstrates how this approach to questioning the reason for a reform program can lead to clear signals for at least some redesign. While the analysis provides strong evidence that the rehabilitation of rural roads improves the welfare of the beneficiary population, the authors argue that the tendency of households living by motorized roads to increase savings rather than consumption suggests that they view the benefits as temporary. This is an implicit message to the authorities to provide adequate assurance that the roads will be maintained and to act on this. And the fact that households near non-motorized roads did not benefit to the same degree points to the need for complementary investments in education and other forms of public infrastructure. As always, the range of reforms plays a critical role.

Omran, in Chapter 10, also constructs a 'control' group to use in his assessment of privatization outcomes in Egypt. Unlike many studies which do not directly test the performance of privatized firms relative to SOEs, he compares the performance of Egyptian privatized and non-privatized firms using industry and firm size as the criteria to construct the two groups. The study examines the performance of 54 newly privatized Egyptian firms against a matching number of SOEs during the period 1994–98. The results of the test do not show a significant improvement in the performance of privatized firms relative to SOEs but rather an improvement in *both* the privatized firms and

SOEs relative to previous performance. The failure to detect an improvement in the privatized firms relative to the SOEs in the Egyptian case does not lead the author to conclude that policymakers should abandon privatization as a vehicle for economic development. Instead, Omran argues that the overall improvement in performance of both privatized firms and SOEs following privatization, appropriately managed, can increase competition and motivate private and public firms alike to better face future changes in the economic system. The study also suggests that interdependence matters to successful divestiture: A number of dimensions must be considered and reformers might need to shift their thinking away from an exclusive focus on ownership to consider the effects of market structure or the power of competition as well.

REFORM AND THE THREE Rs

The varied reform experiences analyzed in this volume constitute a representative sample of the complex problems that policymakers face on the 'battlefield' of reform in developing countries. One particularly important point to emerge is that the outcomes of reforms concerning reach and range can differ substantially from what countries expect because of the influence of initial conditions, idiosyncratic path-dependence effects, the institutional setting and political economy factors. Hence, if we take into account Sen's emphasis on the importance of details and interdependence, we should not be surprised by the frequently observed fact that similar reform initiatives taken in disparate contexts lead to widely different outcomes.

Indeed, this conclusion is in line with the research findings of a related project of the Global Development Network centered on 'Understanding Reform' (Fanelli and McMahon 2005). The main goal of this project is to improve our understanding of the market reforms undertaken by developing and transition countries in the last quarter century. Although the project focused on the market reform process as a whole rather than on specific reforms – as the cases analyzed in this volume mainly do – the conclusions are similar regarding the relevance of the details and the interdependencies associated with the national context, the institutional setting and the political economy. It is worth taking a brief look at such conclusions. To the extent that they refer to the process of market reform as a whole, they will help complement our concluding thoughts on the Three Rs, as well as situate them within a more comprehensive framework.

According to the Understanding Reform Project, the most relevant factors associated with the ability to undertake, sustain and achieve the reform goals have to do with:

1. The ability to deal with the uncertainty concerning policy outcomes. This means that the implementation stage is crucial. Typically important are macroeconomic disequilibria, political unrest and 'technical' problems such as bad sequencing, wrong speed, lobbying at the implementation stage or the lack of an efficient bureaucracy.
2. The intensity of distributional conflicts and social cleavages. Reforms have consequences for the distribution of wealth and political power; hence social, ethnic, regional and cultural cleavages matter in different ways in different contexts.
3. The quality of the state and the institutional setting. Successful states show greater ability to react rapidly and correctly to shocks, to make transfers so as to manage distributional conflicts, and to design and enforce the rules of the game. Unsatisfactory reforms frequently relate to phenomena such as state capture, patrimonialism, and poor regulatory frameworks.
4. The quality of the political system and civil society. This impinges on the ability to solve collective action problems and distributional conflicts, to build institutions, to foster collective learning and to undertake political transactions to insure the legitimacy of reforms.

When viewed in light of Sen's Three Rs, these conclusions have important implications. First, if details are essential, the blueprints for specific reforms cannot be mass-produced. The reach and the range of reforms must be carefully tailored to take into account initial conditions, the characteristics of the institutional setting and stakeholders and the constraints posed by political economy issues. To be sure, this does not mean that the design of reforms can overlook the 'sound' principles of economics and political science. It does, however, suggest that reforms should be context-informed in an essential way.

Second, if social and institutional changes are inherent to reforms and this creates interdependencies, the approach to reform must necessarily be interdisciplinary. From this point of view, the stylized answers about the crucial points of reforms given by economists, political scientists and institutional experts mentioned at the beginning of this introduction are all relevant. But this naturally raises the question of how to integrate these different approaches productively to design, implement and reform the reforms. Some of the most brilliant social scientists have closely scrutinized and analyzed the processes of reforms implemented during the last decades, and our knowledge has substantially improved as a result. We have new analytical tools and a number of context-informed stylized facts about reforms. However, a good part of this knowledge has been produced within the narrow boundaries of each discipline without much cross-fertilization. As a consequence, we still lack a unified view of the social change process. This suggests that investing in multidisciplinary cross-fertilization could pay off well in terms of improving our understanding of reform; reform which should be conceived of as a process of social change in which institutional, political and economic factors interact in complex and sometimes surprising ways.

Third, if reform outcomes can substantially differ from expectations concerning reach and range, it is crucial that we are prepared to 'reform the reforms'. This raises two further questions: How does society learn from experience and manage to put the lessons into practice? What should the criteria for reform of the reforms be?

Although the first question obviously seems urgent, there is scant literature which tackles the issue of how society 'learns'. The papers which analyze reform processes (including the ones in this volume) are full of sensible lessons, and there has been a remarkable analytical effort to model new phenomena, such as those associated with the political economy of reforms. Indeed, given that many countries have made highly visible design and implementation mistakes, one could argue that reformers could even learn from other countries' errors at no cost. However, more often than not, this has not been the case. Many countries have repeated the same mistakes. Hence, it seems that more research is needed on the mechanisms of social learning and, more specifically, on the way in which social consensus on values and norms is built and on the manner by which institutions and organizations of state 'learn'. Since civil society and state organizations do not read papers on reforms, we can hypothesize that learning will take the shape of transformations in social practices and values; changes in the rules of the game and governance structures; and in the allocation of society's resources to improve the functioning of institutions (understood as both players and the rules of the game).

Sen's approach is clear concerning the second question. The reform of reforms should be inherent to the process, because policymakers should constantly scrutinize the reasons for reform in light of the results concerning reach and range. We can take it for granted that technical economic questions – such as whether the reform process is macro-economically sustainable – as well as specific institutional or political issues – such as whether property rights and contracts are firmly enforced – will be part and parcel of the evaluation of the reason dimension. However, in Sen's view all these questions would be instrumental, rather than constitutive. The key question concerning reason is whether reforms are inclusive and person-related. This implies that to assess the reason to reform, policymakers must take into account a number of social facets, especially the consequences of reforms for those individuals that are at the 'bottom of the pyramid'. In this way, while Sen's Three Rs do not deny the importance of technical considerations, evenhandedness and person-relatedness naturally become organizing principles to reform the reforms.

The Three Rs approach to reforms is, of course, very demanding from the analytical point of view. The analysis of the reason dimension naturally calls for an interdisciplinary approach to the extent that evenhandedness and person-relatedness require an analysis which integrates the technical aspects associated with economics and institutions with the study of the effects in several 'domains' of the economy, society and polity. We may have a long way to go before we can confidently articulate reform technologies which do justice to the richness of Sen's approach. We believe, however, that the chapters in this volume have demonstrated convincingly that researchers and policymakers alike have nothing to gain by shirking this task, no matter how demanding.

BIBLIOGRAPHY

Fanelli, José M. and McMahon, Gary (eds) (2005), *Understanding Market Reforms*, New York: Palgrave Macmillan.
Sen, Amartya (1999), *Development as Freedom*, New York: Oxford University Press.
Stern, Nicholas, Jean-Jacques Dethier and F. Halsey Rogers (eds) (2005), *Making Development Happen*, Cambridge, MA: MIT Press.

Acknowledgements

This book is the result of the Global Development Network's efforts to promote policy-relevant social science research on development. Published as part of the GDN Series, it assembles papers from the Global Research Project entitled 'The Impact of Rich Countries' Policies on Poverty: Perspectives from the Developing World'. The editors and contributors to the book owe their gratitude to Isher Ahluwalia, Project Coordinator, for her outstanding management of the research, and to Ramona Angelescu, GDN's Senior Political Scientist, for her tireless efforts in support of this project. Their thanks also go to Ann Robertson, who was invaluable in supervising the copyediting process and preparing the text for publication. Finally, they are indebted to the staff of Edward Elgar Publishing Ltd, whose extraordinary receptivity and tactful advice make preparation of the GDN Series a continually rewarding experience.

PART ONE

Reach: Person-Centered, Evenhanded

1. Economic Transition and Income Distribution in Hungary, 1987–2001

István György Tóth

In his foreword to this book, Amartya Sen uses long periods of Chinese and Indian history to establish his argument that reform must be designed and evaluated on the basis of ethical foundations which emphasize people and inclusion. This chapter focuses on a much shorter period: Hungary's transition from socialism to capitalism, roughly from 1987 to 2001. The institutional coverage, however, is at least as broad as Sen's examples. The 'Great Transformation of Central and Eastern Europe', as János Kornai dubbed the era (2005), influenced all spheres of life, changed way people interact and reshaped the institutions of politics and economics. Since the particular effects of various single reform steps are difficult to isolate, it will not even be attempted here. Rather, I speak about 'reform' in very broad terms, meaning the complex set of transition processes leading from the state redistributive systems to a market economy.

Professor Sen argues that reform should bring something to the lives of people. It should bring improvements for all people, especially those at the bottom of society. Thus, economic reach should include effects on growth, poverty and inequality; social reach should embrace the spread, availability and quality of social services like health care and political reach should include the possibility of criticizing current government practices.

In this chapter I limit the argument to an analysis of economic reach, and I focus on income distribution and the poverty-alleviation effects of broad reforms in Hungary. As Sen predicted, reforms of this magnitude affect all classes of society but in different ways and to different degrees. Using the tools of statistical analysis, I identify structural changes in income distribution and attempt to locate factors affecting the chances of certain subgroups of falling to the 'bottom' of society. The focus is, however, not constrained to the poorest.

The significance of 'reach' cannot be understood in the abstract. The reach of certain policies (whether tax/transfer policies or institutions providing in-kind benefits) can be demonstrated by identifying real contributors or beneficiaries of certain institutional arrangements at a certain point of time. This sort of static incidence (a structure of gains/gainers and losses/losers), however, will require modification in the presence of a broader set of reforms or changes in the policy regime. The reach of a reform, therefore, is best revealed by tracing the incremental impact on all members of society between two separate policy regimes and by comparing the two ends of the process.

In the case of Hungary, the first regime case is socialism, characterized by very limited political freedoms, a shortage economy, merits awards based on loyalty, high levels of economic inefficiency, low productivity and permanent attempts to integrate with similarly inefficient regimes of the Soviet bloc. The second, post-transition regime engendered a much broader set of political freedoms, an almost full-fledged market economy, a greater role for prices as selection signals, more productivity and convergence to Western integration. The transition process affected a range of institutions and dismantled earlier barriers to open up the system and strengthen civil liberties.

The two regimes rewarded different portfolios of skills, resulting in a significant change in the composition of gainers and losers during the transition. It is not only average incomes but also the distribution and the composition of the social structure which changed. Reach will be measured by differential changes alongside basic characteristics such as age, education, employment, number of children and type of settlement. The analysis focuses on the level and dispersion of incomes by various subgroups defined by these dimensions. While the data range from 1962 to 2001, special focus is given to the transition period, defined as 1987 to 2001, and to several critical moments of the transition: 1987 (baseline), 1992 (deep recession), 1996 (austerity program) and 2001 (high GDP growth period).

DATA AND METHODS

Most of the results presented in this chapter are drawn from various household surveys carried out by the Budapest-based TARKI Social Research Institute during the 1990s. I used the cross-sectional and longitudinal datasets of the Hungarian Household Panel for 1992–97 and a cross-section of the TARKI Household Monitor for 1998–2001. In addition, the 1987 Income Survey of the Hungarian Central Statistical Office (KSH) is used as a baseline. All datasets are found in the TARKI Social Science Data Archive (www.tarki.hu). For benchmarks in general macro conditions, KSH census data from 1990 and 2001 are presented.

The fact that income is the central focus here is clearly a limitation. It is well understood that social inequalities between persons may be determined by the distribution of a number of non-income elements like in-kind social benefits, employment opportunities, power relations and symbolic goods. In addition, the relative role of these dimensions may change over time, and their explanatory power may decrease or increase accordingly. These circumstances are not analyzed here, due to space constraints.

The core of the analysis is based on yearly household incomes, a strategy which is good for smoothing out seasonal effects, but poorly captures the fact that households may be in different phases of their life cycles. As a result, the analysis mostly reflects temporary, rather than permanent, income changes. In addition, it uses cross sectional time series, rather than longitudinal panels to assess income changes. Other dimensions of the analysis rely on disposable household income and, for the labor market, the employed/self-employed/ entrepreneur individual. However, the ultimate distribution of income determining the life chances of persons is the result of sharing processes between persons living together, involving shelter, incomes, consumption etc. The basic unit of analysis is thus individuals in a household among whom the shares of consumption are assumed to be equal. This, of course, makes it necessary to adjust incomes for household size, taking into account the economies of scale related to living together and consumption sharing.

Given the availability of time series data since 1962, I present per capita incomes for the last four decades. However, since micro data are available for the period of the transition, there is no need to keep the per capita concept for welfare comparisons of households with various sizes. For the core analysis, therefore, a flatter equivalence scale with elasticity e = 0.73 is used. The choice of this comes from an earlier assessment of objective and subjective equivalence scales gained from consumption surveys, attitude surveys and policy instruments. Tóth (2005) and Förster and Tóth (1997, 1998) arrived at the conclusion that poverty threshold computations in the Hungarian social system are best assessed by this equivalence scale (known as the closest estimate to the 'old' OECD scale). The real importance of this comes when poverty rates will be computed at a later stage, and the choice of equivalence scale will primarily affect those distributional characteristics related to household size.[1]

As for inequality measurement, no really significant difference would arise by switching to per capita incomes or an even flatter equivalence scale like the square root of family size, as suggested by many studies in the international literature.[2] In addition to the percentile ratios, decile shares and Gini coefficients, two other classes of inequality measures are introduced for the rest of the chapter: Atkinson measures and four different indices from the Generalized Entropy (GE) class. All the old and new measures are sensitive to certain parts of the income distribution. For GE (α) measures, the higher α is, the more sensitive the measure is to changes in the upper tail of the income distribution. As for the Atkinson A (ε) measures, a higher ε will give stronger preference to relative income positions of the poor (see Appendix A1 for definitions of the inequality measures).

TRENDS IN AGGREGATE INEQUALITY

This section presents overall trends in inequality. First, long term fluctuations between 1962 and 2001 are presented, followed by a more detailed account for the period between 1987 and 2001.

Long-Run Income Distribution Trends

Hungary's per capita disposable incomes, the part of GDP accessible for households, registered a rapid increase in real terms between 1962 and 1972. Believing they could isolate the country from the effects of the downturn of the world economy at the beginning of the 1970s, leaders delayed structural adjustments in macroeconomic policies, letting real incomes grow beginning in 1972 and continuing until 1987, a period of explicit stagnation in GDP. This pattern of growth led to Hungary's serious foreign indebtedness. This, in turn, meant that the unavoidable transformational recession (due to structural adjustments, trade structure collapse and institutional reforms, see Kornai 1994), was deeper than expected, and macroeconomic balances were on the edge at the moment political reforms began in 1989 and 1990.

In 1990, the freely elected government of József Antall chose a combined strategy of radicalism and gradualism. Radical strategies in economic restructuring (relatively fast privatization policies, stringent bankruptcy laws and withdrawal of the state from economic interventions) were accompanied by gradualist and sometimes hesitant social policy reforms (slow adjustments in pensions and health policies, spreading social benefits to a larger clientele, rather than targeting the needy). An austerity package to get macroeconomic balances back on a sustainable track had to wait until 1995, implemented by the socialist government elected in 1994 (Bokros and Dethier 1998). This package, containing devaluation of the national currency and some real and symbolic social expenditure cuts, however, has led to a reversal of inflation trends, resulting in further sharp decreases in real incomes in the middle of the 1990s. As GDP stagnation (rather than contraction) had already begun in the second half of 1993, this austerity package has contributed to opening the way for relatively strong economic growth between 1998 and 2001. This was further boosted by pro-growth and pro-employment policies of the conservative government of the era. In terms of social policies, this period was characterized by tax-based incentives rather than cash handouts, and by strengthening state pension and health policies rather than further privatizing and cutting social expenditures.

During the period under study, male and female employment rates have shown drastically different patterns. Due to the expansion and maturation of the pension system during the 1950s and the 1970s, male employment rates showed a continuous decrease during the second half of the last century. The growth of female employment was able to overcompensate for that decline until the beginning of the 1980s. Since then, employment for both sexes started to fall, first gradually, then a sharp contraction followed between 1987 and 1996 as a consequence of economic restructuring. As a result of complex factors (e.g., the inherited age and skill composition of the labor force, slow or non-existent adjustments in adult training facilities and counter-incentives created by employment, social and pension policies) there was no significant recovery in employment even in the period of relatively fast economic growth between 1998 and 2001.

In general, trends in income dispersion (as measured by per capita income decile ratios of the uppermost and lowermost deciles of persons) can be divided into distinct periods. Between 1962 and 1982, there was a declining trend of income inequalities, with a local jump in 1972. The general trend may be the result of economic growth in the period, paralleled by continuous efforts of the communist governments to present their success in achieving their basic commitments towards equality. However, this must be understood within the context of a communist system. The communist system's shortage economy, relatively smaller role of money in social inequalities, and the high level of in-kind provisions with rationing techniques had debatable and controversial effects on overall inequalities. The jump in 1972 may be attributed to possible results of some short-lived economic reforms at the end of the 1960s. As mounting foreign debt around 1980 kept the governments under pressure, some economic liberalisation started in the early 1980s. New forms of private incentives were allowed (while the basic economic structure remained untouched), a gradual withdrawal of in-kind provisions started and these together led to an increasing trend in inequality between 1982 and 1987. A relatively large increase in income dispersion took place between 1987 and 1992, followed by a slower increase between 1992 and 1996 and a levelling off between 1996 and 2001.

From the analysis of the internal distribution (which is not particularly easy for the early years as no micro datasets are available), it seems that the change in income distribution in most periods was driven by changes in the relative income position of those at the extreme income deciles. A hint for this may be that drops in the Gini coefficient (a measure relatively less sensitive to changes

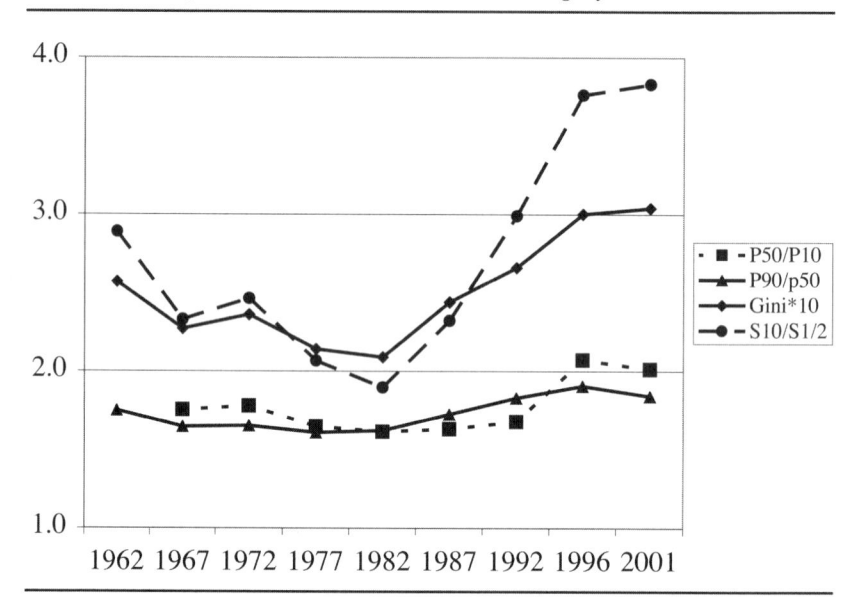

Figure 1.1 Some Inequality Measures for Personal Distribution of Per Capita Net Household Incomes in Hungary, 1962–2001

Source: For 1962–82: Atkinson and Micklewright (1992, Table HI1); for 1987: CSO Income Survey; for 1992 and 1996: Hungarian Household Panel (B), for 2001: TÁRKI Household Monitor, author's calculations.

at the two ends of the income distribution) are milder and jumps are smoother than those for decile ratios (see Figure 1.1).[3] That is, when there is a period of general decline in inequalities, the trend seems more pronounced when measured by decile shares than when measured by Gini coefficients, while in periods of increase jumps seem steeper if measured by decile ratios. The share of the uppermost decile from total incomes shrank between 1962 and 1982 (with a slight drop in 1972), followed by a significant increase until 1996. The share of the poor (the lowermost decile) has shown an opposite pattern, while the share of the middle-income decile has shown consistent monotonic shrinking (see Figure 1.2).

The percentile ratios (less vulnerable to extreme values at the two ends of small sample distributions) show that the period between 1982 and 1992 witnessed an increase in the distance between the uppermost decile and the median, while the distance between the median and the lowest decile changed only a little (that is, the 'rich got richer' argument would find support here, provided it is also confirmed by longitudinal data). In 1992–96, the distance between the middle classes and the poor increased, and the trend in subsequent

Economic Transition and Income Distribution in Hungary, 1987–2001 9

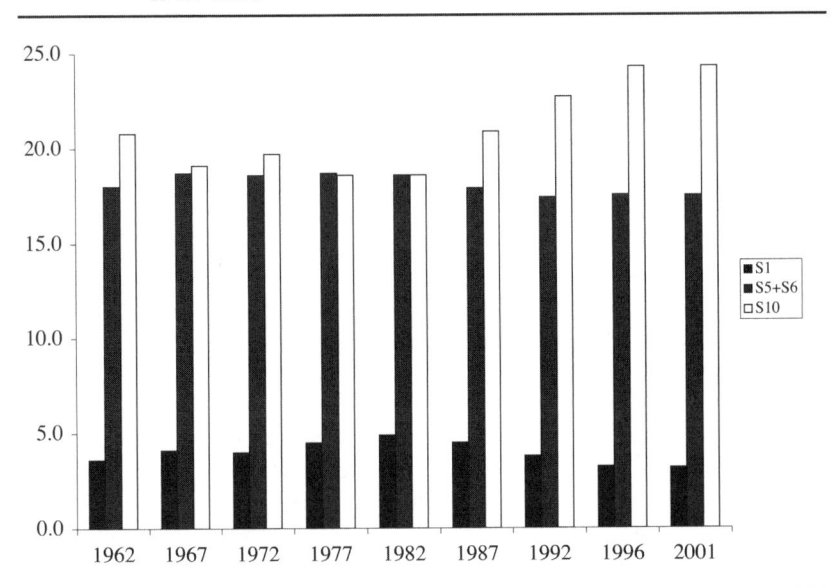

Figure 1.2 Shares of Selected Per Capita Income Deciles from Total Incomes 1962–2001

[Bar chart showing S1, S5+S6, and S10 shares for years 1962, 1967, 1972, 1977, 1982, 1987, 1992, 1996, 2001]

Source: For 1962–82: Atkinson and Micklewright (1992, Table HI1); for 1987: CSO Income Survey; for 1992 and 1996: Hungarian Household Panel (B), for 2001: TÁRKI Household Monitor, author's calculations.

years was, on average, still one of decline or stagnation in real incomes. Thus the 'poor got poorer' argument may find some support here. There is an interesting phenomenon in the last period, as well. As both the P90/P50 and the P50/P10 decile ratios have decreased, while the decile ratio (even if just a little) increased, one might suspect again that the important shift in the income distribution has happened within the extreme deciles rather than between them.

From these trends it could be concluded that, depending on which measure is chosen and which period is observed, the reforms favored the poorest in certain periods and favored the rich in others. Over the long term, the position of the lowermost deciles first improved then deteriorated. However, is worth taking a closer look at the transition years.

Income Dispersion in the Transition Period, 1987–2001

The three periods of the transition are defined by four dates. The baseline is 1987, one of the final years of the socialist regime. That year is still characterized by a shortage economy, tax reforms are about to be introduced in 1988, state firms still dominate economic activity and regulations on private involvement pose high entry barriers in most markets, while there is a high degree of uncertainty for most investments. In political terms it is still uncertain how things will develop, although there are clear signs of political change in the air. In economic terms, it is becoming clearer that at least a reform of the general government expenditures seems inevitable. Finally, this is the year of the last-available, pre-transition KSH income surveys.

The second data point is 1992, with a reference year of April 1991–March 1992, the deepest point of the transition shock. Inflation is at its highest level during the transition (35 per cent in 1991 and 23 per cent in 1992), unemployment is also on the rise (just approaching 13 per cent in February 1993) while the worst contractions in the labor markets are already over (a loss of some 1 million jobs since the second half of the 1980s).

The third data point is 1996, with a reference year April 1995–March 1996. This period is characterized by the Bokros package, the austerity measure named after Lajos Bokros, the finance minister in 1995 and 1996. From the viewpoint of income distribution, the Bokros reform had an immediate effect on real incomes (a decline of 5 per cent), no change in unemployment rates (steady at 10 per cent), and a surge in inflation (from 18 per cent in 1994 to 28 per cent in 1995 and 23 per cent in 1996).

By the fourth data point, 2001, referring to the 12 months between April 2000 and March 2001, the country had experienced a period of 4–5 per cent GDP growth in the previous four years, the annual unemployment rate was down to around 6 per cent and there is real wage growth (some 2 per cent in 1999 and 2000, above 6 per cent in 2001).

The various measures based on equivalent incomes show trends similar to those based on per capita incomes (see Table 1.1). Income inequalities had been increasing at a slower rate during the three consecutive periods. Between 1987 and 1992, all measures (except for P50/P10) show a significant inequality increase (for the difference between the middle class and the poor, the only period when a significant change happened is 1992 to 1996.) This may indicate that, even in a period of large inequality increase, the relative position of the middle class and of the poor did not change. In other words, the initial inequality increase in the beginning years of the transition brought about a relative position gain for the upper classes. In the 1992–96 period, the inequality increase was smaller but also significant for each measure, except for P90/P10, meaning that the gap between upper and middle classes did not widen further in these years.[4] However, from measures of the same class, those that are more sensitive to changes in the upper tail show a greater increase in this period.[5] Finally, the measures are more controversial for the period between 1996 and 2001. Each

Table 1.1 Some Basic Measures of the Distribution of Personal Equivalent (e = 0.73) Incomes in Hungary, 1987–2001

	1987	1992	1996	2001	92/87 (%)	96/92 (%)	01/96 (%)
Panel A: upper-tail sensitivity							
P90/P50	1.69	1.86	1.90	1.92	10.0	2.6	0.7
GE(2)	0.116	0.168	0.236	0.187	45.4	40.3	−21.0
A(0.5)	0.046	0.059	0.071	0.070	29.0	20.4	−1.5
Panel B: middle-tail sensitivity							
P90/P10	2.8	3.1	3.6	3.5	12.0	13.2	−0.3
GE(0)	0.092	0.119	0.143	0.145	29.9	19.7	1.8
GE(1)	0.097	0.127	0.156	0.148	31.7	23.0	−5.2
Gini	0.236	0.263	0.290	0.290	11.5	10.3	0.0
A(1)	0.088	0.112	0.133	0.135	28.1	18.3	1.7
Panel C: lower-tail sensitivity							
P50/P10	0.60	0.59	0.54	0.54	−1.8	−9.5	1.1
GE(−1)	0.098	0.140	0.161	0.199	42.7	15.3	23.7
A(2)	0.164	0.219	0.244	0.285	33.3	11.6	17.0

Source: 1987: KSH Income Survey, 1992, 1996: HHP (B), 2001: Tárki Household Monitor.

of the middle-income-sensitive measures signal an insignificant variation, while the negative signs of change in GE(2) and A(0.5) and the positive signs of GE(−1) and A(2) warrant a change underneath. It seems that an increase in inequality as a result of a relative decline in the position of the poorest did not manifest itself in the middle-income-sensitive measures of inequality, because losses for (or of) the richest 'compensated' for that.

Inequalities increased significantly in the first period of the transition, especially between 1987 and 1992. Then a peak was reached, followed by a leveling off. This occurred well after the market stabilization and the start of a relatively stable growth period (predicted by Coricelli 1997 and documented by others like Milanovic (1998, 1999) and Flemming and Micklewright 1999). If this is the case, the locus for Hungary (and Poland, but not Russia) may be suspected to approach the local maximum of the Kuznets curve (Hölscher 2001).

Although it may be suspected that income positions and well-being for some groups of society have deteriorated, other groups registered an increase during the period. Taking the Rawlsian maximin as a basis for evaluation (focusing on only the 'bottom of society'), the overall situation seems to be deteriorating. However, it is important to stress that from cross-section data alone it is impossible to say whether the deteriorating situation of a certain income bracket would mean a worsening only at the group level or also at the level of the individual. This would only be possible on the basis of a longitudinal study. Furthermore, applying the Rawlsian judgement as a one-shot measure (to compare ex ante and ex post indicators of well-being) would ignore the issue of the sustainability of the starting regime. This, certainly, would mean an oversimplification and a counterfactual with unacceptable preconditions.

Thus the above trends resulted in a different structure of income positions for different social groups that, in turn, resulted in a differential outcome of reforms within the various dimensions. The overall outcome, on balance, may be positive or negative. The next questions to consider are how the outcome of the reforms was spread across the various target groups and whether this led to a greater degree of sustainability of the whole system.

DIFFERENTIAL REACH OF REFORMS: EXPLAINING THE STRUCTURE OF INEQUALITIES

This section analyzes of internal changes in income distribution using a method for the decomposition by population subgroup, followed by a summary of empirical results with special emphasis on structural changes in the age/income dimension.

Methods of Decomposition by Population Subgroups

Overall inequalities (if measured by properly chosen indices) can always be decomposed into within-group and between-group inequalities, where 'group' means a category of society defined by a value of a certain dimension. Figures 1.3 and 1.4 illustrate the logic of the analysis. In Figure 1.3 the personal distribution of equivalent incomes is shown for the two end-years of the observed period, 1987 and 2001. All incomes are normalized to the mean, therefore shifts in the distribution can be attributed purely to the effects of inequality change (and effects of high inflation on real changes are eliminated), but the figure does not mention absolute levels of incomes. The distribution in 2001 shows greater inequality as the density function is flatter, skewed to the right more than in 1987. However, this overall picture might be the result of multiple internal changes.

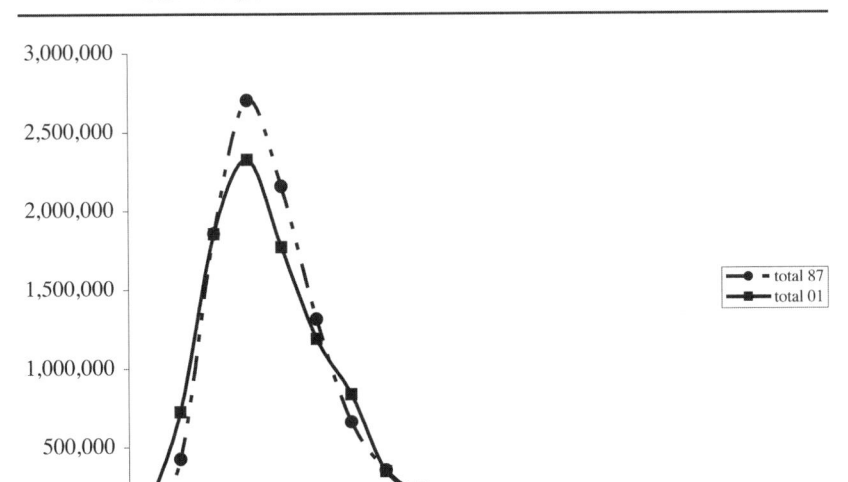

*Figure 1.3 Personal Distribution of Equivalent (e = 0.73) Incomes,
Normalized to the Mean*

Broken down by various dimensions (the figure uses settlement type), changes seem more prevalent. Taking a look at the individual years in Figure 1.4 separately, the overall distribution can be understood as a sum of within-group inequalities for the three subgroups (e.g., among Budapest citizens, among villagers and among those living in cities) and among the three subgroups (village, city and capital inhabitants). This is a static decomposition by subgroups. Comparing the two years with each other, in addition to differences of subgroup means (illustrated by distances of mean values of the subpopulations) and to differences of within-group inequalities (illustrated by the shape of the individual subgroup density functions), a third component comes into the picture, the structural differences within the two overall distributions (illustrated by the relative sizes of areas below the subgroup density functions).[6] The change of inequalities will be shown as a sum of inequality change attributable to changes in these three components in dynamic decomposition (see Appendix 1A for further explanation).

Change in the Size of Population Subgroups

For the decomposition and for the later analyses, I analyze inequalities in three macro-structural dimensions (labor market attachment, education of the head

14   *Economic Reform in Developing Countries*

Figure 1.4   Personal Distribution of Equivalent (e = 0.73) Incomes, Normalized to the Mean, Density Functions by Settlement Type

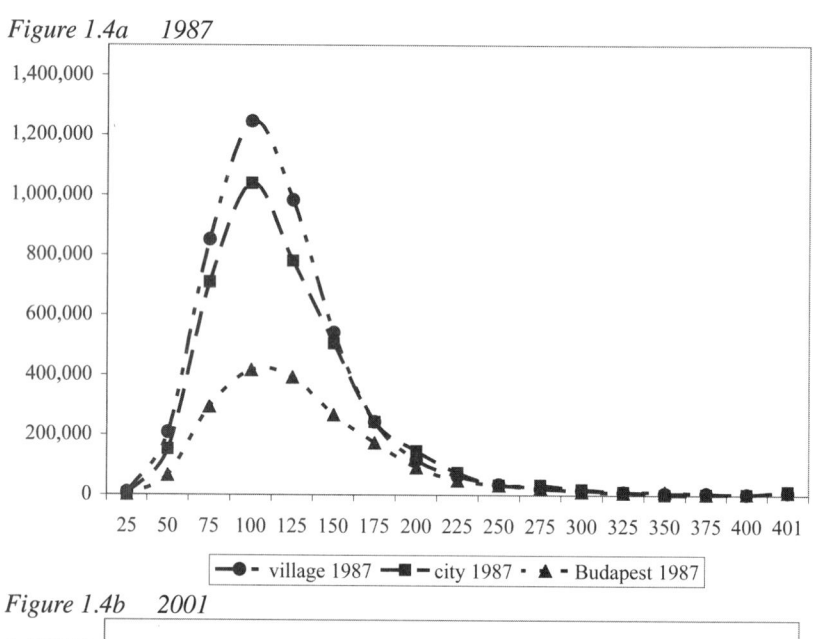

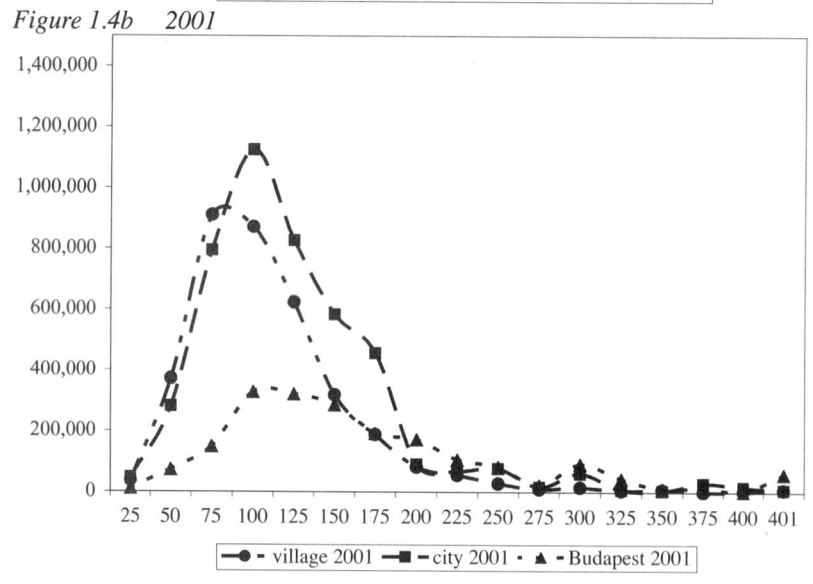

Figure 1.4a   1987

Figure 1.4b   2001

Source: For 1987: KSH Income survey; for 2001: TÁRKI Household Monitor.

of the household and type of settlement) and four demographic characteristics of the respondents and their families (age and gender of the household head, household size and ethnicity).

There has been a significant increase in general education level: the share of those households headed by somebody having primary education almost halved between 1987 and 2001 (from 50 per cent to 25 per cent), while the households headed by a person having higher education has almost doubled (from 12 per cent in 1987 to 21 per cent in 2001). In contrast, the situation with labor market attachments has worsened, as the share of those headed by an inactive or unemployed person went up to 11 per cent by 2001, from almost zero in 1987, while the share of those persons living in households having at least two earners (that is, somebody else besides the head) decreased from 56 per cent to 37 per cent in 1996 and increased only 43 per cent by 2001. General trends in urbanization (measured with the settlement type variable) continued in this period, reflected by a relative shift between those living in cities at the expense of those living in villages.

As for the second group of variables, the gender of the household head means in most cases the gender of the main breadwinner in the household, for which the majority is male (their share ranging from 80 to 85 per cent in the period). By a very broad categorization of the age of the household head (below 35, those in typical active ages of 35–59 and those above 60) there has been no big change in the relative share of those living in households with various age heads. In 2001, some 60 per cent of all households were headed by a 35–59-year old, while the rest were divided equally between the younger and older age groups. Due to differential changes in fertility, aging, marriage and cohabitation patterns, there have been structural shifts in terms of family size and number of dependent children in the households. While the share of those living in childless households increased from 41 per cent to 53 per cent, the share of those having one or two children has decreased, and the share of those living together with at least three children remained largely unchanged between the two end points of the period. Finally, the ethnicity of the head (and of the household) is also taken into account. The census estimate for the Roma population is 1.9 per cent in 2001 in Hungary. Survey estimates for this share vary around 4–6 per cent during the 1990s.[7]

Decomposition by Population Subgroups: Results

Without question, the largest influence on both the level and change of aggregate inequalities was brought about by education of the head of the household. In 1987, differences between groups characterized by different education levels explained some 8 per cent of total aggregate inequalities: this figure jumped to 27 per cent by 2001 (see Table 1A.2).[8] However, the explanation for this increase depends, to different degrees, on change in within-group inequalities, in between-group inequalities and in structural effects. In the period between 1987 and 1996 the change of relative income positions of various subgroups contributed the most to aggregate inequality change. For example, out of a 19 per cent increase in the mean log deviation (MLD), some 12 per cent was explained by that between 1992 and 1996 (see Appendix 1 for the definition of MLD). In contrast, both within-group and between-group inequalities had a decreasing effect on the change of overall inequalities, while structural changes had a positive (increasing) effect between 1996 and 2001 (see Table 1A.3).

Improvement in returns to education may have been driven by three different factors. First, there has been a selective 'clearing' process in labor markets as job destruction may have affected more than the average those low-skill jobs that were relatively overpaid prior to the transition. Second, among those being able to maintain their labor market attachments, artificially maintained communist economic policies to overpay low-skilled work at the expense of high-skilled work have been canceled, following the liberalization of wage setting and the expansion of the private sector. Third, it may also have been very important that new and emerging economic sectors were searching for high-skilled employees during a period with a relative shortage of some special or new skills portfolios existed.[9]

The differential effect of the labor market composition of households on overall inequalities reflects the general labor market adjustment processes in the society. Relative incomes are highest among those where the household contains another employed member in addition to the employed head. However, their relative gain was 11 per cent compared to the average in 1987, while this increased to 21 per cent by 2001 (see Table 1A.1). This should be emphasized, as this is the only subgroup having above average personal equivalent incomes (which is the lowest among those headed by an unemployed or inactive person). Relative income position depends, obviously, on the presence of an employed person in the household even if the head himself is out of the labor force. Among all the subgroups in this respect, those where the head is out of the labor force are the most heterogeneous (Table 1A.1). Within-group inequalities in all groups except pensioner-headed households increased in line with overall inequalities between 1987 and 2001. For pensioner households, within-group inequalities increased between 1987 and 1996, then fell back to the 1987 level by 2001. Knowing that, there is no reason to be surprised that the relative weight of within-group and between-group inequalities did not change in the period (Table 1A.2). In terms of the labor market dimension, changes in inequalities were due to structural shifts, especially in the period between 1987 and 1992, when the most drastic polarization in employment opportunities took place (see Table 1A.3).[10] After 1992 the growth of within-group inequalities had a leading role, with the exception of pensioner households already mentioned.

Differentiation by settlement types also widened in the period. While in 1992 only 2 per cent was explained by settlement hierarchy, this increased to 12 per cent by 2001 (Table 1A.2). The level of inequality increased within all sorts of settlement types and the between-group inequality has also grown (Table 1A.1). This started already back in 1987–92 but accelerated afterwards: While out of the 31 per cent increase in MLD between 1987 and 1992 some 7 per cent was due to change in relative income positions of those living in different settlement types, while out of the corresponding 19 per cent increase between 1992 and 1996 there was also 7 per cent attributable to this factor (Table 1A.3). It is essential to note, however, that the really important changes affected the Budapest-countryside relationship. Budapest caught up to European cities faster than the countryside. Personal equivalent incomes of Budapest inhabitants exceed the national average by some 37 per cent, while the villagers' incomes lag behind the average by some 17 per cent. This should be interpreted together with the fact that inequalities within the capital (MLD = 0.170) are much higher than inequalities in villages (MLD = 0.115).

The gender of the household head explains little of total inequalities. Most of the MLD is explained by within-group rather than between-group inequalities. The relative incomes of female-headed households are estimated invariably to be around 85–90 per cent of those headed by males (Table 1A.1). Though inequalities among male-headed households have risen significantly in the period between 1992 and 2001, this may easily reflect changing composition of other variables like education and employment structure in this group.[11]

Differences between age groups also explain very little of the total inequalities: only 2–6 per cent of total aggregate variance is explained by the household head age variable (Table 1A.2) and there was only a small change in relative income positions of various age groups (Table 1A.1). It should, however, be underlined that within the different age groups changes happened in differing directions. The value of MLD for those living in a household with a head below 35 years of age has increased from 0.092 to 0.195. This means that while, in 1987, inequalities within the households of the young were on par with the average, they became (sometimes very significantly) higher by 2001. Income inequalities within the older households increased between 1987 and 1992, then, in the rest of the 1990s, they decreased. It should be added that the aggregate increase of MLD throughout the period was a result of an increase in within-group rather than between-group inequalities (Table 1A.3). Therefore, it was not only the effect of change in between-group inequality that had a marginal effect but the structural component was also negligible.

The higher the number of children in the household, the larger the observed deterioration in relative incomes during the period. The relative (personal equivalent) income gain of living in a childless household as compared to the national average increased from 5 per cent to 9 per cent between 1987 and 2001, while the relative incomes of three-plus child households decreased from 75 per cent to 65 per cent of the national average (Table 1A.1). This trend paralleled a differential increase in within-group inequalities. The MLD index of the childless households has increased by some 36 per cent (from 0.102 to 0.138) while the MLD index for households with three or more children almost doubled (from 0.079 to 0.156). This partly explains why the between-group component of inequalities did not change much during the period: they took the value of 5 per cent in 1987 and remained at the same level in 2001 (Table 1A.2).

The relative income position of those belonging to the Roma ethnicity has further dropped from an already very low level, from 65 per cent to 45 per cent of the national average between 1992 and 2001 (Table 1A.1). Within this period, the Roma population became poorer and more homogeneous. While inequalities within this group significantly exceeded the overall level of inequalities in 1992, this relationship reversed by 2001.

Results of the decomposition analysis are summarized in Table 1.2. The largest part of aggregate inequalities was explained by the employment composition of the households in 1987. Within-group inequality by education of the head of household was also an important explanatory factor. In 2001 employment structure, education level and settlement types are all more important as explanatory factors than they were in 1987. Taking the whole period as a reference, the largest structural change could be observed in the breakdown by employment categories. Almost half of the increase in the MLD index in the period is attributable to this employment polarization effect. Polarization among social groups is most prevalent in the dimension of education of the household head. Taking a look at the MLD increase from this angle, some 55 per cent of the overall increase is due to differentiation between groups of different education levels. In this respect, the 30 per cent explanatory factor of settlement types is also important to mention.

There is one important element of the analysis presented so far that deserves more attention: the combined effect of age and education structural change on income dispersion change. Some recent analyses of age-earnings profiles of the employed have shown a significant revaluation of human capital investments in the Hungarian labor market during the 1990s. As shown by Köllő (2000), Kézdi and Köllő (2000) and Kézdi (2002), the age-earnings profiles of the employed became flatter between 1986 and 1996. The devaluation of labor market experience was monotonic throughout the period. The appreciation of the skills of the young, educated labor force was significant during the years of

Table 1.2   Decomposition of Inequality Change and the Relative Importance Importance of Some Selected Dimensions of Inequality, 1987–2001 (for Δ% MLD = 58)

In per cent of the change of inequality (Δ%MLD = 100)	Between group inequality 1987	Between group inequality 2001	Components A	B and C	D
Age of household head	6	3	104	−2	−2
Education of household head	8	27	41	−2	55
Employment composition of household	12	14	56	46	−2
Number of children	5	5	88	5	7
Type of settlement	2	12	69	1	30

Notes:
A component = effects of change in inequalities within group.
B and C components = effect of structural changes.
D component = change of relative incomes of various groups.

the systemic change, while relative wage returns to the older and less educated decreased. According to adjusted Mincerian regressions presented by Kertesi and Köllő (2002), the differences in returns to education between the various age cohorts increased after 1993. That is, the returns to education increased the most for the younger cohorts. Tóth (2005) presented similar results from a different dataset. The analysis has shown that the concave character of the age-earnings profile for each level of education became more pronounced. Wage returns for those with medium-length experience have increased relative to those with shorter and longer experiences. The peak of the age-to-earning profile among secondary and higher education levels shifted to the left – towards younger age cohorts. The relative returns to secondary and higher education have gone up compared with those for primary education or less. In general it was found that returns to higher education increased during the period, with a major jump in differences in the early 1990s and maintained advantages thereafter. It can be hypothesized that similar trends would be observed when the incomes of households (rather than earnings of employed) are analyzed. The results shown in Table 1.3 are quite dramatic in this respect. The deterioration of relative income position was the largest among households with primary-educated heads, especially the younger workers. Meanwhile, it was exactly within the group of those households having a maximum 35-

year-old head where income dispersion increased the most. The relative (as compared to the average) income deficit of those with vocational education has increased in each cohort, with income dispersion narrowing among the younger and the older. The largest growth of income dispersion was experienced among the households of the higher-educated workers, regardless of age, under the circumstances of a general relative increase of income level of this group.

SUMMARY OF THE DECOMPOSITION ANALYSES

The change of inequalities was driven by structural, between-group and within-group shifts. In the first third of the period there were large structural changes, mostly in the dimensions of employment composition. Between-group inequalities increased in this period and also between 1992 and 1996 along the lines of educational differentiation. It is particularly interesting to observe this in interaction with various age cohorts (within which there has been a significant increase in differences between various education levels). The relative position of those having vocational education has decreased, while the relative position of those with higher education increased but remained stagnant for those with only secondary school education. These changes affected various age cohorts differently (when controlled for education levels). The younger, if primary educated, lost while the higher educated gained. As a result, the age-income profile among the lower educated has become steeper (that is, the relative gain of an older head with primary education over a younger head with the same education has increased through the period). Among the higher educated, the tide was just the reverse. While in 1987, the members of a household with a higher-educated head of 35 years or younger enjoyed an income of 7 per cent above the average and the members of the household with a higher-educated head of 60 years or more enjoyed an income of 22 per cent above the average, by 2001 these relative gains increased to 52 per cent and 45 percent, respectively. In sum, there has been increased income dispersion among the young in each education subgroup (except those with vocational training where a decrease is observed), the increase being the highest among the higher educated. These data provide strong support to the hypothesis that revaluation of human capital investments in the labor market affected the relative income positions of households.

EVALUATING THE OUTCOME OF THE TRANSITION

The period between 1987 and 2001 is characterized by a specific evolution

Table 1.3 Inequality of Personal Equivalent Incomes and Change of Relative Income Positions, 1987–2001 (MLD = Mean Log Deviation)

Age of household head	Primary	Vocational	Secondary	Tertiary	Total
MLD*1000, 1987					
<35	79	88	88	75	92
36–59	77	72	77	74	82
60>	76	42	106	84	92
Total	86	80	86	81	
MLD*1000, 2001					
<35	174	80	137	176	194.9
36–59	104	110	93	117	139.2
60>	52	38	76	156	88.6
Total	103	94	104	130	
MLD in 2001, in per cent of MLD in 1987					
<35	219	90	156	236	212
36–59	135	153	121	158	170
60>	68	91	72	185	97
Total	119	118	121	162	
Subgroup income averages in per cent of population average, 1987 ($\lambda_k = \mu_k/\mu$)					
<35	74	92	99	107	91
36–59	102	99	117	137	109
60>	78	101	108	122	85
Total	91	96	111	129	
Subgroup income averages in per cent of population average, 2001 ($\lambda_k = \mu_k/\mu$)					
<35	52	78	99	152	90
36–59	74	90	114	149	108
60>	73	85	111	145	88
Total	69	87	110	149	
Subgroup income average in 2001 in % of subgroup income average in 1987					
<35	70	85	100	143	99
36–59	72	90	98	109	99
60>	94	84	102	119	103
Total	76	90	99	116	

of income distribution trends in Hungary. Income inequalities increased significantly between 1987 and 2001. The process involved enrichment and impoverishment, resulting in differential changes in life chances for the various subgroups of society. In addition to the effects of various tax/transfer policies and in-kind benefit systems (which, although important, were not touched upon in this chapter), there were several other important reasons for this.

First, there has been a change in the social distribution of work opportunities. The number of individuals participating in productive employment was significantly lower in 2001 than it was 15 years before. It should be understood, however, that unemployment in Hungary (unlike in some other transition countries) was never extremely high. Rather, inactivity and long term withdrawal from the labor market increased and became very high. These tendencies resulted in a polarization of households by their labor market attachments: there was an increase in the number of households not having an active earner and a decrease in the number of multiple-earner households. Over the whole period the structural change in employment patterns was the main determinant behind the increase in income inequalities.

Second, there has been a permanent race between technological development and the expansion of and quality adjustment in education, especially higher education. On the labor markets, there has been a dramatic skill upgrade in the demand for labor. Job destruction affected low-skill jobs in shrinking sectors (most notably in heavy industries and agriculture). Job creation occurred in high-skill intensive sectors: completely new economic branches emerged and developed (in services, finance, various IT sectors, etc.), providing much better earning possibilities compared to more traditional branches. Two major groups in the labor market benefited the most from these trends: those with convertible modern skills and job starters who successfully converted their higher education degrees into profitable jobs at the very beginning. The structural change between the profitability of various economic sectors, therefore, affected households with different age, education and employment portfolios differently.

What did this mean for the outcome of the reforms? The decomposition analysis presented here shows that the returns from higher education are much greater for younger Hungarians than for earlier entrants to the labor force. This is important not only from the perspectives of equity issues (who gets what) but also from the perspective of sustainability. Among workers already in the labor force at the beginning of the transition, those with a great deal of human and social capital assets (money, skills, information, networks etc.), were able to improve their positions significantly.

At the same time, there were groups in society whose prospects deteriorated. There might be many reasons behind this, ranging from personal and demographic (divorce, illness, loss of family members, etc.) through problems of skill inadequacy (ranging from low education levels to high levels of education but with specialized knowledge only of value in declining sectors) to structural and institutional problems (inadequate income maintenance programs, erosion of in-kind benefit systems, lack of life-long learning options for those otherwise willing and capable to learn, etc.). Certainly, there were numerous groups in society who were pushed out of the labor force with limited chances of ever returning (very low skilled workers, individuals employed earlier in large, inefficient state companies which were sold or closed during the transition process).

The varied, class-specific outcomes of the Hungarian transition demonstrate the importance of 'reach' when considering the design and implementation of reform programs. A narrow focus on mean income (or an exclusive focus on the bottom of the society) would have missed a multitude of class-specific shifts and changes in well being that affected the lives of people throughout Hungary. The decomposition analysis also reveals the varied channels – labor market, human capital and household demographics – which provide the link between reform measures and their ultimate impact on people. This analysis and the evidence of widespread and differentiated impacts point strongly to the need to consider carefully the 'range' of policies. If 'reach' emphasizes the importance of considering the welfare of all members of society, the 'range' of policies must be analyzed with this in mind.

NOTES

I thank Péter Galasi, Orsolya Lelkes, Márton Medgyesi, Péter Szivós for their helpful comments on the first draft. Helpful comments from Robert Holzman and Giovanni Andrea Cornia (the discussants of the earlier version) and José Mariá Fanelli and Lyn Squire (the editors of this book) are also gratefully acknowledged. Special thanks are due to Sándor Sipos for the encouragement to submit the paper to the conference. None of them, however, bears any responsibility for the remaining errors.

1. For recent empirical tests of the effect of equivalence scale choices on poverty rates across social groups and across countries see Förster (2003), Lanjouw and Ravallion (1995) and Lanjouw, Milanovic and Paternostro (1998).
2. See Coulter, Cowell and Jenkins (1992) and, for tests on Hungarian data, Tóth (2005).
3. According to Kattuman and Redmond (1997), the measures sensitive to the two extremes of the income distribution (Theil measure and the coefficient of variation) have increased significantly between 1987 and 1993, while the increase of Gini coefficient (sensitive to the middle of the income distribution) was smaller. As they suggest, income distribution has changed at the extremes, and this led to an overall increase through the period. However, further explanation may be required about why the inequalities decreased between 1989 and 1991 in their analysis.
4. Data drawn from a KSH income survey of 1996, show very similar values for the same period

presented here (KSH 1998; Havasi et al. 1998). In Havasi et al. for example, S10/S1 = 7.58, Éltető–Frigyes index = 2.36, Robin Hood index = 21.0 and Gini = 0.296. These two completely independent estimates, therefore, reconfirm each other. They all consistent with estimates shown by Galasi (1998) also, but direct comparison of the various measures is difficult here as he observes per capita incomes and compares inequalities between households rather than individuals.
5. This reconfirms again that some important changes within the upper classes may be masked by the way we categorize income deciles.
6. The methodology used is similar to the one suggested by Jenkins and van Kerm (2004). They differentiate sliding, stretching and squashing for shifts of the probability density functions along the income line, increase in spread around a constant mean and disproportionate increase in density mass one side of the mode, respectively.
7. Even in the same survey, different estimates can be achieved when using different methods for the assessment of ethnic background. The surveys used here do not contain variable for this in 1987. In other years those households are categorized to be Roma, where the housekeeper (i.e., the person answering the household questionnaire) was categorized to be that by the interviewer. In these surveys, the share of those living in Roma households was about 4–5 per cent.
8. Within group inequality in the dimension of education was measured 18 per cent for 1992 in this analysis. Bailey (1997), however with different equivalence scales ($e = 0.5$), found a very similar result. As she presented results for other countries, it is instructive to look at figures for Slovakia (15 per cent), Czech Republic (13 per cent) and Poland (13 per cent) for between-group inequalities among various education-of-household-head categories.
9. As Kertesi and Köllő (2001) have shown, there have been drastic shifts in relative wages across various sectors. In addition to higher education wage premiums across the economy, employees of firms operating in highly capital intensive, monopolistic sectors and with an organized labor force were also be able to reach significant wage advantages. Putting the Hungarian data into international comparison, the energy sector, transportation, communications and mining are in better position, while education, health and construction were lagging behind in the period they observed. In addition, financial sector appears to have an extra wage premium in international comparisons.
10. Kattuman and Redmond (1997) found similar results on the basis of the KSH Household Budget Survey although direct comparisons, due to different specifications, are hard to make. Nevertheless, they concluded that change in composition by education levels has contributed to a decrease of inequalities between 1987 and 1993. As far as labor market status is concerned, they detected a larger impact of dependency rate in the household, as compared to the labor market status of the household head.
11. Inequalities between males and females were higher in 1987 than later. But this is different from inequalities between households headed by males and females, the topic analyzed here.

BIBLIOGRAPHY

Atkinson, Anthony and John Micklewright (1992), *Economic Transformation in Eastern Europe and the Distribution of Income*, New York: Cambridge University Press.

Bailey, Debra (1997), 'Separate but Equal? Comparing and Decomposing Income Inequality in Central and Eastern Europe', paper presented at the European Bank for Reconstruction and Development conference 'Poverty and Inequality in Transition Countries', London, 23–24 May.

Bokros, Lajos and Jean-Jacques Dethier (eds) (1998), *Public Finance Reform During the Transition: The Experience of Hungary*, Washington, DC: World Bank.

Coricelli, Fabrizio (1997), 'Income Distribution and the Dynamics of Reforms', *Economics of Transition*, **5** (2), 510–5.
Coulter, Fiona, Frank Cowell and Stephen P. Jenkins (1992), 'Equivalence Scale Relativities and the Extent of Inequality and Poverty', *Economic Journal*, **102** (414), 1067–82.
Cowell, Frank A. (1995), *Measuring Inequality*, New York: Prentice Hall/Harvester Wheatsheaf.
Flemming, John and John Micklewright (1999), 'Income Distribution, Economic Systems and Transition', Florence, UNICEF International Child Development Center, Innocenti Occasional Papers, Economic and Social Policy Series, No. 70.
Förster, Michael F. (2003), 'Income Inequalities, Poverty and Effects of Social Transfer Policies in Traditional OECD Countries and Central Eastern Europe: Patterns, Trends and Driving Forces in the 1990s', Ph.D. diss., Université de Liege, Faculté d Économie, de Gestion et de Sceinces Sociales.
Förster, Michael F. and István György Tóth (1997), 'Poverty, Inequalities and Social Policies in the Visegrad Countries', *Economics of Transition*, 5 (2), 505–10.
—— (1998), 'The Effects of Changing Labour Markets and Social Policies on Income Inequality and Poverty: Hungary and the Other Visegrad Countries Compared', Luxembourg Income Study Working Paper No. 177.
Galasi, Péter (1998), 'Income Inequality and Income Mobility in Hungary 1992–1996', Florence, UNICEF International Child Development Center, Innocenti Occasional Papers, Economic and Social Policy Series, No. 64.
Havasi Éva, Ágnes Horváth, Mária Rédey and Lászlóné Schnell (1998), 'A mai magyar háztartások jövedelemeloszlása', (Income Distribution of Current Hungarian Households) *Statisztikai Szemle*, 3, 221–37.
Hölscher, Jens (2001), 'Income Distribution and Convergence in the Transition Process', Luxembourg Income Study Working Paper No. 275.
Jenkins, Stephen P. (1995), 'Accounting for Inequality Trends: Decomposition Analyses for the UK, 1971–86', *Economica*, 62 (245), 29–63.
Jenkins, Stephen P. and Philippe Van Kerm (2004), 'Accounting for Income Distribution Trends: A Density Function Approach', Luxembourg, IRISS Working Paper Series No. 2004-07.
Kapitány Zsuzsa and Gyorgy Molnár (2004), 'Inequality and Income Mobility in Hungary, 1993–1998', *Europe-Asia Studies*, **56** (8), 1109–29.
Kattuman, Paul and Gerry Redmond (1997), 'Income inequality in Hungary, 1987–1993', Cambridge, UK, University of Cambridge, Department of Applied Economics, DAE Working Paper No. 9726.
Kertesi, Gábor and János Köllő (2001), 'Ágazati bérkülönbségek Magyarországon', (Sectoral wage differences in Hungary) Closing study of a research sponsored by the Hungarian Employment foundation (OFA/XLV–45/99, January 2001) Budapest.
—— (2002), 'Economic Transformation and the Revaluation of Human Capital – Hungary, 1986–1999', in Andries De Grip, Jasper Van Loo and Ken Mayhew (eds) *The Economics of Skills Obsolescence*, Amsterdam: JAI Press, pp. 235–73.
Kézdi, Gábor (2002), 'Two Phases of Labour Market Transition in Hungary: Inter-Sectoral Reallocation and Skill-Biased Technological Change', Budapest, Hungarian Academy of Sciences, Working Papers on the Labour Market No. 2002/3.
Kézdi, Gábor and János Köllő (2000): Életkor szerinti kereseti különbségek a rendszerváltás előtt és után' (Age differences in earning before and after the system change), in Júlia Király and András Simonovits (eds), *Racionalitás és méltányosság*.

Tanulmányok Augusztinovics Mária születésnapjára, Budapest: Közgazdasági Szemle Alapítvány, pp. 27–60.

Kornai, János (1994), 'Transformational Recession: The Main Causes', *Journal of Comparative Economics*, **19** (1), 39–63.

—— (2005), 'The Great Transformation of Central Eastern Europe: Success and Disappointment', presidential address at the International Economics Association 14th World Congress Marrakech, Morocco, 29 August.

Köllő, János (2000), 'Iskolázottság és életkor szerinti különbségek: az "emberi tőke" átértékelődése' (Schooling and Age Difference: The Revaluation of Human Capital), in Károly Fazekas (ed.), *Munkaerő-piaci tükör*, Budapest: MTA Közgazdaságtudományi Kutatóközpont, pp. 80–90.

KSH (Hungarian Statistical Office) (1990), *Jövedelemeloszlás Magyarországon. Az 1988. évi felmérés adatai* (Income distribution in Hungary: Data from the 1988 survey), Budapest: KSH.

Lanjouw, Peter, Branko Milanovic and Stefano Paternostro (1998), 'Poverty and Economic Transition: How do Changes in Economies of Scale Affect Poverty Rates of Different Households?', Washington DC, World Bank, Policy Research Working Paper No. 2009.

Lanjouw, Peter and Martin Ravallion (1995), 'Poverty and Household Size', *Economic Journal*, **105** (433), 1415–34.

Milanovic, Branko (1998), *Income Inequality and Poverty during the Transition from Planned to Market Economy*, Washington DC: World Bank.

—— (1999), 'Explaining the Increase in Iinequality during Transition', *Economics of Transition*, **7** (2), 299–341.

Mookherjee, Dilip and Anthony Shorrocks (1982), 'A Decomposition Analysis of the Trend in UK Income Inequality', *Economic Journal*, **92** (368), 886–992.

Shorrocks, Anthony (1980), 'The Class of Additively Decomposable Inequality Measures', *Econometrica*, **48**, (3), 613–25.

Tóth, István György (2005), *Jövedelemeloszlás. A rendszerváltástól az uniós csatlakozásig* (Income distribution. From the change of economic system to the joining of the EU), Budapest: Andorka Társaság – Századvég Kiadó.

APPENDIX 1A: INEQUALITY MEASURES USED IN THE CHAPTER

Variance-Based Measures

Gini: $G = (1/2n((n-1))\Sigma_{i=1,\ldots,n}\Sigma_{j=1,\ldots,n}|y_i - y_j|$.

Generalized Entropy Measure: $GE(\alpha) = (1/(\alpha^2-\alpha))[(1/n)\Sigma_{i=1\ldots n}(y_i/\mu)^\alpha - 1]$, if $\alpha \neq 0,1$ and

$GE(0) = MLD = (1/n)\Sigma_{i=1,\ldots,n}\log(\mu/y_i)$, if $\alpha = 0$ and

$GE(1)$ (Theil-measure) $= (1/n)\Sigma_{i=1,\ldots,n}(y_i/\mu)\log(y_i/\mu)$, if $\alpha = 1$.

$GE(2) = 1/\mu\ [1/n\ (\Sigma_{i=1,\ldots n}(y_i - \mu))^2]^{1/2}$

$GE(-1) =$

Atkinson-measure: $A_\varepsilon = 1 - [(1/n)\Sigma_{i=1,\ldots,n}(y_i/\mu)^{1-\varepsilon}]^{1/(1-\varepsilon)}$, if $\varepsilon \geq 0$, but $\varepsilon \neq 1$

while $A_\varepsilon = 1 - \exp[(1/n)\Sigma_{i=1,\ldots,n}\ln(y_i/\mu)]$, if $\varepsilon = 1$ and $\exp(.) = e^{(.)}$

where n is for the observation units in the sample, y_i is for the income of the ith unit, μ is for the arithmetic mean of all y_i, while α and ε are parameters set depending on our preferential weights given to welfare level of units at different levels of the distribution. With lower level of α the measure will be sensitive to the lower end of the distribution while with higher level of α, the measure will be sensitive more to the upper bounds of the distribution.

Distribution Measures

P10	upper cut point of the lowermost decile in percent of the median (P50) income.
P90	lower cut point of the uppermost decile in percent of the median (P50) income.
S1, S5, S6 and S10	incomes received by the lowest, the fifth, the sixth and the uppermost deciles in percent of total incomes.
Robin Hood index	Difference between actual income shares of below average deciles and a theoretical level of perfect equality.
Éltető–Frigyes index:	ratio of above average and below average incomes.

Method of Decomposition

From the Generalized Entropy (GE) class of measures that satisfy axioms of anonymity, population independence, transfer-sensitivity, scale invariance and decomposability (Cowell 1995), GE(0), the mean log deviation (MLD) can be defined as follows:

$$\text{MLD} = \text{GE}(0) = (1/n)\Sigma_{i=1,\ldots n}\log(\mu/y_i),$$

Where n is the number of observation units in the sample, y_i is the income of the ith -unit, μ is the arithmetic average of all y_i. That is, MLD is the average of the logarithms of mean income divided by individual values of the distribution.

As MLD has the very convenient characteristic of being additively decomposable (Shorrocks 1980), using the terms suggested by Jenkins (1995), decomposition can be described as follows.

Let v_k be the share of k subgroups in total population, $v_k = n_k/n$, and let λ_k be the ratio of average incomes of a k subgroup to the average incomes of the total population, $\lambda_k = \mu_k/\mu$, and let θ_k be the share of k subpopulation from total incomes in the population, $\theta_k = v_k \lambda_k$. Total inequality as measured by MLD index, can be decomposed as a sum of two components:

$$\text{MLD} = \Sigma_k v_k \text{MLD}_k + \Sigma_k v_k \log(1/\lambda_k).$$

The first part of the right hand side is for 'within group' inequalities: it denotes weighted average of inequalities within the subgroups. The second part of the expression denotes 'between group inequalities': that part of inequalities that would be measured, should we replace each individual income in a subgroup by the average of the subgroup. Since the sum of between group and within group inequalities equals total measured inequalities, we can express the various components in percentage terms. Subgroup MLD values and relative income levels are presented in Table 1A.1 and results of these static decompositions (within group and between group inequalities) are shown in Table 1A.2.

In addition to this, a dynamic decomposition of intertemporal *change* (ΔMLD) between two time periods, t and $t + 1$ can be written, following Jenkins (1995) and Mookherjee and Shorrocks (1982):

$$\Delta\text{MLD} \equiv \text{MLD}_{(t+1)} - \text{MLD}_{(t)} = \Sigma_k v_k \Delta\text{MLD}_{(k)} + \Sigma_k \text{MLD}_{(k)} \Delta v_k - \Sigma_k [\log(\lambda_k)] \Delta v_k - \Sigma_k v_k \Delta \log(\lambda_k)$$
$$\cong \Sigma_k \underline{v_k} \Delta\text{MLD}_{(k)} + \Sigma_k \underline{\text{MLD}}_{(k)} \Delta v_k - \Sigma_k [\underline{\lambda_k} - \log(\underline{\lambda_k})] \Delta v_k + \Sigma_k (\underline{\theta_k} - \underline{v_k}) \Delta \log(\mu_k).$$

[A component]   [B component]   [C component]   [D component],

where underlined expressions refer to average values of t and $t + 1$ periods.

For a clearer understanding of decompositions by various dimensions, it is useful to show changes in *relative* terms: the change of inequality between the two periods as a percent of the value measured in period t ($\%\Delta\text{MLD} \equiv \Delta\text{MLD}/\text{MLD}_{(t)}$) is presented in Table 1.A3. Component 'A' is for the 'pure' effect of inequality increase, that is, the effect attributable to increase in within group components, B and C components show structural effects due to change in relative population shares of the various subgroups, while component D measures change in relative mean incomes of the various subgroups (Jenkins 1995).

Table 1A.1 Income Inequality and Relative Income Level in Various Social Subgroups, 1987–2001

	Within-group inequality of personal equivalent incomes (e = 0.73), MLD*1000				Relative income of subgroups in percent of population average ($\lambda_k = \mu_k/\mu$)			
	1987	1992	1996	2001	1987	1992	1996	2001
Total	92	121	143	145	100	100	100	100
Education of household head								
Primary	86	121	107	103	91	80	73	69
Vocational	80	74	106	94	96	96	93	87
Secondary	86	80	107	104	111	110	114	110
Tertiary	81	120	109	130	129	150	163	149
Household employment composition								
Only an employed head	108	123	159	167	88	97	98	96
Head employed, at least one other person also employed	76	96	115	116	111	117	121	121
Inactive or unemployed	262	155	168	206	53	73	65	67
Pensioner, no employed in household	76	89	97	76	75	75	82	79
Pensioner, but with an employed in the household	59	73	83	87	105	103	104	95
Settlement type								
Village	85	119	121	115	96	93	85	83
City	90	93	130	120	100	96	98	97
Budapest	105	141	135	170	111	129	138	137

Table 1A.1 (continued)

	Within group inequality of personal equivalent incomes (e = 0.73), MLD*1000				Relative income of subgroups in percent of population average ($\lambda_k = \mu_k/\mu$)			
	1987	1992	1996	2001	1987	1992	1996	2001
Gender of household head								
Male	n.a.	116	145	149	n.a.	104	102	102
Female	n.a.	119	127	113	n.a.	86	90	86
Age of household head								
<35	92	108	133	195	91	94	93	90
36–59	82	120	164	139	109	107	107	108
60>	92	114	78	89	85	88	89	88
Number of children in the household								
0	102	123	129	138	105	104	112	109
1	79	107	144	137	105	103	100	98
2	76	103	129	122	95	101	97	90
3+	79	147	141	156	75	78	72	69
Ethnicity								
Not Roma		110	131	134		102	103	103
Roma		191	132	128		62	46	45

Source: For 1987: KSH Income survey; for 1992, 1996: HHP (B) 2001. TÁRKI Household Monitor.

31

Table 1A.2 Decomposition of Total Inequality by Various Dimensions, 1987–2001

	MLD*1000	Within group inequality	Between group inequality	Within group inequality, % (total MLD = 100)	Between group inequality, % (total MLD = 100)
Education of household head					
1987	92	84	7	92	8
1992	121	99	21	82	18
1996	143	108	36	75	25
2001	145	106	39	73	27
Employment composition of the household					
1987	92	81	11	88	12
1992	121	104	18	85	15
1996	143	124	20	86	14
2001	145	124	21	86	14
Settlement type					
1987	92	90	1	98	2
1992	121	113	7	94	6
1996	143	128	16	89	11
2001	145	128	17	88	12
Gender of household head					
1987	92				
1992	121	118	3	98	2
1996	143	142	1	99	1
2001	145	143	2	99	1
Age of household head					
1987	92	86	6	94	6
1992	121	117	3	97	3
1996	143	140	3	98	2
2001	145	140	4	97	3
Number of children in household					
1987	92	88	4	95	5
1992	121	118	4	97	3
1996	143	136	10	94	6
2001	145	139	8	95	5
Ethnicity					
1987					
1992	121	117	5	96	4
1996	143	135	11	93	7
2001	145	137	11	93	7

Table 1A.3   Decomposition of Change in Inequality: 1987–2001

	Change of inequality between the start and end of the period ΔMLD *1000	Percentage change of the inequality measure % ΔMLD	A component: effects of change in inequalities (within group)	B and C components: effect of structural changes	D component: change of relative incomes of various groups (between group)
Education of household head					
1987–2001	53	58	24	−1	32
1987–1992	29	31	20	−5	16
1992–1996	23	19	8	−1	13
1996–2001	2	1	−2	5	−2
Employment composition of the household					
1987–2001	53	58	33	27	−1
1987–1992	29	31	15	21	−1
1992–1996	23	19	15	2	1
1996–2001	2	1	1	0	0
Settlement type					
1987–2001	53	58	40	0	17
1987–1992	29	31	26	−1	7
1992–1996	23	19	12	1	7
1996–2001	2	1	0	0	1

Table 1A.3 (continued)

	Change of inequality between start and end of period $\Delta MLD*1000$	Percentage change of the inequality measure % ΔMLD	A component: effects of change in inequalities (within group)	B and C components: effect of structural changes	D component: change of relative incomes of various groups (between group)
Gender of household head					
1987–2001	53	58	na	na	na
1987–1992	29	31	na	na	na
1992–1996	23	19	20	0	−1
1996–2001	2	1	0	0	1
Age of household head					
1987–2001	53	58	60	−1	−1
1987–1992	29	31	34	0	−3
1992–1996	23	19	19	0	0
1996–2001	2	1	1	0	1
Number of children in the household					
1987–2001	53	58	51	3	4
1987–1992	29	31	31	2	−2
1992–1996	23	19	14	1	4
1996–2001	2	1	2	−2	1
Ethnicity					
1987–2001	na	na	na	na	na
1987–1992	na	na	na	na	na
1992–1996	23	19	14	0	5
1996–2001	2	1	1	0	1

Note: Components are to depict internal distribution within an aggregate inequality measure. Sums of columns 3–5, should add up to value in column 2. Alterations are due to rounding.

2. Socioeconomic Vulnerability and Trade Liberalization: Cross-Country Evidence in Central and Eastern Europe

Pierluigi Montalbano, Alessandro Federici, Carlo Pietrobelli and Umberto Triulzi

According to Amartya Sen, policymakers must evaluate the 'reach' of reforms in terms of being person-centered and evenhanded. In particular, he emphasizes that reforms must not overlook the interests and freedoms of any group of people, especially those who are disadvantaged and downtrodden. In practice, however, this is not an easy task. Given our limited knowledge about reform 'technologies', some initiatives which seem to meet these ethical criteria 'ex-ante' can produce undesired effects 'ex-post'. Indeed, this has been true regarding trade reforms, that in some cases increased significantly the level of vulnerability of the economic system, producing unpredicted negative effects. This chapter tries to shed light on this issue by analyzing the relationship between trade liberalization and socioeconomic vulnerability in the case of Central and Eastern Europe during the transition from planned economy.

Substantive cross-country evidence claims that reforms centered on trade liberalization foster income growth and poverty alleviation among trading partners. As Bhagwati and Srinivasan (2002) clearly state: 'Trade does seem to create, even sustain, higher growth'. Likewise, Dollar and Kraay (2001a; 2001b) demonstrate that a group of developing countries, the 'globalizers', has grown faster than the 'non-globalizers' and that trade liberalization benefits the poor, given the positive association between overall growth and income growth among the poor. These results are consistent with trade theory; namely, by eliminating price distortions, trade liberalization improves resource allocation, thereby increasing productivity. Moreover, an open trade regime encourages global integration, modern technology imports and improved productivity.

Some authors, however, cast doubts on the role and direction of causality between trade and growth (Rodriguez and Rodrik 1999). The experience of the East Asian newly industrializing economies reveals, for example, that the adoption of high levels of trade protection and interventionist industrial policies can be a practical way to promote growth, through investment and technological learning (Amsden 1989; Wade 1990; Rodrik 1999). Moreover, as Rodrik (2000) argues, the main trade reforms in at least two of the biggest globalizers – India and China – took place a decade after the onset of robust growth. Furthermore, a huge amount of literature has explored an additional set of key issues about the socioeconomic effects of trade liberalization, including: the heterogeneous impact of trade liberalization on poverty (see, e.g., Timmer 1997; Delgado et al. 1998; Mellor and Gavian 1999); the pervasive effect of trade liberalization on inequality between and within countries (Frankel 2000; Ben-David 1993; Milanovic 2003); the central role of policies and institutions in determining the actual socioeconomic effects on the local population (Krueger 1990, Ades and Di Tella 1997, 1999; Lall and Pietrobelli 2002); and the issue of falling tariff revenues which, in turn, may reduce social expenditures and hurt the poor (McCulloch, Winters and Cirera 2001). More recently, Hertel and Winters (2005) offer a number of additional econometric-based analyses on some key transmission channels to explain the relation between trade and poverty. They underline the importance of price transmission mechanism from the border, the role of cropping choices by farm households, the role of labor market participation decisions and inter-industry movement of labor.

However, scholars are beginning to consider the idea that trade openness and globalization may lead to increased instability, especially in the case of emerging countries. This phenomenon is already known in the case of financial integration and capital mobility. Many authors (Lahiri 2001; Meng and Velasco 1999; Aghion, Banerjee and Piketty 1999) have shown that capital mobility could be destabilizing, since it facilitates intertemporal consumption smoothing and increases the possibility of multiple self-fulfilling expectations equilibria. In the case of trade openness, there is also a growing awareness that it may have non-conventional effects on the level of investment, its cyclical behavior and terms-of-trade volatility (Razin, Sadka and Coury 2003). This phenomenon may help to explain the excessive volatility of the terms of trade of developing countries relative to industrial countries (see, e.g., Mendoza 1995; Razin 1995). The traditional explanation is that the terms-of-trade in developing countries are mostly affected by commodities, whose prices are typically volatile and suffer inadequate infrastructures and scarcity of skilled labor (Razin, Sadka and Coury 2003). Therefore, firms in these countries incur relatively higher setup costs (in terms of training people, setting up infrastructure, etc.) with the result of boom–bust cycles of investment, multiple equilibria supported by self-fulfilling expectations and highly volatile terms of trade.

Along the same lines, Glick and Rose (1999) and Easterly and Kraay (1999) use empirical evidence to demonstrate that the countries most integrated into the world economy have been particularly affected by international crises and that trade linkages could be responsible for regional contagion during currency crises. This issue has been analyzed in depth by Forbes (2001), who demonstrates that trade can transmit crises internationally via different channels and suggests that trade effects are both statistically and quantitatively relevant. Another strand of literature addresses the same issue, using different techniques, in the case of small states, a category which is supposed to be more open and particularly vulnerable to the globalization process and trade openness, among other factors (Atkins and Mazzi 1999; Easterly and Kraay 1999; Kose and Prasad 2002).

In keeping with the above debate, this chapter investigates whether trade liberalization, that usually precedes capital account liberalization in the reform process and economic development, could imply long-term negative socioeconomic effects in the case of the more fragile partner countries. In other words, our aim is to answer the crucial question raised by Winters (2000):

> Where to strike the balance between the advantages of an open economy, and the drawbacks of a greater exposure to shocks – that in turn bring about major socioeconomic costs, and may harm the people's livelihood in social and economic contexts characterized by weak institutional development?

More specifically, we would like to assess whether the occurrence of external negative covariate shocks associated with trade liberalization could imply long-term negative effects on the aggregate welfare of the local population, even within the context of long-term growth.

This is a neglected issue within the debate on the socioeconomic effects of trade liberalization. We believe that a better understanding of the likely long-term effects of the shocks induced by non discriminatory trade liberalization should be an essential part of this debate. This key issue is strongly linked with Sen's central question of what kind of 'ethic' should we choose in implementing the reform process. As Sen strongly points out, reforms are not 'goal-independent institutional requirement which "must be" pursued' (page xi). Rather, they need to be carefully weighed, honed to specific socioeconomic goals and able to include the interests of any group of people involved, particularly those who are disadvantaged or 'vulnerable'. In this respect, socioeconomic vulnerability analysis represents a fundamental step of every reform process, as it considers the long-term effects of policy changes on livelihoods, even in a context of good overall macro performance, by raising their degree of 'uncertainty' toward the future. In other words, a socioeconomic vulnerability analysis strongly relates to the economic, social and political 'reach' of the reforms.

This chapter is an empirical exercise focused on the Central and Eastern European Countries (CEECs). According to EU enlargement strategy, the acronym CEECs includes: Bulgaria, the Czech Republic, Estonia, Hungary, Latvia, Lithuania, Poland, Romania, Slovakia and Slovenia. We chose these cases for two reasons: the CEECs started from an ostensibly 'functioning autarchy' (Holzman 1974) and during the 1990s experienced a dramatic and unprecedented process of political change, economic liberalization and institutional reform (Svejnar 2002). At the same time, they faced severe negative trade shocks, such as the collapse of the Council for Mutual Economic Assistance;[1] the end of traditional trade linkages with the USSR as well as the immediate shift to world prices in foreign trade (Blanchard 1997), while experiencing an economic slowdown of a magnitude never seen during non-war years (Mundell 1997). The above features make the CEECs a useful case study to check whether a pervasive process of trade reform could negatively affect long-term growth performance, consequently affecting the welfare of the people involved. In this respect, this chapter is also a test of the CEECs' socioeconomic vulnerability to trade liberalization. Finally, this study seeks to develop an innovative methodology to detect phenomena of 'macro-vulnerability' induced by trade liberalization and present some preliminary policy remarks related to the 'reach' of reform.

SOCIOECONOMIC VULNERABILITY ANALYSIS: TOWARD A MACRO APPROACH

Vulnerability as a method of analysis does not override traditional approaches; instead, it offers a new lens to focus on the phenomena. Socioeconomic vulnerability can be defined as the 'continuous forward-looking state of expected outcomes' (Alwang, Siegel and Jørgensen 2001). In other words, while ex post losses are the static outcomes of the phenomenon, vulnerability is the continuous process of risk and response. Vulnerability is an ex ante condition that may potentially lead to a negative outcome. Hence, it cannot be directly observed but only predicted. Consequently, what really matters are not the current values of the phenomena analyzed, but the ability to understand their future dynamics and intervene when necessary (Dercon 2001).[2]

After the breakdown of the policy consensus caused by the Asian financial crisis of the late 1990s, the number of risk and vulnerability assessments has been growing, moving toward a more generalized view involving a growing number of developing countries. Most of these efforts have been devoted to assessing the impacts of macroeconomic shocks (such as changes in price, exchange rates and balance of payments), natural disasters (droughts, floods) and health shocks (epidemics, illness, injury) on individuals and households welfare.

Alwang, Siegel and Jørgensen (2001) have provided a clear picture of the various definitions and methodologies of socioeconomic vulnerability. They underline the absence of a complete and systematic theoretical analysis of the phenomenon. According to them, the different approaches tend to be theoretically strong and empirically weak or vice versa, leaving us without a solid, unique method of analysis. An attempt to provide a valuable and holistic conceptual framework to study socioeconomic vulnerability has been provided by Holzmann (2001), Holzmann and Jørgensen (2000), Dercon (2001) and Heitzmann, Canagarajah and Siegel (2002). According to this conceptual framework, socioeconomic vulnerability analysis is determined by the characteristics of the unit of analysis, the correlation, frequency, timing and severity of shocks, and the risk-management instruments applied, both public and private (Heitzmann, Canagarajah and Siegel 2002) and identify relevant negative effect in terms of welfare.

An influential strand of the vulnerability literature typically expresses welfare as consumption. Within this literature we can distinguish three different approaches:

VEP   Vulnerability to Expected Poverty (Chaudhuri, Jalan and Suryahadi 2002; Christiaensen and Boisvert 2000; Pritchett, Suryahadi and Sumarto 2000);
VEU   Vulnerability as low Expected Utility (Calvo and Dercon 2003; Ligon and Schechter 2003);
VER   Vulnerability as Exposure to observed Risks (Amin, Rai and Topa 1999; Dercon and Krishnan 2000; Glewwe and Hall 1998).

These studies adopt primarily a micro approach focused on households (Hoddinott and Quisumbing 2003). More recently, Tesliuc and Lindert (2004) made an additional effort to complete the analysis with qualitative data. Beside these studies, a macro approach to vulnerability analysis is gaining increasing consensus (Thomas 2003; Montalbano et al. 2007). This focus on aggregate variables of socioeconomic vulnerability analysis can be justified by several considerations.

Why a Macro Approach?

First of all, despite the attention paid to the idiosyncratic shocks on individual agents, there are still sizable covariate shocks on aggregate variables which deserve careful consideration. For example, the negative impacts of international crises in the last decade, even if they did not affect local populations disproportionately, proved to be more devastating for those who are poor or nearer the poverty line (Lustig 1999). These crises, resulting from perverse combinations of international turmoil and political economy mismanagement, manifest themselves in various forms (public budget, balance of payments, currency and banking crises, hyperinflation, etc.) and affect primarily the most fragile globalizer countries (Easterly and Kraay 1999). In this new scenario, traditional social relationships and coping mechanisms, along with local market structures in developing countries, are under pressure and a vast proportion of the local population risk being adversely affected because of international competition (Dercon 2001). Similarly, more recent empirical works (e.g., Lundberg and Squire 2003) argue that trade openness erodes income growth in the bottom quintile of the population because of the poor's limited ability to save and their lack of access to general public or private safety net systems (World Bank 2000).

Second, recent events also highlight the paucity of ex-ante international macroeconomic policies capable of properly recognizing and coping with the systemic nature of macroeconomic crises and their actual effects. Current macro policies usually do not take into account a large percentage of the population which has a high probability of falling below the poverty line in the near future (Glewwe and Hall 1998). As a result, there is a clear need to reformulate and redirect current macro policies and foster preventive strategies as well as forward-looking approaches and early warning systems (Holzmann and Jørgensen 2000; Holzmann 2001).

So far, the most important achievements on the role of covariate risks and macro shocks at the macro level have been reached in the literature on volatility. According to this literature, 'Good times do not offset the negative impact of bad times' (Aizenman and Pinto 2005), leading to permanent negative effects. Empirical investigations increasingly show that such asymmetry is reinforced by incomplete markets, sovereign risk, divisive politics, inefficient taxation, procyclical fiscal policy and weak financial market institutions – factors which particularly affect developing countries.

Hence, macro volatility is the main channel through which 'uncertainty' affects aggregate welfare. The current volatility literature has two strands: one which analyzes the effects of volatility and another which focuses on its determinants. While most literature on the effects of volatility suggests a positive relationship between volatility and average growth, there is growing evidence which suggests a negative link in the case of the developing countries. The main explanation here is that particularly 'extreme volatility' (high or low) could be considered, especially in developing countries at the beginning of economic liberalization, as a proxy of greater uncertainty which, in turn, lowers physical and human capital investments, thereby reducing long-term growth (Ramey and Ramey 1995; Martin and Rogers 1997; Talvi and Vegh 2000; Easterly, Islam and Stiglitz 2001; Pallage and Robe 2003; Hnatkovska and Loayza 2004). The theoretical underpinnings for a negative effect of uncertainty on economic growth operate through conditions of risk aversion, aversion to bad outcomes, lumpiness and irreversibility associated with the investment process. Under these conditions, uncertainty is likely to lead firms to underinvest or to invest in the 'wrong' projects (see Bertola and Caballero 1994). Structural country characteristics, such as underdeveloped financial structures, deficiencies in law and procyclical fiscal policy, that usually accompanies large public indebtedness, are bound to worsen the impact of volatility and uncertainty on economic growth (see Caballero 2000).

The second strand of literature examines the determinants of volatility, typically in cross-section analysis (Gavin and Hausmann 1996; Acemoglu et al. 2003; Rodrik 1999). It underlines the potential impact on volatility of political insecurity (Alesina, Roubini and Swagel 1996), macroeconomic instability (Judson and Orphanides 1996), institutional weaknesses (Rodrik 1991; Servén 1997) and also external shocks linked to trade liberalization (Prasad and Gable 1997; Wolf 2005; Hnatkovska and Loayza 2004; Kose 2002; Kose and Yi 2003). Some scholars argue that increasing trade interrelation among economies, especially emerging economies, not only increases inequalities but could also cause an increased risk 'hazard' (i.e. the combination of exogenous risk exposure and the endogenous characteristics of the unit of analysis) which, in turn, could be heading toward a path of underdevelopment. Hence, if markets are not functioning, increasing integration among economies, particularly among the less developed ones characterized by weak infrastructures and fragile institutions, contributes to an environment more susceptible to negative externalities at the macro level (Dercon 2001).

Limits of the Macro Approach

Of course, the macro approach to socioeconomic vulnerability is also subject to a number of caveats. Since the focus is on aggregate variables, mainly in cross-country comparisons, it deals only with covariant macro shocks at the country level (i.e. shocks affecting the variables on average, impacting on the population uniformly), without taking into account the differences between households or income distribution effects. Thus results may differ across social groups within each country, while relative income positions of households will affect their ability to access adequate tools and coping mechanisms. This shortcoming, however, is moderated by the evidence that the aggregated effects hurt the poor disproportionately (Lundberg and Squire 2003; Lustig 1999). Moreover, as the focus is on private consumption, there is no emphasis on the potential smoothing role played by public consumption (Kose, Prasad and Terrones 2003). In addition, the approach should take into account all the limits of cross-section analysis, even though it remains the best choice within the 'cost-benefit tradeoff' of the appropriate sample length (Aizeman and Pinto 2005). In fact, while we could have increased measurement accuracy by using a longer sample, this phenomenon is likely to change over time with diverging characteristics and the performance of shocks and transmission channels. Furthermore, as we will underline below, cross-section comparisons force us to adopt common thresholds within the sample. However, we can easily remove this assumption without invalidating the results. Last but not least, since we aim at presenting a methodology which can be applied across countries and periods, we force ourselves to use macroeconomic data available from official international sources. We acknowledge that this technique risks missing a number of relevant issues, but it lets us enjoy the insights of a clear comparative approach.

ASSESSING SOCIOECONOMIC VULNERABILITY TO TRADE LIBERALIZATION

Volatility is usually measured based on observed realizations of a random variable over time. This is referred to as *realized volatility*, and it is most commonly measured by the standard deviation of the variable analyzed. Since total variability is the sum of two components – 'predictable variability' and 'pure risk volatility', ex-post total variability may overestimate risk. Moreover, the worst negative effects are linked to large or extreme shocks which could be defined as the 'residuals, positive and negative, exceeding a certain cut-off point in magnitude' (Aizenman and Pinto 2005, 3). In fact, while a small negative shock could be easily offset by a traditional coping mechanism, extreme shocks are more likely to have more pervasive effects on the economic system.[3] Following Hnatkovska and Loayza (2004), we decompose the observed total realized volatility of per capita consumption growth into two different variables: the repeated and small cyclical movements around the mean (normal volatility) and the sharp positive or negative fluctuations from the mean (extreme volatility). To carry out this decomposition we define a common threshold, set as the average per capita consumption growth volatility of the sampled countries.[4] It provides absolute (as opposed to relative, country-specific) measures and thus facilitates cross-country comparisons. In this way, we can interpret the portion of standard deviation of consumption change which corresponds to deviations falling within the threshold as 'normal volatility' and the portion of standard deviation of consumption change above and below the same threshold as 'extreme volatility'. Thus only the extreme volatility can be considered as a proxy of pure risk and uncertainty and, consequently, a good measure of covariant shocks.

Having defined our measure of covariant shock, we can now build a sound methodology for computing socioeconomic vulnerability by using macroeconomic data. First, according to the strand of the vulnerability literature which uses per capita consumption as a proxy of welfare (see Hoddinott and Quisumbing 2003), we consider a cross-country linear relationship between the different components of volatility and long-run growth of per capita consumption. The use of the volatility of consumption gives us information about the ability of people to smooth consumption over time. This relationship could be assessed by controlling for other variables that affect a country's per capita growth process:

$$Consgr_i = \beta_0 + \beta_1 Normvol_i + \beta_2 Extvol_i + \beta_4 X_i + \varepsilon \quad (2.1)$$

where *Consgr* represents the average growth rate of per capita consumption; *Normvol* is a measure of normal volatility; *Extvol* is a measure of extreme volatility; X represents a set of control variables, ε is the regression residual, and i is a country index.

The regression analysis is also extended to consider whether the size and statistical significance of the volatility–growth relationship is magnified by procyclical economic policies. Such policies are a clear symptom of a lack of institutional development as well as a key factor explaining why volatility matters and why its effects may be exacerbated in developing countries (Aizenman and Pinto 2005). This effect is taken into account in the model through a 'continuous interaction' term between extreme volatility and a measure of the degree of fiscal policy procyclicality. The regression equation changes as follows:

$$Consgr_i = \beta_0 + \beta_1 Normvol_i + \beta_2 Extvol_i + \beta_3 Extvol_i * fpp_i + \beta_4 X_i + \varepsilon. \quad (2.2)$$

Next, attempting to go beyond the description of mutual relationships, an instrumental-variable technique is used to isolate exogenous changes in each component of volatility induced by trade liberalization and thus gauge their causal impact on per capita consumption growth. In this way, the analysis takes into account the possibility that volatility may be endogenously determined together with long-run growth:

$$Consgr_i = \beta_0 + \beta_1 Normvol_i + \beta_2 Extvol_i + \beta_3 Extvol_i * fpp_i + \beta_4 X_i + \varepsilon$$
$$vol_i = \gamma_i IV_i + u_i \qquad (2.3)$$
$$E(vol_i * \varepsilon_i) \neq 0 \text{ but } E(IV_i * \varepsilon_i) = 0$$

where *IV* represents a set of instrumental variables for each component of volatility, which help explain volatility but at the same time affect long-run growth only through volatility (and the other control variables). The set of instrumental variables includes the volatility of the most common trade indicators as well as the volatility of other selected variables traditionally used in similar studies.

According to this model, cross-country differences in the volatility of a number of aggregate variables can alternatively arise from differences in the exposure to shocks or in the availability of coping mechanisms, producing different welfare conditions. These will be reflected by different elasticities of per capita consumption growth with respect to a given shock (Wolf 2004). It can be related to various factors such as the national incidence of overall macroeconomic instability (Judson and Orphanides 1996), institutional weakness (De Ferranti and Perry 2000; Rodrik 1991), political insecurity (Alesina, Roubini and Swagel 1996), risk aversion and the irreversibility of wrong choices (Hnatkovska and Loayza 2003). What is important to underline, however, is that to deduce the level of welfare loss using per capita consumption as a proxy, we should make assumptions about the relationship between per capita consumption (which is a measure of the middle of the income distribution) and the level of consumption of each quintile. If we are willing to assume that consumption shares of each quintile do not change with changes in per capita consumption, then we can easily predict with this approach the effect of covariate shocks in terms of the population's welfare (see also Thomas 2003; Dollar and Kraay 2001a).

Since vulnerability is a *forward looking* approach, recalling Ligon and Schechter (2003), we thus define socioeconomic vulnerability to trade liberalization of country *i* as the expected value of its welfare loss, calculated as the difference between the expected per capita consumption growth under the hypothesis of no shocks and the expected value of the same variable under the hypothesis of covariate trade shocks:

$$V_i = E[Consgr_i^*] - E[Consgr_i] \qquad (2.4)$$

where V_i is our measure of socioeconomic vulnerability (i.e. the expected value of the welfare loss due to the occurrence of covariate trade shocks); $E[Consgr_i^*]$ is the expected per capita consumption growth under the hypothesis of no shocks – a measure of the potential consumption – and $E[Consgr_i]$ is the expected per capita consumption growth under the hypothesis of covariate trade shocks. Hence, $E[Consgr_i^*]$ represents the benchmark in our socioeconomic vulnerability method. In case of a negative shock, we obviously get $E[Consgr_i^*]$ > $E[Consgr_i]$. The larger the difference between the two measures, the higher socioeconomic vulnerability will be.

TRADE LIBERALIZATION IN THE 1990s

During the 1990s, the countries of Central and Eastern Europe experienced a vast process of trade liberalization, fostered in part by a sympathetic EU trade policy. Beginning 1 January 1995, the EU cut all tariffs and non-tariff restrictions toward the CEECs' imports of industrial goods, boosting bilateral trade between the two geographical areas and fostering the economic development of the transition economies.

As Table 2.1 shows, after the trade liberalization reforms of the 1990s, the CEECs registered an average increase of over 70 per cent of their level of trade openness compared to 1990. This figure was well above the trend not only of the other European countries,[5] that did not benefit from the EU trade liberalization process, but even of the European Economic Area (EEA) members.[6] The same table shows, however, that CEEC trade openness has been accompanied by an increase of trade openness volatility, compared with EEA member countries (more than three times higher, on average). The other European countries did even worse, showing a degree of volatility over seven times the EEA members, even with reduced trade openness. The same happened with the terms-of-trade volatility (Table 2.2), where both the CEECs and the other European countries show a higher degree of volatility compared with EEA members (two times more in the case of CEECs; three times in the case of the other European countries). These results, which are consistent with a number of other empirical studies on the more fragile countries, press us to further investigate the characteristics of the trade liberalization process actually undertaken by the CEECs during the transition.

During the same period the CEECs showed, on average, an initial sharp reduction of their per capita consumption levels.[7] They later recovered following the 'classic' U-shaped path, widely known as the 'transition curve' (Figure 2.1). The consumption performance levels of the CEECs are usually considered to be an example of a successful transition and a positive result achieved by the institutional reforms, including trade liberalization, undertaken with the support of the EU and the other international organizations.

However, during the same period, the CEECs also showed a higher degree of realized volatility, both in the case of per capita consumption and per capita

Table 2.1 Trends and Total Volatility of Trade in Europe in the 1990s (in per cent of GDP)

Trade Openness	1990	1991	1992	1993	1994	1995	1996	1997
Albania		0.18	0.51	0.56	0.48	0.47	0.56	0.48
Austria	0.70	0.71	0.71	0.70	0.72	0.74	0.77	0.85
Belarus	2.11	2.13	1.43	1.21	1.28	1.04	1.10	1.29
Belgium	1.20	1.22	1.25	1.25	1.31	1.34	1.36	1.38
Bulgaria	1.36	0.62	0.76	0.82	0.75	0.91	1.05	1.25
Croatia						0.88	0.90	0.99
Czech Republic	0.73	0.67	0.79	0.95	1.00	1.12	1.19	1.30
Denmark	0.63	0.65	0.64	0.63	0.65	0.67	0.68	0.70
Estonia				1.37	1.50	1.52	1.54	1.81
Finland	0.50	0.48	0.52	0.58	0.63	0.66	0.67	0.71
France	0.37	0.38	0.39	0.39	0.41	0.44	0.44	0.48
Germany	0.44	0.47	0.46	0.44	0.47	0.48	0.50	0.54
Greece	0.37	0.38	0.40	0.40	0.41	0.43	0.44	0.49
Hungary	0.71	0.72	0.75	0.79	0.85	0.89	0.94	1.13
Iceland	0.69	0.68	0.68	0.67	0.69	0.69	0.74	0.76
Ireland	1.04	1.06	1.14	1.20	1.31	1.41	1.47	1.55
Italy	0.41	0.41	0.44	0.43	0.46	0.50	0.50	0.52
Latvia		0.57	0.98	0.79	0.82	0.97	1.16	1.18
Lithuania						1.14	1.33	1.52
Luxembourg	1.95	1.96	1.92	1.94	2.00	2.06	2.12	2.24
Macedonia	0.65	0.45	0.54	0.64	0.73	0.76	0.67	0.84
Netherlands	0.91	0.93	0.94	0.96	1.02	1.09	1.10	1.16
Norway	0.67	0.67	0.67	0.68	0.69	0.70	0.73	0.76
Poland	0.31	0.36	0.38	0.39	0.42	0.48	0.55	0.60
Portugal	0.57	0.57	0.61	0.60	0.64	0.67	0.68	0.71
Romania	0.51	0.43	0.50	0.53	0.56	0.61	0.62	0.72
Russia	0.68	0.43	0.35	0.37	0.46	0.55	0.59	0.58
Slovakia	0.51	0.63	1.00	1.14	1.11	1.13	1.16	1.28
Slovenia				1.03	1.10	1.12	1.11	1.19
Spain	0.33	0.35	0.37	0.38	0.42	0.45	0.48	0.53
Sweden	0.59	0.58	0.60	0.63	0.68	0.72	0.73	0.81
Switzerland	0.62	0.61	0.61	0.62	0.64	0.66	0.68	0.72
Turkey	0.35	0.34	0.36	0.41	0.40	0.44	0.50	0.56
United Kingdom	0.51	0.50	0.53	0.53	0.55	0.57	0.61	0.64
EEA	0.69	0.70	0.71	0.72	0.76	0.79	0.82	0.86
CEECs	0.69	0.57	0.74	0.87	0.90	0.98	1.05	1.18
Other European	0.95	0.71	0.64	0.64	0.67	0.65	0.68	0.75

Source: Authors' estimation based on World Bank World Development Indicators database, 2003.

Table 2.1 (continued)

Trade Openness	1998	1999	2000	Rate of change 1990–2000	Total volatility*
Albania	0.45	0.50	0.45	1.54	0.60
Austria	0.87	0.92	1.00	0.43	0.04
Belarus	1.13	1.13	1.20	-0.43	0.14
Belgium	1.45	1.47	1.53	0.27	0.01
Bulgaria	1.24	1.24	1.38	0.02	0.21
Croatia	0.95	0.94	0.98	0.12	0.05
Czech Republic	1.43	1.50	1.70	1.32	0.08
Denmark	0.73	0.77	0.84	0.34	0.03
Estonia	1.95	1.91	2.28	0.67	0.08
Finland	0.73	0.74	0.83	0.66	0.05
France	0.51	0.51	0.56	0.51	0.03
Germany	0.57	0.60	0.65	0.48	0.04
Greece	0.51	0.52	0.59	0.56	0.04
Hungary	1.29	1.39	1.61	1.27	0.06
Iceland	0.81	0.81	0.82	0.20	0.03
Ireland	1.76	1.80	1.98	0.91	0.03
Italy	0.55	0.55	0.59	0.43	0.03
Latvia	1.26	1.16	1.17	0.21	0.24
Lithuania	1.49	1.30	1.34	0.17	0.11
Luxembourg	2.41	2.52	2.67	0.37	0.03
Macedonia	0.88	0.87	1.01	0.57	0.16
Netherlands	1.20	1.22	1.31	0.44	0.02
Norway	0.77	0.76	0.76	0.13	0.02
Poland	0.66	0.63	0.73	1.38	0.07
Portugal	0.76	0.78	0.80	0.40	0.03
Romania	0.78	0.81	1.01	1.01	0.10
Russia	0.57	0.53	0.57	-0.17	0.17
Slovakia	1.42	1.39	1.52	1.95	0.17
Slovenia	1.24	1.24	1.30	0.26	0.03
Spain	0.56	0.60	0.63	0.92	0.02
Sweden	0.86	0.87	0.93	0.58	0.04
Switzerland	0.75	0.78	0.84	0.36	0.03
Turkey	0.58	0.58	0.66	0.90	0.06
United Kingdom	0.66	0.69	0.74	0.47	0.02
EEA	0.91	0.94	1.01	0.47	0.03
CEECs	1.25	1.23	1.37	0.76	0.11
Other European	0.72	0.72	0.78	0.48	0.23

Note: Total volatility is measured by the standard deviation of trade (% of GDP) rate of change.

Table 2.2 *Trends and Total Volatility of Terms of Trade Adjustment in Europe in the 1990s (in per cent of GDP)*

Country	1990	1991	1992	1993	1994	1995
Albania		−2.1	−3.5	−3.9	−1.6	−1.3
Austria	−0.3	−0.5	−0.4	−0.5	−0.5	0.0
Belarus	0.0	2.8	−5.0	−8.7	−11.2	−10.5
Belgium	−1.0	−1.1	0.0	1.0	0.6	0.0
Bulgaria	11.4	−0.7	−3.2	−3.3	−3.3	−4.0
Croatia						−1.8
Czech Republic	3.3	−5.9	−4.9	−2.2	−0.2	0.0
Denmark	−0.8	−1.2	−0.1	0.0	−0.1	0.0
Estonia				−4.8	−4.8	−3.1
Finland	0.0	−0.8	−1.3	−2.1	−1.6	0.0
France	−0.3	−0.4	−0.1	0.1	0.0	0.0
Germany	−0.9	−1.3	−0.8	−0.3	−0.3	0.0
Greece	−0.8	−0.5	−0.9	−0.6	−0.2	0.0
Hungary	−1.7	−2.5	−2.6	−1.6	−1.0	1.3
Iceland	0.0	1.2	1.0	−0.5	−0.4	0.0
Ireland	2.8	1.4	1.1	2.6	1.3	0.0
Italy	0.9	1.6	1.6	0.8	0.5	0.0
Latvia		11.6	4.6	0.5	−2.0	1.7
Lithuania						−6.5
Luxembourg	−1.5	−2.7	−3.7	−1.3	−0.3	0.0
Macedonia	−5.3	−1.8	−3.4	−4.4	−3.1	0.0
Netherlands	0.2	0.1	−0.4	−0.5	−0.4	0.0
Norway	3.0	2.8	0.8	1.0	−0.4	0.0
Poland	−0.1	−1.4	−0.5	0.6	1.3	1.8
Portugal	−2.9	−2.3	−1.1	−1.0	−0.5	0.0
Romania	0.3	1.5	1.4	1.6	1.3	−0.8
Russia	10.8	2.3	4.9	2.4	0.4	1.1
Slovakia	1.1	−5.1	−8.0	−0.4	−0.7	0.0
Slovenia				−2.2	−0.7	0.1
Spain	−0.6	−0.1	0.2	0.0	−0.3	0.0
Sweden	0.7	1.1	1.1	−0.3	−0.4	0.0
Switzerland	−3.7	−2.7	−3.1	−2.2	−0.7	0.0
Turkey	−0.6	−0.5	−0.6	0.7	1.0	−0.5
United Kingdom	0.3	0.7	1.1	1.2	0.7	0.0
EEA	−0.3	−0.3	−0.3	−0.1	−0.2	0.0
CEECs	2.4	−0.4	−1.9	−1.3	−1.1	−1.0
Other European	1.2	0.1	−1.5	−2.8	−2.9	−2.3

Source: Authors' estimation based on World Bank World Development Indicators database, 2003.

Table 2.2 (continued)

Country	1996	1997	1998	1999	2000	Total volatility
Albania	0.0	−1.3	0.9	3.4	2.4	0.0228
Austria	−0.4	−0.9	−0.9	−0.9	−1.5	0.0038
Belarus	−10.6	−14.1	−10.4	−11.4	−12.1	0.0508
Belgium	−0.6	−1.2	−0.3	−0.9	−2.4	0.0090
Bulgaria	−4.7	−7.3	−3.0	−2.2	−0.1	0.0456
Croatia	−1.5	0.0	0.8	0.3	0.7	0.0104
Czech Republic	0.9	1.3	4.9	4.6	3.0	0.0343
Denmark	0.6	1.0	1.0	1.7	1.6	0.0088
Estonia	−3.3	−2.7	−1.1	−1.1	0.0	0.0165
Finland	−0.5	−1.1	−0.5	−1.8	−3.6	0.0101
France	−0.1	0.0	0.3	0.3	−0.5	0.0024
Germany	−0.1	−0.6	0.0	0.1	−1.4	0.0050
Greece	0.1	0.3	0.3	0.4	0.1	0.0045
Hungary	0.9	0.8	1.4	0.2	−0.7	0.0142
Iceland	−1.1	−0.2	1.9	1.5	0.5	0.0090
Ireland	0.2	0.6	1.3	1.4	−0.1	0.0092
Italy	1.1	0.8	1.5	1.4	−0.7	0.0070
Latvia	0.5	−2.5	−0.3	1.2	0.0	0.0384
Lithuania	−4.8	−3.3	−4.7	−2.2	0.0	0.0210
Luxembourg	0.7	1.2	3.1	3.4	3.7	0.0236
Macedonia	−0.1	−0.9	−1.3	−0.1	−0.2	0.0182
Netherlands	−0.4	−0.2	−0.1	−0.8	−0.8	0.0033
Norway	2.3	3.1	−0.9	3.8	15.9	0.0440
Poland	1.3	1.0	1.7	1.3	0.0	0.0098
Portugal	−1.0	−1.1	−0.5	−0.3	−1.3	0.0083
Romania	−1.0	−1.0	0.0	0.8	1.9	0.0106
Russia	1.9	0.0	−1.6	−2.5	6.1	0.0359
Slovakia	−1.4	−2.2	−0.9	−2.3	−2.3	0.0243
Slovenia	0.2	0.6	1.8	2.2	0.0	0.0129
Spain	0.2	0.2	0.5	0.4	−0.3	0.0030
Sweden	−0.2	−0.6	−1.0	−2.3	−3.6	0.0135
Switzerland	0.1	−0.5	0.7	1.8	0.5	0.0169
Turkey	−1.9	−0.5	−0.9	−0.1	−2.5	0.0095
United Kingdom	0.4	1.4	2.1	2.4	3.0	0.0090
EEA	0.1	0.1	0.5	0.6	0.5	0.011
CEECs	−1.2	−1.4	0.1	0.3	0.2	0.022
Other European	−2.1	−3.4	−2.7	−2.2	−1.3	0.027

Note: Total volatility is measured by the standard deviation of trade (% of GDP) rate of change.

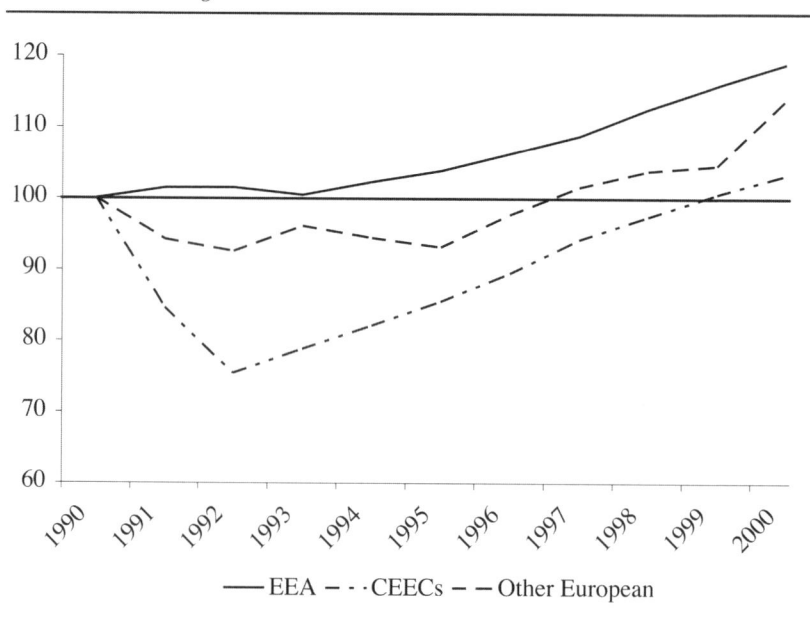

Figure 2.1 The U-shaped Curve of Per Capita Consumption in Europe during the 1990s

——— EEA – · · CEECs – – Other European

Source: World Bank World Development Indicators database, 2003.

GDP growth rates (Table 2.3). Moreover, the ratio of per capita consumption growth rate over per capita GDP growth rate has been much greater than one for the majority of the CEECs. This result, consistent with a number of other empirical studies (see Kose, Ayhan and Yi 2003; Wolf 2004; De Ferranti and Perry 2000), indicates that the local population has limited capacity to maintain a stable consumption path during the decade investigated.

Is this inability to smooth consumption over time a symptom of the local population's socioeconomic vulnerability to the 'first-type' institutional reforms carried out at the beginning of the transition period?[8] If this is the case, can this socioeconomic vulnerability eventually be related to trade liberalization reforms?

To shed light on this phenomenon, we must determine how much of the observed higher total consumption volatility can be linked to actual situations of 'uncertainty' and 'pure risk'. To this end, we applied the decomposition method mentioned above. As Table 2.4 clearly shows, not only are the emerging European countries (Baltic States, other CEECs and other European) more volatile compared to the EEA member countries, but also the CEECs'

Table 2.3 Per Capita Consumption Volatility and Per Capita GDP Volatility: A Comparison

2.3a Volatility of the Rates of Change of Per Capita Consumption

Estonia	0.098	Austria	0.009
Latvia	0.179	Belgium	0.011
Lithuania	0.033	Denmark	0.018
Baltic States	0.103	Finland	0.037
		France	0.012
Albania	0.124	Germany	0.015
Belarus	0.096	Greece	0.012
Croatia	0.058	Iceland	0.043
Macedonia	0.069	Ireland	0.023
Russia	0.072	Italy	0.020
Turkey	0.045	Luxembourg	0.018
Other European	0.078	Netherlands	0.015
		Norway	0.011
Bulgaria	0.094	Portugal	0.017
Czech Republic	0.085	Spain	0.017
Hungary	0.041	Sweden	0.023
Poland	0.019	Switzerland	0.011
Romania	0.075	United Kingdom	0.019
Slovakia	0.105	EEA	0.018
Slovenia	0.070		
CEECs 7	0.070		

Source: Authors' estimation based on World Bank World Development Indicators database, 2003.

higher level of volatility is primarily due to an elevated level of 'extreme volatility' (i.e. uncertainty and pure risk). Notwithstanding the fact that almost all of the emerging European countries suffered from extreme volatility, the most (extreme) volatile countries are Latvia, Albania, Slovakia, Belarus and Estonia, while only five (out of 18) EEA member countries showed signs of extreme volatility. Conversely, the level of 'normal volatility' of the emerging European countries is, on average, very low compared with that of EEA members, except in Lithuania and Poland (which did not register 'extreme volatility') and Hungary.

This suggests that the path of economic convergence of the CEECs' per capita consumption to the EEA levels has probably occurred at the cost of increasing uncertainty and risk (proxied by the extreme volatility of per

Table 2.3 (continued)

2.3b Volatility of the Rates of Change of Per Capita GDP

Estonia	0.086	Austria	0.011
Latvia	0.121	Belgium	0.014
Lithuania	0.096	Denmark	0.014
Baltic States	0.101	Finland	0.040
		France	0.012
Albania	0.120	Germany	0.012
Belarus	0.082	Greece	0.018
Croatia	0.098	Iceland	0.029
Macedonia	0.039	Ireland	0.031
Russia	0.068	Italy	0.011
Turkey	0.048	Luxembourg	0.020
Other European	0.076	Netherlands	0.010
		Norway	0.013
Bulgaria	0.053	Portugal	0.020
Czech Republic	0.046	Spain	0.014
Hungary	0.049	Sweden	0.024
Poland	0.039	Switzerland	0.016
Romania	0.058	United Kingdom	0.017
Slovakia	0.062	EEA	0.018
Slovenia	0.047		
CEECs 7	0.051		

capita consumption). This is a very important point: emerging countries at the beginning of their liberalization process show more volatility than the developed and more integrated countries.

Figure 2.2 illustrates two representative case studies: Austria, an EEA member which did not experience episodes of extreme volatility during the entire period analyzed, and Bulgaria, a CEEC which experienced at least four separate events of extreme volatility during the same period (even, recently, during the so-called recovery period of 1997–2000).[9]

We want to know if there is a clear cut relationship between the 'extreme' volatility of trade openness and the volatility of per capita consumption able to determine permanent effects in the welfare of the local population. In other words, did the trade liberalization reforms of the 1990s make CEECs more vulnerable in their socioeconomic conditions?

Table 2.3   (continued)

2.3c Volatility of Per Capital Consumption/Volatility of Per Capita GDP

Estonia	1.136	Austria	0.796
Latvia	1.482	Belgium	0.820
Lithuania	0.341	Denmark	1.296
Baltic States	0.987	Finland	0.915
		France	0.957
Albania	1.031	Germany	1.275
Belarus	1.175	Greece	0.663
Croatia	0.596	Iceland	1.498
Macedonia	1.748	Ireland	0.759
Russia	1.062	Italy	1.846
Turkey	0.942	Luxembourg	0.880
Other European	1.092	Netherlands	1.506
		Norway	0.855
Bulgaria	1.759	Portugal	0.839
Czech Republic	1.831	Spain	1.187
Hungary	0.833	Sweden	0.959
Poland	0.487	Switzerland	0.729
Romania	1.277	United Kingdom	1.139
Slovakia	1.681	EEA	1.051
Slovenia	1.507		
CEECs 7	1.339		

Therefore, we seek to explore empirically the relationship between consumption volatility and long-term growth, and its effects in terms of socioeconomic vulnerability to covariate trade shocks.

SOCIOECONOMIC VULNERABILITY TO TRADE LIBERALIZATION: AN EMPIRICAL ASSESSMENT

Our assessment of socioeconomic vulnerability to covariant trade shocks has been tested for 34 European countries,[10] in the period 1990–2000, the decade when the major 'first type' reforms and trade liberalization have been implemented (Svejnar 2002). While an empirical exercise on CEECs during the transition era could represent, in principle, a useful way of analyzing socioeconomic vulnerability to covariate trade shocks, we cannot benefit from

Table 2.4 Decomposition of Per Capita Consumption Volatility

	Total	Normal	Extreme		Total	Normal	Extreme
Estonia	0.098	0.005	0.092	Austria	0.009	0.009	0.000
Latvia	0.179	0.000	0.179	Belgium	0.011	0.011	0.000
Lithuania	0.033	0.033	0.000	Denmark	0.018	0.018	0.000
Baltic States	**0.103**	**0.013**	**0.091**	Finland	0.037	0.007	0.029
				France	0.012	0.012	0.000
Albania	0.124	0.003	0.121	Germany	0.015	0.015	0.000
Belarus	0.096	0.002	0.094	Greece	0.012	0.012	0.000
Croatia	0.058	0.005	0.054	Iceland	0.043	0.005	0.037
Macedonia	0.069	0.000	0.069	Ireland	0.023	0.023	0.000
Russia	0.072	0.007	0.065	Italy	0.020	0.005	0.015
Turkey	0.045	0.004	0.041	Luxembourg	0.018	0.018	0.000
Other European	**0.078**	**0.003**	**0.074**	Netherlands	0.015	0.015	0.000
				Norway	0.011	0.011	0.000
Bulgaria	0.094	0.006	0.088	Portugal	0.017	0.017	0.000
Czech Republic	0.085	0.004	0.081	Spain	0.017	0.017	0.000
Hungary	0.041	0.015	0.026	Sweden	0.023	0.014	0.009
Poland	0.019	0.019	0.000	Switzerland	0.011	0.011	0.000
Romania	0.075	0.002	0.073	United Kingdom	0.019	0.006	0.012
Slovakia	0.105	0.006	0.099	**EEA**	**0.018**	**0.013**	**0.006**
Slovenia	0.070	0.007	0.063				
CEECs 7	**0.070**	**0.008**	**0.061**				

Source: Authors' estimation.

*Figure 2.2 Volatility Decomposition of Per Capita Consumption:
A Comparison between Austria and Bulgaria in the 1990s*

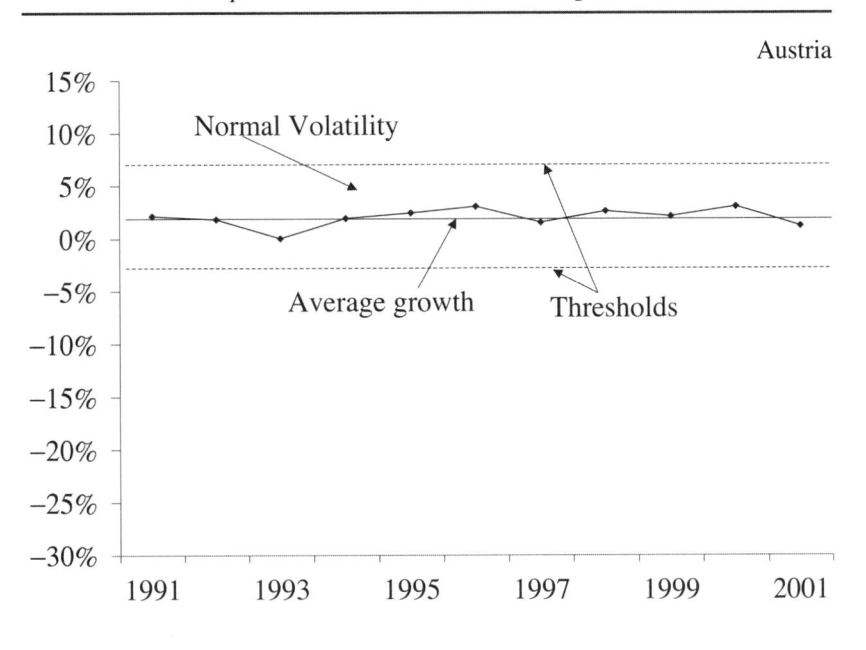

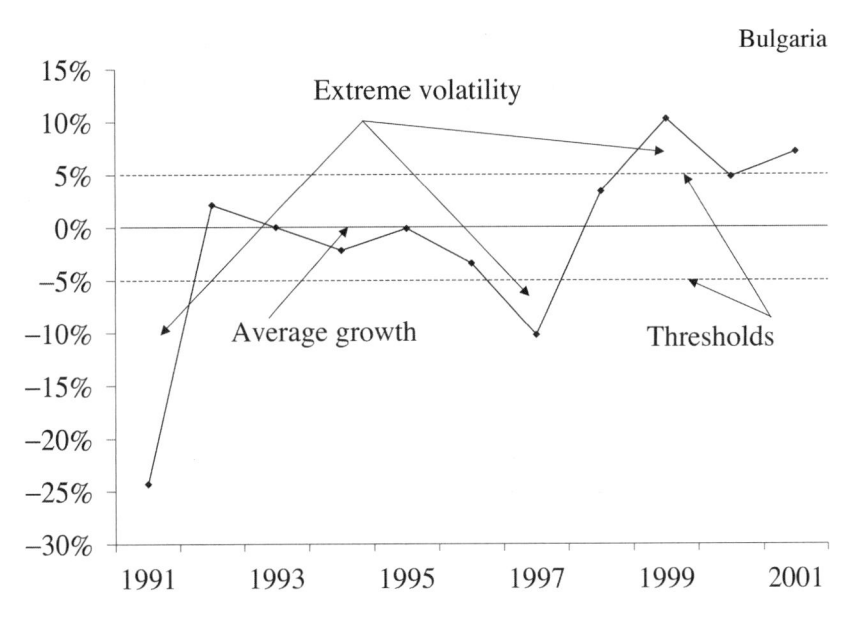

reliable long-term series of data; hence, we should rely on single observations of the phenomena actually experienced in the past decade.

Using Equation 2.3, we test whether higher levels of extreme consumption volatility actually worsen the macroeconomic performance of countries in terms of consumption growth. We used the instrumental variable technique to take into account the possibility that volatility may be endogenously determined together with long-run growth. This is a two-step procedure. First we tested the determinants of per capita consumption volatility in order to isolate exogenous changes in volatility and thus gauge their causal impact on per capita consumption growth; afterwards, we used the estimated values as instrumental variables in the final regression. Hence, we tested three instrumental variables: the standard deviation of terms of trade adjustment (per cent of GDP), trade openness and current account balance. We also tested the volatility of selected other variables traditionally used in similar studies, such as the standard deviation of the inflation rate, real interest rate and real exchange rate. We also considered a non-EEA dummy to isolate the effect in the case of non-EEA member countries. The results of the instrumental variable technique first step are presented in Appendix 2A.1 and 2A.2 and emphasize the role played by the volatility of trade openness rates of change and terms-of-trade adjustment, especially in the case of extreme volatility.

As Table 2.5 shows, regression results reveal a negative and significant relationship between consumption volatility and its growth rate, that proves to be particularly relevant in the case of extreme volatility. We also considered the continuous interaction effects on extreme volatility with a measure of fiscal policy procyclicality (equation 2.3).[11] We also tested the continuous interaction effects on extreme volatility of a set of structural characteristics, such as average per capita consumption (as a proxy for overall economic development), average ratio of private domestic credit to GDP (as a proxy for financial depth), a subjective index of investor perceptions, the International Country Risk Guide (ICRG) index (as a proxy of institutional development) and trade openness (per cent of GDP). Among all those tested variables, only fiscal policy procyclicality turned out to be robust and statistically significant (see Table 2A.2). As the model clearly highlights, a procyclical behavior in the management of policy tools is closely associated with the worsening macroeconomic performance of the countries analyzed. This point is particularly relevant, since it underlines the fundamental role of policy reforms and efficient coping mechanisms. Besides, the coefficient associated with the initial level of per capita consumption demonstrates, in a significant way, the presence of a convergence process among the European countries during the transition era.[12]

Table 2.5 Effects of Volatility on Per Capita Consumption Growth

Dependent variable	\multicolumn{3}{c}{Average per capita consumption growth rate}		
	(1)	(2)	(3)
Constant	0.1706511***	0.1961619***	0.1755771***
	0.047759	0.0611729	0.04834
Total volatility	−0.5876046***		
	0.1516663		
Normal volatility		−1,197	
		2,137	
Extreme volatility		−0.6902593***	−0.6184464***
		0.2045621	0.1575628
Interaction Volatility*Pro-cyclicality	−0.451776***	−0.4384365**	−0.4834059***
	0.1499331	0.1738781	0.1524579
Per capita consumption in 1990, in logs	−0.0153654***	−0.0170121***	−0.0163785***
	0.0049249	0.005276	0.005094
Test Breusch-Pagan/Cook-Weisberg (Prob>chi^2)			
	1.22	0.93	1.56
p-value	0.2687	0.3345	0.2113
R^2	0.37	0.38	0.38
Observations	34	34	34

Notes: Standard errors are reported below the corresponding coefficients. ***Significant at the 1% level; **significant at the 5% level; *significant at the 10% level.
Source: Authors' estimation.

The above results clearly underline the negative role that economic uncertainty (proxied by extreme volatility) induced by trade liberalization has on the socioeconomic performance (proxied by per capita consumption growth) of these countries. In other words, trade liberalization, bringing an entirely new set of shocks and incentives, may have increased the degree of CEECs' socioeconomic vulnerability, which translated itself retroactively in

Table 2.6 *'Ex-Post' Impact of Extreme Volatility on Consumption Growth in Europe during the 1990s (per cent)*

	Impact of extreme volatility		Impact of extreme volatility
Estonia	–3.45	Austria	–0.09
Latvia	–6.07	Belgium	–0.12
Lithuania	–3.93	Denmark	–0.28
Baltic States	–4.484	Finland	–0.50
		France	0.03
Albania	–8.84	Germany	–0.19
Belarus	–5.69	Greece	–0.15
Croatia	–2.85	Iceland	–0.27
Macedonia	–4.32	Ireland	–0.32
Russia	–5.25	Italy	–0.22
Turkey	–2.98	Luxembourg	–0.93
Other European	–4.989	Netherlands	0.05
		Norway	–1.81
Bulgaria	–6.14	Portugal	–0.22
Czech Republic	–4.28	Spain	0.07
Hungary	–3.12	Sweden	–0.54
Poland	–3.02	Switzerland	–0.61
Romania	–3.36	United Kingdom	–0.22
Slovakia	–4.70	EEA	–0.350
Slovenia	–2.80		
CEECs 7	–3.918		

Source: Authors' estimation.

an actual worsening of CEECs' welfare, proxied by a reduction of per capita consumption growth.

Table 2.6 contains an ex-post evaluation of the actual socioeconomic vulnerability to trade liberalization. We simply calculated, for each country i, the actual welfare loss experienced during the last decade induced by the extreme volatility of consumption and linked it to the volatility of trade variables. This welfare loss is measured by the difference between the registered value of per capita consumption growth and the expected per capita consumption growth under the hypothesis of no shocks – a measure of the *potential* consumption growth. It is easy to detect that the effect of volatility has been particularly relevant in the case of the Baltic states (almost 4.5 per cent of their potential annual per capita consumption growth has been actually lost because of extreme volatility), in the case of the group of 'other European countries' (they lost almost 5 per cent) and in the case of the seven CEECs7 (almost 4 per cent), the group which also includes the new EU member states. The countries most harmed by extreme volatility have been Albania, Bulgaria and Latvia. Conversely, among EEA member countries, the effect of volatility is quite negligible.

Practically speaking, if the CEECs7, Baltic states and the other European countries group had been able to reduce their degree of consumption volatility related to trade volatility, they would have achieved higher consumption growth rates during the 1990s (about 4–5 per cent more). Consequently, we must go beyond the apparent positive association between trade liberalization and good economic performance in Eastern Europe.

From the analysis of the determinants of the volatility, we know that part of the registered extreme volatility is affected by trade volatility (see Table 2.A1). Hence, we can derive a measure of the CEECs' relative vulnerability to trade liberalization with respect to Western European countries. To do so, we need to estimate, for each country i, the expected value of its welfare loss induced by uncertainty derived from trade openness. Therefore, we have to estimate the expected value of per capita consumption growth under the hypothesis of covariate trade shocks and, consequently, the probability of covariate trade shocks.

Because of the lack of observations, we cannot adequately model future volatility. However, we do know that the historical volatility provides the best estimate of the future (Dehn 2000). Hence, we simply assumed that past observations may also be observed in the future. Practically speaking, we assume the existence of a stable underlying process. Accordingly, our measure of socioeconomic vulnerability to trade covariate shocks has been derived by simply calculating for each country i the probability that extreme volatility of consumption increases because of a 25 per cent improvement of the total volatility of terms-of-trade and trade openness[13] and by computing the associated expected welfare loss, proxied – according to Equation 2.4 – by the difference between the predicted and the potential per capita consumption growth. The higher the probability of a trade covariate shock and the magnitude of its likely negative impact on per capita consumption growth, the higher the degree of vulnerability for a given country.

Table 2.7 reports the results for each country in the sample. The last column of the table shows the degree of socioeconomic vulnerability given by the product between the probability and its negative effect on per capita consumption growth. These results clearly confirm that EEA member countries are structurally less vulnerable than the other countries sampled, both in the case of increased volatility of trade openness and in terms of trade. They show,

Table 2.7 Socioeconomic Vulnerability to Trade Shock

	Trade Openness Shock		
	Probability (%)	Final Effect (%)	Vulnerability
Estonia	16.17	−0.19	0.307
Latvia	21.44	−0.59	1.258
Lithuania	20.68	−0.26	0.530
Baltic States	19.43	−0.34	0.698
Albania	21.94	−1.46	3.209
Belarus	20.67	−0.34	0.713
Croatia	0.00	−0.11	0.000
Macedonia	21.65	−0.39	0.841
Russia	21.97	−0.41	0.902
Turkey	6.05	−0.16	0.095
Other European	15.38	−0.48	0.960
Bulgaria	22.71	−0.52	1.178
Czech Republic	16.13	−0.19	0.304
Hungary	3.06	−0.14	0.042
Poland	12.14	−0.16	0.196
Romania	19.00	−0.24	0.452
Slovakia	21.37	−0.41	0.876
Slovenia	0.00	−0.07	0.000
CEECs 7	13.49	−0.25	0.435
Austria	0.00	−0.09	0.000
Belgium	0.00	−0.03	0.000
Denmark	0.00	−0.07	0.000
Finland	8.02	−0.11	0.092
France	0.00	−0.07	0.000
Germany	0.00	−0.10	0.000
Greece	0.00	−0.10	0.000
Iceland	0.00	−0.07	0.000
Ireland	0.00	−0.08	0.000
Italy	0.00	−0.08	0.000
Luxembourg	0.00	−0.07	0.000
Netherlands	0.00	−0.06	0.000
Norway	0.00	−0.04	0.000
Portugal	0.00	−0.07	0.000
Spain	0.00	−0.06	0.000
Sweden	0.00	−0.09	0.000
Switzerland	0.00	−0.06	0.000
United Kingdom	0.00	−0.06	0.000
EEA	0.45	−0.07	0.005

Source: Authors' estimation.

Table 2.7 *(continued)*

	Terms of Trade Shock		
	Probability (%)	Final Effect (%)	Vulnerability
Estonia	15.54	-0.20	0.303
Latvia	21.34	-0.45	0.967
Lithuania	17.28	-0.25	0.428
Baltic States	18.05	-0.30	0.566
Albania	19.77	-0.27	0.531
Belarus	20.28	-0.60	1.215
Croatia	0.00	-0.12	0.000
Macedonia	14.70	-0.21	0.315
Russia	22.01	-0.42	0.933
Turkey	3.63	-0.11	0.041
Other European	13.40	-0.29	0.506
Bulgaria	22.25	-0.54	1.197
Czech Republic	21.73	-0.40	0.879
Hungary	7.45	-0.17	0.124
Poland	0.00	-0.12	0.000
Romania	0.00	-0.12	0.000
Slovakia	19.69	-0.29	0.565
Slovenia	14.85	-0.15	0.226
CEECs 7	12.28	-0.26	0.427
Austria	0.00	-0.04	0.000
Belgium	6.02	-0.11	0.064
Denmark	0.00	-0.10	0.000
Finland	5.21	-0.12	0.062
France	0.00	-0.03	0.000
Germany	0.00	-0.06	0.000
Greece	0.00	-0.05	0.000
Iceland	0.00	-0.11	0.000
Ireland	13.22	-0.11	0.143
Italy	0.00	-0.08	0.000
Luxembourg	21.81	-0.28	0.607
Netherlands	0.00	-0.04	0.000
Norway	21.80	-0.52	1.132
Portugal	10.64	-0.10	0.104
Spain	0.00	-0.03	0.000
Sweden	14.67	-0.16	0.233
Switzerland	21.24	-0.20	0.423
United Kingdom	0.00	-0.11	0.000
EEA	9.76	-0.17	0.270

on average, a limited probability to being hurt by a shock in terms of extreme volatility and even in these unlucky episodes the induced negative effects on annual consumption growth remain small (on average no more than −0.5 per cent in the case of trade openness shocks and −0.17 per cent in the case of terms of trade). Relevant exceptions in the case of a terms-of-trade shock are Ireland, Luxembourg, Norway and Switzerland. These countries show levels of probability of extreme volatility and likely dimensions of negative effects on annual consumption similar to that of the Baltic states. Not surprisingly the first two are the most open EU member countries, while the latter are not members of the European single market.

The most vulnerable groups in the sample are the Baltic states and the other European countries, that have a probability of experiencing extreme volatility of almost one out of five. However, the situation is highly diversified among countries within each group. For instance, among the CEECs7, while Bulgaria, the Czech Republic and Slovakia show one of the highest probabilities of extreme volatility and the worst results in terms of consumption performance, Hungary and Slovenia, for trade openness, and Poland and Romania, for terms of trade, register one of the best results. Similarly, among the other European countries, Albania, Russia and Belarus show one of the worst performances, while Turkey and, above all, Croatia register a performance similar to most of the Western European countries.

The actual measurement of the estimated vulnerability of the CEECs7, however, needs a more careful approach. We need to take into account that these countries are new EU member states.[14] Could these countries experience a different volatility path in the future because of EU economic and political integration? In other words, are the new member countries likely to experience a sort of synchronization with EEA member countries' socioeconomic performance as well as a process of stabilization of their degree of volatility?

To test this hypothesis, the obvious reference is the past experience of Greece, Portugal and Spain, the Mediterranean EU countries which joined EEC in the 1980s. Actually, these countries did show an overall increased synchronization with the older EU member countries (Table 2.8),[15] with the relevant exceptions of Spain (trade openness) and Greece (trade volatility). It is also worth noting the situation in terms of reduction of extreme volatility: since accession neither Portugal nor Greece have experienced a period of sharp fluctuations from the point of view, respectively, of trade openness and terms of trade volatility.

Assuming that the new EU member countries of Central and Eastern Europe will experience a trade volatility pattern similar to the average of the pattern of the Mediterranean EU member countries, we can calculate for these countries

Table 2.8 Volatility Patterns Before and After EU Accession

	Normal volatility			Extreme volatility			Total volatility		
	Before accession	After accession	Difference (%)	Before accession	After accession	Difference (%)	Before accession	After accession	Difference (%)
Trade openness										
Greece	3,467	2,232	−35.61	4,254	1,579	−62.88	7,721	3,811	−50.63
Portugal	2,169	4,378	101.86	7,398	0.000	−100.00	9,566	4,378	−54.24
Spain	2,924	3,941	34.75	4,367	5,242	24.21	7,291	9,365	28.44
Average	2.853	3.517	23.26	5.339	2.334	−56.28	8.193	5.851	−28.58
Terms of trade										
Greece	0.004	0.007	76.32	0.003	0.000	−100.00	0.007	0.007	2.99
Portugal	0.004	0.001	−78.29	0.013	0.011	−14.1	0.017	0.012	−30.58
Spain	0.004	0.001	−65.41	0.01	0.009	−12.55	0.014	0.01	−27.16
Average	0.004	0.003	−24.72	0.009	0.007	−22.78	0.013	0.010	−23.40

Source: Authors' estimates.

Table 2.9 Socioeconomic Vulnerability of CEECs after EU Accession

	Trade Openness Shock			Terms of Trade Shock		
	Probability (%)	Final Effect (%)	Vulnerability	Probability (%)	Final Effect (%)	Vulnerability
Czech Republic	6.64	−0.14	0.095	21.91	−0.37	0.808
Estonia	6.67	−0.14	0.096	15.72	−0.18	0.280
Hungary	0.50	−0.10	0.005	7.58	−0.15	0.116
Latvia	10.73	−0.44	0.477	21.52	−0.41	0.890
Lithuania	10.09	−0.19	0.196	17.46	−0.23	0.395
Poland	4.16	−0.12	0.051	0.00	−0.11	0.000
Slovakia	10.67	−0.31	0.331	19.87	−0.26	0.520
Slovenia	0.00	−0.05	0.000	15.03	−0.14	0.208

Source: Authors' estimates.

new probabilities of per capita consumption volatility and the likely impacts on their macroeconomic performances. The results are presented in Table 2.9.

After EU accession, the CEECs will show a lower degree of vulnerability than in the previous exercise, regarding a trade openness volatility shock, while in the case of shocks in terms of trade volatility the results are quite surprising: the CEECs, following the hypothesis of EU synchronization, will register a decrease of extreme volatility proportionately less than total volatility and will show a higher degree of vulnerability, notwithstanding the reduction of total volatility.

CONCLUSION

This chapter offers a substantive contribution to the debate on the effects of trade liberalization on emerging countries, with an empirical focus on the CEECs. It presents a sound methodology to assess the effect in terms of socioeconomic vulnerability of covariate trade shocks on aggregate welfare and, even, on the poor, since we assume that consumption shares of each quintile do not change with changes in per capita consumption. The main result of the empirical exercise is that, in spite of the registered growth of per capita consumption, during the 1990s the CEECs experienced a clear worsening of their socioeconomic well-being, following trade shocks which occurred at the beginning of the transition era, when they undertook a dramatic process of institutional and economic liberalization.

As the empirical results clearly show there is robust evidence on the adverse effects of trade covariate shocks on consumption growth. Shocks on terms-of-trade and trade openness (proxied by their extreme volatility) directly reduce the resources available for private investment and consumption. This is linked to a poor use of adequate policy tools to cope with or mitigate trade shocks and their repercussions on the domestic economy. It also underlines the limited ability of the more fragile countries in terms of their economy and institutional capacity to cope with a higher degree of uncertainty. These empirical results spur some general and relevant implications regarding reach and the need to undertake policy reforms to reduce the degree of vulnerability induced by trade liberalization as well as design policies to cope or mitigate its negative impacts.

First, to reduce the vulnerability of more fragile countries, we should improve the governance of the globalization process. The pervasive role of covariant trade shocks points to a specific role for international policy coordination. Countries with weak institutions and imperfect and incomplete internal markets risk being adversely affected by international competition and globalization. Hence, international policies must be redirected and designed to be able to limit the size and frequency of macro shocks. Multilateral agreements and international institutions should play a role in reducing the degree of risk exposure within the current international framework. In other words, we need to implement a new culture of prevention at the international level.

Second, countries should adopt a new generation of forward-looking national policies to support the trade liberalization process, such as policies able to mitigate the impact of trade shocks on the national economy and to enhance the coping mechanisms of the population in the face of external shocks. In this light, some authors underline the central role of insurance tools. Indeed, particularly for those shocks that tend to recur, such as those related to commodity price cycles, it would be better to incur the cost of insurance rather than the cost of a shock. Moreover, since the poor are especially prone to suffer from shocks, explicit or implicit insurance may be considered an important form of pro-poor expenditure of national governments. At the same time, the pervasive negative effect of covariate shocks demonstrates that a micro approach which limits policy intervention to risk insurance tailored to specific target groups would appear to be insufficient. Covariate shocks which occur at the aggregate level – but with pervasive effects on the poorest and most vulnerable social categories – call for an overall reform of national policies based on a deeper analysis of specific transmission channels of shocks into the domestic economy.

The purpose of this analysis is not to support a new protectionism, that indeed would have additional negative socioeconomic impacts; rather, it is to help policymakers draw more attention to the hidden negative effects that follow trade liberalization reforms. In this respect, the study suggests that macro policy tools may play an effective role in reacting to such events and, in the case of the CEECs, to catch up, if not to the EU average levels of well-being, at least to their own potential well-being. In this light, socioeconomic vulnerability analysis of trade covariate macro shocks is a clear guideline for the 'reach' of any trade liberalization reform.

NOTES

This study was produced under the GDN-IPALMO Research Program on Macroeconomic Vulnerability, directed by Umberto Triulzi. Financial support by the Italian Ministry of Foreign Affair (Development Cooperation Directorate General) is gratefully acknowledged. Preliminary drafts of this chapter were presented at the Fifth Annual Global Development Conference 'Understanding Reform', New Delhi, India, 28–30 January 2004, and at the University of Reading (UK) at the University of Lucca (Italy). We thank Andrea Cornia, Robert Holzmann, Luca De Benedictis, Ethan Ligon, Emil Tesliuc and Silvia Nenci for their useful comments.

1. The Council for Mutual Economic Assistance (CMEA) was established in 1949 to foster economic, scientific and technological cooperation and develop the economic integration among the socialist member countries: USSR; Bulgaria, Czechoslovakia, Hungary, Poland, Romania and Albania (joined in 1949); East Germany (1950), Mongolia (1962), Cuba (1972) and Vietnam (1978).
2. This is a central point. Some disciplines call vulnerability something which is very similar to ex-post poverty outcome assessments. Instead, a proper vulnerability assessment requires an ex-ante analysis of exogenous risk factors and risk management tools. While many international organizations (e.g., UN Food and Agriculture Organization, World Bank, United Nations Development Programme, US Agency for International Development) have made significant strides in improving our understanding of vulnerability, a proliferation of multiple methodologies, terminology and approaches to vulnerability is apparent, involving as diverse areas of interest as food security, conflict prevention, etc.
3. Take the example of a terms-of-trade shock. In the case of a single event, countries may use their foreign-exchange reserves as an efficient coping mechanism, but in the case of 'extreme' shocks, the capacity of the country to cope may be exhausted and lead to severe economic disruption (Aizenman and Pinto 2005).
4. This threshold is set equal to the average standard deviation of per consumption growth of the sampled countries. In this way, we define as 'extreme volatility' the volatility of each country which exceeds the average volatility of the sample.
5. Albania, Belarus, Croatia, Macedonia, Russian Federation and Turkey.
6. Austria, Belgium, Denmark, Finland, France, Germany, Greece, Iceland, Ireland, Italy, Luxembourg, Netherlands, Norway, Portugal, Spain, Sweden, Switzerland and United Kingdom.
7. Data on household final consumption expenditure per capita in constant prices, 1995, US dollars (World Development Indicators Database, 2003).
8. 'First-type reforms' typically focus on macro stabilization, price liberalization and dismantling the institutions of the communist system. During the first period of the transition process, the institution governing the Soviet bloc trading area, the CMEA, was abolished and most CEECs opened up rapidly to international trade. 'Second-type' reforms, undertaken later, involved the development and enforcement of laws, regulations and institutions in order to ensure a successful market-oriented economy (Svejnar 2002)
9. Following the decomposition procedure described above, 'extreme volatility' has been detected using the average per capita consumption growth volatility of the sampled countries as common threshold.
10. The 34 European countries are the following: Austria, Belgium, Denmark, Finland, France, Germany, Greece, Iceland, Ireland, Italy, Luxembourg, Netherlands, Norway, Portugal, Spain, Sweden, Switzerland, United Kingdom (the group EEA); Bulgaria, Czech Republic, Estonia, Hungary, Latvia, Lithuania, Poland, Romania, Slovak Republic, Slovenia (the group of CEECs); Albania, Belarus, Croatia, Macedonia, Russian Federation and Turkey (the group 'Other European').
11. The degree of fiscal policy pro-cyclicality is approximated by the correlation coefficient between the growth rate of GDP and the growth rate of government consumption as share of GDP.
12. Following Levine and Renelt (1992) we tested a set of additional control variables chosen in consideration of their role in the new empirical growth literature: the average ratio of domestic private credit to GDP (as a proxy for financial development) and the average secondary school enrollment ratio (as a proxy for human capital investment). They turn to be not statistically significant in our empirical exercise.
13. Under the hypothesis of a normal distribution of the rates of change of the trade variables, we test the following hypothesis: H_0: $s^2 \leq \sigma^2$ against H_1: $s^2 > \sigma^2$. Under the null hypothesis $\frac{s^2(n-1)}{\sigma^2} \approx \chi^2_{n-1}$ where n is the number of years considered in the forecast, s^2 is the extreme volatility observed over sample and σ^2 is the assumed higher extreme volatility.

14. The Czech Republic, Estonia, Hungary, Latvia, Lithuania, Poland, Slovakia and Slovenia joined the EU on 1 May 2004.
15. This result is consistent with other similar empirical evidence. For example, in the case of the NAFTA Agreement implementation, Mexico appears to have recorded a larger synchronization of its macro volatility with the United States and Canada (Kose, Meredith and Towe 2004).

BIBLIOGRAPHY

Acemoglu, Daron, Simon Johnson, James A. Robinson and Yunyong Thaicharoen (2003), 'Institutional Causes, Macroeconomic Symptoms: Volatility, Crises and Growth', *Journal of Monetary Economics*, **50** (1), 49–123.
Ades, Alberto and Rafael Di Tella (1997), 'National Champions and Corruption: Some Unpleasant Interventionist Arithmetic', *Economic Journal*, **107** (443), 1023–42.
—— (1999), 'Rents, Competition and Corruption', *American Economic Review*, **89** (4), 982–93.
Aghion, Phillipe, Abhijit Banerjee and Thomas Piketty (1999), 'Dualism and Macroeconomic Volatility', *Quarterly Journal of Economics*, **114** (4), 1359–97.
Aizenman, Joshua and Brian Pinto (eds) (2005), *Managing Volatility and Crises: A Practitioner's Guide*, New York: Cambridge University Press.
Alesina, Alberto, Nouriel Roubini and Philip Swagel (1996), 'Political Instability and Economic Growth', *Journal of Economic Growth*, **1** (2), 189–213.
Alwang, Jeffrey, Paul B. Siegel and Steen L. Jorgensen (2001), 'Vulnerability: A View from Different Disciplines', Washington, DC, World Bank Social Protection Discussion Paper No. 0115.
Amin, Sajeda, Ashok S. Rai and Gorgio Topa (1999), 'Does Microcredit Reach the Poor and Vulnerable? Evidence from Northern Bangladesh', Cambridge, MA, Harvard University Center for International Development Working Paper No. 28.
Amsden, Alice H. (1989), *Asia's Next Giant: South Korea and Late Industrialization*, New York: Oxford University Press.
Atkins, Jonathan P. and Sonia Mazzi (1999), 'Small States: A Composite Vulnerability Index', Report Presented to the Advisory Board to the Joint Commonwealth Secretariat/World Bank Task Force on Small States.
Ben-David, Dan (1993), 'Equalizing Exchange: Trade Liberalization and Economic Convergence', *Quarterly Journal of Economics*, **108** (3), 653–79.
Bertola, Giuseppe and Ricardo J. Caballero (1994), 'Cross Sectional Efficiency and Labor Hoarding in an Matching Model of Unemployment', Cambridge, MA, National Bureau of Economic Research Working Paper No. 4472.
Bhagwati, Jagdish and T.N. Srinivasan (2002), 'Trade and Poverty in the Poor Countries', *American Economic Review*, **92** (2), 180–83.
Blanchard, Olivier (1997), *The Economics of Post-Communist Transition*, Oxford: Clarendon Press.
Caballero, Ricardo J. (2000), 'Macroeconomic Volatility in Latin America: A View and Three Case Studies', Washington, DC, National Bureau of Economic Research Working Paper No. 7782.
Calvo, Cesar and Stefan Dercon (2003), 'Vulnerability: An Axiomatic Approach', Oxford University, Department of Economics, unpublished paper.

Chaudhuri, Shubham, Jyotsna Jalan and Asep Suryahadi (2002), 'Assessing Household Vulnerability to Poverty from Cross-sectional Data: A Methodology and Estimates from Indonesia', New York, NY, Columbia University, Department of Economics, Discussion Paper.
Christiaensen, Luc J. and Richard N. Boisvert (2000), 'On Measuring Household Food Vulnerability: Case Evidence from Northern Mali', Ithaca, NY, Cornell University, Department of Agricultural, Resource and Managerial Economics, unpublished paper.
De Ferranti, David M. and Guillermo Perry (2000) *Securing our Future in a Global Economy*, Washington, DC, World Bank.
Dehn, Jan (2000), 'The Effects on Growth of Commodity Price Uncertainty and Shocks', Washington, DC, World Bank, Policy Research Working Paper No. 2455.
Delgado, Christopher L., Jane Hopkins, Valerie A. Kelly, Peter Hazell, Anna A. McKenna, Peter Gruhn, Behjat Hojjati, Jayashree Sil and Claude Courbois (1998), 'Agricultural Growth Linkages in Sub-Saharan Africa', Washington, DC, International Food Policy Research Institute (IFPRI) Report No. 107.
Dercon Stefan (2001), 'Assessing Vulnerability to Poverty', Oxford, UK, Oxford University, Department of Economics, unpublished paper. Available at: http://www.economics.ox.ac.uk/members/stefan.dercon/assessing%20vulnerability.pdf.
Dercon, Stefan and Pramila Krishnan (2000), 'Vulnerability, Seasonality and Poverty in Ethiopia', *Journal of Development Studies*, **36** (6), 25–53.
Dollar, David and Aart Kraay (2001a), 'Growth Is Good for the Poor', Washington, DC, World Bank Policy Research Working Paper No. 2587.
―― (2001b), 'Trade, Growth, and Poverty', World Bank, Development Research Group Working Paper No. 2615.
Easterly William R., Roumeen Islam and Joseph E. Stiglitz (2001), 'Shaken and Stirred: Explaining Growth Volatility', in Boris Pleskovic and Nicholas Stern (eds) *Annual World Bank Conference on Development Economics, 2000*, Washington, DC: World Bank, pp. 191–211.
Easterly, William R. and Aaart Kraay (1999), 'Small States, Small Problems?', Washington, DC, World Bank, Policy Research Working Paper No. 2139.
Forbes, Kristin (2001), 'Are Trade Linkages Important Determinants of Country Vulnerability to Crises?', Cambridge, MA, National Bureau of Economic Research (NBER) Working Paper No. 8194.
Frankel, Jeffrey A. (2000), 'Globalization of the Economy', Cambridge, MA, National Bureau of Economic Research (NBER) Working Paper No. 7858.
Gavin, Michael and Ricardo Hausmann (1996), 'Sources of Macroeconomic Volatility in Developing Economies', Washington, DC, Inter-American Development Bank, Office of the Chief Economist, unpublished paper.
Glewwe, Paul and Gilette Hall (1998), 'Are Some Groups More Vulnerable to Macroeconomic Shocks Than Others? Hypothesis Tests Based on Panel Data from Peru', *Journal of Development Economics*, **56** (1), 181–206.
Glick, Reuven and Andrew K. Rose (1999), 'Contagion and Trade. Why Are Currency Crises Regional?', *Journal of International Money and Finance*, 'Sources of Macroeconomic Volatility in Developing Economies' (4), 603–17.
Heitzmann, Karin, R. Sudharshan Canagarajah and Paul B. Siegel (2001), 'Guidelines for Assessing the Sources of Risk and Vulnerability', Washington, DC, World Bank, Social Protection Discussion Paper No. 218.
Hertel, Thomas W. and L. Alan Winters (2005), 'Poverty Impacts of a WTO Agreement:

Synthesis and Overview', in Thomas W. Hertel and L. Alan Winters (eds), *Poverty and the WTO: Impacts of the Doha Development Agenda*, Washington, DC: World Bank, pp. 3–30.

Hnatkoska, Viktoria and Norman Loayza (2004), 'Volatility and Growth', Washington, DC, World Bank, Policy Research Working Paper No. 3184.

Hoddinott, John and Agnes Quisumbing (2003), 'Methods for Microeconometric Risk and Vulnerability Assessments: A Review with Empirical Examples', World Bank, Social Protection Discussion Paper No. 324.

Holzman, Franklyn D. (1974), *Foreign Trade Under Central Planning*, Cambridge, MA: Harvard University Press.

Holzmann, Robert (2001), 'Risk and Vulnerability: The Forward Looking Role of Social Protection in a Globalizing World', Washington, DC, World Bank, Social Protection Discussion Paper No. 109.

Holzmann, Robert and Steen Jorgensen (2000), 'Social Risk Management: A New Conceptual Framework for Social Protection and Beyond', Washington, DC, World Bank, Social Protection Discussion Paper No. 0006.

International Monetary Fund (2003), *World Economic Outlook*, Washington, DC: International Monetary Fund.

Judson, Ruth and Athanasios Orphanides (1996), 'Inflation, Volatility and Growth', Washington, DC, Board of Governors of the Federal Reserve System, Finance and Economic Discussion Series No. 96-19.

Kose, M. Ayhan (2002), 'Explaining Business Cycles in Small Open Economies: How Much Do World Prices Matter?', *Journal of International Economics*, **56** (2), 299–327.

Kose, M. Ayhan and Eswar Prasad (2002), 'Thinking Big: How Can Small States Hold Their Own in an Increasingly Globalized Economy?', *Finance and Development*, **39**, 38–41.

Kose, M. Ayhan and Kei-Mu Yi (2003), 'The Trade-Comovement Problem in International Macroeconomics', New York, NY, Federal Reserve Bank of New York, Staff Report No. 155.

Kose, M. Ayhan, Eswar Prasad and Marco Terrones (2003), 'Volatility and Comovement in a Globalized World Economy: An Empirical Exploration', Washington, DC, IMF Working Paper No. 03/246.

Kose, M. Ayhan, Guy Meredith and Christopher M. Towe (2004), 'How Has NAFTA Affected the Mexican Economy? Review and Evidence', Washington, DC, IMF Working Paper No. 04/59.

Krueger, Anne O. (1990), 'Asian Trade and Growth Lessons', *American Economic Review*, **80** (2), 108–12.

Lahiri, Amartya (2001). 'Growth and Equilibrium Indeterminancy: The Role of Capital Mobility', *Economic Theory*, **17** (1), 197–208.

Lall, Sanjaya and Carlo Pietrobelli (2002), *Failing to Compete: Technology Development and Technology Systems in Africa*, Cheltenham, UK and Northhampton, MA: Edward Elgar.

Levine, Ross and David Renelt (1992), 'A Sensitivity Analysis of Cross-country Growth Regressions', *American Economic Review*, **82** (4), 942–63.

Ligon, Ethan and Laura Schechter (2003), 'Measuring vulnerability', *Economic Journal*, **113** (486), 95–102.

Lundberg, Mattias and Lyn Squire (2003), 'The Simultaneous Evolution of Growth and Inequality', *Economic Journal*, **113** (487), 326–44.

Lustig, Nora (1999), 'Crises and the Poor: Socially Responsible Macroeconomics, Sustainable Development Department', Washington, DC, Inter-American Development Bank, Technical Paper.

Martin, Philippe and Carol Ann Rogers (1997), 'Stabilization Policy, Learning-by-Doing and Economic Growth', *Oxford Economic Papers*, **49** (1), 152–66.

McCulloch, Neil, L. Alan Winters and Xavier Cirera (2001), *Trade Liberalization and Poverty: A Handbook*, London: Centre for Economic Policy Research.

Mellor, John and Sarah Gavian (1999), 'The Determinants of Employment Growth In Egypt: The Dominant Role of Agriculture And the Rural Small Scale Sector', Cambridge, MA, Abt Associates Inc, Impact Assessment Report No. 7.

Mendoza, Enrique G. (1995), 'The Terms of Trade, the Real Exchange Rate and Economic Fluctuations', *International Economic Review*, **36** (1), 101–37.

Meng, Qinglai and Andres Velasco (1999), 'Can Capital Mobility be Destabilizing?', Cambridge, MA, National Bureau of Economic Research (NBER) Working Paper No. 7263.

Milanovic, Branko (2003), 'Worlds Apart: International and World Inequality 1950–2000', lecture notes presented at the Siena Summer School, July.

Montalbano, Pierluigi, Alessandro Federici, Carlo Pietrobelli and Umberto Triulzi (2007), 'Trade Openness and Vulnerability in Central and Eastern Europe', in Machiko Nissanke and Erik Thorbecke (eds), *The Impact of Globalization on the World's Poor: Transmission Mechanisms*, New York: Palgrave, pp. 204–34.

Mundell, Robert A. (1997), 'Great Contractions in Transition Economies', in Mario I. Blejer and Marko Skreb (eds), *Macroeconomic Stabilization in Transition Economies*, New York: Cambridge University Press, pp. 73–99.

Pallage, Stephane and Michel A. Robe (2003), 'On the Welfare Cost of Economic Fluctuations in Developing Countries', *International Economic Review*, **44** (2), 677–98.

Prasad, Eswar S. and Jeffrey A. Gable (1997), 'International Evidence on the Determinants of Trade Dynamics', *IMF Staff Papers*, **45** (3), 401–39.

Pritchett, Lant, Asep Suryahadi and Sudarno Sumarto (2000), 'Quantifying Vulnerability to Poverty: A Proposed Measure, with Application to Indonesia', Canberra, East Asian Bureau of Economic Research, Development Economics Working Paper No. 83.

Ramey, Garey and Valerie A. Ramey (1995), 'Cross-Country Evidence on the Link between Volatility and Growth', *American Economic Review*, **85** (5), 1138–51.

Razin, Assaf (1995), 'The Dynamic-Optimizing Approach to the Current Account: Theory and Evidence', in *Understanding Interdependence: The Macroeconomics of the Open Economy*, Peter B. Kenen (ed.), Princeton, NJ: Princeton University Press, pp. 169–98.

Razin Assaf, Efraim Sadka and Tarek Coury (2003), 'Trade Openness, Investment Instability, and Terms-of-Trade Volatility', *Journal of International Economics*, **61** (2), 285–306.

Rodríguez, Francisco and Dani Rodrik (1999), 'Trade Policy and Economic Growth: A Skeptic's Guide to the Cross-national Evidence', London, Centre for Economic Policy Discussion Paper No. 2143.

Rodrik, Dani (1991), 'Policy Uncertainty and Private Investment in Developing Countries', *Journal of Development Economics*, **36** (2), 229–42.

—— (1999), 'Where Did All the Growth Go? External Shocks, Social Conflict and Growth Collapses', *Journal of Economic Growth*, **4** (4), 385–412.

—— (2000), 'How Far Will International Economic Integration Go?', *Journal of Economic Perspectives*, **14** (1), 177–86.

Servén, Luis (1997), 'Irreversibility, Uncertainty and Private Investment: Analytical Issues and Some Lessons for Africa', *Journal of African Economies*, **6** (3), 229–68.

Svejnar, Jan (2002) 'Transition Economies: Performance and Challenges', *Journal of Economic Perspectives*, **16** (1), 3–28.

Talvi, Ernesto and Carlos A. Vegh (2000), 'Tax Base Variability and Procyclical Fiscal Policy', Cambridge, MA, National Bureau of Economic Research (NBER) Working Paper No. 7499.

Tesliuc, Emil and Kathy Lindert (2002), 'Vulnerability: A Quantitative and Qualitative Assessment', Washington, DC, World Bank Guatemala Poverty Assessment Program.

Thomas, Timothy (2003), 'A Macro-Level Methodology for Measuring Vulnerability to Poverty, with a Focus on MENA Countries', paper presented at the Fourth Annual Global Development Network Conference, Cairo, 21 January.

Timmer, C. Peter (1997), 'How Well Do the Poor Connect To the Growth Process?', Cambridge, MA, Harvard Institute for International Development, CAER Discussion Paper No. 17.

Wade, Robert (1990), *Governing the Market: Economic Theory and the Role of Government in East Asian Industrialization*, Princeton, NJ: Princeton University Press.

Winters, L. Alan (2000), 'Trade, Trade Policy and Poverty: What are the links?', Canberra, Australian National University, Research School of Statistics, CEPR Discussion Paper No. 2382.

Wolf, Holger (2004), 'Accounting for Consumption Volatility Differences', *IMF Staff Papers*, **51** (special issue), 109–25.

—— (2005), 'Volatility: Definitions and Consequences', in Joshua Aizenman and Brian Pinto (eds), *Managing Volatility and Crises: A Practitioner's Guide*, New York: Cambridge University Press, pp. 45–64.

World Bank (2000), *World Development Report 2000/2001: Attacking Poverty*, New York: Oxford University Press.

Table 2A.1 Instrumental Variable First Step: Determinants of Volatility

Dependent variable	Total Volatility of the annual rates of change of consumption					
Constant	0.006743* 0.004375	-0.0000468 0.0093103	0.0054535 0.0052406	0.0077678* 0.0046465	0.010188*** 0.0045524	
Dummy non-EEA	0.0350919*** 0.0094839	0.0307337*** 0.0107659	0.0380008*** 0.0098717	0.0352693*** 0.0116753	0.0266079** 0.0088003	
Rates of change of trade openness volatility	0.1431774*** 0.0457061	0.1342683*** 0.0420448	0.1385019*** 0.0455428	0.1415275*** 0.0469311	0.3119070** 0.0898157	
TOT adjustment (% GDP) volatility	0.6949499* 0.3890764	0.6048715 0.369622	0.8354209 0.5284034	0.6847735 0.4313535	0.1643135 0.2666624	
CAB (% GDP) volatility		0.0037033 0.0034654				
Inflation rate volatility			-0.0000293 0.0000317			
Real interest rate volatility				-0.000112 0.0002099		
Real exchange rate volatility					-0.0774872 0.0648186	
Test Breusch-Pagan/Cook-Weisberg (Prob>chi²) p-value	13.87 0.0002	15.51 0.0001	13.45 0.0002	11.81 0.0006	2.04 0.1536	
R² Observations	0.74 34	0.75 34	0.75 34	0.74 34	0.82 27	

Notes: Standard errors are reported below the corresponding coefficients; in the first four regressions they are robust; **significant at 5% level; *significant at 10% level; ***significant at 1% level.
Source: Authors' estimate.

Table 2A.1 (continued)

Dependent variable	Normal volatility of the annual rates of change of consumption							
Constant	0.0121348*** 0.0014917	0.013024*** 0.0016489	0.0133734*** 0.0019254	0.0133169*** 0.0025374	0.0124273*** 0.0015354	0.0117466*** 0.0015463	0.0139948*** 0.0016216	
Dummy non-EEA		-0.0033818 0.0027629						
Rates of change of trade openness volatility	-0.0239355** 0.0108917		-0.015603 0.0127731	-0.0188893 0.0120897	-0.0207444* 0.0123088	-0.0215025* 0.0112911	-0.0243703** 0.0104249	-0.0502867* 0.0257848
TOT adjustment (% GDP) volatility				-0.101551 0.099891				
CAB (% GDP) volatility					-0.0004845 0.0008367			
Inflation rate volatility						-0.0000072 0.00000833		
Real interest rate volatility							0.0001864** 0.0000885	
Real exchange rate volatility								-0.0045314 0.0252445
Test Breusch-Pagan/Cook-Weisberg (Prob>chi^2) p-value	0.1 0.748	1.25 0.2631	0 0.9635	0.07 0.7946	0.05 0.8258	0.03 0.8592	0.11 0.7376	
R^2	0.10	0.12	0.10	0.08	0.10	0.21	0.18	
Observations	34	34	34	34	34	34	34	

Notes: Standard errors are reported below the corresponding coefficients; ***significant at 1% level; **significant at 5% level; *significant at 10% level.
Source: Authors' estimate.

Table 2A.1 (continued)

Dependent variable	Extreme volatility of the annual rates of change of consumption					
Constant	−0.0070997 0.0050264	−0.013784 0.0100863	−0.0082929 0.0059789	−0.0078012 0.0056363	−0.0045393 0.0050277	
Dummy non-EEA	0.0380134*** 0.0117078	0.0337229** 0.0130118	0.0407048*** 0.012094	0.0423267** 0.0166299	0.0281685* 0.0143883	
Rates of change of trade openness volatility	0.1566533*** 0.0503722	0.1478826*** 0.0467923	0.1523274*** 0.0501903	0.1703643*** 0.0587344	0.3118068** 0.1304627	
TOT adjustment (% GDP) volatility	0.7626687* 0.4181344	0.6739898* 0.4040241	0.8926368 0.5561459	0.9279313 0.5658649	0.1863309 0.312008	
CAB (% GDP) volatility		0.0036458 0.0038075				
Inflation rate volatility			−0.0000271 0.0000359			
Real interest rate volatility				−0.0006581 0.0009093		
Real exchange rate volatility					−0.0002131 0.0011395	
Test Breusch-Pagan/Cook-Weisberg (Prob>chi²) p-value	11.02 0.0009	12.34 0.0004	10.63 0.0011	8.61 0.0033	1.15 0.2833	
R^2	0.70	0.71	0.71	0.72	0.78	
Observations	34	34	34	34	27	

Notes: Robust standard errors are reported below the corresponding coefficients; ***significant at 1% level; **significant at 5% level; *significant at 10% level.
Source: Authors' estimate.

Table 2A.2   The Continuous Interaction Effects on 'Extreme Volatility' of Various Structural Characteristics

Dependent variable	Consumption annual rate of change				
Structural variable	Average per capita consumption	Trade openness	ICRG	Private credit	Pro-cyclicality
Constant	0.1156703**	0.1420328***	0.1389319**	0.1349502**	0.1755771***
	0.05355	0.0527624	0.0561941	0.0555603	0.04834
Extreme volatility	0.9568506	−0.2161119	−0.1799673	−0.3550371**	−0.6184464***
	0.7539849	0.2042858	0.5448696	0.1802073	0.1575628
Interaction extreme volatility*struct	−0,181169*	−0.2134665	−0.0032799	−0.0018012	−0.4834059***
	0.0986943	0.1519367	0.0078167	0.0032877	0.1524579
Per capita consumption in 1990, in logs	−0,0097003*	−0,0127936**	−0,0124645**	−0,0120112**	−0,0163785***
	0.0057032	0.0055615	0.0059524	0.005901	0.005094
Breusch-Pagan/Cook-Weisberg test for heteroskedasticity	0.53	0.32	0.02	0.03	1.56
p-value	0.4687	0.5722	0.9022	0.8546	0.2113
R^2	0.18	0.14	0.09	0.09	0.31
Observations	34	34	33	34	34

Notes: Standard errors are reported below the corresponding coefficients; ***significant at 1% level; **significant at 5% level; *significant at 10% level.
Source: Authors' estimate.

3. Market Failures in Human Development: The Intergenerational Poverty Trap in Mexico

David Mayer-Foulkes

Health and education investment in Mexico are subject to barriers which create a long-term intergenerational poverty trap which slows economic growth. Specifically, a major portion of the population cannot tap into the increasing returns from investment in education. The role of health is twofold: first, early child health and nutrition are strongly associated with the probability of obtaining a higher education later in life, over and beyond parental education, income and wealth. Second, adult health contributes to adult income. However, the returns from policies for improving early child development are large enough to help overcome the barriers to investment in higher education, and therefore to overcome the human development trap.

This chapter illustrates the two dimensions of Amartya Sen's notion of 'reach' using the specific case of Mexico. First, it is 'person-related' in that it demonstrates the benefits of early child development for future educational attainment and income-earning capability. The second element of reach, inclusiveness, implies that reforms must be conceived in a manner which explicitly accounts for the poor and the barriers they face. In one of the few empirical investigations of the poverty trap, this study shows that increasing returns to adult education hold especially at higher educational levels in Mexico. However, lower-income households rarely attain these levels, pointing to the presence of a poverty trap. When human development traps are present, economic forces do not lead to social integration but generate distinct social classes instead. Unlike past efforts, future reforms must expand their range to emphasize human capital investment, including early child development, and public funds are needed to reach lower income groups.

Historical and macroeconomic studies have identified how nutrition and health affect long-term income and economic growth. Nevertheless, disentangling the underlying causal channels has presented a major challenge to microeconomic research. Studies on the productivity effects of adult health on income have accounted for only a small proportion of the impact. The magnitude found here for the effect of child nutrition and health on education – and therefore on adult income – accounts for an important part of the impact of health on economic growth detected at the macroeconomic and historical levels. These results are supported by recent related research on the 'gradient' of adult health along income using databases for developed countries which place childhood health at the origin of the gradient (Case, Fertig and Paxson 2003; Case, Lubotsky and Paxson 2002). There are two elements in the relationship between development and growth: the intergenerational nature of human capital accumulation, in which early child development plays a key role, and the market failures and traps which characterize such investment. Policies aimed at achieving long-term growth must focus on intergenerational human capital accumulation and on early child development.

In today's globalized world, most people's income depends directly on their skills. Therefore, emergence from poverty can only occur through a population-wide accumulation of human capital. The diffusion and use of knowledge in economic activities have become crucial determinants of cross-country economic growth. Pro-market reforms tending to ease restrictions on capital and trade and to augment technology flows have made the accumulation of skills – as well as the production, adoption and use of knowledge – even more crucial to economic growth. For these reasons, closing the gap in education and technology has become a central focus for development policy. The presence of an intergenerational poverty trap has important implications for policy. For example, although a series of pro-market reforms implemented in Mexico since the mid-1980s led to rises in the returns to education, the distribution of schooling in the adult population remained almost unchanged. The reforms had insufficient reach and range and their potential benefits only materialized for those able to obtain an education. If leading economic institutions acknowledged the existence of poverty traps and integrated the corresponding policies with those promoting globalization, there would be enormous welfare benefits.

In the following discussion I first develop a conceptual framework for understanding the relation between human development and economic growth. This framework provides a natural context for a discussion of the effects of pro-market reforms on the poor. I will first review the evidence on the historical and macroeconomic relation among nutrition, health and economic growth. This nexus motivates a long-term conception of human development including technophysio evolution (Fogel 2002). The relation between human development and economic growth is characterized by a series of intergenerational market failures in human capital accumulation, in which early child development plays an important role.

The second, empirical part of the chapter shows that for Mexico, the intergenerational human development traps discussed here actually exist. As far as I am aware, there are no empirical counterparts establishing the existence of low human capital traps available in the literature. The next section discusses possible market failures leading to the shortfall in human capital investment. Finally, the disappointing results of pro-market reforms carried out in Mexico, reforms which excluded education and health, are reviewed in relation to the ongoing poverty trap.

NUTRITION, HEALTH AND ECONOMIC GROWTH

In recent studies, health has joined education to form a unified conception of human capital. Nobel Prize winning historical studies by Robert W. Fogel (1993, 1994a, 1994b) and Fogel and Wimmer (1992) find that one-third or even one-half of the economic growth in England over the last 200 years is due to improvements in nutrition and health. Arora (2001) finds comparable results for seven advanced countries using 100 to 125-year time series of diverse health indicators. According to this research, the synergy between technological and physiological improvements has produced a rapid, culturally transmitted form of human evolution which is biological but not genetic. Fogel (2002) calls this process, that continues in both rich and developing societies, 'technophysio evolution'. A series of macroeconomic studies has also examined the contemporary role of health in raising income and education.[1] However, their microeconomic counterparts measuring the impact of adult health on productivity[2] tend to find a smaller impact than expected from the macroeconomic and historical studies. This study shows that the impact of nutrition and health on the productivity of education – and therefore on income – is much stronger.

The momentous long-term rises in stature, weight, life expectancy, education[3] and other human capabilities (Sen 1999), such as cognitive development, fertility preferences and ethical development, give a whole new meaning to the concept of long-term human development, as a process of technophysio evolution to which are added educational and cultural dimensions of achievement in the modern world. The scope for human development can itself explain the universal emergence from stagnation to growth (Cervellati and Sunde 2003).

The process of human development can be understood as an intergenerational cycle of investment in nutrition, health and education, that is beset by market failures. This process provides the labor, skills and knowledge inputs for production and technological change, and it also is a determinant of capital accumulation. In turn, the intensity of intergenerational human development depends on the resulting income and technology levels.

Economic growth is dynamic. Both the forces which accelerate growth (human and physical capital accumulation and technological change) and the forces which hold it back can change. In addition to market failures in human capital accumulation, other dampers on growth include institutional failures and low technology traps which may result from knowledge thresholds (Howitt and Mayer-Foulkes 2002) or underdeveloped financial systems (Aghion, Howitt and Mayer-Foulkes 2004). These forces, whether due to market failures or non-convexities in production, accumulation or technological change, are strong enough to induce deficient steady states, causing poverty traps or slow transitions which prevent individual and national incomes from converging to higher equilibria. They account for the historical and contemporary divergence of global income levels (Pritchett 1997; Quah 1993; Maddison 2001; Mayer-Foulkes 2002) and the possible presence of global convergence clubs (Mayer-Foulkes 2001a, 2001b, 2002). Public policy is necessary to overcome these barriers. If there are not appropriate institutions to generate a flow of private funding for investment, then public funding must be put into place. One of the hallmarks of advanced countries' institutions is their ability to promote market functions and to overcome economy-wide market failures.[4] For example, public education and research systems have been crucial to capitalist development throughout history.

Pro-market reforms facilitating economic growth will only realize their full potential if they are accompanied by policies overcoming the market failures slowing economic growth, including those for human development.

THE ROLE OF EARLY CHILDHOOD HEALTH IN HUMAN CAPITAL FORMATION

Fogel and others have focused attention on the long-term rise in nutrition, health and longevity, its relation to economic growth and its interconnections with indicators like stature and weight. Related research has found that most loss of height is determined irreversibly in the first two years of life and is a predictor of life-long health and longevity (Schürch and Scrimshaw 1987; Steckel 1995). A wave of research has focused on the biological mechanisms through which these interconnections occur and have led to a focus on early child development, the combination of physical, mental and social development in the early years of life. Numerous links are now known between malnutrition beginning in utero, early infection and the crucial period of brain development in utero and shortly after birth (Barker 1998; Ravelli 1999) and adult ailments such as high blood pressure, diabetes, asthma, Parkinson's disease, multiple sclerosis and cardiovascular disease (see Van der Gaag 2002).

Early child development is now understood to be a crucial component of human capital formation. Children participating in ECD programs receive psychosocial stimulation, nutritional supplementation and health care, while their parents receive training in effective childcare. There is extensive scientific evidence that ECD is important for school performance and rapid brain development (see Van der Gaag 2002). The effects of health and nutrition on education in developing countries have also been studied in some detail in an attempt to detect specific links which may be addressed cost-effectively (World Bank 1993). UNDP, UNESCO, UNICEF and the World Bank have conducted numerous surveys on how poor nutrition affects education (Levinger 1994). Deficiencies in nutrition and health contribute to inattentiveness, poor cognitive ability and lower general conceptual ability.

Micronutrients are especially important for school performance. Iodine deficiencies, for example, are associated with reduced intelligence, psycho-motor retardation, mental and neurological damage and cretinism. Iron-deficiency anemia affects 1.3 billion people, of whom 210 million are school-age children, and is associated with lower mental and motor development test scores. Vitamin A deficiencies are associated with eyesight problems and other conditions. Parasites generate high levels of morbidity associated with impaired cognitive function, absenteeism, under enrollment and attrition. Untreated sensory impairments, such as vision or auditory problems, constitute significant educational risk factors. In 21 Latin American countries 42.8 per cent of the children under age five show moderate and severe stunting, a clear sign of malnutrition associated with poorer educational performance.[5]

In a study with some parallels to this one, Case, Lubotsky and Paxson (2001) and Case, Fertig and Paxson (2003) find that early childhood health is a critical link through which household wealth is transmitted to the next generation, forming the basis for future adult income and health and clarifying the origin of the income gradients observed in adult health. I use stature as a direct indicator of early child development, because it plays an important role in the intergenerational transmission of poverty.

EMPIRICAL EVIDENCE OF A LOW HUMAN CAPITAL TRAP

The concept of a poverty trap is very well established and is usually based on the existence of convexities and market failures. Nonetheless, the empirical counterpart to this concept is almost absent in the econometric literature. While estimates exist on the determinants and mechanisms of poverty and the economic discussions include many references to poverty traps and market failures, there are very few – if any – specific empirical demonstrations that these exist.

Galor and Zeira (1993) describe a typical poverty trap in their work on the credit constraint trap in human capital accumulation. However, two related concepts are often overlooked: a dynamic poverty trap and a prolonged transition. With a dynamic poverty trap multiple steady states exist, but the variables defining these states (e.g. income, human capital or technology) are subject to long-term growth. Income in a low equilibrium may grow, but maintains a permanent proportional lag – or worse – to income in a higher equilibrium. Dynamic traps will not necessarily be weakened by growth, unlike absolute poverty traps, whose threshold must eventually be overcome by growth. Howitt and Mayer-Foulkes (2002) and Aghion, Howitt and Mayer-Foulkes (2004) provide examples of dynamic traps and models of technological convergence in which growth in the leading technological edge drives growth in each of the multiple steady states through technology transfer. The lower equilibria grow at rates slower or equal to the higher equilibria, therefore defining dynamic traps.

The concept of prolonged transition is weaker than the concept of a static or dynamic poverty trap and refers to dynamics which may remain at a near steady state for a long time, with faster growth occurring along the transition to a higher steady state.

How do these concepts apply to Mexico? Since market failures slow the transition to equilibrium, I shall refer to an empirical situation of systematic, prolonged, under-investment in human capital as a prolonged transition. The transition corresponding to the perfect market counterpart would be faster. If the convexities or market failures are strong enough, lower equilibria – static or dynamic – should appear. Here the concept of dynamic trap is useful, because it removes the objection that in a poverty trap there must be absolute stagnation. Empirically, what must be shown is the evidence for multiple equilibria. This is provided, for example, by multiple peaks in the distribution of schooling, or by evidence that no transition is occurring from lower to higher levels of education, in particular, privately funded increases in schooling are negligible at lower steady states.

Part of the difficulty of revealing a human capital poverty trap lies in the intergenerational nature of human capital accumulation, since the education and health of the young is determined by the wealth, health and education of their parents. These interrelationships are difficult to disentangle. The long-term nature of these processes means that the appropriate data is not usually available and the theoretical concept, especially of a poverty trap, is limited to playing the role of a parable. Microeconomic data do not usually include information like parental educational levels and place of birth for current workers. Under these conditions, any strategy for constructing empirical evidence for possible poverty traps or slow transitions is very dependent on available data.

To construct evidence for the presence of a low human capital trap (which may or not be dynamic) in Mexico, I decompose the concept of a poverty trap in the acquisition of health and education – the main dimensions of human development – into their constituent elements and find empirical support for the existence of each. In view of the lack of more specific data on human capital investment problems, an appeal to theory argues that a class of market failures must be present to explain the empirical findings. Childhood nutrition turns out to play an important role for education and holds the key for overcoming the barriers to higher secondary and tertiary education. Specifically, I find empirical evidence for the following constituent elements:

- Increasing returns to education in adult income (the essential assumption in Galor and Zeira, 1993).
- Substantial returns to children's health in the acquisition of education, as measured by school permanence.
- Transmission from parental wealth, health and education to the health and education of their young (an essential assumption in any intergenerational model of human capital accumulation).

The increasing returns hold at educational levels higher than those achieved by most of the population.[6]

These constituent elements imply a functional relationship between parental wealth (including human capital assets) and their children's future income which has a region of increasing returns. The only remaining distinction between a poverty trap and a slow transition is whether multiple equilibria exist or not. I use the following evidence to distinguish between these alternatives, based on the study of eight national surveys:[7]

- The distribution of households according to spouses' education is multiple-peaked, with the main separations occurring between lower and higher secondary schooling.
- Changes in the distribution of schooling in the low group have occurred almost exclusively in response to increased availability of public schooling.

Thus, the main empirical findings are: (1) education has increasing returns for adult income, (2) early childhood health has a strong, probably causal relation on permanence in school throughout the educational career and (3) the population divides itself into two social classes, those with lower secondary schooling or less and those above. Schooling within the lower groups reflects almost entirely public investment in education.[8]

Nutrition improvements generate considerable increases in higher education. A rough calculation shows that nutritional supplementation programs are valuable from the ensuing gains in education alone. Improving child nutrition and early child development provides a viable economic policy for improving human capital formation and weakening the hold of the human capital trap.

The empirical work has three main implications. First, social welfare can be improved by promoting the education of the majority of the Mexican population, which underinvests in human capital. Second, improvements in early child development, an area subject to underinvestment, will promote education and help overcome the barrier to higher education.[9] Finally, the empirical evidence supports the existence of a poverty trap in Mexico. The bulk of the population is unable to invest enough in nutrition and schooling to benefit from the higher returns of higher education.

POSSIBLE MARKET FAILURES

From the point of view of economic theory, it would be simplest if babies were born with a bank account and an omniscient trust manager decided how much to invest in food, medicine, stimulation and schooling to maximize the expected utility. According to received theory, any important and systematic deviation from this standard is due to some kind of market failure such as imperfect credit markets or missing markets with important consequences for social welfare and justifying public policies. Of course, any attempt at public intervention must be tempered by the efficiency problems inherent in public policy implementation.

Leaving human capital investment decisions to the market fails for many reasons. For example, parents may be unavailable, malnourished, unhealthy, unknowledgeable or uncaring. Families with credit constraints may be unable to obtain proper nutrition, health, education or complementary inputs such as social capital or early child development programs. These are accentuated by indivisibilities present in the educational system, such as uncertainty, lack of information or foresight on the relevant benefits of early child development. There may be excessive impatience or risks due to poverty or the unavailability of necessary public goods in health or education.

It may be impossible to identify only one or two main market failures holding back human capital investment. If increasing returns to human capital create economic forces which generate distinct social classes instead of social integration, surmounting the barriers between them may involve complex cultural changes.

PRO-MARKET REFORM AND HUMAN CAPITAL MARKET FAILURES

How do pro-market reforms work in the presence of human capital market failures? How do they affect the poor? My conceptual framework points to some of the answers. Assume that pro-market reforms lead to rises in production, technological change and higher returns to human capital. There will be higher incentives and more resources for investment in human capital. Families in higher equilibria who already supply human capital will benefit both in the present and in the future. Families in lower equilibria will benefit less in the present, and if these benefits are insufficient, they will not supply additional human capital in the future. Inequality will increase and the growth process – which could accelerate convergence to a higher steady state – will subside.

Thus, a well conceived reform must consider education and health. However, this was not the case with the pro-market reforms undertaken in Mexico between its entry into GATT in 1986 and the North American Free Trade Agreement (NAFTA) in 1994. Consequently, as Legovini, Bouillon and Lustig (2001) show, the rise in returns to tertiary education in Mexico increased income inequality. This rise in returns, seen in Mexico and other Latin American countries, was due to increased demand for skills. Mexico has exhibited increasing returns for education since at least 1984.[10] The returns to higher education increased through several mechanisms promoted by pro-market reforms, such as skill-biased technological change and opening to trade and investment.[11] However, even though these higher returns should have led to higher investment in higher education, the evidence presented below shows that this did not occur. As Scott (2003a) notes, NAFTA has failed to deliver the accelerated convergence predicted by traditional growth and trade theory. Although these benefits have occurred in fairly comparable countries like Portugal, in Mexico the post-NAFTA period has been characterized by regional (north–south), sectoral (urban–rural) and even intra-sectoral polarization and increasing income inequality at the household level. Scott argues that convergence failed to materialize because of a deficit in human capital, a lack of infrastructure and poor institutions.[12] The reforms did not include human capital investment, provision of public goods and improvement of institutions, limiting their benefits.

THE DATA

Mexico's 2000 National Health Survey includes the following variables for household members 12 years and older: height, gender, age, income and type of work, health insurance, health institution preference, educational level and first language, as well as household composition, type of construction (walls, roof, floor, finishings, kitchen, number of rooms, water source, bathroom, drainage), electricity and telephone (ENSA 2000). Stature was the main health variable used, although parental weight was also used as a control.[13] Most other health variables in the survey reflected recent medical treatment not covering every individual and were therefore not used.[14]

The relevance of stature as an indicator of population-wide welfare has been extensively studied (see, for example, Steckel 1995). Height is known to reflect early childhood nutrition and to predict life-long health. Glewwe and Jacoby (1995) and Larrea, Freire and Lutter (2001) show that stunting due to malnutrition becomes established in the first two to three years of life. Stunting has been shown to be cumulative and non-reversible and therefore provides an excellent, if perhaps noisy, measure of chronic malnutrition and its effects.

Two databases were constructed using the ENSA 2000 data, one for adults (aged 20 and above) and one for adolescents (12 to 19 years old), containing 42,970 and 19,493 observations, respectively, covering both health and education. The database for adolescents includes parental characteristics. It is worth mentioning that, by comparison with the 2000 National Income and Expenditure Survey (ENIGH 2000), the ENSA 2000 survey under represents an already small sample of male household heads with higher education. Compared to what would be predicted by the ENIGH sample, the ENSA sample contains only 48 per cent of male household heads with 17 years of schooling (1,102 observations) and 77 per cent with 19 years of schooling (74 observations).

ECONOMETRIC ANALYSIS

The analysis consists of three parts. The first is a fairly standard Mincerian estimate including health and shows that schooling has increasing returns for adult income. The second is a probit analysis of decisions for the young to continue in school for further three-year periods from lower primary to higher secondary school. The results show that early childhood health plays a strong, probably causal, role in school permanence. These two analyses imply that there is significant underinvestment in education and nutrition and suggest possible market failures holding up human capital investment. The third is an analysis of the schooling distribution showing that its shape and dynamics conform to the presence of a human capital accumulation trap in Mexico. Finally, the role that nutrition may play as a policy lever for education is briefly evaluated.

Adult Income Estimates

The returns to education and health in adult income were evaluated using Mincerian (1962, 1974) regressions. These are carried out for each gender separately. It is customary to instrument for health, because this variable may be jointly determined with education (Schultz 1997; see Savedoff and Schultz 2000 for details). In this case, however, since the variable representing health is stature, its instrumentation was found to be either unnecessary or infeasible. The reason is that adult stature conveys information about conditions far in the past, which reduces the endogeneity problem, and that health instruments were only available for the present and were not very powerful. To control for local conditions which could be correlated to both income and health, however, local fixed effects referred to municipal residence were included. It is also customary to correct the estimates for selection bias due to labor participation, using the Heckman correction method, for example (Savedoff and Schultz 2000). Two specifications were used for the selection correction, that was nevertheless not very reliable for men or for women. However, the qualitative nature of the results was robust to all of the specifications, and coincides with those obtained by other authors. The following control variables were included, partly addressing heterogeneity: type of employment, indigenous language dummy and wealth variables such as type of walls, roof, floor, water supply, drainage, number of rooms and presence of electricity, telephone and kitchen. Many of the control variables for wealth obtained significant coefficients. This control is for assets, other than education, which may be contributing to income. Instrumental variables may also be used to address these problems. Using family background instrumental variables, Patrinos (2003) finds slightly higher earnings (10 per cent) for education. Overall, the results are fairly standard and supported by other research in the literature (cited below). The variables and regressions were defined specifically to obtain marginal returns for human capital assets, by interacting the health and experience human capital variables with dummies for the three-year educational levels and by assigning to each adult a system of 'marginal educational dummies', each having a value of one for each completed educational period.[15]

The main finding of the income regressions is that the returns of additional three-year periods of education and its associated complementary inputs are increasing for both men and women after completing lower secondary schooling. Two standard deviation corridors for the coefficients are shown in Figures 3.1a

Figure 3.1 Human Capital Marginal Returns for Adult Income by Educational Level (Two Standard Deviation Corridors for OLS coefficients)

Marginal Human Capital Returns Asociated with Three-Year Periods of Schooling

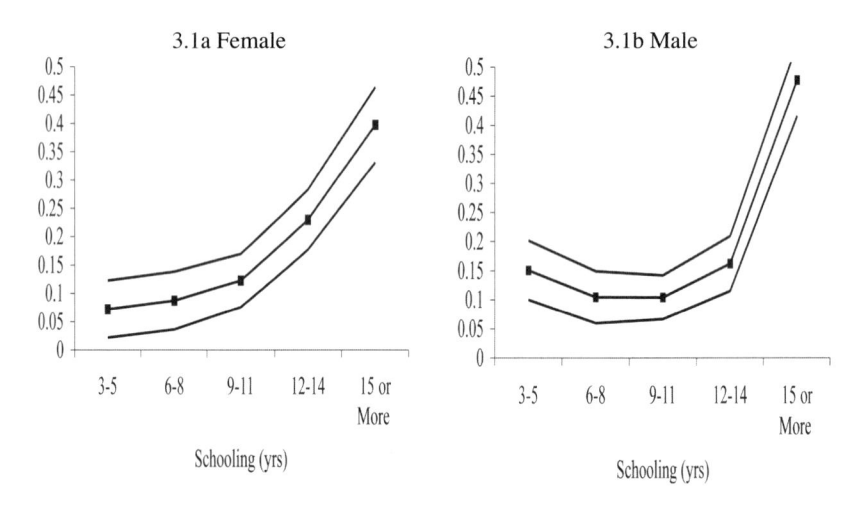

3.1a Female

3.1b Male

Marginal Returns of Stature by Schooling Levels

3.1c Female

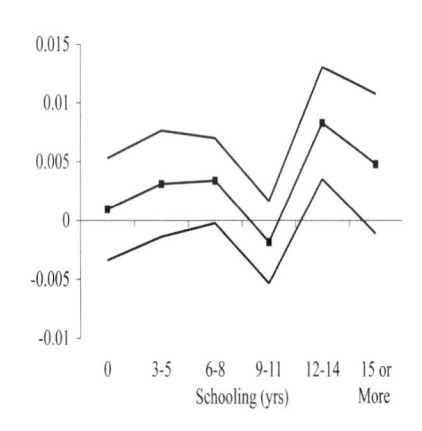

3.1d Male

and 3.1b.[16] The returns to health are small but significant and similar to those found in other microeconomic studies (Savedoff and Schultz 2000), yielding a maximum of about 1 per cent increase for stature increases of 1 centimeter. They show no clear tendency according to educational level (Figures 3.1c, 3.1d). These findings are obtained consistently in the OLS regressions and in both applications of the Heckman selection correction model.[17]

Good instruments for why women or men might decide to participate in the labor workforce are, unfortunately, not available. The main instruments used in the selection equation were number of dependent children and dependent adolescents. The first application includes the human capital variables in the selection equation, while the second excludes them. In both cases the selection correction was insignificant for men, as expected since most men work, so that the OLS estimates are more efficient and therefore preferred. For women, however, the selection correction was significant in both cases, with different implications with respect to the role of human capital. When human capital is included in the selection model 'Heckman I', it appears significantly and therefore the estimation of the productivity of female human capital is corrected downward. In the second application, 'Heckman II', these variables are not included in the selection model and are therefore corrected upwards. If more educated women participate in the labor market because they are more productive, schooling should not be considered to bias the productivity estimates. Then the Heckman II model, whose estimates of female productivity more closely correspond to the estimates of male productivity, is more reliable. If instead it is considered that the educational indicators are signals for ability, and that therefore the productivity estimates are biased upwards, then additional indicators of ability would be needed for the correction, but these are unavailable. The OLS estimates fall between the two Heckman estimates and therefore also seem the most reliable in the case of women. In a study on Mexico by Zamudio and Bracho (1994), the Heckman correction is found to increase the returns for women and urban zones.

The experience variables, when significant, exhibit the expected signs. These variables are not significant for lower levels of education, when health and strength can be expected to be more important to labor capacity and may be inversely related to experience. If this is the case, the expected sign for experience would be negative. This can explain its insignificant results for low levels of education and would also bias the coefficient for stature downwards, since stature is correlated with age.

Increasing returns to education since 1994 are found in several other studies on Mexico, as mentioned above. Results by Mayer-Foulkes and Stabridis-Arana (2003), based on seven ENIGH surveys estimating marginal returns to

Figure 3.2 Marginal Returns to Schooling in Mexico, 1984–2000

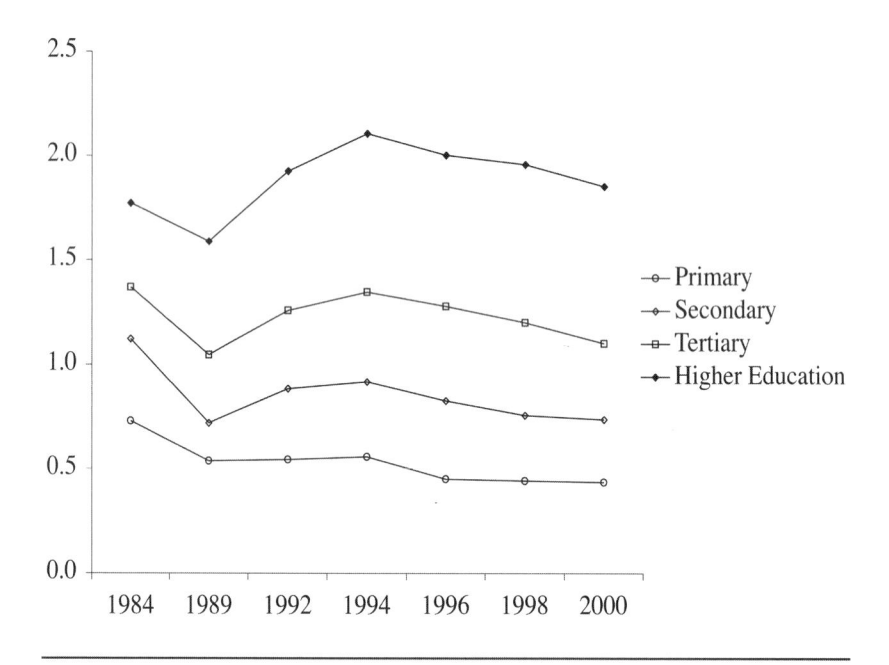

Source: Mayer-Foulkes and Stabridis-Arana (2003). Estimates based on ENIGH surveys.

education, are shown in Figure 3.2; marginal returns to tertiary education are higher than for other levels and tend to increase during the period.

Adolescent Schooling Decisions

Preliminary examination of the distribution of schooling by ages for the ENSA 2000 sample of children and adolescents shows that the young drop out of school mostly at the end of primary, lower secondary or upper secondary school, as expected. Schooling has definite jumps at six, nine and 12 years of education. The critical decisions for achieving schooling occur at the end of these educational cycles and consist of deciding to continue on to another three-year period of schooling. They are thus best represented as separate 0–1 variables for subsequent stages of education. Hence probit regressions were estimated to study the impact of child nutrition and parental schooling, income and wealth on the decision to acquire an additional three years of education.[18]

In the ENSA 2000 survey, stature is only available for adolescents, not for children. Thus to evaluate the schooling decisions of the young in a homogeneous manner, I analyzed the sample of 17 to 19 year old adolescents for their probability to continue on a further three years of study. I thus have a homogenous group of people born between 1980 and 1982 whose educational career can be followed, and who are still at home so data is available on their parents. Most of the people in the sample started primary school at age six or seven, so schooling decisions up to higher secondary are well represented in the sample. Chronic malnutrition is definitely present in the sample. Weighting for representativity, 20.3 per cent of the women and 18.1 per cent of the men aged 17 to 19 had height for age Z-scores less than −2.0.

For each adolescent i, the following variables J_{bi} are defined to indicate when a further three-year period of study was attempted, given that the child entered the previous three-year period:

$$\text{If } s_i > b, \text{ then } J_{bi} = 1 \text{ or if } b-3 < s_i \leq b, \text{ then } J_{bi} = 0. \tag{3.1}$$

With J_{bi} defined as missing if, where s_i is the adolescent schooling level (so that the sample is $s_i \geq b$), and $b = 3$, 6 and 9, corresponding to continuing into higher primary, lower secondary and higher secondary school. The probit estimate is the following:

$$P(J_{bi}=1)=F(X_i, Gender_i, \times X_i, W_i, \eta_{mun(i)}) \tag{3.2}$$

The variables X_i include children's stature, constant and age dummies, mother's and father's schooling, total household income, mother's proportion of income, non-parental proportion of income and number of children. In a final set of regressions, X_i also included one parent's stature and weight. ENSA 2000 only contains this information for one adult, so a dummy was included indicating the gender of this adult. $Gender_i$ is a gender dummy, and each of the variables in X_i was interacted with $Gender_i$. The variables W_i include an indigenous language dummy; wealth variables including type of walls, roof, floor, water supply, drainage, number of rooms and presence of electricity, telephone and kitchen.[19] The variable $\eta_{mun(i)}$ represents municipal fixed effects defined by residence. These control at least partially for local availability of schooling and health services and for local differences in wealth, tastes for child rearing and so on, for example defined by Mexico's diverse cultural geography. Since current parental nutrition and health decisions have a negligible impact on child stature, parental weight variables control for the ability and taste for producing nutrition at the family level which could be correlated with educational ability, while the parental stature variables control for long-term nutritional and health assets, possibly inherited in the parents' family of origin.

Two main econometric issues arise when using stature as a health indicator. The first and most prominent is that stature is a very noisy health indicator. For example, Glewwe, Jacoby and King (2001) find in their sample that a regression of current children's stature on stature at age two, age and sex has an R^2 of only 0.49, just the right amount of noise to explain the huge bias toward zero of their OLS as compared to their instrumented coefficients for stature, a common finding for stature. The second is endogeneity, arising because health and education investments may be determined simultaneously. This issue is described by Schultz (1997) and Savedoff and Schultz (2000), who recommend using health policy variables as instruments if possible. With Mexico two factors reduce the endogeneity issue. First, much of the effect of nutrition on stature is determined before the age of three (Glewwe and Jacoby 1995; Larrea, Freire and Lutter 2001; Schürch and Scrimshaw 1987), while the educational decisions studied below occur later on in childhood and hence are influenced by independent events, reducing the correlation of errors.[20] The second is the educational variable used here is a binary decision variable. Thus the correlation between its errors and stature will concentrate on a much smaller region and therefore be much smaller than in the case of a continuous variable.

The estimates deal with the noise and endogeneity issues together by instrumenting stature. This requires instruments correlated with stature but not directly influencing decisions on education. To choose them, I rely on the observation that stature is mostly determined in early childhood, before the educational decisions studied here are made. By age six, much of the variation in stature has been determined by genetic factors, history of nutrition, illnesses and health inputs. The instruments used were membership and preferences over public health insurance institutions as available in the dataset. The membership variables were dummies running over the following health insurance categories: Instituto Mexicano del Seguro Social (IMSS); Instituto de Seguridad y Servicios Sociales de los Trabajadores del Estudio (ISSSTE); social security provided by the government petroleum monopoly (PEMEX); Secretaría de la Defensa Nacional (SEDENA); Secretaría de la Marina (SEMAR); Secretaría de Salud y Asistencia (SSA); Private Worker; Private User; State and none. The preference variables were dummies running over: IMSS, ISSSTE, PEMEX, SSA, IMSS-Solaridad, Private-Worker, Private-User, none and other. Some of these institutions, mainly IMSS, also provide early child care services which may be correlated with education decisions. A child who has received child care service may be more likely to continue on to school. Therefore I chose instrument sets which survived the Basman-

Sargan test for overidentifying restrictions, meaning that the instruments had no significant effects on education which did not work through stature.

A few additional comments on the instrumentation should be noted. First, since the probit estimate is nonlinear, it may be more appropriate to think that in the first stage a less noisy and less endogenous component of stature indicating nutrition and health was constructed, to be used instead of rather than to approximate the original, noisy indicator. Second, in constructing this component, the parental stature and weight variables were excluded. This made the final results more significant because by excluding these variables, the noise related to the genetic endowment of weight and height was excluded. Instead, the selected component, a linear combination of economic and health service variables, picks up the economic and health component of stature.

The estimation of the stature coefficients is subject to an additional econometric issue, namely unobserved child or household-specific factors, whose correction escapes the possibility of the ENSA 2000 database, that is used to determine the state of the human development process in Mexico. Careful comparison with the magnitudes obtained for these coefficients by Glewwe and Jacoby (1995) and Glewwe, Jacoby and King (2001), who correct for these effects, finds very comparable magnitudes, however, confirming that no strong biases are present. A direct coefficient comparison for stature is impossible, because primary enrollment decisions differ from continued education decisions. Nevertheless, these decisions are similar enough for it to be plausible that the ratio (relative magnitude) between stature and the mother's schooling (an essential variable in human capital formation) coefficients should be similar. Table 3.1 compares the coefficient ratios obtained in this study (with stature coefficients rescaled to female Z-score coefficients) and the two results in Glewwe and Jacoby's (1995) study for which the two necessary coefficients are reported, corresponding to a full instrument set (preferred) and to a reduced one.

The similarity between the ratios obtained for delayed enrollment in primary and for continuing to upper primary or lower secondary education in this study is remarkable. They are within 10 per cent of each other. Granted, the stature coefficients here might be slightly biased upward according to this comparison. On the other hand, Glewwe and Jacoby (1995) also compare their own coefficients, including child and household fixed effects, with an estimate only controlling for mother's height, similar to one reported here (which also includes municipal fixed effects) and find that in this case their Z-score coefficient is underestimated by about one-third. Thus it can broadly be concluded that the order of magnitude of the estimates presented here is correct.

Three sets of probit estimates (see equation 3.2) were performed for adolescents to examine the decision to continue from lower to higher primary,

Table 3.1 Ratio of Z-score (Stature) to Mother's Schooling Coefficients

	Present Study			Glewwe and Jacoby (1995)	
	Stature not instrumented	Stature instrumented		Full Instrument Set	Reduced instrument set
		Parent's stature and weight not included as controls	Parent's stature and weight included as controls		
Lower to higher primary	0.48	10.16	**9.67**	**8.87**	7.18
Primary to lower secondary	1.88	11.97	**9.13**	na	na
Lower to higher secondary	3.26	73.25	**30.49**	na	na

Note: Results converted to Z-score units for comparability. Preferred results in bold.

94

primary to lower secondary, lower to higher secondary and higher secondary to tertiary schooling. The first set was not instrumented while the second and third were. The second set excludes and the third set includes parental stature and weight variables as controls for parental abilities, tastes and (possibly genetic) assets for nutrition and health.

There are also several variables other than stature which obtained significant, credible results in the instrumented probit test.[21] Male adolescents are less likely to continue to higher secondary school when the mother's proportion of income is high (4 per cent to 6 per cent significance). Adolescents are less likely to continue to higher secondary school when the proportion of income not provided by household head and spouse is high (better than 1 per cent significance), but concomitantly it is more likely that younger males continue to upper primary school than do females (9 per cent significance). Mother's schooling contributes to females' continuing higher primary and lower secondary, and father's schooling to males continuing in school (both better than 1 per cent). Father's schooling contributes to continuing to higher secondary schooling in the case of both genders (better than 1 per cent). When the household reports more children, it is more likely that more stages of schooling will be attempted (1 per cent at lower levels, 4 per cent for higher secondary) although this is somewhat less true for males at lower levels of schooling (4 per cent). Parental stature variables are mostly less significant than parental weight variables, which is consistent with weight reflecting current conditions as they affect the children (the significance pattern is hard to interpret). Other variables obtaining positive significant (better than 10 per cent) results include the indigenous language dummy, kitchen, number of rooms, electricity, wood, tile or other finishings. Variables obtaining negative significant results include wooden, adobe or non-reported housing walls, cardboard, metal sheet or asbestos sheet roofs, earthen or non-reported floors and septic tank, non-reported or no drainage.[22]

Table 3.2 shows the results on stature, comparing the three sets of regressions. It includes the marginal probabilities associated with a 1 centimeter increase in stature and presents the Wu-Hausman test for endogeneity and the Basman-Sargan tests for overidentifying restrictions. The results show a considerable rise in the magnitude of the stature coefficients when this variable is instrumented, as is common in many studies. Although the individual significance of the stature variables falls, the joint significance remains better than 1 per cent after instrumenting in all cases. Once the marginal probabilities are calculated (recall that probit is non-linear) the 90th percentile level rises from about 1 per cent to 4 per cent and above in all cases. Second, when parental stature and weight variables are introduced as controls, the magnitude remains stable for continuing to higher primary or lower secondary but somewhat decreases for continuing

Table 3.2 *Comparison of the Effects of Stature in Several Probit Estimates for School Permanence (Adolescents Ages 17–19 of Both Genders, Municipal Fixed Effects in ENSA 2000 Database for Individuals)*

	Lower to higher primary	Primary to lower secondary	Lower to higher secondary
	Stature not instrumented		
Stature (cm)	0.024	0.037	0.024
	(0.137)	(0)	(0.001)
Stature * male dummy	−0.044	−0.039	−0.009
	(0.091)	(0.001)	(0.389)
Joint p for stature	0.1977	0.0001	0.0005
Marginal probability (p10, p90), female	(0, 0.009)	(0.001, 0.014)	(0.002, 0.01)
Marginal probability (p10, p90), male	(−0.005, 0)	(−0.001, 0)	(0.001, 0.006)
Observations	928	2060	2061
	Stature instrumented, parent's stature and weight not included as controls		
Stature (cm)	0.262	0.135	0.181
	(0.033)	(0.055)	(0.002)
Stature * male dummy	−0.131	0.001	0.066
	(0.578)	(0.996)	(0.514)
Joint p for stature	0.0033	0.0004	0
Marginal probability (p10, p90), female	(0, 0.068)	(0.005, 0.052)	(0.024, 0.072)
Marginal probability (p10, p90), male	(0.001, 0.033)	(0.002, 0.052)	(0.036, 0.097)
Wu-Haussman p	0.9941	0.0489	0
Basman-Sargan p	0.6196	0.1214	0.0062
Observations	3349	5212	4612

to higher secondary school. I therefore regard these results as my preferred, conservative estimate on the effect of stature on the decision to continue in school. In this case the Basman-Sargan test shows that the instruments do not affect success in school through any other channels than stature, while the Wu-Hausman results reject exogeneity of stature except for continuing to higher secondary schooling. Thus in the case of continuing to higher primary or lower secondary schooling, the instruments are mostly correcting for noise. In the case of higher secondary, when parents must exercise a more purposeful

Table 3.2 (continued)

	Lower to higher primary	Primary to lower secondary	Lower to higher secondary
	Stature instrumented, parent's stature and weight included as controls		
Stature (cm)	0.315	0.141	0.113
	(0.04)	(0.086)	(0.085)
Stature * male dummy	−0.113	−0.002	0.164
	(0.701)	(0.989)	(0.156)
Joint p for stature	0.0018	0.0013	0
Marginal probability (p10, p90), female	(0, 0.088)	(0.004, 0.055)	(0.014, 0.045)
Marginal probability (p10, p90), male	(0.001, 0.06)	(0.002, 0.053)	(0.039, 0.109)
Wu-Haussman p	0.9672	0.143	0.0003
Basman-Sargan p	0.5185	0.5091	0.1333
Observations	2363	3998	3620

Note: Coefficients show 1% confidence in bold, 10% confidence in italics, p values in parenthesis. Confidence for marginal probability intervals, percentiles 10 and 90, not marked.

choice,[23] they are also correcting for some degree of endogeneity. These results also hold for the case that does not include the parental stature and weight variables as controls, except for the Basman-Sargan test. In this case, if the 'culprit' instruments are eliminated the coefficients remain almost identical in magnitude, with a somewhat reduced significance.

The magnitude of the effect of early childhood nutrition and health on education is much larger than what has been found for the effect of health on income and is therefore more commensurate with other studies of the long-term economic effects of nutrition and health.

Market Failures

All children are born equal, at least potentially. However, malnutrition can begin in utero with life-long health consequences including impaired cognitive development (Van Der Gaag 2002). Investments in nutrition, health, early child development and education are needed to help babies grow into productive adults realizing their full potential. As mentioned above, *any* important and systematic deviation from this standard is due to failure of the market system, such as imperfect credit, incomplete markets or imperfect expectations and has important consequences for social welfare.

Do the regressions on adult income and school performance provide evidence that there is an important and systematic degree of underinvestment in health and education? The evidence is unequivocal: The regression on adult income shows that investment in education and its complementary inputs is highly rewarding. Every additional three-year period of education gives additional returns and thus has a larger net return than the previous three-year investment, assuming that costs are proportional to forgone income and educational level.[24] Moreover, this has been true at least since 1984 (see Figure 3.2), so that informed, rational decisions in pursuing secondary and higher education would have taken this fact into account. The probit estimates on school permanence also identify underinvestment in nutrition which would yield higher probabilities for continuing in school beyond primary level.

To summarize, there are returns to education and nutrition which go untapped by many children in the population, children whose human capital investment decisions depend on their family situation and parental assets. This implies that the market mechanisms for human capital investment fail, and that returns may be obtained from appropriate public policy. Human capital accumulation transition is occurring slower rather than faster, with more of the intergenerational steps spent in poverty.

Slow Transition or Poverty Trap?

The above empirical and theoretical analyses establish the presence of failures in health and education investment in Mexico. Increasing returns to education in income and to nutrition and health in schooling imply that these failures cause a considerable slowdown in the investment on health and education and that the income of the more educated tends to rise faster than that of the less educated, a temporary divergence in incomes with effects which may last several generations. Thus the transition to an educated society is prolonged. However are the failures severe enough to cause a poverty trap?

To answer this question, I first examine the distribution of households according to female and male spouses' schooling, using ENSA 2000 data (Figure 3.3a) and also data from the seven ENIGH surveys from 1984 to 2000 (Figure 3.3b). This distribution has two main peaks. The first one occurs with both spouses having lower secondary education or less. The second occurs with both spouses having higher education. A comparison of the figures based on the ENSA and ENIGH surveys show that their representativity is somewhat different. In the case of the ENSA 2000 survey (Figure 3.3a), a third peak occurs due to gender bias in acquiring higher education: male spouses with

Figure 3.3a   Distribution of Households According to Female and Male Spouses' Schooling

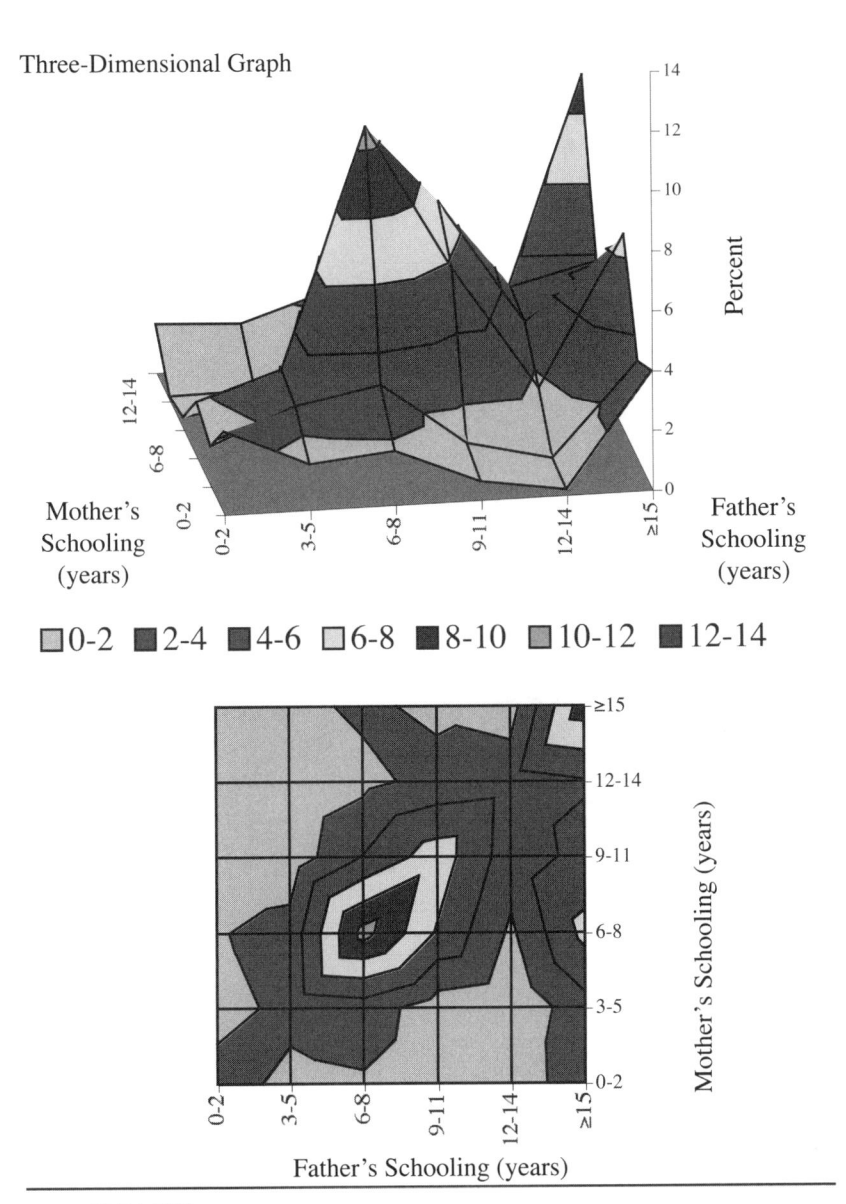

Three-Dimensional Graph

☐ 0-2   ■ 2-4   ■ 4-6   ☐ 6-8   ■ 8-10   ■ 10-12   ■ 12-14

Source: ENSA 2000.

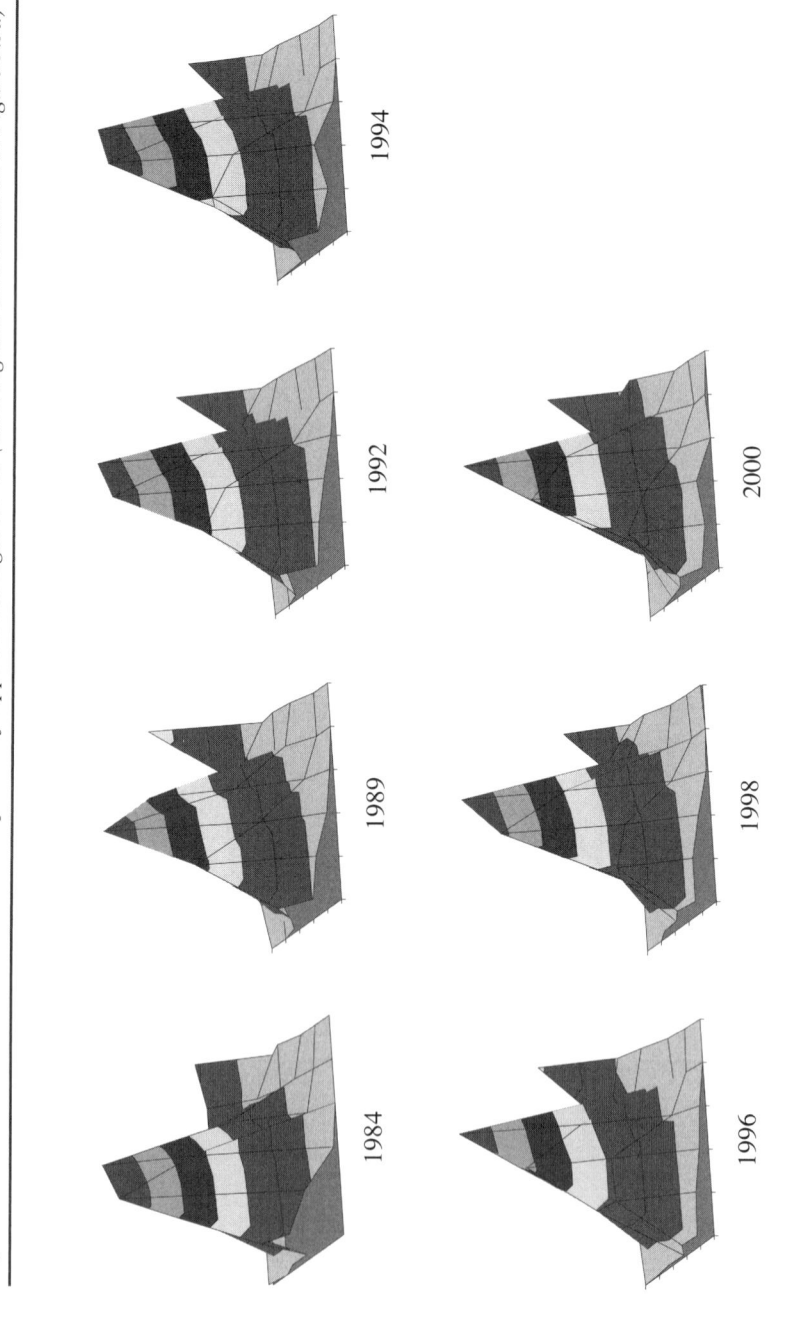

Figure 3.3b Households Restricted to Two Spouses of Opposite Sex Ages 25–30 (coloring and orientation as in Figure 3.3a)

100

higher education and female spouses with lower secondary education or less. A fourth but very small peak holds the opposite relation. In Figure 3.3b, it can be appreciated that the 'lower class' peak is in transition from incomplete to complete primary education in 1984, centers at complete primary school in 1989, and then shifts through the years to a peak at complete secondary school education in 1996 and 2000. Spouses with no schooling, perhaps belonging to rural areas, cease to be present; their progress may be reflected in the high primary frequency in 1998.

Marriage creates a matching between men and women which is at least partially hierarchical according to economic status (Fernandez, Guner and Knowles 2001). However, this matching need not be multiple-peaked. Here, the multiple-peaked figures show that the population categorizes itself into two classes of people which can be identified by their educational status: a low one with completed lower secondary school or less, and a higher one with 15 or more years of schooling.[25]

Next, I examine the distribution of schooling for adults between 25 and 30. Figure 3.4, based on the same ENIGH surveys, shows this distribution to be remarkably steady except for a very clear pattern of changes. As can be seen in Figure 3.5, that plots the profile of the trends of change in the distribution from 1989 to 2000,[26] the main changes are that a higher proportion of men and women have completed lower secondary school (higher in the case of men) instead of having no schooling or incomplete or complete primary schooling. These changes have been similar for men and women. However, throughout the period the proportion of men with completed lower secondary schooling or less (the lower class) has remained approximately constant at an average of 75.02 per cent (with no significant trend). The corresponding proportion of women has shown a tendency to decrease about 0.5 per cent per year. However, these could be women in the upper class who are catching up with men, a trend which is also occurring in higher education (see Figure 3.5).

Turning to Figure 3.6, showing the population of students in public and private schools by level of schooling, it becomes apparent that most of the increases in adult schooling correspond to a higher population of students in public schooling. Higher investment in education at all levels is occurring thanks to public investment. In fact, between 1989 and 2000 the relative level of private-to-public investment as measured by student population decreased at the lower and upper secondary levels from 8.7 per cent and 32.5 per cent respectively to 8.3 per cent and 27.2 per cent respectively. The corresponding changes were 6.0 per cent to 8.0 per cent at the primary level and 21.7 per cent to 58.6 per cent at higher levels of education. The latter increase is due to a decreased population enrolled in public schools.[27] Moreover, 58.2 per cent of public education expenditure at tertiary levels of education was received

102   *Economic Reform in Developing Countries*

Figure 3.4   Distribution of Schooling for Adults 25 to 30

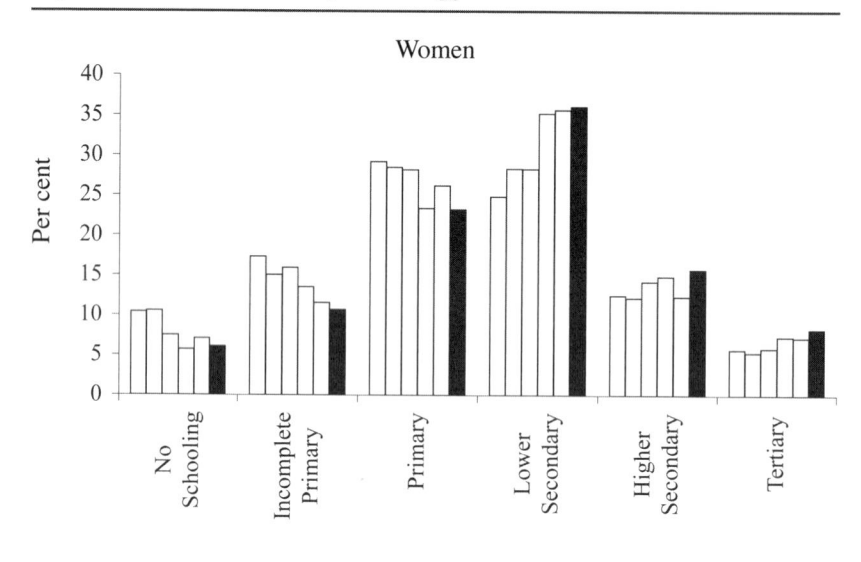

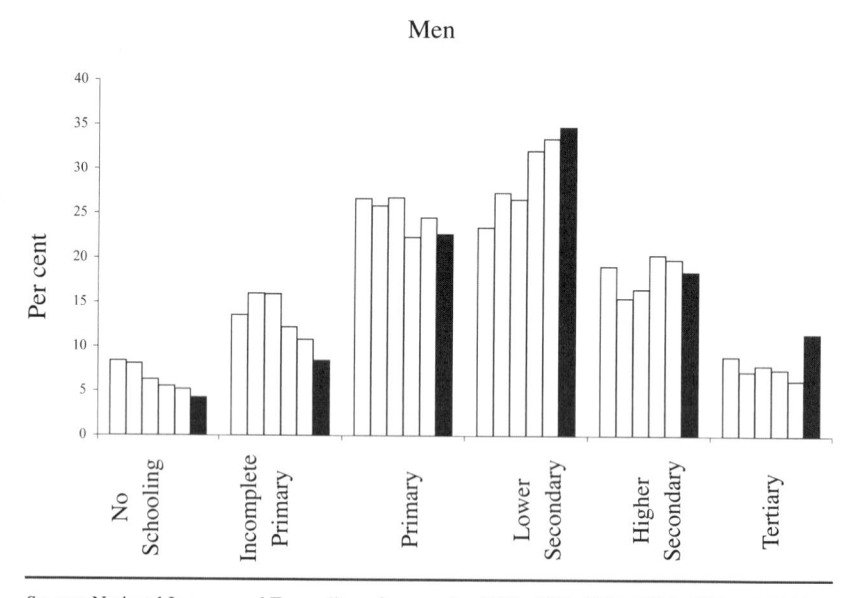

Source: National Income and Expenditure Surveys for 1989, 1992, 1994, 1996, 1998 and 2000.

Figure 3.5 Tendency for Change in Distribution of Adult Schooling for Adults 25 to 30, 1989–2000

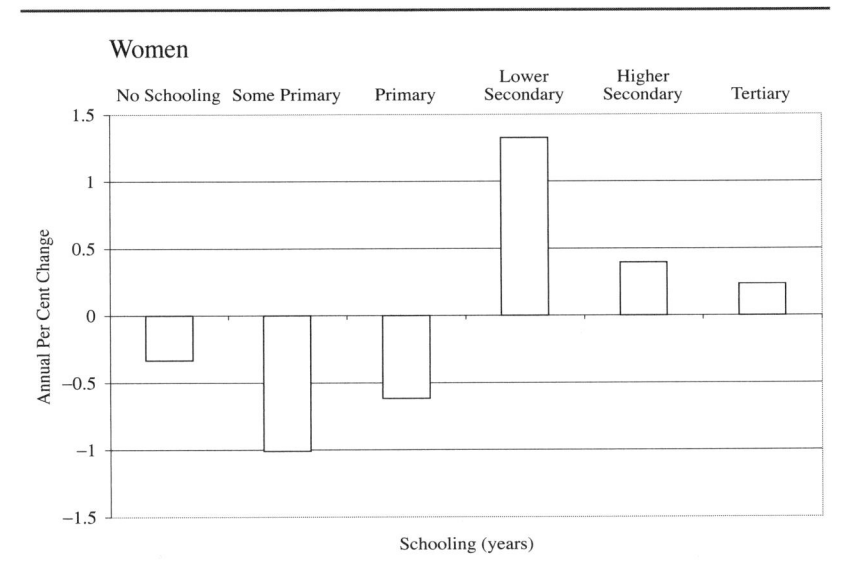

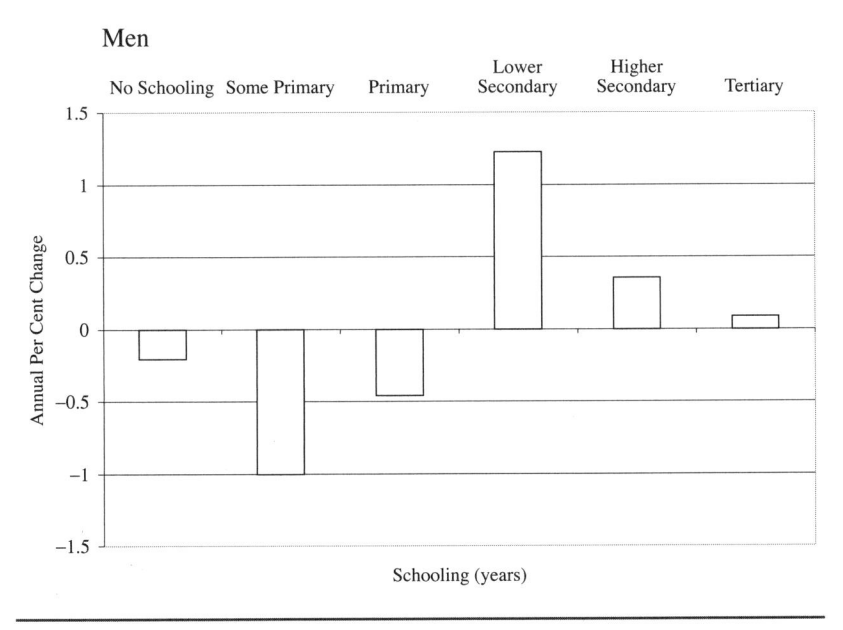

Source: National Income and Expenditure Surveys for 1989, 1992, 1994, 1996, 1998 and 2000.

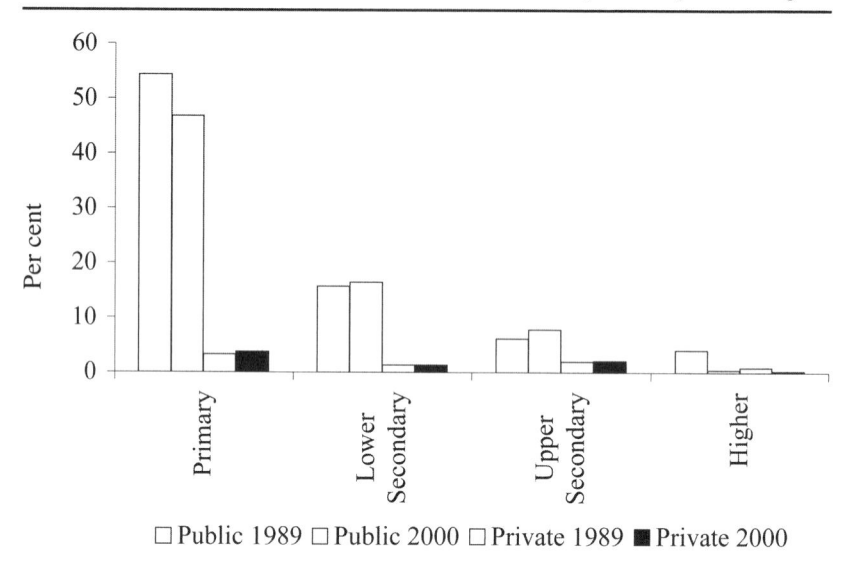

Figure 3.6   Students in Public and Private Schools, by Level of Schooling

□ Public 1989   □ Public 2000   □ Private 1989   ■ Private 2000

Source: Estadística Histórica del Sistema Educativo de la Nación, Mexico City: Ministry of Education.

by students in deciles VIII and above (Figure 3.7). Thus it is quite possible that much of the higher education in Mexico would not occur without public support.[28]

Three conclusions can be drawn from this analysis. First, the population divides itself into two social classes, those with lower secondary schooling or less and those above. Second, the proportion of adults between 25 and 40 with completed lower secondary schooling or less remained almost unchanged. Third, in the lower portion of the population, more adults reached lower secondary education because of the increased availability of public schooling at that level rather than through private investment. These three propositions support the presence of a low human capital accumulation trap with a barrier at lower secondary schooling, rather than a single-peaked, slow transition.

The overall finding of a barrier for higher secondary schooling is supported by De Ferranti et al. (2003, 86) who argue that in most Latin American countries there is a 'bottleneck' at the secondary education level, requiring a policy focus to facilitate transitions to higher education. However, although these authors recommend policies helping individuals to overcome market failures, they do not analyze the role of early child nutrition and health in determining the

Figure 3.7 Distribution of Public Education Expenditure in 2000

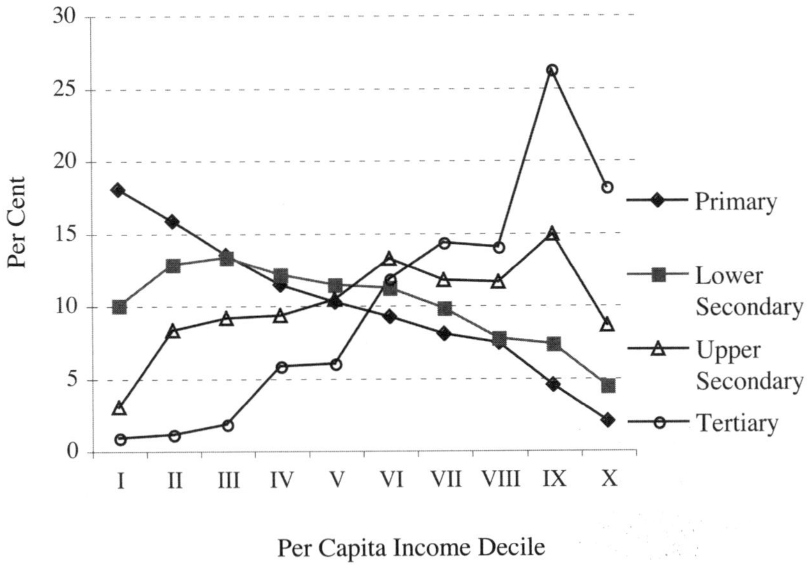

Source: John Scott (2003b), 'Public Spending and Inequality of Opportunities in Mexico: 1992–2000', Lomas de Santa Fé, Mexico, Centro de Investigación y Docencia Económicas (CIDE) Working Paper No. 235, revised version.

educational potential of the young, nor do they consider the full implications of the presence of a poverty trap.

The dynamics and shape of the distribution of adult schooling are consistent with multiple equilibria and therefore indicate the presence of a human capital accumulation poverty trap in Mexico, rather than a slow transition. Since education and wealth have increased somewhat in both classes (albeit with public intervention) the poverty trap may be considered to be *dynamic* in the sense defined above.

CONCLUSION

The process of human development is subject to a series of market failures. The Mincerian estimates on labor income show increasing returns to education in Mexico at levels not achieved by most of the population and, therefore, that there is substantial underinvestment in education. The probit estimates show that school permanence is more likely with higher child nutrition and health, for which there is evidence of substantial returns. Thus there is also substantial underinvestment in these factors. Barriers to education which the market system cannot surmount on its own pose a problem to social welfare and economic growth, since they give rise to substantial underinvestment in human capital across most of the Mexican population.

The presence of substantial increasing returns implies that a poverty trap or a slow transition exists, with the income of the less educated growing more slowly. The distribution of schooling across household partners, however, is multi-peaked, providing evidence of two classes of people: those with complete lower secondary education and below and those above. Moreover, the proportion of the population in the lower group has remained almost unchanged and the group's educational investment has only improved in response to public investment. This supports the hypothesis that there is a barrier to education beyond lower secondary schooling.

The probit results show that improvements in nutrition could have considerable impact on the schooling distribution, with high improvement rates in higher education. The increasing marginal rates of return to education suggest that almost 90 per cent of the population – those with less than higher education – would benefit from increased levels of nutrition, health and education. Although there may be a premium to higher education caused by the present low supply of human capital (itself accentuated by the low investment trap), it is unlikely that in today's high technology production environment the demands for human capital will be saturated very soon. Indeed, the tendency has been for returns to primary and secondary education to decrease, while those of higher education increase.

In common sense terms, since education is essential for adult income, today's young must be raised with adequate nutrition and quality education if the cycle of poverty is to be broken. The reach of reform must be broadly conceived and inclusive of all people, especially the poor. In the case analyzed here, this translates into a need for investment flows beyond those generated by the market.

While it is true that the low institutional quality of public health and school systems have lead to widespread inefficiencies, achieving the institutional capacity to overcome failures in the market system by, for example, streamlining efficient investment flows, require government intervention and should be an integral part of reform. Pro-market reforms facilitating economic growth will only realize their full potential if their range includes policies for human development. In Mexico, as in many countries, the educational advances of previous generations were based on government action. These advances will only continue if public action responds to the continuing nutritional, educational and health demands of the young. More generally, optimal strategies for economic growth must be two-pronged. First, they must establish the appropriate conditions for markets to function; otherwise, who will have the appropriate incentives in production and technological change to effectively employ the supplied human capital? Second, the main market failures holding back economic growth must be overcome through government policies to supply human capital. Only such dual strategies will rally the productive forces needed to emerge from poverty. Without appropriate public policy, human capital accumulation will be slow, human potential will be wasted, the coming generation will continue to be poor and Mexico – as well as many other countries – will experience low rates of development.

NOTES

A previous version of this chapter, 'Market Failures in Health and Education Investment for the Young, Mexico 2000', was written as a research project for the Pan American Health Organization, 'Nutrition and Human Capital in Mexico: Returns and Intergenerational Transmission' and was awarded Gold Medal for Research on Development in the Pro-market Reform and the Poor category at the Fifth Global Development Network Conference, New Delhi, 2004.

1. See, e.g. Knowles and Owen (1995, 1997); Bhargava, Jamison, Lau and Murray (2001); Gallup and Sachs (2001); Mayer (2001a, 2001b) Sachs and Warner (1997a, 1997b).
2. See, e.g. Schultz (1992, 1997, 1999); Thomas, Schoeni and Strauss (1997); Strauss and Thomas (1998) Savedoff and Schultz (2000).
3. Average stature rose from 164 to 181cm in Holland (1860–2002) and from 161 to 173cm in France and Norway (1705–1975). Average weight rose from 46 to 73 kg in Norway and France (1705–1975). Life expectancy rose from 41 to 78 years in England (1841–1998); and from 29 to 60 years in India (1930–1990) (Fogel 2002; Cervellati, Matteo and Uwe Sunde 2003).
4. It is enough to recall the names Roosevelt, Marshall and Keynes for policies addressing badly or insufficiently functioning markets. Present day financial regulation also plays a significant role.
5. See Micronutrient Initiative and United Nations Children's Fund (2004) for a recent study on deficiencies, their consequences and the technology of vitamin and micronutrient provision.
6. Regressions not reported here also support increasing returns to parental education in the acquisition of education, in the sense that parental support for their children to reach their own level of education is significantly higher. A poverty trap model can be built on this assumption alone.
7. The seven ENIGH income and expenditure surveys in the period 1984 to 2000 and ENSA 2000.
8. These findings are supported in the literature. See Zamudio (1999), Rojas, Angulo and Velásquez (2000), Mayer-Foulkes and Stabridis (2003), De Ferranti et al. (2003, 88) and Legovini, Bouillon and Lustig (2001) for increasing returns to education. See Moock and Leslie (1986) and Jamison (1986), Glewwe and Jacoby (1995) and Glewwe, Jacoby and King (2001) for the impact of stature on education. Mother's stature also influences her cognitive ability (Rubalcava and Teruel, 2004). For the higher secondary schooling barrier in Latin America see De Ferranti et al. (2003, 86).
9. According to unreported regressions, education of the young beyond the level achieved by

their parents, at which point there appears to be a barrier to continuing education, must also be promoted.
10. See footnote 8 for the references. Note that parents in our sample who did not invest in higher education for their children could have had the foresight to do so.
11. De Ferranti et al. (2003, Chapter 3); Hanson and Harrison (1995); Revenga (1995); Tan and Batra (1997); Cragg and Epelbaum (1996) and Robertson (2000).
12. Of course, achieving convergence in the European Union is facilitated by a series of programs in regional and infrastructure support and by the free flow of labor.
13. Jamison (1986) and Moock and Leslie (1986) find height-for-age is more closely associated with school performance than weight-for-height, that measures acute malnutrition.
14. Note that the absence of appropriate health status indicators results in a higher emphasis on nutrition, as compared to health, than may be warranted.
15. Thus an adult having completed lower but not higher secondary school would have a one in the 'marginal dummies' for incomplete or complete primary and lower secondary and a zero for the higher secondary dummy. The marginal returns for education remain almost identical if stature is not interacted with the educational dummies, implying that the estimate is unaffected by the possibly nonlinear returns to stature.
16. The t-statistic testing the schooling coefficient relations C15 or more ≥ C12 or more ≥ C9 or more for the OLS income regressions are 3.95, 3.025 for women and 8.14, 1.93 for men.
17. Detailed regression results can be consulted in the working paper version of this document at www.cide.edu.
18. A multiprobit on schooling is not appropriate, because the educational decisions are not simultaneous but sequential and therefore independent. The relation between subsequent educational decisions is also quite nonlinear (as would be predicted by a poverty trap model). Although this multiprobit was nevertheless attempted, it did not converge.
19. Interacting each of the variables in Wi with Genderi would sacrifice too many degrees of freedom. Instead it may be thought that some of the wealth variables, such as those related to kitchen and water availability or to wealth in general, are sufficiently related to ongoing gender distinctions and discrimination that the full set in fact adjusts for gender effects.
20. This argument is also made by Glewwe and Jacoby (1995), who find for their database that most of the shortfall in height for age Z-score occurs before the age of two. Also, Martorell et al. (1988) find that, across the population, stature at age five is not correlated with changes in stature after age five.
21. Among the significant variables are gender, mother's schooling, household income, mother's proportion of income, proportion of income not parents', indigenous language dummy, number of rooms, telephone, and several of the instrumental variables, IMSS and PEMEX coverage, and preferences for IMSS, PEMEX, SSA, IMSS-Solidaridad.
22. Income variables are not very significant (except for mother's presence at home or employment of some of the children). In some studies this is taken as poor evidence for the credit constraint hypothesis. However, this is true only in a marginal sense: a little more income does not change the decisions very much. A much higher income, though, might lead to an outcome corresponding to another equilibrium.
23. Primary school was 'obligatory' for all children in the sample. Lower secondary school became obligatory in 1993, before most of the children in the sample graduated from primary school.
24. A more careful argument is needed if the returns do not increase. For example, at a discount rate of 5 per cent, a group of 30 people with a given salary and level of education, expecting to work or study for another 40 years, would pool up to 45 of their salaries for three years to receive the services of an educational institution yielding a salary increase of 10 per cent per year studied.
25. I use the term 'class' sparingly because of its strong connotations, although it may well be that human development traps lie at the origin of class systems.
26. These trends are obtained by regressions on the data in Figure 3.4. I exclude the 1984 survey because it is an outlier at every level of the distribution, either because of sampling issues or

because of the objective differences in the state of education observed in Figure 3.2.
27. Figures based on SEP (Ministry of Education) statistics on public and private education.
28. The changes in the distribution of schooling observed across time in Figure V are very similar to those which result from comparing adults aged 19 to 24 with adults aged 25 to 40 using the ENSA 2000 data.

BIBLIOGRAPHY

Aghion, Philippe, Peter Howitt and David Mayer-Foulkes (2004), 'The Effect of Financial Development on Convergence: Theory and Evidence', Cambridge, MA, National Bureau of Economic Research (NBER) Working Paper No. 10358.

Arora, Suchit (2001), 'Health Human Productivity and Long-Term Economic Growth', *Journal of Economic History*, **61** (3), 699–748.

Barker, D.J.P. (1998), *Mothers, Babies and Health in Later Life*, Edinburgh: Churchill Livingstone.

Bhargava, Alok, Dean Jamison, Lawrence Lau and Christopher Murray (2001): 'Modeling the Effects of Health on Economic Growth', *Journal of Health Economics*, **20** (3), 423–40.

Bracho, Teresa (1994), 'Gasto Privado en Educación. México, 1984–1992'[Private Expenditure in Education. Mexico, 1984–1992], Lomas de Santa Fé, Mexico, Centro de Investigación y Docencia Económicas (CIDE) Political Science Working Paper No. 21.

Bracho, Teresa and Andrés Zamudio (1994a), 'Rendimientos económicos a la escolaridad I: Discusión Teórica y Métodos de Estimación' [Returns to Schooling I: Theoretical Discussion and Estimation Methods], Lomas de Santa Fé, Mexico, Centro de Investigación y Docencia Económicas (CIDE) Economics Working Paper No. 30.

—— (1994b), 'Rendimientos económicos a la escolaridad II: Estimaciones para el Caso Mexicano 1989' [Returns to Schooling II: Estimates for the Mexican Case, 1989], Lomas de Santa Fé, Mexico, Centro de Investigación y Docencia Económicas (CIDE) Economics Working Paper No. 31.

Case, Anne, Angela Fertig and Christina Paxson (2003), 'From Cradle to Grave? The lasting impact of childhood health and circumstance', Cambridge, MA, National Bureau of Economic Research (NBER) Working Paper 9788.

Case, Anne, Darren Lubotsky and Christina Paxson (2002), 'Economic Status and Health in Childhood: The Origins of the Gradient', *American Economic Review*, **92** (5), 1308–34.

Cervellati, Matteo and Uwe Sunde (2003), 'Human Capital Dormation, Life Expectancy and the Process of Economic Development', Bonn, Institute for the Study of Labor, Discussion Paper No. 585.

Cragg, Michael I. and Mario Epelbaum (1996), 'Why Has Wage Dispersion Grown in Mexico? Is It the Incidence of Reforms or the Growing Demand for Skills?', *Journal of Development Economics*, **51** (1), 99–116.

De Ferranti, David, Guillermo Perry, Indermit Gill, J. Luis Guasch, William Maloney, Carolina Sánchez-Páramo and Norbert Schady (2003), *Closing the Gap in Education and Technology*, Washington, DC: World Bank.

ENIGH (2000), 'National Household Income and Expenditure Surveys', Mexico City: Instituto Nacional de Estadistica, Geographica e Informática.

ENSA (2000), 'National Health Survey', Mexico City: Instituto Nacional de Salud Pública.
Fernandez, Raquel, Nezih Guner and John Knowles (2001), 'Love and Money: A Theoretical and Empirical Analysis of Household Sorting and Inequality', Cambridge, MA, National Bureau of Economic Research (NBER) Working Paper No. 8580.
Fogel, Robert W. (2002), 'Nutrition, Physiological Capital, and Economic Growth', Washington, DC, Pan American Health Organization, Program on Public Policy and Health, at http://www.paho.org/English/HDP/HDD/fogel.pdf.
—— (1994a), 'Economic Growth, Population Theory, and Physiology: The Bearing of Long-Term Processes on the Making of Economic Policy', *American Economic Review*, **84** (3), 369–95.
—— (1994b), 'The Relevance of Malthus for the Study of Mortality Today: Long Run Influences on Health, Morality, Labor Force Participation, and Population Growth', in Kerstin Lindahl-Kiessling and Hans Landberg (eds), *Population, Economic Development, and the Environment*, New York: Oxford University Press, 231–84.
—— (1993), 'New Sources and New Techniques for the Study of Secular Trends in Nutritional Status, Health, Mortality, and the Process of Aging', Cambridge, MA, National Bureau of Economic Research (NBER) Historical Working Paper No. 26.
Fogel, Robert W. and Larry T. Wimmer (1992), 'Early Indicators of Later Work Levels, Disease, and Death', Cambridge, MA, National Bureau of Economic Research (NBER) Historical Working Paper No. 38.
Gallup, John Luke and Jeffrey D. Sachs (2001): 'The Economic Burden of Malaria', *American Journal of Tropical Medicine and Hygiene*, **64** (1/2), 85–96.
Galor, Oded and Joseph Zeira (1993), 'Income Distribution and Macroeconomics', *Review of Economic Studies*, **60** (1), 35–52.
Glewwe, Paul and Hanan G. Jacoby (1995), 'An Economic Analysis of Delayed Primary School Enrollment in a Low Income Country: The Role of Early Childhood Nutrition', *Review of Economics and Statistics*, **77** (1), 156–69.
Glewwe, Paul, Hanan Jacoby and Elizabeth King (2001), 'Early Childhood Nutrition and Academic Achievement: A Longitudinal Analysis', *Journal of Public Economics*, **81** (3), 345–68.
Hanson, Gordon H. and Ann Harrison (1995), 'Trade, Technology and Wage Inequality in Mexico', Cambridge, MA, National Bureau of Economic Research (NBER) Working Paper No. 5110.
Hertzman, Clyde (1999), 'Population Health and Human Development', in Daniel P. Keating and Clyde Hertzman (eds), *Developmental Health and the Wealth of Nations: Social, Biological, and Educational Dynamics*, New York: Guilford Press, pp. 21–40.
Howitt, Peter and David Mayer-Foulkes (2002), 'R&D, Implementation and Stagnation: A Schumpeterian Theory of Convergence Clubs', Cambridge, MA, National Bureau of Economic Research (NBER) Working Paper No. 9104.
Jamison, Dean (1986), 'Child Malnutrition and School Performance in China', *Journal of Development Economics*, **20** (2), 299–309.
Knowles, Stephen and Owen, P. Dorian (1995), 'Health Capital and Cross-country Variation in Income Per Capita in the Mankiw Romer Weil-Model', *Economics-Letters*, **48** (1), 99–106.
—— (1997), 'Education and Health in an Effective-Labor Empirical Growth Model', *Economics-Record*, **73** (223), 314–28.

Larrea, Carlos, Wilma B. Freire and Chessa Lutter (2001), *'Equidad desde el principio, situación nutricional de los niños ecuatorianos'* [Equity from the beginning, nutritional situation of children in Ecuador], Pan American Health Organization.

Legovini, Arianna, Bouillon, César and Lustig, Nora (2001), 'Can Education Explain Changes in Income Inequality in Mexico?', Inter-American Development Bank Working Paper.

Levinger, Beryl (1994), 'Nutrition, Health and Education for All', New York: UNDP Education Development Center, p. 73. Available at http://www.edc.org/INT/NHEA/index.html.

Maddison, Angus (2001), *The World Economy: A Millennial Perspective*, Paris: Organization for Economic Cooperation and Development.

Martorell, Reynaldo and Guillermo Arroyave (1988), 'Malnutrition, Work Output, and Energy Need', in K.J. Collins and D.B. Roberts (eds), *Capacity for Work in the Tropics*, New York: Cambridge University Press, pp. 57–75.

Mayer, David (2001a), 'The Long-Term Impact of Health on Economic Growth in Mexico, 1950-1995', *Journal of International Development*, **13** (1), 123–26.

—— (2001b), 'The Long-Term Impact of Health on Economic Growth in Latin America', *World Development*, **29** (6), 1025–33.

Mayer-Foulkes, David (2002), 'Global Divergence', lecture at Brown University, Providence, RI, April 9, available at http://papers.ssrn.com /sol3/papers. cfm?abstract_id=335140.

Mayer-Foulkes David and Omar Stabridis-Arana (2003), 'Estimaciones de los Retornos Privados a la Escolaridad y Cálculo Del PIB Educativo para México', unpublished paper.

Micronutrient Initiative and United Nations Children's Fund (2004), *Vitamin and Mineral Deficiency: A Global Progress Report*, Ottawa: Micronutrient Initiative and New York: UNICEF.

Mincer, Jacob (1974), *Schooling, Experience and Earnings*, Cambridge, MA, National Bureau Economic Research NBER).

—— (1962), 'On the Job Training', *Journal of Political Economy*, 70, 50–79.

Mirrlees, James A. (1975), 'A Pure Theory of Underdeveloped Economies', in L. Reynolds (ed.), *Agriculture in Development Theory*, New Haven, CT: Yale University Press.

Moock, Peter and Joanne Leslie (1986), 'Childhood malnutrition and schooling in the Teri region of Nepal', *Journal of Development Economics*, **20** (1), 33–52.

Patrinos, Harry (2003), 'Economic Volatility and Returns to Education in Venezuela: 1992–2002', mimeo.

Pritchett, Lant (1997), 'Divergence, Big Time', *Journal of Economic Perspectives*, **11** (3), 3–17.

Quah, Danny T. (1993), 'Empirical cross-section dynamics in Economic Growth', *European Economic Review*, **37** (2/3), 426–34.

Ravelli, A.C.J. (1999), 'Prenatal Exposure to the Dutch Famine and Glucose Tolerance and Obesity at Age 50', Thela Thesis Amsterdam: University of Amsterdam.

Revenga, Ana (1995), 'Employment and Wage Effects of Trade Liberalization: The Case of Mexican Manufacturing', Washington, DC, World Bank Policy Research Working Paper No. 1524.

Robertson, Raymond. (2000), 'Trade Liberalization and Wage Inequality: Lessons from the Mexican Experience', *World Economy*, **23** (6), 827–49.

Rojas, Mariano, Humberto Angulo and Irene Velásquez (2000), 'Rentabilidad de la

Inversión en Capital Humano en México' [Returns to Human Capital Investment in Mexico], *Economía Mexicana*, **9** (2), 113–42.
Rubalcava, Luis N. and Graciela M. Teruel (2004), 'The Role of Maternal Cognitive Ability on Child Health', mimeo.
Sachs, Jeffrey D. and Andrew M. Warner (1997a), 'Fundamental Sources of Long-Run Growth', *American Economic Review*, **87** (2), 184–88.
—— (1997b), 'Sources of Slow Growth in African Economies', *Journal of African Economies* **6** (3), 335–76.
Savedoff, William D. and T. Paul Schultz (eds) (2000), *Wealth from Health: Linking Social Investments to Earnings in Latin America*, Washington, DC: Inter-American Development Bank.
Schultz, T. Paul (1999), 'Health and Schooling Investments in Africa', *Journal of Economic Perspectives*, **13** (3), 67–88.
—— (1997), 'Assessing the Productive Benefits of Nutrition and Health: An Integrated Human Capital Approach', *Journal of Econometrics*, **77** (1), 141–58.
—— (1992), 'The Role of Education and Human Capital in Economic Development: An Empirical Assessment', New Haven, CT, Yale University Economic Growth Center Discussion Papers No. 670.
Schürch, Beat and Nevin S. Scrimshaw, N.S. (eds) (1987), *Effects of Chronic Energy Deficiency on Stature, Work Capacity and Productivity*, Lausanne: International Dietary Energy Consultancy Group.
Scott, John (2003a), 'Poverty and Inequality', in Sidney Weintraub (ed.), *NAFTA at Ten: Strengthening the North American Community*, Washington, DC: Center for Strategic and International Studies.
—— (2003b), 'Public Spending and Inequality of Opportunities in Mexico: 1992–2000', Lomas de Santa Fé, Mexico, Centro de Investigación y Docencia Económicas (CIDE) Working Paper No. 235, revised version.
Sen, Amartya (1999), *Development as Freedom*, New York: Alfred A. Knopf.
Smith, James P. (1999), 'Healthy Bodies and Thick Wallets: The Dual Relation between Health and Economic Status', *Journal of Economic Perspectives,* **13** (2), 145–66.
Steckel, Richard H. (1995), 'Stature and the Standard of Living', *Journal of Economic Literature*, **33** (4), 1903–40.
Strauss, John and Duncan Thomas (1998), 'Health, Nutrition, and Economic Development', *Journal of Economic Literature*, **36** (2), 766–817.
Tan, Hong and Geeta Batra (1997), 'Technology and Firm Size-Wage Differentials in Colombia, Mexico, and Taiwan (China)', *World Bank Economic Review*, **11** (1), 59–83.
Thomas, Duncan, Robert E. Schoeni and John Strauss (1997), 'Parental Investments in Schooling: Gender and Household Resource Allocation in Urban Brazil', Santa Monica, CA, RAND Labor and Population Program Working Paper No. DRU-1303-NICHD.
Van Der Gaag, Jacques (2002), 'From Child Development to Human Development', in Mary Eming Young (ed.), *From Early Child Development to Human Development: Investing in Our Children's Future*, Washington, DC, World Bank, Human Development Network, Education Sector available at http://www.worldbank.org/children/ECDtoHumanDevelopment.pdf.
World Bank (1993), *World Development Report 1993: Investing in Health*, Washington DC, World Bank.
Zamudio, Andrés (1999), 'Educación y distribución condicional del ingreso: una

aplicación de regresión cuantil' [Education and conditional distribution of income: an application of quantile regressions], Lomas de Santa Fé, Mexico, Centro de Investigación y Docencia Económicas (CIDE) Economics Working Paper No. 163.

—— (1995), 'Rendimientos a la educación superior en México: ajuste por sesgo utilizando máxima verosimilitud' [Returns to higher education in Mexico: maximum likelihood correction of bias], Lomas de Santa Fé, Mexico, Centro de Investigación y Docencia Económicas (CIDE) Economics Working Paper No. 44.

Zamudio, Andrés and Teresa Bracho (1994), 'Rendimientos económicos a la escolaridad III: El problema de Sesgo por elección' [Returns to schooling III: selection bias], Lomas de Santa Fé, Mexico, Centro de Investigación y Docencia Económicas (CIDE) Economics Working Paper No. 32.

PART TWO

Range: Institutional Reform, Policy Change

4. Government Policies and FDI Inflows of Asian Developing Countries: Empirical Evidence

Rashmi Banga

According to Amartya Sen, social change creates interdependence. This is why the methods used in the process of economic reform must have a wide range. Policymakers must understand that restructuring the rules of the game concerning specific dimensions of economic activity can have important repercussions in the broader economy. This ripple effect is particularly apparent concerning the reforms which bring the national economy in contact with the rest of the world. The process of integration into the world economy has increased the range of domestic market-oriented reforms, that now include instruments and policies to attract foreign direct investment (FDI). Developing countries no longer regard FDI with suspicion, and controls and restrictions over the entry and operations of foreign firms are now being replaced by selective policies which aim at encouraging FDI. In fact, the developing countries of Asia are now competing with each other to attract FDI.

These changes have spawned an extensive network of bilateral and regional investment agreements which seek to promote and protect FDI coming from the partner countries.[1] This process thus induces changes not only in the behavior of domestic agents, but also changes in the behavior of foreign agents, and the institutional and policy framework must be correspondingly adapted. For example, authorities must evaluate whether FDI coming from developed and developing countries responds to incentives in the same way. Given this broad context, it is not surprising that the range of methods which reformers have used to influence the behavior of foreign investors has widened.

The growing integration and competition among host countries to attract FDI leads to doubts regarding the consensus reached in the literature about multinational corporations investing in specific locations mainly because of the availability of economic fundamentals like large market size, skilled labor and stable macroeconomic policy.[2] It is quite possible that economic fundamentals may no longer be sufficient to attract FDI; instead, government policies specifically aimed at FDI may be playing a more important role.

The literature on how policies affect FDI inflows is mixed. Brewer (1993) discuses various government policies which can directly and indirectly influence FDI through their effects on market imperfections. Specifically, he argues that a single government policy can increase or decrease market imperfections and thereby increase or decrease FDI inflows. Correspondingly, the empirical evidence on the impact of selected government policies on FDI inflows is ambiguous. Grubert and Mutti (1991), Loree and Guisinger (1995), Taylor (2000) and Kumar (2002) find a positive effect from investment incentives and a negative effect from performance requirements imposed by the host governments on inward FDI. UNCTAD (1996) reports that incentives can attract FDI only at the margin, varying according to the type of incentive and project. Several studies find that fiscal incentives affect location decisions, especially for export-oriented FDI, although other incentives seem to play a secondary role (Hines 1996).

But some studies (e.g., Contractor 1991) find that policy changes have a weak influence on FDI inflows. Caves (1996) and Villela and Barreix (2002) conclude that incentives are generally ineffective once the role of fundamental determinants of FDI is taken into account. This view is also supported by Hoekman and Saggi (2000), who conclude that although useful for attracting certain types of FDI, incentives do not seem to work when applied at a macro level. Nunnenkamp (2002) argues that little has changed since the 1980s and traditional market-related determinants are still dominant factors in attracting FDI. Further, Blomstrom et al. (2000) have discussed whether FDI incentives are justified for the host economies, given the fact that they involve a transfer of resources from host countries to foreign firms.[3]

This chapter adds to the existing literature on location determinants of FDI by empirically examining the response of FDI inflows to selected national and international FDI policies of Asian developing countries, after controlling for the economic fundamentals of host countries. With the growth of FDI outflows from developing countries in the last two decades, there are reasons to believe that FDI from developed and developing countries may seek to fulfill distinct objectives and therefore may be attracted by different sets of host government policies.[4] This hypothesis, however, has not been empirically tested until now.

This study uses panel data to estimate how government FDI policies and investment agreements affect inflows for 15 developing countries of South, East and Southeast Asia for the period 1980–81 to 1999–2000. In addition, FDI is disaggregated into FDI from ten developed and developing countries, after which their responses to government policies and investment agreements are examined for the period 1986–87 to 1996–97. The resulting Random Effects Model and the Fixed Effects Model are also estimated using panel data.

FDI FLOWS TO DEVELOPING COUNTRIES IN ASIA

The last two decades have witnessed a tremendous increase in global FDI flows. This growth has been accompanied by a slow shift in the pattern of FDI, that has gradually become more favorable to the developing countries. Table 4.1 presents the percentage of global FDI flows into developed and developing countries and from developed and developing countries in this period. The data indicate that the share of developing countries in total inward FDI has increased steadily. The average annual percentage flow of FDI into developing countries rose from 25 per cent in the 1980s to 30 per cent in the 1990s. Privatization, that took place simultaneously in many Asian developing countries, is largely responsible for the higher inflow of FDI in the 1990s.

The average inflow of FDI would have been much higher in the 1990s if the Asian economic crisis had not slowed the Asian economies after 1997. The worst-hit countries were the Southeast Asian countries which experienced a dramatic fall in both FDI inflows and outflows. In spite of the drastic reduction in the latter half of the 1990s, average annual outflow of FDI from developing countries almost doubled in the 1990s as compared to 1980s. However, an increasing proportion of FDI outflows, around 88 per cent, still came from the developed countries.

Among developing regions, the share of Asian countries in global FDI flows has steadily increased in the last two decades (UNCTAD 2003). The average annual inflow of FDI into Asia and the Pacific region increased to around 54 per cent in the 1980s and around 61 per cent in the 1990s. But the distribution of FDI flows to Asia and the Pacific region is biased heavily towards the Asian countries (99 per cent in the 1990s). Within Asia, on average 72 per cent of total FDI went to South, East and Southeast Asia in the 1980s and around 97 per cent in the 1990s. Therefore it makes sense to analyze FDI flows into South, East and Southeast Asia. The sample here includes Bangladesh, China, China–Hong Kong, India, Malaysia, Nepal, Pakistan, Philippines, Singapore, South Korea, Sri Lanka, China–Taiwan, Indonesia, Thailand and Vietnam.

Within the Asian countries, there has been a substantial change in the pattern of FDI inflow over the last two decades (Table 4.2). China has seen a substantial increase in its average share of total FDI inflow in the 1990s. The average share of FDI inflow has also increased in the 1990s for countries like Bangladesh, India and Vietnam, although their overall share still remains very low. However, the average share of Malaysia declined from around 15 per cent to 8 per cent

Table 4.1 Percentage of Global FDI Inflows and Outflows: 1980–2001

Year	FDI inflows into Developed countries	FDI inflows into Developing countries	FDI outflows from Developed countries	FDI outflows from Developing countries
1980	84.68	15.25	93.79	6.17
1981	66.04	33.91	96.08	3.92
1982	54.04	45.93	90.20	9.79
1983	65.40	34.53	95.39	4.60
1984	69.44	30.53	95.66	4.32
1985	74.13	25.82	93.15	6.85
1986	81.04	18.97	94.75	5.22
1987	83.37	16.62	95.20	4.80
1988	81.40	18.57	93.24	6.74
1989	84.49	15.26	92.82	7.18
Average	74.40	25.54	94.02	5.96
1990	81.16	18.53	92.82	7.16
1991	70.60	27.71	93.97	6.01
1992	62.67	34.60	87.43	12.53
1993	60.28	36.61	83.69	16.18
1994	55.71	41.86	83.35	16.48
1995	61.51	34.05	85.34	14.46
1996	56.95	39.54	84.15	15.52
1997	56.05	39.96	83.33	15.78
1998	69.73	27.02	92.29	7.35
1999	76.98	20.69	92.70	7.07
2000	82.27	15.95	92.16	7.55
2001	68.44	27.86	93.54	5.89
Average	66.86	30.36	87.79	11.00

Source: UNCTAD 2003. Total FDI flows are divided between developed countries, developing countries and Central and Eastern Europe.

and Hong Kong from 22 per cent to 17 per cent in the 1990s. Some fall is also seen in the average shares of Taiwan, Indonesia, Pakistan, Sri Lanka and Thailand during this period.

However, the average shares of these countries in the total stock of FDI in this region between 1980 and 2001 show a very different picture. Hong Kong has received around 50 per cent of the total stock of FDI in these two decades. While 15 per cent of the total FDI stock has gone into China, followed by

Table 4.2 Average Share of Countries in Total FDI Inflows and Total FDI Stock in South, East and Southeast Asia, 1980–2001

	Average share in total FDI inflow 1980–1990	Average share in total FDI inflow 1991–2001	Average share in total FDI inward stock 1980–2001
Bangladesh	0.04	0.08	0.05
China	16.46	40.62	15.35
China, Hong Kong	22.13	16.87	50.96
China, Taiwan	4.73	3.03	2.49
India	1.29	2.07	0.90
Indonesia	4.12	2.68	10.23
Korea	3.43	3.98	1.97
Malaysia	14.88	8.18	0.01
Nepal	0.0001	0.0001	0.00
Pakistan	1.11	0.77	0.68
Philippines	1.49	1.90	1.16
Singapore	23.83	11.82	8.49
Sri Lanka	0.62	0.25	0.24
Thailand	5.38	4.84	2.10
Vietnam	0.13	1.59	0.52
Others	0.36	1.32	4.84
Total	100.00	100.00	100.00

Source: UNCTAD 2003.

Indonesia (around 10 per cent) and Singapore (around 8 per cent). Thailand and Taiwan received about 2 per cent of total FDI stock and all others received less than 1 per cent.

Table 4.3 reports the average share of FDI inflows from developed and developing countries into the Asian developing countries in the period 1986–87 to 1996–97.[5] During this period Singapore received the largest share of FDI from the developed countries, followed by Hong Kong, South Korea and Indonesia. Countries like Taiwan, India, Thailand, Philippines, Malaysia and Pakistan received more than half of their FDI from developed countries. But the rest have a larger share of FDI from developing countries; China and Vietnam, for example, have more than 60 per cent of FDI inflows from developing countries.

Table 4.3 Average Share of FDI Inflows from Developed and Developing Countries, 1986–87 through 1996–97

Country	FDI from developed countries	FDI from developing countries	Total
Bangladesh	36.02	63.98	100
China	23.64	76.36	100
China, Hong Kong	83.32	16.68	100
China, Taiwan	63.05	36.95	100
India	68.47	31.53	100
Indonesia	81.26	18.74	100
Korea, Rep.	86.50	13.50	100
Malaysia	57.55	42.45	100
Nepal	46.92	53.08	100
Pakistan	73.27	26.73	100
Philippines	72.41	27.59	100
Singapore	96.36	3.64	100
Sri Lanka	36.77	63.23	100
Thailand	63.72	36.28	100
Vietnam	33.51	66.49	100

Source: World Investment Directory, volume VII, parts 1 and 2: Asia and the Pacific. The figures are based on Approvals for FDI.

MEASURING FDI POLICY

There three leading schools of thought on the emergence of FDI. First, the market imperfections hypothesis (Hymer 1976) postulates that FDI is the direct result of an imperfect global market. Second, the internalization theory (Rugman 1986) argues that multinationals use FDI to replace external markets with more efficient internal ones. Third, the eclectic approach to international production (Dunning 1988) sees FDI emerging due to ownership, internalization and locational advantages.

But what determines the cross-country pattern of FDI? There is an extensive empirical literature on determinants of inward FDI which emphasize the economic conditions or fundamentals of the host countries relative to the home countries. This literature is in line with Dunning's eclectic paradigm (1993), that suggests it is the locational advantages of the host countries which determine a cross-country pattern of FDI. However, the location-specific advantages sought by mobile investors may be changing due to globalization. Dunning (2002) suggests these advantages may differ for FDI from developed and developing countries. This, however, remains to be tested empirically. Therefore, I construct a model which controls for economic fundamentals and examines the impact of government policies on FDI inflows in developing countries and then use it to analyze locational determinants from developed and developing countries separately.

Government policies that may influence the inflow of FDI can be broadly categorized into three types. First, overall economic policies which increase locational advantages by improving the economic fundamentals of the host country; second, national policies which reduce the transaction costs of foreign firms; and third, international policies which deal with agreements (bilateral, regional or multilateral) on foreign investments.

The overall economic policies work at the macro level and aim to improve the fundamentals of the economy like market size, availability of skilled labor, infrastructure, etc. The national FDI policies work at the domestic level by regulating FDI entry and exit along with creating incentives and restrictions on operations of foreign firms. International FDI policies work at the international level and deal with agreements on the issue of treatment of FDI from a particular partner or region. These investment agreements may ensure that FDI from a particular partner or region receives treatment under most-favored nation standards and national treatment standards.

The following model is used to estimate effects of host government national and international FDI policies in developing countries (after controlling economic fundamentals):

$FDI_{it} = f\,[(\text{Economic Fundamental})_{it-1}, (\text{National FDI Policies, e.g., Tariff Policies, FDI Incentives and Removal of Restrictions on FDI})_{it},$
$(\text{International FDI Policies e.g. Regional Investment Agreements})_{it}$ (4.1)

where i stands for country and t stands for the time period (1980–81, 1981–82 through 1999–2000.

The impact of economic fundamentals is estimated with a lag of one period to avoid simultaneity with the dependent variable. A similar model is estimated for FDI from developed countries and FDI from developing countries for the period 1986–87 to 1996–97 based on FDI approvals. Specifically, the impact of two regional investment agreements is examined: the non-binding investment principles (NBIP) agreed among Asia-Pacific Economic Cooperation (APEC) members and the investment area agreement (AIA) of the Association of Southeast Asian Nations (ASEAN). These are captured by a dummy variable for the country's membership in APEC and ASEAN. The next section discusses in detail the methodology, variables and data.

OVERALL ECONOMIC POLICIES

Overall economic policies help strengthen the fundamentals of an economy. A vast literature has analyzed the impact of economic fundamentals on the inflow of FDI. Table 4.4 provides a list of variables used by the earlier studies and those which have been considered here as determinants of inward FDI along with their expected signs. Studies have found variables like market-size, quality of human capital, macroeconomic stability, financial health and infrastructure availability to have a positive impact on FDI inflows, while cost variables are expected to be negatively related to FDI inflows (UNCTAD 1992). The definitions of the above variables along with their sources of data are reported in Table 4A.1 and Table 4A.2, respectively, of the Appendix.

Market Size

The most important economic fundamentals are market-related variables which may affect market-seeking FDI: current market size and potential market size. While a large market size generates scale economies, a growing market improves the market's potential prospects and thereby attracts FDI flows (Chen and Khan 1997; Mbekeani 1997). I use the log of GDP and the growth rate of GDP to capture the impact of current and potential market size on FDI and expect this to have a positive impact on inward FDI.

Cost Factors

The relative cost of labor, capital and infrastructure may create cost differentials across countries which, in turn, may significantly influence the choice of an investment location for resource-seeking and efficiency-seeking FDI.[6]

To capture cost of labor and availability of skilled labor, I use efficiency wage rates, i.e., the real wage rate as a ratio of the productivity of labor, defined as value added per unit of labor. Many studies use only real wage rates as an estimate of the cost of labor, but these studies fail to capture the efficiency of labor in the host country. I expect lower efficiency wages in the host country to attract inward FDI. The availability of skilled labor is also captured by the secondary school enrolment rate.

The impact of the cost of capital (i.e. lending interest rates) on FDI inflows is ambiguous and often statistically insignificant. On one hand, it can be argued that higher lending rates may have a positive impact on FDI inflows, i.e., the higher the cost of capital in the host country the more capital is brought in by foreign firms as equity. Alternatively, it can be argued that the host country's cost of capital directly affects domestic consumption. Thus, the lower the interest rates, the higher the domestic consumption and hence the higher the FDI inflows (Bende-Nabende et al. 2000). I therefore do not hypothesize any particular relationship between the two variables.

Regarding infrastructure costs, the availability of cheap infrastructure increases the host country's ability to attract FDI. Different studies have used different measures to capture infrastructure availability and cost. Some of the variables used in the literature are land and property rents, fuel costs, index of infrastructure, transport costs and share of transport and communication to GDP. I use two variables: transport and communication as a ratio of GDP and electricity consumed as a ratio of GDP across countries. Electricity consumed reflects both the availability and cost of electricity in host countries. However, the variables used as indicators of efficiency wage rates and the cost of capital are only rough indicators, as markets in developing countries are severely segmented.

Real Exchange Rates

There is mixed evidence about how depreciating real exchange rates in the host country affect FDI inflows. Foreign investors may gain or lose from a devalued exchange rate. They may gain due to larger buying power in host countries and because a devalued exchange rate would imply cheaper production and easier exports. This may attract resource-seeking and efficiency-seeking FDI. However, foreign firms may not enter if they believe that depreciation may continue after they enter a country, as this would imply that costs are too high to justify their investments (Trevino et al. 2002). I expect a devalued exchange rate to encourage the inflow of FDI in the host countries, as this would reduce the cost of investment to the foreign firms.

Macroeconomic Stability

FDI faces fluctuations of basic macroeconomic variables (like budget deficits, inflation, exchange rates, etc.) across countries. The volatility of macroeconomic policy creates problems for international firms, requiring them to manage the risk inherent in volatile countries, but it also presents an opportunity to move production to lower cost facilities.

If exchange-rate fluctuations merely offset price movements so that real purchasing power parity is maintained, the exchange-rate movements would

Table 4.4 Economic Determinants

Determinants	Variables used in the literature	Empirical studies	Variables used in this study	Expected signs
1. Current market size and potential market size	1. Log GDP 2. Per capita income 3. GDP growth rate 4. Per capita growth rate	Root and Ahmed 1979, Bhattacharya et al. 1996, Chen and Khan 1997	1. Log GDP 2. GDP growth rate	+
2. Cost of labor	1. Real wage rate	Woodward and Rolfe 1993	Efficiency wage rate	−
3. Availability of skilled labor	1. Literacy rates 2. Secondary enrollment rate	Schneider and Frey 1985	Secondary enrollment rate	+
4. Cost of capital	1. Local credit ratio 2. Log annual average lending rates	Bende-Nabende, et al. 2000	Log annual average lending rates	?
5. Availability of infrastructure	1. Ratio of commerce, transport and communication to GDP 2. Energy production (equivalent tons of coal per 1,000 population)	Bende-Nabende, et al. 2000	1. Proportion of electricity consumed/GDP 2. Transport and communication/GDP	+
6. Real exchange rate	1. Real exchange rate	Goldberg and Klein 1998, Trevino, et al. 2002	Real exchange rate	−

have little real effect. Nevertheless, there is empirical evidence to indicate that purchasing power parity does not hold for all time periods and thus exchange-rate fluctuations can affect the competitiveness of plants in different countries. I expect high volatility of the exchange rate of the host country currency to

Table 4.4 (continued)

Determinants	Variables used in the literature	Empirical studies	Variables used in this study	Expected signs
7. Exchange rate stability	1. Percentage change in annual average exchange rate between local currency and $1 2. Exchange rate volatility using monthly data	Froot and Stein 1991	Percentage change in annual average exchange rate between local currency and $1	−
8. Rate of inflation	Percentage change in consumer prices	Schneider and Frey 1985		−
9. Financial health	1. Current account deficit 2. Ratio of external debts to exports	Schneider and Frey 1985	Ratio of external debts to exports	−
10. Overall economic stability, including political stability	1. Credit ratings 2. Budget deficit/ GDP	Trevino, et al. 2002	Budget Deficit / GDP	−

discourage investment by foreign firms, as it increases uncertainty regarding the future economic and business prospects of the host country. To capture the volatility in exchange rates, that may negatively affect FDI inflows, I use the percentage change in the annual average exchange rate between local currency and the US dollar.[7]

Economic Stability

The financial health of the host economy is captured by the ratio of external debts to exports. As this ratio decreases, economic stability in the country should increase. Studies have used country credit ratings given by various institutions as an indicator of overall economic stability (which includes political and macroeconomic stability). However, subjectivity is a potential problem, as the ranking of countries based on these ratings differ across estimates provided by different agencies. To avoid the problem of subjectivity I prefer to use the budget deficit as a ratio of GDP in the host country as an indicator. As a large and continuous budget deficit in an economy may reflect economic instability in the host country, I expect it to have a negative impact on FDI inflows.

Rate of Inflation

A low inflation rate should be a sign of internal economic stability in the host country. High inflation indicates that the government is unable to balance its budget and the central bank has failed to conduct appropriate monetary policy (Schneider and Frey 1985). Due to a high correlation between the inflation rate in the economy and the extent of budget deficit, I do not use this variable explicitly here.

I thus control for the market variables (market size and potential market size), cost variables (cost of labor in terms of efficiency wages and cost of capital), skill availability (education), macroeconomic stability (real exchange rate and exchange-rate stability), financial health (budget deficit and level of external debt) and infrastructure availability (transport and communication and electricity consumed) in the economy.

NATIONAL FDI POLICIES

The national policies host governments use to encourage FDI have assumed greater importance in the current liberalized regime. However, as observed by Globerman and Shapiro (1999), it is difficult to statistically examine the impact of FDI-specific policies like incentives offered and the removal of restrictions on the operations of foreign firms, since they are hard to isolate from other factors, 'often because they are more implicit than explicit'. Another obstacle to empirical analysis is the difficulty in quantifying these policies.

Studies which empirically test for the impact of government policies on FDI flows are generally based on benchmark surveys at a particular point in time (Kumar 2002; Loree and Guisinger 1995). Although these kinds of studies give an insight into what determines the pattern of FDI flows at a particular point in time, they do not capture the influence of change in the FDI policies in a particular country and its comparative attractiveness to inward FDI into that region over time.

FDI may flow into a country not only because the host country now provides certain investment incentives, but also because they seem more attractive compared with the incentives provided by competing host countries. Another important consideration is that although different incentives offered by a host country may have significant influence on FDI when considered individually, when considered as a entire package they may lose their significance.

In an attempt to quantify policies which are not captured by proxy variables and to make them comparable across countries, I assign scores to different countries for the policies offered by them over time. These scores range from 0 to 2, where a zero score is allotted to a country at a time when it offers no incentives. The score 1 or 2 is allotted for different incentives offered depending upon how conducive they are to attracting FDI. For example, the score for tax holidays is based on duration. A zero score means no tax holidays are offered, 1 means the tax holidays are offered for less than five years and 2 means tax holidays are offered for five or more years.

Different scores have been allotted to different countries over time depending on the number of incentives offered and the number of sectors covered. The influence of the composite score (i.e., the sum of all the scores allotted to it in a particular year) on FDI inflows is then tested empirically. The influence of the combined score on FDI flows demonstrates the importance of the entire package of incentives offered by the host country. A similar exercise is undertaken with respect to lifting restrictions.

Tariff Policies

Following Mundell (1957) it was long thought that FDI substitutes for trade. Agmon (1979) challenged this proposition and subsequently a number of studies emphasized the potential complementarities between FDI and trade.[8] Earlier literature suggests that FDI and trade are either substitutes (in the case of tariff-hopping investment) or complementary to each other (in the case of intra-firm trade). However, the relationship between FDI and trade has become far more complex in the WTO regime wherein several developing countries have initiated import liberalization processes which have drastically reduced trading costs and encouraged international vertical integration and intra-industry trade.

As trade barriers decline and the importance of networks increases, foreign investors find barriers to entry and less competitive environments less appealing. More recent studies have found that foreign investment is deterred by high tariffs or non-tariff barriers on imported inputs and is attracted to more open economies. In reviewing cross-country regressions on the determinants of FDI, Chakrabarti (2001) argues that after market size, openness to trade has been the most reliable indicator of a location's attractiveness for FDI. I therefore expect greater openness to trade to attract higher FDI inflows.

Some studies have used the ratio of the sum of exports and imports as a share of GDP as an indicator of openness to trade. I prefer to use an exogenous variable which is average tariff rates (TARIFF) across countries. The sources of average tariff rates for the countries in the sample are UNCTAD's Trains database and the WTO's Trade Policy Reviews and Integrated Data Base (IDB).

Investment Incentives

Developing countries use both fiscal and financial incentives to attract FDI inflows. Fiscal incentives are designed to reduce the tax burden of a firm, such as tax concessions in the form of a reduced corporate income-tax rate, tax holidays, accelerated depreciation allowances on capital taxes, exemption from import duties and duty drawbacks on exports. Financial incentives include direct contributions to the firm from the government, including grants, subsidized loans and loan guarantees, publicly funded venture capital used for high-risk commercial investments and government insurance at preferential rates.

Almost all of the countries in the sample have such schemes, but developing countries prefer fiscal incentives. Unlike financial incentives, these can be easily granted without incurring any financial costs at the time of their provision.[9] The study therefore focuses on fiscal incentives, specifically:

1. Tax holidays ($TAXH_{it}$): A zero score is allotted to country i, in period t, if no tax holidays are declared. If tax holidays are declared for less than five years a score of one is allotted and five or more years receive a score of two.
2. Tax concessions in number of industries ($TAXCON_{it}$): A zero score is allotted to a country i, in period t, if there are not tax incentives for industries. If tax incentives are declared for a restricted number of industries, then a score of one is allotted and if it is declared for all industries, a score of two is allotted.
3. Repatriation of profits and dividends ($REMITS_{it}$): A score of zero is allotted to a country for the period when approvals are required to repatriate remittances, one if some restrictions are imposed and two if no permission is required.

The role of incentives in attracting FDI has been questioned on theoretical and empirical grounds, as discussed earlier. The results with respect to the impact of incentives offered by host countries to inward FDI are ambiguous. Several studies find that fiscal incentives do affect location decisions, especially for export-oriented FDI, although other incentives seem to play a secondary role. However, fiscal incentives appear unimportant for FDI which is geared primarily towards the domestic market. Instead, such FDI appears to be more sensitive to the extent to which it will benefit from import protection. However, as discussed earlier, incentives must be considered as a package and this requires a more nuanced view.

The impact of incentives on inward FDI flows is expected to be positive. But, it is interesting to see whether FDI from developed and developing countries respond in a similar way to the investment incentives offered to foreign firms in the developing countries.

Removal of Restrictions

Various forms of restrictions were applied to FDI in the developing countries in the pre-liberalized era. These were related to admission and establishment, ownership and control and other operational measures. Admission and establishment restrictions included restricting certain sectors, industries or activities to FDI; screening, authorization and registration of FDI and minimum capital requirements. Ownership and control restrictions existed in various forms, for example, allowing only a fixed percentage of foreign-owned capital in an enterprise; compulsory joint ventures, mandatory transfer of ownership to local private firms, usually over a period of time and restrictions on reimbursement of capital upon liquidation. Even after entry, foreign firms could face certain restrictions on their operations, such as restrictions on employment of foreign key personnel; and performance requirements such as sourcing or local content requirements, training requirements and export targets.

However, under the WTO regime, many of these restrictions have now been withdrawn in a large number of countries in Asia due to the enforcement of TRIMS (Trade-Related Investment Measures). In many countries today FDI does not require approval or licensing except in a few sectors which are closed to FDI (mainly for security reasons). I study the impact of removing the following restrictions:

1. Access to industries ($ACCESS_{it}$): a score of zero is allotted to country i in year t if there is restricted entry to foreign firms in a number of industries. A score of one or two is allotted depending upon whether the entry is restricted or free (excluding defense).
2. Foreign ownership restrictions ($OWNERSHIP_{it}$): a score of zero is allotted

to country i in year t if there are high ceilings on foreign ownership, i.e., foreign firms are not allowed. A score of one or two is allotted depending upon whether the ceiling is limited or absent.
3. Ease of entry ($ENTRY_{it}$): a score of zero is allotted to country i in year t if there is restricted entry to foreign firms in terms of required approvals or licensing. A score of one or two is allotted depending upon whether the entry is made easier by reducing administrative procedures or by giving free access to foreign firms and if no approvals are required.
4. Performance requirements ($PERFORMANCE_{it}$): a score of zero is allotted if many performance requirements exist. A score of one is allotted if the number and degree of performance requirements are reduced and a score of two is allotted if no performance requirements exist.

I examine the impact of the combined score for incentives, the sum of scores given for incentives, and the combined score for removal of restrictions on inward FDI. Higher scores should be associated with higher inflows of FDI. I also analyze this dimension separately for FDI from developed and developing countries.

The policies with respect to incentives and restrictions on FDI for each country in the sample have been collected from the United Nations' *Economic and Social Survey of Asia and the Pacific*, the Asian Development Bank's *Asian Development Outlook and Country Economic Review* and *Country Reports on Economic Policy and Trade Practice*, released by the Bureau of Economic and Business Affairs, US Department of State.

INTERNATIONAL FDI POLICIES: REGIONAL INVESTMENT AGREEMENTS

In contrast to the number of trading agreements, there are very few existing investment agreements. In general, such agreements deal exclusively with investments, establishing specific standards of investment protection and transfer of funds. They contain provisions for the settlement of disputes both between the treaty partners and between investors and host states. They also cover a number of other areas, including non-discrimination in the treatment – and in some cases the entry – of foreign-controlled enterprises.

Following the negotiations on TRIMS in the Uruguay Round of multilateral trade negotiations under the GATT (WTO), some regional trade bodies have also taken the initiative to improve the investment environment to make it more conducive to the free flow of FDI. One such agreement was reached among the APEC members in 1994, namely, the non-binding investment principles (NBIP). A similar agreement was also reached by the Association of Southeast Asian Nations (ASEAN) in 1999. The ASEAN Investment Area (AIA) has been signed by all the member countries which are committed to opening up industries and granting national treatment to all ASEAN investors immediately, except for some industries of national interest. The next section examines the impact of these two regional investment agreements on FDI inflows into developing countries, expecting them to have a positive effect. A dummy variable is used to capture the impact.

DETERMINANTS OF AGGREGATE FDI

After controlling for the economic fundamentals, random effects as well as fixed effects models have been estimated to gauge the impact of national and international FDI policies on FDI inflows. However, the analysis is based on the random effects model, since it is found to be more suitable by the Hausman Statistic.[10] The estimations have been undertaken at two levels. First, using data for 15 developing countries of South, East and Southeast Asia for the period 1980–81 to 1999–2000, an attempt is made to control for the economic fundamentals of the host country and to analyze the impact of FDI policy on FDI inflows. Second, the impact of FDI policy on FDI inflows from developed and developing countries is analyzed separately using panel data for ten developing countries for the period 1986–87 to 1996–97.[11] List-wise deletion is undertaken in the case of missing data. All results presented are corrected for auto-correlation and heteroscedasicity.

To test the significance of economic fundamentals on FDI inflows, the model is first estimated with only economic fundamentals. The results of the impact of fundamentals of the economy are reported in column 1 of Table 4.5. A number of equations are presented which include policy variables as determinants.[12] Most of the variables reported in column 1 of Table 4.5 have the expected signs and are consistent with the literature. FDI is found to be attracted to large market size; low labor cost, in terms of efficiency wages; availability of high skill levels captured by the secondary enrollment ratio in the economy; lower external debt, reflecting the financial health of the economy, and extent of electricity consumed in the economy. However, cost of capital reflected by domestic lending rates, macroeconomic stability captured by exchange rate stability and the budget deficit-to-GDP ratio are not found to be significant.

However, recent econometric studies emphasize that there has been a shift in the relative importance of the determinants of foreign investment decisions away from fundamentals toward FDI policies which aim at attracting higher flows in particular sectors. These studies suggest that the effects of FDI

Table 4.5 Impact of Selective Government Policies and Investment Agreements on Aggregate FDI (dependent variable = log of aggregate FDI inflows)

Variables	(1)	(2)	(3)
MKTSIZE	0.60***	0.20***	0.02**
	(3.46)	(5.34)	(2.11)
GRTHMKT	−0.003	0.007	0.002
	(−0.55)	(1.10)	(0.88)
EFFWAGE	−0.004**	−0.003	−0.001
	(−1.98)	(−0.08)	(−0.26)
EDU	0.08***	0.05***	0.001***
	(9.27)	(4.82)	(2.88)
EXRATE	−0.01	−0.001	−0.002
	(−0.71)	(−1.13)	(−1.40)
EXTDEBT	−0.35***	−0.13	−0.89
	(−4.00)	(−1.36)	(−0.93)
T&C	−0.26	0.12	0.21
	(−0.16)	(0.08)	(0.14)
ELECT	0.001***	0.001***	0.001***
	(4.82)	(5.14)	(4.69)
LDRATE	0.0003	0.0003	0.0001
	(0.97)	(1.08)	(0.38)
EXGVOL	−0.003	−0.008	−0.007
	(−0.42)	(−1.23)	(−1.02)
BUDGETDEF	−0.0002	−0.003	−0.0003
	(−0.71)	(−1.03)	(−1.06)

incentives, in particular fiscal incentives, and other governmental domestic FDI policies have become more important in the integrated world economy. One of the most discussed policies involves the openness of the economy, measured using average tariff rates.

Column 2 of Table 4.5 shows that tariff rates have a significant negative impact on FDI inflows. This result is robust in the sense that inclusion and exclusion of other variables does not affect its significance and sign. The result, as expected, corroborates the results of the earlier studies (e.g., Chakrabarti 2001) which find that openness to trade attracts FDI after controlling for other factors. The result therefore suggests that the FDI which went to developing countries during this time was not 'tariff-jumping' in nature. Rather, countries with high average tariffs were at a disadvantage compared with countries with lower average tariffs.

Table 4.5 (continued)

Variables	(1)	(2)	(3)
TARIFF		−0.02***	−0.02***
		(−3.12)	(−3.99)
REST		0.11***	0.13***
		(3.02)	(3.68)
INCENTIVES		0.11	0.10
		(1.37)	(1.66)
APEC			0.94***
			(4.57)
ASEAN			−0.71
			(−0.59)
CONSTANT	2.28***	3.35***	4.55***
	(3.40)	(2.45)	(3.33)
Adjusted R-Squared of OLS	0.50	0.54	0.59
N.	270	255	255
Fixed vs Random	3.59	3.28	3.28

Notes:
1. Results of Random Effects Model is presented.
2. Autocorrelation and Hetroscedasticity are corrected for.
3. List-wise deletion is made for missing values.
4. Hausman test supports random effect model. Figures in parenthesis are t-statistic.
***Significant at 1% level; **significant at 5% level and *significant at 10% level.

The impact of incentives offered as a package by the host countries and the removal of restrictions on the operation of foreign firms are studied separately, based on the presumption that these may have separate effects on inward FDI. Removing restrictions on entry, ownership, access to industries, etc. may in fact be more important to foreign firms than the actual fiscal incentives offered. The results here indicate that although incentives have a positive impact on inward FDI, they are not significant determinants of FDI. Various studies show that incentives play a minor role in attracting FDI once the impact of economic fundamentals has been controlled (Caves 1996; Villela and Barreix 2002). Perhaps most countries eventually offer identical or similar incentives as competition for external resources intensifies. As a result, investors become less sensitive to these measures in their decisions to locate their investments.

Table 4.6 *Impact of Government Policies on FDI Inflows from Developed Countries in Developing Countries: Random Effects Model*

Explanatory variables	FDI from developed countries	FDI From developing countries
MKTSIZE	2.03***	2.28***
	(4.57)	(6.57)
GRTHMKT	0.03	0.08***
	(0.85)	(2.48)
EFFWAGE	−0.006	−0.003**
	(−0.12)	(−2.08)
EDU	0.02**	0.01
	(2.40)	(1.00)
EXRATE	−0.001*	−0.0003***
	(−1.67)	(−4.13)
EXTDEBT	−0.11	−0.10
	(−1.08)	(−1.24)
T&C	36.23***	32.31***
	(2.46)	(2.59)
ELECT	0.0002	0.0001
	(0.65)	(0.34)
LDRATE	−0.001***	−0.008**
	(−2.46)	(−2.02)
BUDGETDEF	−0.003	−0.55
	(−0.96)	(−1.00)
EXGVOL	−0.01	−0.005**
	(−1.04)	(−1.91)

However, the results show that removing restrictions has a significant positive impact on FDI inflows into developing countries. This is supported by the results arrived at by a growing body of literature which documents difficulties that foreign firms face in establishing their operations in developing countries. Djankov, Hart and Nenova (2002) suggest that stricter regulation of entry is correlated with more corruption and a larger informal economy, and therefore restrictions on entry may have a negative impact on FDI inflows. Also, it has been found that healthy economies have a high 'churn rate' of firms, and research indicates a strong positive link between entry and exit (Love 1996).[13] The results arrived at by Friedman et al. (2000) also suggest that very often it

Table 4.6 (continued)

Explanatory variables	FDI from developed countries	FDI From developing countries
TARIFF	−0.004	−0.005**
	(−0.45)	(−2.00)
REST	0.18***	−0.23
	(2.26)	(−1.27)
INCENTIVES	−0.16	0.33***
	(−0.77)	(4.81)
CONSTANT	−49.37***	−56.75***
	(−4.42)	(−6.52)
Adjusted R^2 (OLS)	0.56	0.65
N	150	130
Fixed vs. random (Hausman)	2.37	

Notes:
1. Results of Random Effects Model is presented.
2. Autocorrelation and Hetroscedasticity are corrected for.
3. List-wise deletion is made for missing values.
4. Hausman test supports random effect model. Figures in parenthesis are t-statistic.
***Significant at 1% level; **significant at 5% level and *significant at 10% level.

is the arbitrary array of obstacles to starting and running a business which are the more significant barriers to foreign investors.

A emerging strand of literature examines the impact of regional trading agreements on FDI flows (Worth 2002). Most of these studies argue that the determinants of FDI and trade are similar. However, these studies have exclusively focused on the impact of trade agreements on FDI and not investment agreements. Regarding regional investment agreements, the results here show that the impact varies depending on the agreement. APEC membership has had a significant impact on FDI inflows, but ASEAN membership has not influenced the inflow of FDI into a member country.

These results are, however, expected since the ASEAN AIA agreement is still new and may take effect with a lag. There are several multilateral agreements in force which include clauses on incentives and investment, but their coverage remains limited. For example, the WTO regulates FDI incentives in its agreements on Subsidies and Countervailing Measures (SCMs) and TRIMS, but these agreements leave much to the discretion of national decision makers and apply only to 'specific subsidies' which are directed to individual enterprises.[14]

DETERMINANTS OF FDI FROM DEVELOPED AND DEVELOPING COUNTRIES

The results for the determinants of FDI from developed and developing countries are reported in Table 4.6. Focusing first only on the fundamentals of the economy, the results indicate that economic fundamentals are still significant determinants of FDI from developed countries (FDIDC) and FDI from developing countries (FDIDGC), but the importance of the variables differ between the two groups.

Large market size is found to be an important determinant of FDI from developed and developing countries. Apart from the market variables, variables which attract FDI are higher education levels, better financial health, greater transport and communications and lower domestic lending rates in the host countries. However, among the determinants of FDI from developing countries, cost factors are found to be more important; it is not the availability of skilled labor but the lower cost of labor along with devalued exchange rates that are significant determinants of FDI from developing countries.

Lower capital costs attract FDI from both developed and developing countries. However, lower lending rates can be taken as an indicator of higher investment and consumption and therefore larger markets. Although transport and communications are an important determinant of FDI from both developed and developing countries, exchange rate stability is more important for FDI from developing countries. On the whole, the results indicate that cost factors play a more dominant role in attracting FDI from developing countries. However, the economic fundamentals which indicate a higher degree of development in the host economies, e.g., higher education levels and lower external debts, attract FDI from developed countries.

Along with the significance of fundamentals as determinants of FDI, the FDI policies of the host governments also have a differential impact on FDI flows from developed and developing countries. Policies with respect to trade barriers, i.e., low tariff rates, encourage FDIDGC but are not found to be significant for the FDIDC. Fiscal incentives offered by the host countries attract FDIDGC but are not important for developed countries. What appears to be more important to the FDIDC is the removal of restrictions on their operations. These results also support the findings which emphasize the importance of cost factors for FDI from developing countries.

The study presented here provides empirical evidence on the impact of governmental policies and regional investment agreements on FDI flows into 15 developing countries of South, East and Southeast Asia, for the period 1980–81 to 1999–2000, after controlling for economic fundamentals of the host country. The impact is also analyzed separately for FDI coming from developed and developing countries into ten developing countries of this region for the period 1986–87 to 1996–97.

The results highlight the importance of government policies in attracting FDI inflows into the developing countries of Asia. These results illustrate the need for taking the 'range' dimension of reforms into account. The FDI policies of the host governments and investment agreements both play important roles. Removing restrictions on the operations of foreign firms in the host country is the most important FDI policy that governments can adopt, especially for FDI coming from the developed countries. While cost factors are found to have higher relevance as determinants of FDI from developing countries, regional investment agreements like that among APEC countries is also found to be an important policy instrument for attracting FDI inflows.

Policies with respect to cost factors (lower tariff rates, tax concessions, tax holidays, etc.) play an important role in attracting FDI from the developing countries but not necessarily from developed countries. What matters more to FDI coming from developed countries are the policies which facilitate the operations of foreign firms in the host country.

Thus, the chapter brings into focus the role played by reforms in the post-liberalized era in accelerating the pace of opening of the economy and integrating it with the rest of the world. But, it also calls attention to the importance of the range dimension: Specific policies with respect to FDI need to be complemented with a wide range of reforms in other sectors. Reforms in the areas of financial liberalization, macroeconomic adjustments, privatization and domestic regulations are all needed to successfully implement specific policies to attract inward FDI flows.

NOTES

I thank the Indian Council for Research on International Economic Relations (ICRIER) for funding this study. I am extremely grateful to Dr. Arvind Virmani (ICRIER), Prof. K.L. Krishna (ICRIER) and Prof. B.N. Goldar (ICRIER) for their valuable insights and suggestions.

1. The main provisions of these agreements, whether bilateral or regional, are linked with the gradual decrease or elimination of measures and restrictions on the entry and operations of foreign firms and application of positive standards of treatment with a view toward eliminating discrimination against foreign enterprises.

2. See Dunning (1993), Globerman and Shapiro (1999) and Shapiro and Globerman (2001).
3. A subset of these studies has also tested the impact of openness to trade and regional agreements in trade on FDI inflows and found them to be important determinants (e.g., Gastanaga, Nugent and Pashmova 1998; Taylor 2000; Chakrabarti 2001; and Asiedu 2002).
4. This has also been observed by Dunning (2002).
5. These averages are based on FDI approvals and not actual inflows.
6. Efficiency-seeking FDI engages more in international vertical integration and seeks to minimize total production costs.
7. See Chakrabarti and Scholnick (2002), who argue that the magnitude of change in exchange rates is more important than standard deviation, since a large devaluation in a single year may suggest an expected future appreciation of the host country's currency which, in turn, benefits the foreign investors. Therefore larger FDI may flow to countries after sudden large devaluations in their exchange rates.
8. This literature has been summarized by Ethier (1996) and Markusen (1995).
9. Using a study of 71 developing countries Bora (2002) concludes that fiscal incentives are the most popular, accounting for 19 out of 29 most frequently used incentives.
10. In most of the cases the results do not differ qualitatively between the Fixed Effects model and the Random Effects Model.
11. The choice of the period and countries depended on the availability of data. The countries chosen are a subset of countries in the earlier analysis.
12. The overall explanatory power of the corresponding OLS models improves as policy variables are included.
13. Entry barriers can also become exit barriers (World Bank 2003).
14. The SCM agreement prohibits subsidies which are contingent on export performance and use local inputs, and restricts the use of firm-specific subsidies exceeding 15 per cent of total investment cost.

BIBLIOGRAPHY

Agmon, Tamir (1979), 'Direct Investment and Intra-Industry Trade: Substitutes or Complements?', in Herbert Giersch (ed.), *On the Economics of Intra-Industry Trade*, Tubingen, Germany: JCB Mohr.

Asiedu, Elizabeth (2002), 'On Determinants of Foreign Direct Investments to Developing Countries: Is Africa Different?', *World Development*, **30** (11), 107–19.

Bende-Nabende, Anthony, James L. Ford, Somnath Sen and Jim R. Slater (2000), 'FDI Locational Determinants and the Linkage between FDI and other Macro-Economic Factors: Long-run Dynamics in Pacific Asia', Birmingham, UK, University of Birmingham, Department of Economics Discussion Paper No. 11.

Bhattacharya, Amar, Peter J. Montiel and Sunhil Sharma (1996), 'Private Capital Flows to Sub-Saharan Africa: An Overview of Trends and Determinants', Washington DC, World Bank, unpublished paper.

Blomstrom, Magnus, Ari Kokko and Mario Zejan (2000), *Foreign Direct Investment: Firm and Host Country Strategies*, New York: St. Martin's.

Bora, Bijit (2002), 'Investment Distortions and the International Policy Architecture', Geneva, World Trade Organization, unpublished paper.

Brewer, Thomas L. (1993), 'Government Policies, Market Imperfections and Foreign Direct Investment', *Journal of International Business Studies*, **24** (1), 101–21.

Caves, Richard E. (1996), *Multinational Enterprise and Economic Analysis*, 2nd ed., New York: Cambridge University Press.

Chakrabarti, Avik (2001), 'The Determinants of Foreign Direct Investment: Sensitivity Analyses of Cross-Country Regressions', *Kyklos*, **54** (1), 89–113.

Chakrabarti R. and Barry Scholnick (2002), 'Exchange Rate Expectations and FDI Flows', *Weltwirtschaftliches Archiv/Review of World Economics*, **138** (1), 1–21.

Chen, Zhaohui and Mohsin Khan (1997), 'Patterns of Capital Flows to Emerging Markets: A Theoretical Perspective', Washington, DC, International Monetary Fund, Working Paper WP/97/13.

Contractor, Farok (1991), 'Government policies towards Foreign Investment: An Empirical Investigation of the Link between National Policies and Foreign Direct Investment Flows', *Journal of International Business Studies*, **24** (1), 101–20.

Djankov, Simeon, Oliver Hart and Tatiana Nenova (2002), 'Efficiency Insolvency, Background Paper for Doing Business in 2003', Washington, DC, World Bank, Report of Private Sector Advisory Services.

Dunning, John H. (1988), *Explaining International Production*, Boston: Unwin Hyman.

—— (1993), *Multinational Enterprises and the Global Economy*, Reading, MA: Addison-Wesley.

—— (1999), 'A Rose By Any Other Name? FDI Theory in Retrospect and Prospect', Reading, UK and New Brunswick NJ, University of Reading and Rutgers University, unpublished paper.

—— (2002), 'Determinants of Foreign Direct Investment: Globalization Induced Changes and the Role of FDI Policies', London, World Investment Prospects.

Ethier, Wilfred J. (1996), 'Theories about Trade Liberalisation and Migration: Substitutes or Complements', in P.J. Lloyd and Lynne Williams (eds), *International Trade and Migration in the APEC Region*, New York: Oxford University Press, pp. 50–68.

Friedman, Eric, Simon Johnson, Daniel Kaufmann and Pablo Zoido-Lobaton (2000), 'Dodging the Grabbing Hand: The Determinants of Unofficial Activity in 69 Countries', *Journal of Public Economics*, **76** (3), 457–93.

Froot, Kenneth A. and Jeremy C. Stein (1991), 'Exchange Rates and Foreign Direct Investment: An Imperfect Capital Markets Approach', *Quarterly Journal of Economics*, **10** (4), 1191–1217.

Gastanaga, Victor M., Jeffrey B. Nugent and Bistra Pashmova (1998), 'Host Country Reforms and Foreign Direct Investment Inflows: How Much Difference do They Make?', *World Development*, **26** (7), 1299–1314.

Globerman, Steven and Daniel M. Shapiro (1999) The Impact of Government Policies on Foreign Direct Investment: The Canadian Experience', *Journal of International Business Studies*, **30** (3), 513–32.

Goldberg, Linda and Michael Klein, (1998), 'Foreign Direct Investment, Trade and Real Exchange Rate Linkages in Developing Countries', in Reuven Glick (ed.), *Managing Capital Flows and Exchange Rates*, New York: Cambridge University Press, pp. 73–100.

Grubert, Harry and John Mutti (1991), 'Taxes, Tariffs and Transfer Pricing in Multinational Corporate Decision Making', *Review of Economics and Statistics*, **73** (2), 285–93.

Hines, James R. (1996), 'Altered States: Taxes and the Location of Foreign Direct Investment in America', *American Economic Review*, **86** (5), 1076–94.

Hoekman, Bernard and Kamal Saggi (2000), 'Assessing the Case for Extending WTO Disciplines on Investment Related Policies', *Journal of Economic Integration*, **15** (4), 588–610.

Hymer, Stephen (1976), *The International Operations of National Firms: A Study of Direct Investment*, Cambridge, MA: MIT Press.
Kumar, Nagesh (2001), 'WTO's Emerging investment regime and developing countries: The way forward for TRIMS review and Doha Ministerial Meeting', *Economic and Political Weekly*, **36** (33), 315–58.
—— (2002), *Globalization and the Quality of Foreign Direct Investment*, New York: Oxford University Press.
Loree, David and Stephen E. Guisinger (1995), 'Policy and Non-policy Determinants of U.S. Equity Foreign Direct Investment', *Journal of International Business Studies*, **26** (2), 281–99.
Love, James H. (1996), 'Entry and Exit: A Country-Level Analysis', *Applied Economics*, **28** (4), 441–51.
Markusen, James R. (1995), 'The Boundaries of Multinational Enterprises and the Theory of International Trade', *Journal of Economic Perspectives*, **9** (2), 169–89.
Mbekeani, K.K. (1997), 'Foreign Direct Investment and Economic Growth', Johannesburg, South Africa, National Institute for Economic Policy (NIEPO) Occasional Paper No. 11.
Mundell, Robert A. (1957), 'International Trade and Factor Mobility', *American Economic Review*, **47** (3), 321–35.
Nunnenkamp, Peter (2002), 'Determinants of Foreign Direct Investment Inflows: Has Globalization Changed the Rules of the Game?', Kiel, Germany, Kiel Institute for World Economics Working Paper No. 1122.
Root, Franklin R. and Ahmed A. Ahmed (1979), 'Empirical Determinants of Manufacturing Direct Investment in Developing Countries', *Economic Development and Cultural Change*, **27** (4), 751–67.
Rugman, Alan M. (1986), 'New Theories of the Multinational Enterprise: An Assessment of Internalization Theory', *Bulletin of Economic Research*, **38** (2), 101–18.
Schneider, Friedrich and Bruno Frey (1985), 'Economic and Political Determinants of Foreign Direct Investment', *World Development*, **13** (2), 161–75.
Shapiro, Daniel and Steven Globerman (2001), 'National Infrastructure and Foreign Direct Investment', Vancouver, BC, Simon Fraser University, draft paper.
Taylor, Christopher T. (2000), 'The Impact of Host Country Government Policy on U.S. Multinational Investment Decisions', *World Economy*, **23** (5), 635–48.
Trevino, Len J., John D. Daniels and Harvey Arbelaez (2002), 'Market Reform and FDI in Latin America: An Empirical Investigation', *Transnational Corporations*, **11** (1), 30–48.
UNCTAD (1992), 'The Determinants of Foreign Direct Investment: A Survey of the Evidence', New York, United Nations Conference on Trade and Development, Division of Transnational Corporations and Investment.
—— (1996), 'Incentives and Foreign Direct Investment', New York, United Nations Conference on Trade and Development, Current Studies Series A, No. 30.
—— (2003), *FDI Policies for Development: National and International Perspectives*, New York: United Nations World Investment Report.
United Nations, *UN International Financial Statistics Yearbook*, Various Issues, New York: United Nations.
United Nations, *UNESCO Statistical Yearbook,* Various Issues, New York: UNESCO.
Villela, Luiz and Alberto Barreix (2002), 'Taxation and Investment Promotion: Background Note for Global Economic Prospects 2003', Washington, DC: Inter-American Development Bank.

Woodward, Douglas and Robert J. Rolfe (1993), 'The Location of Export-Oriented Foreign Direct Investment in the Caribbean Basin', *Journal of International Business Studies*, **24** (1), 121–44.

World Bank (2003), *Global Economic Prospects and Developing Countries: Investing to Unlock Global Opportunities*, Washington, DC: World Bank.

World Investment Report (1998), 'Trends and Determinants', New York: United Nations Conference on Trade and Development.

Worth, Thomas (2002), 'Regional Trade Agreements and Foreign Direct Investment', Washington, DC, US Department of Agriculture, Economic Research Division, AER-771, U 77.

Table 4A.1 Variables and Definitions

Variables	Abbreviation	Definition
1. Log of FDI		Log of foreign direct investment inflows
2. Market size	MKTSIZE	Log of real gross domestic product
3. Potential market size	GRTHMKT	Growth rate of real GDP
4. Efficiency wage rate	EFFWAGE	Labor cost/ labor productivity
5. Education	EDU	Log of Secondary Enrolment Ratio
6. Real exchange rate	EXRATE	Real Effective Exchange Rates
7. Financial health	EXTDEBT	Ratio of external debts to exports
8. Budget deficit	BUDDEF	Budget deficit / GDP
9. Transport and communication	T&C	Transport and communication/ GDP
10. Electricity consumed	ELECT	Electricity consumed/ GDP
11. Lending rate	LDRATE	Log of real domestic interest rates
12. Exchange rate volatility	EXGVOL	Percentage change in annual exchange rate between local currency and US $1

Table 4A.2   Variables and Data Sources of Economic Fundamentals

Variables	Source
1. FDI	United Nations, *World Investment Directory*, Vol VII, Part I & II: Asia and the Pacific; UNCTAD, Division on Investment, Technology and Enterprise Development statistics on foreign direct investment (FDI).
2. Market size	Asian Development Bank, *Key Indicators of Developing Asian and Pacific Countries*, various issues.
3. Potential market size	Asian Development Bank, *Key Indicators of Developing Asian and Pacific Countries*, various issues.
4. Labor costs	ILO, *Yearbook of Labour Statistics*, various issues, UNIDO CD-ROM versions of UNIDO's Industrial Statistics Database at the 3– and 4–digit level of the ISIC classifications and ASI, Government of India, for wages in India.
5. Labor productivity	UNIDO CD-ROM versions of UNIDO's Industrial Statistics Database at the 3– and 4–digit level of the ISIC classifications.
6. Efficiency wage	Computed.
7. Education	UNESCO.
8. Real exchange rate	IMF, *International Financial Statistics*, various issues.
9. Financial health	IMF, *International Financial Statistics*, various issues.
10. Macroeconomic stability	IMF, *International Financial Statistics*, various issues.
11. Transport and communication	World Bank, *World Bank and World Development Indicators*, World Tables.
12. Electricity consumed	Asian Development Bank, *Key Indicators of Developing Asian and Pacific Countries*, various issues.
13. Lending rate	Global Development Finance and World Development Indicators.

Note: Gross enrollment ratio at the secondary level is the ratio of total enrolment, regardless of age, to the population of the age group which officially corresponds to the secondary level of education. Data for Taiwan for some of the variables have been collected from *Taiwan Statistical Data Book* (CEPD) various issues. See: United Nations Educational Scientific and Cultural Organization (UNESCO) Institute for Statistics, *World Education Indicators*, Paris: UNESCO, 2002.

Table 4A.3 Correlation between Economic Fundamentals

	LOGFDI	MKTSIZE	GDPGRTH	EFFWG	EDU	EXRATE
LOGFDI	1.00	0.41	0.33	0.26	0.49	0.04
MKTSIZE	0.41	1.00	0.21	0.23	0.01	0.14
GDPGRTH	0.33	0.21	1.00	0.08	−0.03	0.15
EFFWG	0.26	0.23	0.08	1.00	0.08	−0.13
EDU	0.49	0.01	−0.03	0.08	1.00	0.18
EXRATE	0.04	0.14	0.15	−0.13	0.18	1.00
	LOGFDI	MKTSIZE	GDPGRTH	EFFWG	EDU	EXRATE
ELECT	0.17	0.37	0.07	0.18	0.11	−0.07
LDRATE	−0.08	−0.02	−0.12	−0.21	−0.27	0.16
BDGETDEF	−0.44	0.17	0.14	−0.04	0.30	0.06
EXGVOL	0.05	0.04	0.08	−0.05	−0.08	−0.21

5. The Effect of Free-Trade Agreements on Foreign Direct Investment and Property Rights Protection

Lorenza Martínez Trigueros and Roberto Romero Hidalgo

Amartya Sen defines 'range' as the methods policymakers use to achieve specific goals, and he emphasizes that range involves a variety of institutions. Following his admonition to consider the interactions between reform initiatives and institutions, this chapter focuses on the effects which a trade-reform initiative (a trade agreement) can have on institutions (property rights). More specifically, we analyze the negative impact of weak property rights protection on foreign direct investment (FDI) as well as the role of multilateral trade agreements as an alternative to overcome this effect.[1] Such agreements affect commercial flows and have the potential to improve property rights protection in these countries.

Specifically, multilateral trade agreements have greater impact on FDI going to countries which lack adequate property rights protection. When these agreements include a chapter about conflict resolution through an arbitrage panel, they help mitigate some of the defects of weak domestic institutions by allowing some conflicts to be solved in panels formed by international members. Foreign investors can appeal to this more transparent authority whenever their property rights are violated. This option offers a level of security for investors when legal institutions in a country are corrupt or incompetent. Put another way, these treaties allow countries lacking a clear definition or strong protection of property rights to free ride on the protection offered by more efficient international institutions. This mechanism might even have positive externalities, if it imposes greater discipline on domestic authorities, by diminishing the probability of arbitrary actions even against domestic investors. However, testing for the last effect is beyond the scope of this chapter and will be analyzed in future research.

Although similar ideas have been present in the literature, they have not been addressed from an empirical perspective. We analyze this hypothesis using a 38-country panel which includes 203 free-trade or investment agreements. After controlling for variables such as year, country-specific effects and bilateral exchange rates, the results show that the effect of free-trade agreements on FDI flows is greater in countries with weak property rights protection than in countries with more efficient legal institutions. The results corroborate our hypothesis about the positive role which these treaties play.

Figure 5.1a shows how the growth rate of world FDI flows has experienced a significant increase, especially since 1992, while the growth rate of world gross domestic product (GDP) even decreased. The annual average growth rate of GDP from 1970 to 1990 was 4.2 per cent and from 1990 to 2000 was 0.6 per cent, while for FDI these figures were 9.8 per cent and 16.1 per cent, respectively.

In addition to the rapid growth of FDI three stylized facts motivate the hypothesis analyzed in this chapter. First, the increasing number of free-trade agreements reflects the globalization process. Second, such agreements should impact FDI more than portfolio investment, a fact confirmed by the increasing share of FDI in total international investment flows. Figure 5.1b shows how the share of FDI flows in total investment flows has increased. Third, the growth of FDI flows directed to emerging countries has been greater than that directed to the rest of the world.[2] Since emerging countries are also characterized by inefficient institutions, the evidence supports our theory (see Figure 5.2).

We need a deeper analysis to find out to what extent these treaties have contributed to the increased capital flows. The present chapter is limited to formally testing the hypothesis concerning the differentiated effect of free-trade agreements on FDI according to the quality of the institutions of the receiving country.

RELEVANT LITERATURE

Three categories of literature inform this analysis; namely, discussions of property rights, FDI and free-trade agreements.

Property Rights

The definition and protection of property rights in a market economy affect the way production factors are assigned and used. Only with efficient protection of these rights is it possible to guarantee efficient allocation of productive resources. North and Thomas (1973), Scully (1988) and Barro and Sala-i-

Free-Trade Agreements, Foreign Direct Investment and Property Rights 149

Figure 5.1a   FDI and World GDP Evolution

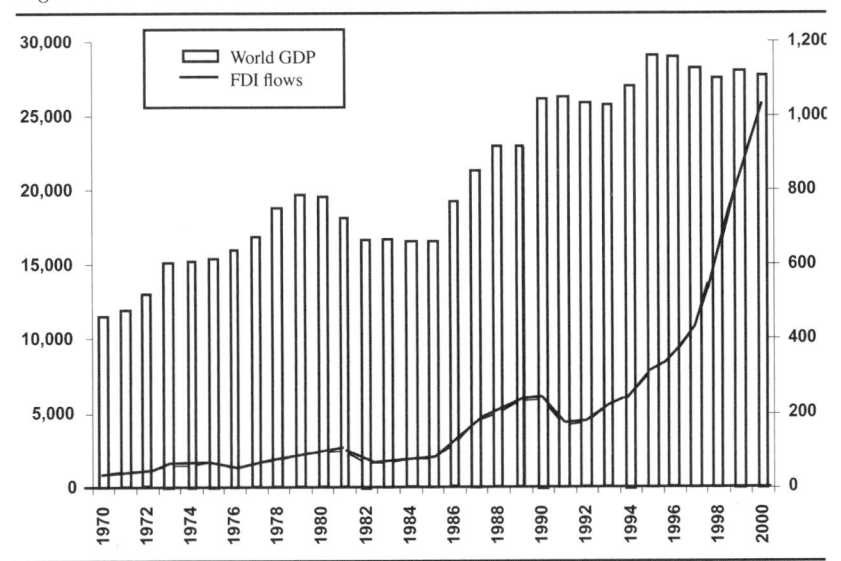

*Billions of 1995 dollars.
Source: World Bank.

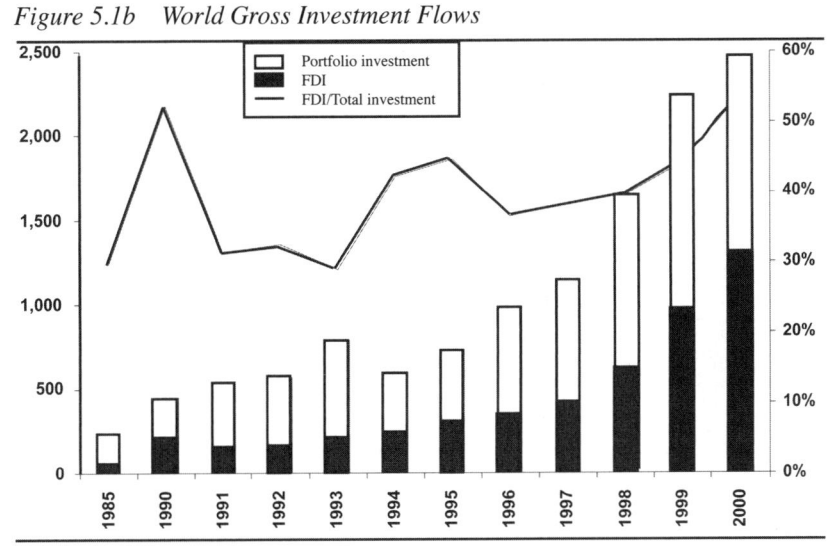

Figure 5.1b   World Gross Investment Flows

Note: Total investment includes portfolio and FDI; billions of US Dollars.
Source: IMF balance of payments statistics.

150   *Economic Reform in Developing Countries*

Figure 5.2a   FDI to Emerging Countries/Total FDI

Source: IMF balance of payments statistics.

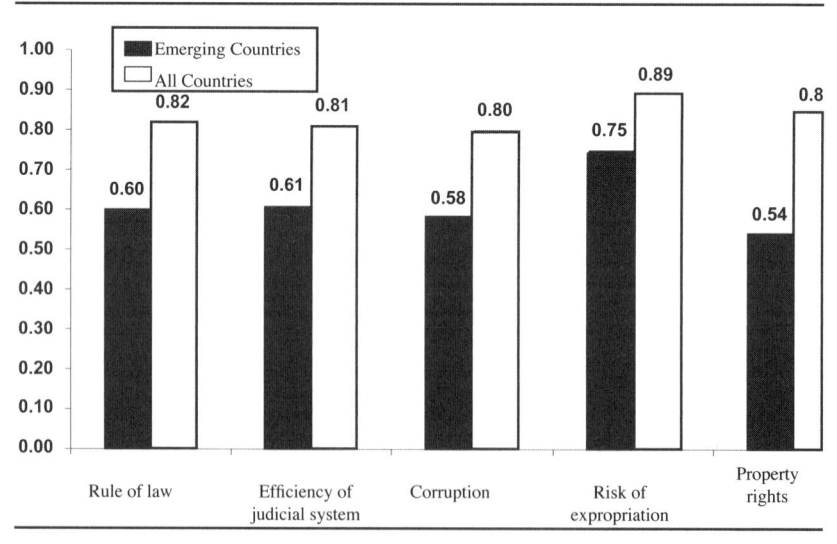

Figure 5.2b   Institutional Quality Indexes

Sources: International Country Risk Guide, Business International Corporation and Index of Economic Freedom Country Ranking, 1997.

Martin (1999) find that efficient organizations and protected property rights are essential to economic growth. Furthermore, they argue that the high growth rates experienced by Western Europe are due to efficient institutions which guarantee efficient organization. However, these studies do not solve the problem of the endogeneity of institutions. Acemoglu, Johnson and Robinson (2000) use an original instrumental variable to estimate the impact of institutions on economic development. After controlling for the endogenous component of institutions, they find that although institutions are important, some of the variables used as determinants are no longer relevant. La Porta et al. (1997) analyzed the impact which the efficiency of the legal system has on the development of capital markets and the channels through which efficient legal institutions affect economic growth.

Sarkar (1999) finds that a key determinant for the development experienced in the New Industrialized Countries such as Korea, Malaysia[3] and Taiwan is the type of rights granted to foreign investors, such as the guarantee to repatriate their earnings and tax exemptions and the guarantee that these rights would be respected. Blumenthal (1999) affirms that corruption has a negative effect on an economy because 'special payments', to guarantee that property rights are respected, increase the total cost of a project. Since some agents cannot afford these costs, some socially optimal projects are not undertaken because of the increase in private costs, hence reducing the welfare of the economy as a whole. However, it may also be in the interest of a corrupt or populist government to promote overinvestment by foreign investors for at least three reasons. First, while undergoing privatization, some governments promote foreign investment by giving investors certain privileges, like insuring a level of market power, either to obtain higher fiscal revenues or for political profit. Second, national and local governments frequently grant subsidies to foreign investors when competing with other countries or regions to attract capital. Third, foreign investors might be more prone to undertake certain actions – try to bribe, lobby and pressure their governments, finance political campaigns – with corrupt governments for privileges and 'inflate' the level of investment.

Castelar and Cabral (1999) and Cristini, Moya and Powell (2001) emphasize the importance of law enforcement by analyzing the development of the financial system in Argentina and Brazil, respectively. In these countries, the efficiency of the judicial system differs significantly among provinces despite having the same laws, because the judicial system in each province is autonomous. The authors find that improving the effectiveness of the legal system would bring huge economic benefits because it would substantially increase credit as a proportion of GDP, deepening the financial system and enhancing growth.

Foreign Direct Investment and Its Determinants

International capital inflows bring many advantages to a country, especially in increasing the supply of financial resources. FDI also transfers the latest technological innovations to developing countries. However, the extent of this effect depends on the level of human capital, that has to be high enough to absorb technological spillovers. This channel might also increase domestic investment by improving productivity through these spillovers, eliminating the crowding-out effect of domestic investment (Borensztein, De Gregorio and Lee 1995).

The rapid growth of FDI flows has increased interest in understanding its determinants. Before Helpman (1984), theories of general equilibrium with international trade did not consider FDI or multinational firms in the models used to explain trade flows. Since then, several models explaining FDI flows have emerged. Following Lizondo (1991), these theories can be divided into ones assuming perfect capital markets and others assuming capital market imperfections. Under perfect capital markets, capital flows from capital-abundant countries to the rest of the world will benefit from the differences in rates of return. However, this does not explain capital flows from emerging economies to developed countries or FDI flows in both directions in most countries.[4] Theories assuming some market imperfections, such as transaction costs and economies of scale, offer more satisfying explanations for the empirical evidence. For example, Hymer (1976) stated that multinational firms exist because of market imperfections, particularly structural and transaction costs.

Helpman (1985) complemented these theories with two integration models. In the horizontal integration model, multinational firms produce in several countries, and the corporate sector is located in one of these countries. Production in each country focuses only on the domestic market. The presence of economies of scale at the corporate level represents the principal advantage of multinational firms over domestic ones. In the absence of trade costs, firms would produce in one country, export to the rest, and take advantage of economies of scale. But as transport costs and barriers to trade increase, firms turn to foreign production to avoid these restrictions, so multinational activity arises between countries with similar factor endowments; otherwise, higher production costs in some countries may hamper the benefits of avoiding trade restrictions.

In the vertical integration model, the firm locates its corporate headquarters and at least one productive plant in different places without additional costs. The corporate sector is more capital intensive than the productive sector, so firms locate each part of their operation in different places to take advantage of lower factor prices. This model implies that FDI would only arise between countries with different relative factor endowments, so that the low production cost compensates for transport costs and trade barriers.

Empirically, it has been shown that not all FDI falls within these two integration categories. Hart (1988) extended the integration theory, stating that a firm reaches new markets either through exports or by producing locally, depending on the cost of each option. Local production takes the form of FDI or licensing, depending on the protection of property rights. If property rights are poorly protected, a foreign firm with special technology will serve the domestic market mainly through FDI, because if licenses are not respected it will lose significant profits. Countries with well-protected property rights are cheaper to serve by licensing local producers, as these will be respected. Therefore, effective protection of property rights induces FDI, but there is a threshold above which foreign firms will prefer to serve the market through licenses, and thus negatively impact FDI. This theory differs from the integration models, as it states that even if a firm decides to produce directly in the new market to avoid trade costs or to take advantage of the difference in relative prices, production will not always imply an FDI flow and can depend on the level of property rights protection in the country.

Tinbergen (1962) originally proposed a gravity model to explain the determinants of bilateral trade flows. In its simplest formulation, the gravity model states that bilateral trade flows depend positively on the GDP of both countries and negatively on the distance between them. The underlying theory is that the size of an economy determines the size of the potential market. However, transport costs depend on the distance between the two countries. Despite the obvious differences between trade and FDI, the gravity model has been used very successfully to analyze bilateral FDI flows.

Free-Trade Agreements and Investment Treaties

During the last 20 years, the number and depth of regional integration agreements around the world have significantly increased. The former European Economic Community evolved into a single market with a common currency, the European Union. Other European countries have formed free-trade areas with the EU. Countries from the Asia-Pacific region signed an economic cooperation agreement (APEC) in 1989. Likewise, countries in Southeast Asia agreed to form the ASEAN free-trade area. The United States has been no exception, involving itself with a number of regional integration agreements, like Latin America's MERCOSUR in 1991 or the North American Free Trade Agreement (NAFTA) in 1994, while others have been strengthened, like the Andean Community, which created a free-trade area in 1993.

This chapter considers only treaties which include the option of solving disputes between foreign investors and domestic authorities through an international arbitrage panel. The mechanism followed to solve these disputes is very straightforward. Parties agree on the number of arbitrators and the method for their appointment. If they do not reach an agreement, the tribunal will be formed of three arbitrators. Each party will name an arbitrator and will propose a president of the tribunal from a different country than the two involved. In case they do not reach an agreement, the authorities will proceed to name the president.

The treaty should have a greater effect for countries with poorly protected property rights – generally less developed countries. However, these treaties are not a substitute for efficient laws or institutions, because only foreign investors have the possibility of going to international tribunals. That is, the treaty places foreign investors in a privileged position with respect to domestic investors. However, treaties may impose greater discipline on authorities, diminishing the probability of arbitrary actions even against domestic investors. Therefore, more general effects could include the improvement of domestic institutions.

Theoretically, these agreements have an ambiguous effect on FDI. On one hand, if foreign trade and investment are two alternative ways to reach a given market, signing a free-trade agreement and decreasing trade barriers would imply a decline in FDI flows between treaty signatories. On the other hand, if the relative price of factors between countries differs significantly, and production involves intangible assets, FDI is the best method to reach a market. In this sense, the existence of free-trade agreements would increase FDI flows, a prediction confirmed by the data.

According to the two integration models previously described, free-trade agreements may have different effects on FDI. If FDI follows the reasons described in the horizontal integration model, it turns out to be an international trade substitute, so a free-trade agreement should decrease these flows between the signing countries. The opposite happens when FDI responds to vertical integration, where the firm produces in the labor-abundant country and exports to the other country. In this case, FDI flows and international trade are complements, so a free-trade agreement would increase these flows. A free-trade agreement also has an indirect effect on countries which are not members of a particular treaty. The most important is that by increasing the size of the market, it can generate investment in activities with economies of scale.

The empirical results on the effect of international agreements on FDI are mixed. Blomström and Kokko (1997) found a positive impact which depends on the original openness of the signing countries. According to these authors, the effect is greater in countries where trade barriers were low before the treaty was signed, indicating that there were fewer FDI-substituting imports in countries with a favorable geographical location. Levy-Yeyati, Stein and Daude (2002) also found a positive effect, determined by the size of the market generated. Vallejo and Aguilar (2002) found that a preferential agreement does not effect the overall FDI flow. Rather, there is a reallocation of FDI flows.

Klein and Olivei (1999) find that the impact of capital account liberalization depends on the quality of that country's institutions, measured by the level of development. Their results indicate that capital account liberalization in developed countries deepens the financial system and therefore increases growth, while for emerging economies the effect was not significant. Their results indicate that adequate economic, legal and social institutions are required, so that opening the capital account results in a deeper financial system. This differs from our methodology, as they measure the internal development of the financial system resulting from opening the capital account, while we consider external flows, that are affected not only by a capital account liberalization which does not imply any change in domestic institutions – but also by the fact that foreign investors' rights are protected by more efficient international arrangements.

Other empirical works have found that bilateral agreements serve as a commitment device for governments to forestall deviation from rules. Hellman (1997) affirmed that it is very easy for a government to acquire a bad reputation once it has behaved arbitrarily, leading to suboptimal resource allocation. International treaties impose a high cost for violating the law, therefore reducing government incentives to expropriate investments or undertake similar actions. The mere existence of arbitration panels and other bilateral sanctions imposes discipline on governments and contributes to improving domestic institutions. Therefore, this brings an additional positive externality which could affect domestic investment.

DATA AND EMPIRICAL ANALYSIS

We constructed a 38-country panel to estimate the effect of bilateral treaties on FDI. The number of origin-receiving country pairs is 1,316 (see Appendix 5A.1). We used the nominal bilateral FDI from the 2002 edition of the OECD *International Direct Investment Statistics Yearbook* for each pair. We only consider treaties signed after 1985. The panel consists of yearly observations from 1980 to 2001, yielding a total of 28,952. It includes 203 international agreements (Appendix 5A.2). Appendix 5A.3 presents a brief description of the different types of treaties considered in this chapter.

Table 5.1 shows the number of regional integration agreements and the evolution of FDI, GDP and GDP per capita for the 38 receiving countries

Table 5.1   FDI, GDP, GDP Per Capita and Agreements in the Sample

Year	Number of treaties	FDI by receiving country* [a]	Receiving country GDP* [a]	Receiving country per capita GDP* [b]
1980	0	526	413,353	5,934
1981	0	605	514,669	7,213
1982	0	2,458	1,381,219	13,554
1983	0	2,702	1,530,865	13,745
1984	0	2,866	1,396,881	13,255
1985	4	2,422	1,233,088	12,721
1986	8	2,508	1,275,465	15,270
1987	15	2,908	1,192,233	17,794
1988	22	3,228	1,186,755	18,815
1989	32	3,454	1,310,762	20,875
1990	43	3,719	1,274,371	20,869
1991	54	3,234	1,259,121	20,456
1992	181	3,101	1,372,539	19,994
1993	101	2,717	1,213,677	18,867
1994	125	2,544	1,112,977	19,520
1995	144	3,171	1,027,176	19,260
1996	158	3,441	1,013,921	19,079
1997	177	3,276	954,194	17,549
1998	194	3,475	937,163	18,437
1999	201	5,229	1,207,589	17,078
2000	203	7,644	1,786,745	18,900

Notes:
*Means.
[a] Millions of US$.
[b] Means in 1995 US$.

included in the sample during the 21 years considered. The average FDI underestimates the real figure, because the total flows going to emerging countries is not covered; the OECD data specifies that at least one country in each pair of countries has to be a developed country; therefore, we are not considering pairs of developing countries.

Given its high explicative power, we adopt the gravity model to test our hypothesis. The model, in its simplest formulation, states that bilateral FDI flows depend positively on the size of both economies and negatively on the distance between them. We considered the logarithm of nominal GDP in US dollars as a measure of size, using data from the IFS. For example, we consider the distance between the capital cities of both countries. This proxy can present some problems, especially if the countries share a common border, but their capital cities are far away. As a solution, dummy variables indicating if each pair of countries shares a common border or language were included. These variables take the value of 1 if both countries share a common border or language. The language variable captures other cultural issues like similar legal system origins, because countries with the same language usually share the same legal origin. We would expect both variables to have a positive coefficient.

The logarithm of a bilateral real exchange rate index, constructed with IFS data, between the origin and the receiving country is also included as a control variable. The index of the real exchange rate takes 1998 as a base year to homogenize the scale for every pair of countries. Country-fixed effects interacted with yearly dummies are also included to control for a more general effect of globalization, that could be inducing the significant increase of FDI flows over the last years.

To determine the degree of property rights protection, we considered five variables, as shown in Table 5.2.

Table 5.3 shows the correlation coefficient between these five variables. There is a high correlation between four of them, of more than 80 per cent in almost all cases, while the correlation of the Property Rights Definition with the other four is weaker. Despite the high correlation between these variables, we might expect that the expropriation and property rights indexes should be the most relevant variables for the analysis, as these are the kinds of problems which are easier to solve with an international panel of dispute resolution.

The expected effect of these variables on FDI is positive, since better protection of property rights makes a country more attractive to foreign investors. However, as stated in the model of the theory of the firm, where intellectual property is respected or when property rights are well defined, some firms will rather enter a market through licenses rather than FDI.

We use two alternative variables to account for the effect of free-trade agreements. The first is a dummy which takes the value of 1 if the receiving and origin countries have a common treaty and 0 otherwise. As mentioned above, the expected sign is ambiguous. To the extent that FDI is an international trade substitute, as proposed by the horizontal integration model, the sign should be negative. If the dominant effect is that proposed by the vertical integration model, it should have a positive sign. The second variable takes the value of 0 if the receiving and origin countries do not have a common treaty, and takes the value of 1 for the first year after the treaty is signed, the value of 2 for the second year after the treaty is signed and so on. This variable is more appropriate to capture the effect of free-trade agreements on FDI if it acts gradually. Since we

Table 5.2 Definition of Variables

Name	Description	Scale	Source
Rule of Law	Assessment of the law and order tradition in a country. It considers the average of the months of April and October of the monthly index between 1982 and 1995.	0–1, with 1 being the highest	International Country Risk guide
Efficiency of the Judicial System (EJS)	Assessment of the efficiency and integrity of the legal environment as it affects business, particularly foreign firms. Average between 1980 and 1983.	0–1, with 1 being the most efficient	Business International Corp.
Risk of Expropriation (Exprop)	Assessment of the risk of outright confiscation or forced nationalization. Average of the months of April and October of the monthly index between 1982 and 1995.	0–1, with 0 being the highest risk	International Country Risk guide
Corruption (Corrup)	Assessment of the corruption in a government. Lower scores indicate that high government officials are likely to demand 'special' and illegal payments in the form of bribes connected with import and export licenses, exchange controls, tax assessment, policy protection or loans. Average of April and October of the monthly index between 1982 and 1995.	0–1, with lower scores indicating higher levels of corruption	International Country Risk guide
Property Rights Definition (Prop. Right)	Index of private property protection based on the legal protection of private property, the probability of government expropriation and the efficiency of the government to enforce laws which protect private property.	0–1, where 1 is the highest protection	Index of Economic Freedom – Country Ranking, 1997

Table 5.3 Correlation between Variables of Property Rights Protection

	Rule of law	EJS	Expropriation	Corruption
EJS	0.87			
Expropriation	0.90	0.79		
Corruption	0.84	0.87	0.77	
Property Rights	0.78	0.64	0.72	0.67

have a relatively short period of time after the signing of the treaties (7.5 years on average with a median of 7.0 years), it is likely that this linear specification could be acting as an approximation of a more general functional form. This will be the case if several years after signing a treaty its effect vanishes. If this happens after seven years, then our approximation will be satisfactory.

Finally, to test our hypothesis we include the interaction of the variable indicating the level of protection of property rights in the receiving country with the variable for a free-trade agreement. We expect this variable to have a negative coefficient because the effects of the treaty should be greater for countries with a poor definition of property rights.

The equation to estimate is the following:

$$\ln(1 + FDI_{ijt}) = a + b_1 \ln GDP_{it} + b_2 \ln GDP_{jt} + b_3 \ln Dist_{ij} + b_4 Bord_{ij} + b_5 Lang_{ij} + b_6 \ln IRER_{ijt} + b_7 t_{ijt} + b_8 Char_j + b_9 t_{ijt} * Char_j + b_{it} + b_{ijt} \quad (5.1)$$

where:

$\ln(1+FDI_{ijt})$ is the logarithm of 1 + FDI in millions of dollars from country i to country j in year t.

$\ln GDP_{it}$ is the logarithm of country i's nominal GDP in millions of dollars in year t.

$\ln Dist_{ij}$ is the logarithm of the distance in kilometers between the capital cities of country i and country j.

$Bord_{ij}$ and $Lang_{ij}$ indicate if countries i and j share a common border and language respectively.

$\ln IRER_{ijt}$ is the logarithm of the index of the bilateral real exchange rate between country i and country j in year t.

t_{ijt} is one of the two variables indicating if country i and country j have a common treaty in year t.

$Char_j$ is one of the five measures of the level of property rights protection in country j.

Our null hypothesis is conformed by $b_9 = 0$ and $b_7 = 0$, with an alternative defined as $b_9 < 0$ and $b_7 > 0$. Coefficient b_8 is not relevant for testing our hypothesis.

In choosing the specification, it was taken into account that the distribution of FDI is not normal and there is a concentration in null levels of FDI (Figure 5.3). This implies two problems. The first is that taking the logarithm of FDI would lead to losing an important number of observations and a reduction in degrees of freedom. The second is that an ordinary least squares (OLS) estimation is inadequate in this case, because the dependent variable does not follow a normal distribution.

A common solution to the first problem is adding a constant, $b > 0$, to FDI, that can be optimally solved by maximum likelihood estimation. Alternatively, several authors (Levy-Yeyati, Stein and Daude 2002; Vallejo and Aguilar 2002) use the natural solution $d = 1$, having the advantage that when FDI_{ijt} takes large values, $\ln(1 + FDI_{ijt}) \approx \ln(FDI_{ijt})$. In these cases coefficients can be interpreted as elasticities or semielasticities depending on the scale of the independent variables. To address the second problem, we use a Tobit model which considers a truncated normal distribution for the dependant variable to obtain consistent estimations.

EMPIRICAL EVIDENCE

Table 5.4 shows the results using the variable indicating the years since the signing of the treaty. The coefficient of the interacted variable is negative and significant with three of the five property rights protection variables, while the coefficient is negative but not significant for the other two. In these three specifications the variable which measures the time since the signing of the treaty is positive and significant, while in the other two specifications it is positive but not significant.

Our estimations validate the gravity model: the source country GDP is positive and significant, while the distance between countries is negative and significant. Clearly, under this specification, the year–country fixed effects capture the effect of the receiving country GDP. Having a common border or language has a positive effect on the bilateral FDI flow between a pair of countries. The coefficient of the real exchange rate is negative and significant; this might indicate that FDI responds to the long run real exchange rate and

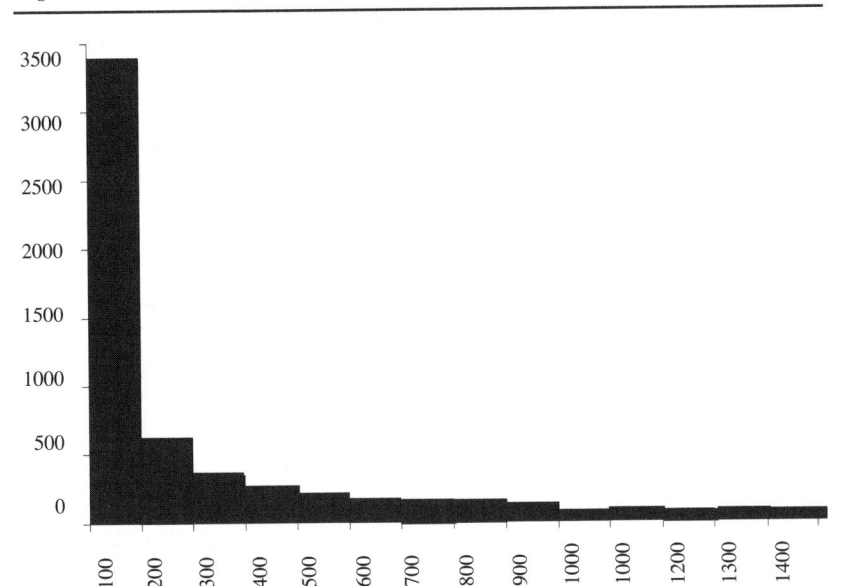

Figure 5.3   FDI Distribution* in Millions of US$

[Histogram showing FDI distribution with bins from 100 to 1400, with the first bin (100) reaching approximately 3500, and rapidly decreasing thereafter.]

*Includes only 75 per cent of the observations, the rest are outliers.

is not affected by shorter term fluctuations. This is different from the case of exports which might adjust easily when market conditions change. While the real exchange rate is not the most appropriate measure for the country risk premium, this might be a tentative explanation for the negative sign.[5]

We can conclude that signing a treaty has a positive overall impact on FDI flows, and that this impact is greater in countries with poor property rights protection. We present the F-statistic of the sum of the interacted variable with the treaty variable to show that, even though the effect of the treaty is differentiated, adding up the coefficients of the interacted variable with the treaty variable demonstrates that sometimes the effect of the treaty is negative even for countries with perfect institutions, while sometimes it is not significant. This could be explained by the fact that before signing the treaty, FDI was mainly motivated by barriers to trade, that are eliminated with the treaty. Consequently, this kind of FDI is no longer attractive, and the other country's market is served through trade.

We repeat the same exercise, but using the treaty dummy variable, instead of years since signing the treaty. The five interacted variables are now negative and significant, and the treaty variable is positive and significant in the five

Table 5.4 *Effects of Years after the Signing of a Treaty on FDI Flows, Including Receiving Country Dummies Interacted with Year Dummies*

	1	2	3	4	5
Log. source country GDP	1.26**	1.27**	1.26**	1.26**	1.266**
	(70.81)	(71.02)	(70.92)	(70.66)	(69.60)
Log. distance	−1.17**	−1.17**	−1.17**	−1.16**	−1.18**
	(36.73)	(36.67)	(36.66)	(36.58)	(37.00)
Border	0.21*	0.22*	0.22*	0.21*	0.17
	(1.99)	(2.04)	(2.03)	(2.00)	(1.62)
Language	1.21**	1.21**	1.21**	1.21**	1.22**
	(15.94)	(15.92)	(15.93)	(15.91)	(16.00)
Log. real exchange rate index	−0.14**	−0.14**	−0.14**	−0.14**	−0.14**
	(9.22)	(9.22)	(9.22)	(9.21)	(9.14)
T	0.08*	0.01	0.02	0.27**	0.11**
	(2.25)	(0.29)	(0.91)	(3.89)	(4.41)
T * rule of law	−0.11*				
	(2.55)				
T * efficiency of judicial system		−0.02			
		(0.67)			
T * corruption			−0.04		
			(1.27)		
T * risk of appropriation				−0.30**	
				(4.04)	
T * property rights					−0.14**
					(9.14)
Constant	−0.40	5.71	−0.47	5.67	2.10
	(0.32)	(1.32)	(0.37)	(1.32)	(0.77)
Observations	6389	6389	6389	6389	6368
Pseudo R^2	0.22	0.22	0.22	0.22	0.22
F (T + T * institutions)	6.35*	1.53	2.67	11.68**	16.84**

Notes:
Dependent variable = log(1 + FDI).
Estimation using Tobit model.
Absolute value of t–statistics in parentheses.
*Significant at 5 per cent level; **significant at 1 per cent level.

estimations. The coefficients for the rest of the variables are qualitatively the same as the ones in Table 5.4. Once again, our results confirm our hypothesis that free-trade agreements have a differentiated effect on FDI according to the level of protection of property rights in the receiving country, and that this effect is greater for countries with weak legal institutions. These estimations also show that signing a treaty has an overall positive impact on FDI flows, even though it can be negative in countries with 'near perfect institutions'.

In our next analysis, we exclude the interaction of the receiving-country dummies with the year dummies and include the variables which measure the level of property rights protection in the receiving country to see how efficient protection of these rights affects FDI flows. One potential drawback of the sample is that it might be biased by not including bilateral FDI between pairs of developing countries. As already mentioned, the data come from OECD countries, so each pair must include an industrial country either as origin or receiving. This represents a problem, because most of the industrial countries in the sample are close to each other (i.e., European countries) and have more efficient legal institutions. Therefore, there is a correlation between distance and rule of law. Due to the mentioned bias in our sample, the variable for distance could be capturing the effect of the quality of institutions. Despite the caveat of overestimating the effect of the legal system variables, we did the same estimations but excluding the distance between the pair of countries, and the results are presented in Table 5.5.

The results using the trend variable are shown in Table 5.5. The coefficient for four of the five property rights protection variables is positive and significant, while for the other one it is not significant. Moreover, the net effect of signing a treaty is negative for countries with 'perfect' institutions. The gravity model implications stand, while the border variable is not significant in two of the specifications. Having a common language has a positive and significant effect on FDI in all the specifications. The coefficient of the bilateral real exchange index is again negative and significant. The treaty variable is positive and significant, while the coefficient of the interacted variable is negative and significant in all five cases, confirming our hypothesis of the differentiated effect of the treaty, this being greater in countries with poor protection of property rights. The F-statistic of the sum of the interacted variable with the years since the signing of the treaty variable and with the institutions variable shows that the effect of the treaty is negative and significant for countries with perfect institutions.

The results are qualitatively the same if we use the treaty dummy variable instead of the years since the signing of the treaty variable. This provides further evidence in favor of our theory of a differentiated effect from signing a treaty according to how well property rights are protected in the receiving country. In

Table 5.5 Effects of Signing of a Treaty on FDI for Each Year after Signing

	1	2	3	4	5
Log. receiving country GDP	0.56**	0.56**	0.58**	0.58**	0.63**
	(26.46)	(26.78)	(27.42)	(25.91)	(28.02)
Log. source country GDP	1.32**	1.33**	1.39*	1.33*	1.33*
	(65.04)	(65.01)	(64.91)	(65.08)	(64.75)
Log. distance	−0.89**	−0.91**	−0.94**	−0.93**	−1.01**
	(27.62)	(28.28)	(28.63)	(27.77)	(30.38)
Border	0.16	0.17	0.11	0.14	0.04
	(1.32)	(1.35)	(0.39)	(1.13)	(0.34)
Language	1.59**	1.57**	1.61**	1.61**	1.69**
	(19.07)	(18.65)	(19.03)	(19.28)	(20.29)
Log. real exchange rate index	−0.12**	−0.11**	−0.12**	−0.12**	−0.1**
	(6.52)	(6.14)	(6.43)	(6.39)	(6.29)
T	0.66*	0.36**	0.43**	1.22**	0.48**
	(7.95)	(4.87)	(5.62)	(9.57)	(6.02)
Rule of law	1.3988				
	(7.86)				
Efficiency of the judicial system		1.02**			
		(6.04)			
Corruption			0.41*		
			(2.30)		
Risk of expropriation				1.34**	
				(4.33)	
Property rights					0.02
					(0.13)
T * rule of law	−0.84**				
	(9.24)				
T * efficiency of judicial system		−0.51**			
		(6.28)			
T * corruption			−0.61**		
			(7.01)		
T * risk of appropriation				−1.42**	
				(10.39)	
T * property rights					−0.62**
					(7.49)
Constant	−9.88**	−12.05**	−8.78**	−9.8**	−11.39**
	(10.75)	(18.41)	(9.52)	(10.32)	(17.69)
Observations	6051	6051	6051	6051	6051
Pseudo R^2	0.15	0.15	0.15	0.15	0.15
F (T + T * institutions)	91.52**	65.15**	77.98**	105.44**	71.43**
F (T + T * institutions + institutions)	10.13**	9.85**	1.45	0.06	15.93**

Notes:
Dependent variable = log(1 + FDI).
Estimation using Tobit model.
Absolute value of t-statistics in parentheses.
*Significant at 5 per cent level; **significant at 1 per cent level.
Includes year dummies even though they are not reported.

this second exercise, the coefficient of the treaty variable is always larger than the coefficient of the rule of law and of the rest of these variables. A country with 'terrible' institutions would attract more FDI by signing a regional agreement than would a country with 'perfect' institutions. This somewhat puzzling result can be explained by the 'preferential' treatment given to foreign investors with respect to domestic ones in countries with poor quality institutions, by having the opportunity of solving their conflicts in other forums than the domestic ones. The sample bias problem could also be reflected in an underestimation of the coefficient on the rule of law variables.

As discussed above, the degree of government corruption could have opposite effects on FDI flows. On one hand, there is the effect of reducing these flows because of the uncertainty it creates for foreign investors about the possibility of arbitrary actions against their investments. On the other hand, many corrupt governments might find it in their best interest either to increase fiscal revenues or to secure the political success of a privatization tender to promote overinvestment by giving benefits like market power to foreign investors. As long as the trade agreement does not increase rent-seeking behavior, the proposed specification directly tackles this effect by measuring the differentiated effect between FDI coming from countries with which the receiving country has a free-trade agreement and those with which they do not. The privatization effect would apply both to countries with and without free trade agreements; therefore, the proposed specification controls for this effect.

As mentioned above, distance was excluded in some specifications. It is important to point out that in this exercise the effect of the distance variable will be captured by the common border dummy, not by the legal system variables.

Table 5.6 shows the results using the trend variable. As expected, the five property rights protection variables are positive and significant, and their coefficients are higher than in the previous exercise. The interaction with the years since signing the treaty variable is negative and significant in all cases, corroborating our hypothesis of a greater impact of the treaties on countries with poorly protected property rights. The coefficient of the common border dummy is now positive and significant in all cases. Now, the sum of the coefficients of the interacted variable with the institutions variable becomes positive, while the sum with the treaty variable is not significant or negative, but with a lower coefficient. Distance was evidently capturing some of the effect of the rule of law variables.

The results using the treaty dummy are qualitatively the same as those presented in Table 5.6, once again confirming the differentiated effect that signing a free-trade agreement has on FDI flows, according to the level of property rights protection in the receiving country. The results do not change if we include only the treaties signed when the receiving country had its

Table 5.6 Effects of Signing of a Treaty on FDI for Each Year after Signing, Including Restrictions to Capital Flows Dummy

	1	2	3	4	5
Log. receiving country GDP	0.49**	0.49**	0.50**	0.54**	0.58**
	(22.81)	(22.76)	(23.22)	(24.09)	(25.23)
Log. source country GDP	1.30**	1.31**	1.31**	1.30**	1.31**
	(63.62)	(63.51)	(64.00)	(63.77)	(63.58)
Log. distance	−0.92**	−0.93**	−0.97**	−0.99**	−1.03**
	(28.49)	(29.04)	(29.65)	(29.62)	(31.12)
Border	0.19	0.17	0.12	0.14	0.09
	(1.55)	(1.37)	(0.96)	(1.17)	(0.71)
Language	1.55**	1.55**	1.57**	1.55**	1.59**
	(18.26)	(18.17)	(18.52)	(18.42)	(18.77)
Log. real exchange rate index	−0.13**	−0.13**	−0.14**	−0.13**	−0.13**
	(7.11)	(7.10)	(7.32)	(7.14)	(7.06)
Controls	−0.89**	−0.97**	−1.02**	−1.06**	−0.95**
	(11.73)	(12.46)	(14.11)	(13.70)	(13.19)
T	0.59**	0.28**	0.36**	0.96**	0.43**
	(7.13)	(3.88)	(4.82)	(7.55)	(5.57)
Rule of law	0.21**				
	(1.02)				
Efficiency of the judicial system		−0.26**			
		(1.34)			
Corruption			−0.69**		
			(3.75)		
Risk of expropriation				−1.32**	
				(3.68)	
Property rights					−0.82**
					(5.03)
T * rule of law	−0.78**				
	(8.62)				
T * efficiency of judicial system		−0.45**			
		(5.57)			
T * corruption			−0.56**		
			(6.48)		
T * risk of appropriation				−1.16**	
				(8.55)	
T * property rights					−0.60**
					(7.25)
Constant	−7.36**	−6.91**	−6.21**	−5.76**	−8.34**
	(7.89)	(7.40)	(6.71)	(5.88)	(15.68)
Observations	5870	5870	5870	5870	5870
Pseudo R^2	0.16	0.15	0.16	0.16	0.16
F (T + T * institutions)	104.02*	77.84**	91.22**	113.48**	87.19**
F (T + T * institutions + institutions)	8.70**	14.56**	49.15**	53.98**	76.63**

Notes:
Dependent variable = log(1 + FDI).
Estimation using Tobit model.
Absolute value of t-tatistics in parentheses.
*Significant at 5 per cent level; **significant at 1 per cent level.
Includes year dummies even though they are not reported.

capital account open. If a country has restrictions on FDI, and signs a treaty with another country, the flow of FDI would increase not as a result of the improvement in institutions, but as a result of the possibility to invest, that was not present before signing the treaty. This result supports our theory that the effect of the treaty comes not because investment constraints are relaxed, but because of an improvement in the conditions for foreign investors.

ROBUSTNESS OF RESULTS

In order to address some potential critiques of the analysis presented in the previous section and to verify the robustness of the results, we estimated four additional sets of specifications. The first exercise included a dummy variable (*Control*)[6] for the years in which the recipient country had any restrictions on FDI, using our two treaty variables. As expected, Control has a negative and significant coefficient; results are once again in line with our hypothesis of a differentiated effect of the treaties, even when controlling for the receiving country having some controls on FDI flows, confirming our hypothesis that free-trade agreements increase FDI flows because of an improvement in institutions, and not because of an elimination of restrictions on FDI in the receiving country. Table 5.7 presents the estimations using the trend variable. We observe that the coefficients that measure the quality of institutions are now either negative or not significant. The results are the same if we use the treaty dummy variable between the receiving and origin country.

As mentioned previously, our data sample is biased because it omits pairs of emerging countries. An implication of this bias is the negative correlation between distance and the rule of law of the recipient country. This explains the low significance or even the negative sign of some of the variables measuring the quality of legal institutions, especially when we include restrictions on FDI. We made the same estimations, omitting distance, and the property rights protection variables recovered their positive and significant coefficient.

For this same reason the negative and significant sign of the interaction between the agreement variables and the indicators of law enforcement might be capturing the effect of the omitted interaction with distance. Table 5.8 reports the results, including the mentioned interacted variables, using the trend variable. The results indicate that the effect of the agreements is higher when countries are closer to each other; however in several cases the coefficient is not significant. The rest of the coefficients are almost the same and the ones concerning our hypothesis are not affected.

Since our database includes some outlier observations which are biased toward the right tail of the distribution, it is important to test if the results are

Table 5.7 Effects of Signing of a Treaty on FDI for Each Year after Signing, Including Distance Interacted with the Years after the Signing Variable

	1	2	3	4	5
Log. receiving country GDP	0.56**	0.56**	0.58**	0.57**	0.63**
	(26.32)	(26.70)	(27.29)	(25.77)	(27.88)
Log. source country GDP	1.33**	1.33**	1.33**	1.33**	1.33**
	(65.11)	(65.04)	(64.96)	(65.21)	(64.88)
Log. distance	−0.86**	−0.89**	−0.92**	−0.88**	−0.97**
	(24.76)	(25.84)	(25.93)	(24.63)	(27.25)
Border	0.16	0.17	0.11	0.14	0.04
	(1.32)	(1.35)	(0.86)	(1.14)	(0.31)
Language	1.90**	1.57**	1.61**	1.61**	1.69**
	(19.09)	(18.65)	(19.03)	(19.30)	(20.35)
Log. real exchange rate index	−0.12**	−0.12**	−0.12**	−0.12**	−0.12**
	(6.62)	(6.18)	(6.51)	(6.51)	(6.43)
Controls	−0.89**	−0.97**	−1.02**	−1.06**	−0.95**
	(11.73)	(12.46)	(14.11)	(13.70)	(13.19)
T	1.00**	0.51**	0.69**	1.76**	0.92**
	(6.38)	(3.57)	(4.48)	(8.76)	(5.77)
T * distance	−0.03**	−0.02	−0.03[1]	−0.05**	−0.04**
	(2.54)	(1.25)	(1.93)	(3.47)	(3.20)
Rule of law	1.43**				
	(8.07)				
Efficiency of the judicial system		1.03**			
		(6.12)			
Corruption			0.45**		
			(2.65)		
Risk of expropriation				1.47**	
				(4.71)	
Property rights					0.07
					(0.63)
T * rule of law	−0.91**				
	(9.59)				
T * efficiency of judicial system		−0.53**			
		(6.41)			
T * corruption			−0.66**		
			(7.27)		
T * risk of appropriation				−1.58**	
				(10.96)	
T * property rights					−0.71**
					(8.12)
Constant	−10.10**	−9.75**	−11.72**	−10.19**	−8.86**
	(10.94)	(10.55)	(17.69)	(10.66)	(9.73)
Observations	6051	6051	6051	6051	6051
Pseudo R²	0.15	0.15	0.15	0.15	0.16
F (T + T * institutions)	0.72	0.04	0.05	2.72[1]	3.37[1]
F (T + T * institutions + institutions)	9.38**	9.69**	1.63	0.14	17.79**

Notes: Dependent variable = log(1 + FDI); Estimation using Tobit model.
Absolute value of t-tatistics in parentheses.
1. Significant at 10 per cent level; *significant at 5 per cent level; **significant at 1 per cent level.
Includes year dummies even though they are not reported.

Table 5.8 Estimations Excluding 5 per cent of the Observations, Including Receiving Country Dummies Interacted with Year Dummies

	1	2	3	4	5	6
Log. source country GDP	1.22**	1.21**	1.21**	1.21**	1.21**	1.21**
	(62.93)	(62.79)	(61.83)	(62.97)	(62.95)	(62.13)
Log. distance	−1.15**	−1.15**	−1.17**	−1.17**	−1.17**	−1.20**
	(34.68)	(34.54)	(34.93)	(34.64)	(34.74)	(35.02)
Border	0.34**	0.35**	0.31**	0.32**	0.33**	0.28*
	(3.02)	(3.03)	(2.68)	(2.85)	(2.89)	(2.48)
Language	1.25**	1.24**	1.24**	1.22**	1.69**	1.24**
	(15.46)	(15.42)	(15.49)	(15.37)	(15.22)	(15.38)
Log. real exchange rate index	−0.14**	−0.14**	−0.14**	−0.15**	−0.14**	−0.15**
	(9.29)	(9.29)	(9.23)	(9.35)	(9.32)	(9.28)
T	0.061	0.22**	0.10**			
	(1.75)	(3.19)	(3.95)			
Treaty				1.46**	3.78**	1.08**
				(4.21)	(6.31)	(4.22)
T * rule of law	−0.07[1]					
	(1.72)					
T * risk of expropriation		−0.24**				
		(3.17)				
T * property rights			−0.12**			
			(4.13)			
Tr * rule of law				−1.84**		
				(4.62)		
Tr * risk of expropriation					−4.27**	
					(6.54)	
Tr * property rights						−1.45**
						(5.03)
Constant	−0.58	1.40	2.42	3.82	−3.60	2.78
	(0.25)	(0.36)	(0.89)	(1.02)	(0.91)	(1.02)
Observations	6025	6025	5910	6025	6025	5910
Pseudo R²	0.20	0.20	0.20	0.20	0.20	0.20
F (T + T * institutions)	0.87	3.22[1]	5.86*	17.07**	28.50**	19.71**

Notes:
Dependent variable = log(1 + FDI).
Estimation using Tobit model.
Absolute value of t-statistics in parentheses.
[1]Significant at 10 per cent level; *significant at 5 per cent level; **significant at 1 per cent level.
Includes year dummies even though they are not reported.

robust enough to eliminate these observations. Table 5.8 presents the original specification, eliminating 5 per cent of the observations. The first three columns include the trend variable and the last three columns include the treaty dummy. Under these estimations, the robustness of our results is confirmed.

It is important to mention that even though the recent literature analyzing the effect of institutions on economic development adopts instrumental variables to correct for endogeneity, we do not find this problem in our analysis. While total FDI might have a positive effect on institutions, it is hard to imagine that bilateral flows would have an impact on these. Despite that, we used the instrumental variables proposed by Acemoglu, Johnson and Robinson (2000) and by La Porta et al. (1997) to run two-stage least squares. The results are not affected, and with the Hausman specification test we cannot reject the hypothesis that the OLS estimator is consistent.

We only include the treaties signed after 1985 in order to have enough observations to control for the pre-treaty period. But our results do not change qualitatively if we include treaties signed before 1985. An additional test for robustness was to take into account free-trade agreements, monetary unions and customs union without making any distinction between them. However, it is likely that FDI might have a stronger effect on countries with relatively weak institutions when entering a monetary union than on countries with better institutions. This will be the case if firms perceive that relative prices will be more stable under the agreements. Since the only monetary union included is the European Union, we run the same regressions excluding the countries involved in that agreement. The results do not change in a significant way, although the magnitude of the relevant effect is lower, indicating that, in fact, the European Union has benefited countries like Ireland and Spain more than others like Germany, at least in terms of FDI. With this simple analysis it is not possible to determine how much of this effect can be attributed to the perceived stabilization of relative prices and how much to institutional improvements.

NAFTA AND FDI IN MEXICO

Mexico started moving toward the global economy with its entrance into GATT in 1985, and by 1987 Mexico's trade barriers in all sectors, except for agriculture, were among the world's lowest. The capital account was liberalized between 1989 and 1991, as restrictions on portfolio investment and FDI were relaxed.[7] After this liberalization, portfolio inflows skyrocketed, achieving an average annual growth of 119 per cent from 1990 to 1994, just before the Mexican crisis. The same figure was 33 per cent for the 1980–89 period. FDI also experienced a significant increase in its growth rate from 9 per cent during the 1980–89 period to 12 per cent for 1990–94. However, the real shift in the slope of FDI took place in 1994, following the approval of NAFTA in December 1993. FDI grew at an annual average rate of 17 per cent from 1994 to 2000 (Figure 5.4). That is, even when Mexico had no significant restrictions on international trade or investment, the average annual growth of FDI increased by 5 percentage points in these two periods. FDI as a share of GDP increased from 0.1 per cent during 1980–88, to 1.2 per cent during 1989–93 and 3.1 per cent during 1994–2001.

Figure 5.4 FDI in Mexico (in millions of US$)

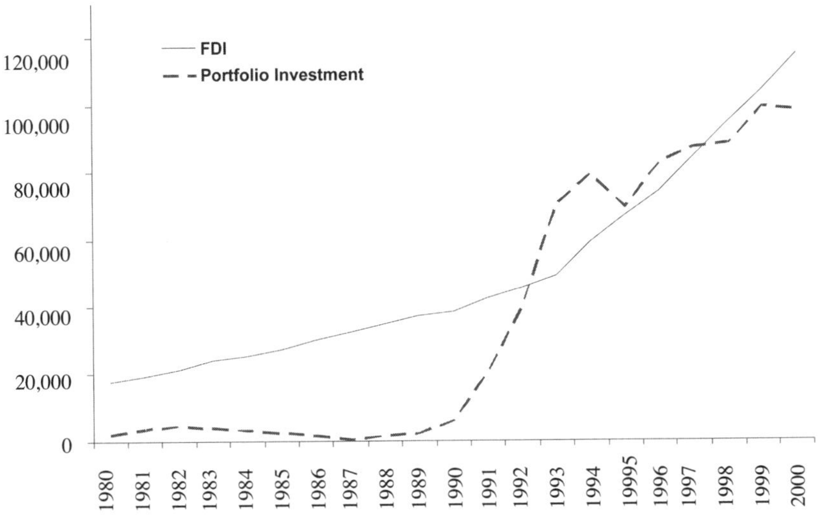

[Chart showing FDI (solid line) and Portfolio Investment (dashed line) in Mexico from 1980 to 2000. FDI rises steadily from about 20,000 in 1980 to over 120,000 in 2000. Portfolio investment remains near zero until around 1989, then rises sharply to about 100,000 by 2000.]

Source: OECD and Banco de Mexico.

The delay in the upward trend observed with respect to portfolio investment is not surprising, considering that almost all of the portfolio investment during the period was on short-term government bonds. What is interesting is the change in the slope of the FDI trend after NAFTA. According to our hypothesis, and as mentioned by Esquivel and Tornell (1995), NAFTA established a supranational body to settle disputes. Only in this framework did foreign investors perceive that their interests would be protected even when the current government is no longer in power.

The effect of NAFTA on FDI going from the United States to Mexico is especially notable. After the signing of NAFTA the flow of FDI going from the United States to Mexico experienced a significant increase. The average FDI flows as a share of GDP during the period 1995–2000 increased by 3.32 per cent from its level in the period 1990–94. According to the estimations, more than half of this increase (1.82 per cent of GDP) was motivated by the signing of NAFTA. An additional increase of 2.1 per cent was due to the effect of growth in the US economy, while other variables such as the real exchange rate have had a negative impact of 0.6 per cent.

A natural question following the argument raised in this chapter is: Do foreign investors, actually use this opportunity against a national government which has violated their rights?

In Mexico there have been many FDI-related disputes between international investors and domestic parties, in which international investors have gone to international panels. In five of the six concluded cases, the result favored the international investor.[8] Mexican authorities have lost more than $25 million in these cases. Although the process through which the federal government passes on the penalty to local governments is not clearly established, it can be deducted from the fiscal revenues distributed to them. To the extent that local governments internalize these costs, there could be additional benefits from these trials.

As local institutions improve their performance and act more carefully to avoid these disputes, domestic investors might also benefit. That is, foreigners taking the opportunity of using international panels to solve their disputes may impose more discipline on domestic institutions. Therefore, as long as local authorities pay for violating property rights, they will have an incentive to respect the rights of international investors, knowing that if these actions go to international panels they will have to compensate investors. Eventually this could improve conditions both for domestic and international investors. Some of the cases are still awaiting a decision, and it has been clear that this type of process could take more time than expected, even four years or more. Appendix 5.A4 shows the conflicts and resolutions which have arisen between international investors and domestic stances in Mexico since 1995.

CONCLUSION

This chapter analyzed the relationships among property rights, free-trade agreements and bilateral FDI flows. In particular, it considered the hypothesis that poorly defined property rights reduce FDI inflows to countries, and that a possible way to provide that definition is through an international agreement which includes an option to solve controversies via an international panel. Thus, these international agreements have a differentiated effect on FDI depending on the definition of property rights in the receiving country, and an international agreement has a greater impact on FDI when the receiving country has poorly protected property rights.

We used the specification proposed in the gravity model as a starting point to test our hypothesis. We found that an increase in both receiving and source country GDP has a differentiated impact on bilateral FDI flows, and that the closer the two countries are located, the greater the FDI will be between them. Results hold even after including other variables such as both countries having a common language or border. Having a common language has a positive effect on FDI, indicating that having some kind of cultural affinity between two countries and having similar legal traditions should have a positive effect on their bilateral FDI flows. The real exchange rate has a negative effect on FDI which is explained by the fact that a real depreciation in the receiving country, on top of reducing the relative production costs, also implies a higher country risk.

According to the theory of the firm, as tested by Blyde and Acea (2003), the impact of property rights protection on FDI is positive for countries with inadequate property rights protection but negative for countries with good law enforcement. Blyde and Acea find that this result might be explained by the effect which improving property rights has on licensing. According to their results, it might be the case that a foreign firm prefers to serve the market of countries with high protection of property rights through licensing, because the investor knows these licenses will be respected. This theory is consistent with the results obtained in this chapter. The effect is also observed when we interact the treaty variable with the institution variables, as we get a negative effect for countries with 'near perfect' legal institutions. The effect of treaties is differentiated, having a stronger impact on countries with poor property rights protection. Moreover, the estimated coefficients imply that the effect of the agreement is null or even negative for countries with 'near perfect' legal institutions.

Although treaties are not a substitute for efficient institutions in a country, they do constitute a more reliable alternative than local institutions for foreign investors to protect property rights. The large magnitude of the effect of regional agreements for countries with weak property rights protection also reflects the advantage given by these treaties to foreign investors relative to domestic ones. This mechanism may impose greater discipline on authorities and therefore diminish the probability of arbitrary actions, even for domestic investors. Therefore the more general effect could even include the improvement of domestic institutions.

In sum, we believe that this chapter provides valuable evidence in favor of Sen's view that the range of reforms is critical to designing consistent reform programs. We have shown how intervention in one area – trade – has a positive effect in another area – FDI. Reformers should take these interactions into account when designing reform packages and considering the range of reforms.

NOTES

The authors are grateful to the comments of Daniel Chiquiar, Gustavo Carvajal, Gordon Hanson, César Hernández and participants of the Fifth Annual Global Development Conference, New

Delhi, January 2004. We also want to thank an anonymous referee and Lyn Squire for their very helpful suggestions and advice. The views expressed here are those of the authors and should not be attributed to Banco de México.

1. In this analysis we consider any trade agreement which includes a chapter on conflict resolution for FDI and gives the option of solution through an international panel. Clearly the effect on FDI of Monetary Union differs from the effect of a Free Trade Union.
2. The growing trend of the share of FDI directed to emerging markets with respect to total FDI was temporarily interrupted in 1998 by the Russian and Asian financial crises, but apparently since 2001 the share of FDI to emerging countries resumed its growth rate.
3. Although Malaysia established a capital control regime in 1998, the rights of foreign investors had been respected earlier.
4. These puzzles have been addressed frequently in the literature. Feldstein and Horioka (1980) affirm that the arbitrage theory holds for short-term capital flows, when investors take advantage of the difference in return rates and invest in the country with the higher rates to take advantage of this spread. But they find that longer-term flows, such as direct investment, is made to enhance trade positions or to take advantage of a special knowledge, and that this type of investment does not react to differences in the rates of return.
5. The inclusion of the spread between a domestic interest rate and Libor rate as an alternative control for country risk was tested; however, it was never significant.
6. This variable was constructed using data from the IMF Annual Report on Exchange Arrangements and Exchange Restrictions, and takes the value of 1 if there were restrictions to capital transactions in the receiving country in a given year and 0 if there were no restrictions.
7. Martínez and Werner (2003) and Babatz and Conesa (1997).
8. The only case in which a foreign investor has lost against Mexican authorities was that demanded by Halcheted Distribution and it was completely unjustified.

BIBLIOGRAPHY

Acemoglu, Daron, Simon Johnson and James A. Robinson (2000), 'The Colonial Origins of Comparative Development: An Empirical Investigation', Cambridge, MA, National Bureau of Economic Research (NBER) Working Paper No. 7771.

Babatz, Guillermo and Andrés Conesa (1997), 'The Effect of Financial Liberalization on the Capital Structure and Investment Decisions of Firms: Evidence from Mexican Panel Data', Cambridge, MA, Harvard University, unpublished paper.

Barro, Robert and Xavier Sala-i-Martin (1999), *Economic Growth*, Cambridge, MA: MIT Press.

Blomström, Magnus and Ari Kokko (1997), 'Regional Integration and Foreign Direct Investment', Cambridge, MA, National Bureau of Economic Research (NBER) Working Paper No. 6019.

Blumenthal, Michael W. (1999), 'Capital Flows to Eastern Europe', in Martin Feldstein (ed.), *International Capital Flows*, Chicago: University of Chicago Press, pp. 97–102.

Blyde, Juan and Cristina Acea (2003), 'How Does Intellectual Property Affect Foreign Direct Investment in Latin America?', at http://www.iadb.org/intal/aplicaciones/uploads/publicaciones/i_INTAL_IYT_19_2003_Blyde-Acea.pdfmimeo.

Borensztein, Eduardo, José De Gregorio and Jong-Wha Lee (1995), 'How Does Foreign Direct Investment Affect Economic Growth?', Cambridge, MA, National Bureau of Economic Research (NBER) Working Paper No. 5057.
Burki, Shahid Javed and Guillermo E. Perry (eds) (1999), *Annual World Bank Conference on Development in Latin America and the Caribbean, 1998 Proceedings: Banks and Capital Markets*, Washington, DC: World Bank.
Castelar, Armando and Celia Cabral (1999), 'Credit Markets in Brazil: The Role of Judicial Enforcement and Other Institutions', Washington, DC, Inter-American Development Bank Working Paper No. R-368.
Cristini, Marcela, Ramiro Moya and Andrew Powell (2001), 'The Importance of an Effective Legal System for Credit Markets: The Case of Argentina', Washington, DC, Inter-American Development Bank Working Paper No. R-428.
Esquivel, Gerardo and Aaron Tornell (1995), 'The Political Economy of Mexico's Entry to NAFTA', Cambridge, MA, National Bureau of Economic Research (NBER) Working Paper No. 5322.
Feldstein, Martin and Charles Horioka (1980), 'Domestic Saving and International Capital Flows', *Economic Journal*, **90** (358), 314–29.
Hart, Oliver (1988), 'Incomplete Contracts and the Theory of the Firm', *Journal of Law, Economics and Organization*, **4** (1), 119–39.
Hellman, Joel S. (1997), 'Constitutions and Economic Reform in the Post-Communist Transitions', in Jeffrey D. Sachs and Katharina Pistor (eds), *The Rule of Law and Economic Reform in Russia*, Boulder, CO: Westview Press, Colorado, pp. 55–78.
Helpman, Elhanan (1984), 'A Simple Theory of International Trade with Multinational Corporations', *Journal of Political Economy*, **92** (3), 451–71.
—— (1985),'Multinational Corporations and Trade Structure', *Review of Economic Studies*, **52** (3), 443–57.
Hymer, Stephen (1976), *International Operations of National Firms: A Study of Direct Foreign Investment*, Cambridge, MA: MIT Press.
International Monetary Fund (1993), *Balance of Payments Manual*, 5th ed., Washington, DC: International Monetary Fund.
Klein, Michael and Giovanni Olivei (1999), 'Capital Account Liberalization, Financial Depth and Economic Growth', Cambridge, MA, National Bureau of Economic Research (NBER) Working Paper No. 7384.
La Porta, Rafael, Florencio López de Silanes, Andrei Shleifer and Robert Vishny (1997), 'Legal Determinants of External Finance', Cambridge, MA, National Bureau of Economic Research (NBER) Working Paper No. 5879.
Levy-Yeyati, Eduardo, Ernesto Stein and Christian Daude (2002), 'Regional Integration and the Location of FDI', Washington, DC, Inter-American Development Bank Working Paper No. 491.
Lizondo, J. Saul (1991), 'Foreign Direct Investment' in *Determinants and Systemic Consequences of International Capital Flows*, Washington, DC, International Monetary Fund Occasional Paper No. 77, pp. 68–82.
Martínez, Lorenza and Alejandro Werner (2003), 'Capital Markets in Mexico: Recent Developments and Future Challenges', Mexico City, Banco de México, Working Paper.
North, Douglass and Robert Thomas (1973), *The Rise of Western World*, New York: Cambridge University Press.
Organization for Economic Cooperation and Development (1996), *OECD Benchmark Definition of Foreign Direct Investment*, 3rd ed., Paris: OECD.

Sarkar, Rumu (1999), *Development Law and International Finance*, London: Kluwer Law International.

Scully, Gerald W. (1988), 'The Institutional Framework and Economic Development', *Journal of Political Economy*, **96** (3), 652–62.

Tinbergen, Jan (1962), *Shaping the World Economy*, New York: Twentieth Century Fund.

Vallejo, Hernán and Camila Aguilar (2002), 'Economic Integration and the Attraction of Foreign Direct Investment: The Case of Latin America', paper presented at the Latin American and Caribbean Economic Association 7th annual meeting, Madrid, Spain, 11–13 October.

Vernon, Raymond (1966), 'International Investment and International Trade in the Product Cycle', *Quarterly Journal of Economics*, **80** (2), 190–207.

APPENDIX 5A.1 BILATERAL FDI AVAILABLE FOR RECEIVING AND SOURCE COUNTRIES

Countries	Receiving	Origin	Complete Data*
Argentina	X	X	
Australia	X	X	X
Austria	X	X	X
Belgium-Lux.	X	X	X
Brazil	X	X	
Canada	X	X	
Chile	X	X	
China	X	X	
Czech Republic	X	X	X
Denmark	X	X	X
Finland	X	X	X
France	X	X	X
Germany	X	X	X
Greece	X	X	X
Hong Kong	X	X	
Hungary	X	X	X
Iceland	X	X	X
Indonesia	X	X	
Ireland	X		
Italy	X	X	X
Japan	X	X	X
Korea	X	X	X
Mexico	X	X	X
Netherlands	X	X	X
New Zealand	X	X	X
Norway	X	X	X
Poland	X	X	X
Portugal	X	X	X
Singapore	X	X	
South Africa	X	X	
Spain	X		
Sweden	X	X	X
Switzerland	X	X	X
Thailand	X	X	
Turkey	X		
United Kingdom	X	X	X
United States	X	X	X
Venezuela	X	X	

* Corresponds to OECD countries except Ireland, Spain and Turkey. For the Non-OECD countries bilateral FDI is only available to/from OECD countries.

APPENDIX 5A.2a BILATERAL INVESTMENT TREATIES INCLUDED IN THE CHAPTER

Countries	Date came into force	Countries	Date came into force
China & Germany	18/03/1985	Austria & Czech Republic	01/10/1991
China & France	19/03/1985	Hungary & Thailand	18/10/1991
China & Norway	10/07/1985	Czech Republic & Finland	23/10/1991
China & Thailand	13/12/1985	Austria & Korea	01/11/1991
China & Finland	26/01/1986	Czech Republic & Spain	28/11/1991
China & UK	15/05/1986	Austria & Turkey	01/01/1992
Belgium/Lux. & China	05/10/1986	Greece & Hungary	01/02/1992
Austria & China	11/10/1986	Belgium/Lux. & Czech	13/02/1992
China & Netherlands	01/02/1987	Canada & Czech Republic	09/03/1992
China & Switzerland	18/03/1987	Australia & Poland	27/03/1992
Hungary & Sweden	21/04/1987	Argentina & Turkey	08/05/1992
China & Italy	28/08/1987	Australia & Hungary	10105/1992
Hungary & UK	28/08/1987	Italy & Korea	25/06/1992
France & Hungary	30/09/1987	China & Greece	25/06/1992
Germany & Hungary	07/11/1987	Denmark & Turkey	01/08/1992
Poland & UK	14/04/1988	Hungary & Spain	01/08/1992
Denmark & Netherlands	01/06/1988	Czech Republic & Germany	02/08/1992
Denmark & Korea	02/06/1988	Czech Republic & Norway	06/08/1992
Australia & China	11/07/1988	Argentina & Belgium/Lux.	26/08/1992
Belgium/Lux. & Hungary	23/09/1988	Argentina & Poland	01/09/1992
Denmark & Hungary	01/10/1988	Czech Republic & Denmark	19/09/1992
Hungary & Korea	01/01/1989	Argentina & Spain	28/09/1992
China & Poland	08/01/1989	Argentina & Sweden	28/09/1992
China & New Zealand	25/03/1989	Czech Republic & Netherlands	01/10/1992
Finland & Hungary	12/05/1989	Czech Republic & UK	26/10/1992
China & Japan	14/05/1989	Argentina & Switzerland	06/11/1992
Hungary & Switzerland	16/05/1989	China & Portugal	01/12/1992
Austria & Hungary	01/09/1989	China & Czech Republic	01/12/1992
Korea & Thailand	30/09/1989	China & Korea	04/12/1992
Austria & Poland	01/11/1989	Hungary & Norway	04/12/1992
Netherlands & Turkey	01/11/1989	Czech Republic & US,	19/12/1992
Poland & Sweden	04/01/1990	Czech Republic & Greece	31/12/1992
Korea & Poland	02/02/1990	Italy & Poland	10/01/1993
France & Poland	10/02/1990	Indonesia & Sweden	18/02/1993
Switzerland & Turkey	21/02/1990	Argentina & UK	19/02/1993
Hungary & Italy	23/02/1990	Argentina & France	03/03/1993
Poland & Switzerland	17/04/1990	Japan & Turkey	12/03/1993
Belgium/Lux. & Turkey	04/05/1990	China & Hungary	01/04/1993
Turkey & US	18/05/1990	Argentina & Canada	29/04/1993
Norway & Poland	24/10/1990	China & Spain	01/05/1993
Denmark & Poland	30/10/1990	Poland & Spain	01/05/1993
Canada & Poland	22/11/1990	Indonesia & Poland	01/07/1993
Germany & Poland	24/02/1991	Australia & Indonesia	29/07/1993
Finland & Poland	29/03/1991	Poland & Thailand	10/08/1993
Belgium/Lux. & Poland	02/08/1991	Hong Kong & Netherlands	01/09/1993
Czech Republic & Switzerland	07/08/1991	Argentina & Italy	14/10/1993
Czech Republic & Sweden	23/09/1991	Australia & Hong Kong	15/10/1993
Czech Republic & France	27/09/1991	Netherlands & Venezuela	01/11/1993

APPENDIX 5A.2a *(continued)*

Countries	Date came into force	Countries	Date came into force
Argentina & Germany	08/11/1993	Finland & Thailand	18/05/1996
Canada & Hungary	21/11/1993	Chile & Finland	14/06/1996
Poland & Singapore	23/12/1993	Czech Republic & Venezuela	23/07/1996
Netherlands & Poland	01/02/1994	UK & Venezuela	01108/1996
Denmark & Hong Kong	04/03/1994	Korea & Portugal	1110811996
Indonesia & Korea	10/03/1994	Denmark & Venezuela	19/09/[1996
Chile & Spain	29/03/1994	Argentina & Korea	25/09/[996
Argentina & Hungary	02/06/1994	Chile & Czech Republic	0511011996
Korea & Turkey	04/06/1994	Turkey & UK	2211011996
Hong Kong & Sweden	26/06/1994	Argentina & Australia	11/01/1997
Australia & Czech Republic	29/06/1994	Indonesia & Spain	12/0211997
Korea & Spain	19/07/1994	China & Iceland	01/03/1997
Poland & Portugal	03/08/1994	Mexico & Spain	19/03/1997
Czech Republic & Poland	03/08/1994	Denmark & South Africa	23/04/1997
Czech Republic & Portugal	03/08/1994	France & Hong Kong	30/05/1997
Poland & US	06/08/1994	Finland & Indonesia	07/06/1997
China & Turkey	19/08/1994	Korea & Sweden	18/06/1997
Poland & Turkey	19/08/1994	Hong Kong & Japan	18/0611997
Chile & Norway	08/09/1994	France & South Africa	22/06/1997
Argentina & Netherlands	01/10/1994	Chile & UK	23/06/1997
Indonesia & Norway	01/10/1994	Korea & South Africa	28/06/1997
Argentina & US	20/10/1994	Czech Republic & Ireland	01/08/1997
Hong Kong & Switzerland	22/10/1994	Czech Republic & Turkey	01/08/1997
Hungary & Turkey	01/11/1994	Spain & Venezuela	10/09/1997
Switzerland & Venezuela	30/11/1994	Hungary & Portugal	08/10/1997
Chile & France	05/12/1994	Czech Republic & Italy	01/11/1997
Argentina & Austria	01/01/1995	South Africa & Switzerland	29/11/1997
Argentina & Denmark	02/01/1995	Austria & Hong Kong	01/01/1998
Chile & Italy	08/02/1995	Austria & South Africa	01/01/1998
Greece & Poland	20/02/1995	Sweden & Venezuela	05/01/1998
Czech Republic & Korea	16/03/1995	Canada & Venezuela	28/01/1998
Finland & Turkey	23/04/1995	Hong Kong & Italy	02/02/1998
Czech Republic & Thailand	04/05/1995	Germany & Hong Kong	19/02/1998
Portugal & Venezuela	11/05/1995	Chile & Portugal	24/02/1998
Czech Republic & Hungary	25/05/1995	Spain & Turkey	03/03/1998
Hungary & Poland	16/06/1995	Germany & South Africa	10/04/1998
Indonesia & Italy	24/06/1995	South Africa & UK	27/05/1998
Indonesia & Netherlands	01/07/1995	Argentina & Czech Republic	23/07/1998
Hong Kong & New Zealand	05/08/1995	Argentina & Mexico	28/08/1998
Czech Republic & Singapore	08/10/1995	Sweden & Turkey	08/10/1998
Chile & Denmark	03/11/1995	Germany & Venezuela	16/10/1998
China & Denmark	03/11/1995	Hungary & Singapore	01/01/1999
Greece & Korea	04/11/1995	Hong Kong & UK	12/04/1999
Chile & Sweden	30/12/1995	Netherlands & South Africa	01/05/1999
Chile & Switzerland	30/12/1995	Chile & Germany	18/06/1999
Hungary & Indonesia	13/02/1996	Belgium/Lux. & Chile	05/08/1999
Mexico & Switzerland	14/03/1996	Australia & Chile	18/11/1999
Argentina & Finland	03/05/1996	Chile & Korea	18/11/1999
Argentina & Portugal	03/05/1996	Chile & Poland	22/09/2000
Finland & Korea	11/05/1996	Austria & Chile	17/11/2000

APPENDIX 5A.2b OTHER TREATIES INCLUDED IN THE CHAPTER

Countries included	Date came into force	Type
Austria, Belgium/Lux. Denmark, Finland, France, Germany Greece, Ireland, Italy, Netherlands, Portugal, Spain, Sweden and UK	01/11/1993	European Union
Canada and Thailand	01/11/1998	Foreign investment protection and promotion agreement
Australia and New Zealand	1998*	Free-trade agreement
Canada, Mexico and US	01/01/1994	Free-trade agreement
Canada and Chile	05/07/1997	Free-trade agreement
Chile and Mexico	28/07/1999	Free-trade agreement
Brazil and Canada	June 1998	Trade and investment cooperation agreement
Canada and South Africa	September 1998	Trade and investment cooperation agreement

Note: The treaty was signed in 1983, but the part related to investment did not enter into force until 1988.

APPENDIX 5A.3 DESCRIPTION OF FREE-TRADE AGREEMENTS INCLUDED IN THE CHAPTER

Bilateral Investment Treaties

- Guarantees signing countries that their investors will receive Most Favored Nation treatment, that implies that the investors of the other country must receive at least the same treatment as the investors of any other country, except for specific areas specified in the treaty.
- An expropriation can only happen according to international rules; that is, when it is for a common benefit and the investor has to be fairly compensated.
- It guarantees investors that they can freely transfer their money both outside and within the country without delay.
- In guarantees that the government will not ask an investor to carry out trade distorting activities. For example, it will not ask for an export quota or establish origin rules among others.
- It guarantees foreign investors the possibility of going to an international panel to solve their disputes with domestic authorities according to International Center for Settlement of Investment Disputes (ICSID) rules. It also gives the investor the possibility of going to domestic stances, but is not obligatory.
- It gives investors the right to hire any person they want, regardless of his nationality.

Foreign Investment Protection and Promotion Agreements

- A bilateral agreement which has as its objective to protect and promote foreign investment from the other member of the treaty by creating favorable conditions.
- Not all restrictions must be eliminated, but from the signing of the agreement and so on it is prohibited to increase restrictions to investors from the other country, unless it is specified in the agreement. As the restrictions regarding foreign investment are gradually dropped, those liberties will be the minimum for other country's investors, guaranteeing that conditions for foreign investors will continuously improve or at least they will not deteriorate.
- It establishes three ways in which foreign investment can be treated: the minimum, that guarantees that foreign investment cannot receive a treatment under certain international standards internationally accepted,

and that varies through time. Domestic treatment, that guarantees that the foreign investor has to receive the same treatment as the domestic one and the most-favored nation.
- An expropriation can only happen according to international rules; that is, when it is for a common benefit and the investor has to be fairly compensated.
- A dispute between a foreign investor and a domestic stance has to be settled in an international panel, and according to ICSID rules.

European Union

- Member countries accord the application of internal economic policies as well as external and security policies common to all of them. Citizens of different countries are EU citizens, so investors of one country are not considered foreigners in another.
- They have formed a common market and the free circulation of people, goods and services between member countries has been established.
- They even have a monetary union and a common Central Bank.

Free-Trade Agreements

- It stimulates the expansion and diversification of goods and services trade between the signing countries.
- It promotes free competence conditions within the free-trade area.
- It reciprocally eliminates trade restrictions for goods and services originally from the region.
- It eliminates barriers to capital and to businessmen in the trade area.
- It also establishes a mechanism to solve a probable controversy between a foreign investor and a domestic stance, although there is the possibility of going to local stances if the foreign investor wants to.

Trade and Investment Cooperation Agreement

- It is a bilateral treaty which establishes a legal framework for greater cooperation to strengthen both bilateral investment and trade. Each treaty specifies both the mechanisms to achieve this economic integration and the regulation to which the members of the treaty will be subject.

APPENDIX 5A.4 FDI DISPUTES IN MEXICO SOLVED IN INTERNATIONAL PANELS

Investor	Nationality	Date	Amount	Violation	Resolution
Halchette Distribution	?	1995	?	Acts or omissions regarding an airport concession.	Case dismissed.
Metalclad Corp.	USA	1996	90	Denial of a license to construct a dangerous residues confinement in Guadalcazar, and the declaration of a Protected Natural Area in that same county.	Solved in favor of investor, with $16 million settlement.
Robert Azinian	USA	1996	19	Concession dealing with county residues in Naucalpan, Mexico, revoked.	Solved unanimously in tribunal.
Marvin, Roy, Feldman, Karpa	USA	1998	50	Modification and application of certain fiscal dispositions which denied investor a refund of special tax related to cigarette exports.	Solved by the majority of the tribunal in favor of the investor, 17 million peso settlement.
Waste Management, Inc.	USA	1998	60	Revoked concession dealing with county residues in Acapulco by the county and by BANOBRAS, as a public credit institution.	Solved in favor of the participants.
Waste Management, Inc.	USA	2000	?	Apparently same as above.	Pending.
Adams et al.	USA	2001	75	Supreme Court ordered restitution of land in Coronel Esteban Cantu Ejido, BC, where investors had developed a tourist complex.	Pending.
Lomas Santa Fe Investments	USA	2001	210	Expropriation of land in Mexico City for road construction.	Pending.
Fireman's Fund Insurance	USA	2001	50	Banco de Mexico denied an assistance package which would allow Grupo Financiero Bancrecer to buy back obligations it had issued.	Pending.
Calmark Commercial Dev.	Canada	2002	0.4	Penal, judicial and administrative authorities in Baja California refused to punish parties which had defrauded the investor.	Pending.

183

APPENDIX 5A.4 (*continued*)

Investor	Nationality	Date	Amount	Violation	Resolution
Robert J. Frank	USA	2002	1.5	Investor deprived of land on the coast of Baja California.	Pending.
GAMI Investments	USA	2002	55	Expropriation of sugar-producing plants owned by investor, under supposedly discriminatory conditions; renegotiation of the debt of the investor under supposedly discriminatory conditions.	Pending.
International Thunderbird Gaming	Canada	2002	?	Closure of three 'virtual casinos' by the Secretaria de Gobernacion in Nuevo Laredo, Matamoros and Reynosa.	Pending.
Corn Products International	USA	2003	250	Impossition and application of a special 20% tax on soft drinks and hydrating and rehydrating drinks made with sweeteners other than cane sugar.	Pending.
Tecnicas Medioambientales Tecmed	Spain	2000	52	Request to renew an authorization granted in 1997 to operate a dangerous residues reservoir denied; storage facility ordered to close.	Settlement in favor of the investor, including payment of $5.5 million plus interest.
Henry Davis–Renave	France	2003	250	The imposition and application of a special tax of 20% on soft drinks, hydrating and rehydrating drinks made with sweeteners other than cane sugar.	Pending.

¹Date of notification of intention of arbitrage.

6. Attending School, Reading, Writing and Child Work in Rural Ethiopia

Assefa Admassie and Arjun Singh Bedi

International Labor Organization Convention 138 and the UN Convention on the Rights of the Child (CRC) are often used as benchmarks to provide a working definition of child labor. According to the CRC, the main criterion for deciding whether a particular activity should be considered 'labor' is the nature of the work. The convention states that children should be protected from hazardous work which interferes with their education, is harmful to their health and compromises their physical, mental, spiritual, moral or social development.

However, the idea that work should be considered labor if it is harmful for a child still does not provide a definition of 'child labor'. Apart from the most egregious types of work which no doubt harm a child, there may be a wide range of activities carried out by children, especially in rural areas, which may not harm their overall development. Before labeling all types of work as child labor, it may be important to identify the potentially different effects of different kinds of work activities carried out by children. Furthermore, it is not just the incidence of work which needs to be considered, but also whether there is a threshold beyond which the number of hours of work provided by children begins to harm their development.

In this chapter we use information on the work activities of children in rural Ethiopia to investigate these issues. We concentrate on the formal human capital development of children and whether the number of hours they work has an effect on school attendance and on their ability to read and write. We also go beyond the aggregate effect of the number of hours worked to investigate the effect of different types of work on school attendance and reading and writing ability.[1]

We also identify the factors which determine the allocation of children's time to work. In particular, we assess the link between access to modern agricultural technologies and child labor. Information about the potential link between the adoption of improved agricultural practices and child work is particularly relevant, as Ethiopia is currently engaged in an aggressive extension program aimed at introducing farmers to new methods of agricultural production.

This extension program is one component of a wide-ranging set of reforms and strategies undertaken by the Ethiopian government to encourage growth and reduce poverty. Since 1988 the government has followed a policy of moving from central control to a more market-based economy. In 1992 these reforms became part of a structural-adjustment program sponsored by international financial institutions which included a large currency devaluation in 1992, easing foreign exchange controls, simplifying licensing procedures, removing price restrictions on agricultural outputs and inputs, ending compulsory grain deliveries to an agricultural cooperative and removing restrictions on the private grain trade.

Overall, the government has adopted a strategy of agriculture-led industrialization to increase productivity on small farms. In addition to the market-oriented reforms discussed above, one crucial aspect of the growth strategy has been an extension program called the Participatory Demonstration and Training Extension System (PADETES) introduced in 1994–95. This new program merged the extension and management principles of the Training and Visit system with the technology-diffusion experiences of the Sasakawa–Global 2000 program, emphasizing the provision of fertilizers, improved seeds, pesticides, herbicides and modern farming methods.

While the extension program does not directly address child labor and educational outcomes, there are potential links between the increased availability of inputs and child welfare. In the spirit of Sen's remarks in the foreword to this book on the need for a 'range' of methods to capture the 'reach' or aims of policy, this chapter examines the link between access to modern agricultural inputs and the use of child labor, that, in turn, is linked to educational outcomes. In the Foreword to this volume, Sen argued that like reach, the range of policies had to be 'person-centered' and 'evenhanded'. This chapter's focus on education and the concern that some of Ethiopia's children may be excluded from educational opportunities fits both dimensions perfectly.

This study, however, also illustrates another, analytically more interesting aspect of range. Sen remarks that there is no 'magic bullet'; indeed, a variety of means may often be required and interdependencies have to be recognized. In line with this observation, this chapter shows that trying to influence educational outcomes with a narrow focus on educational policy alone is unlikely to be successful in a context where child labor is widely prevalent. Influencing educational outcomes requires an understanding of the links among educational policy, agricultural policies, child labor and educational outcomes. Additionally, it is important to study the direct and indirect effects of reform packages. While the direct effect of the agricultural reform package is to enhance agricultural productivity, the indirect effects of the reform program need to be assessed as well.

A REVIEW OF THE LITERATURE

Agricultural Technology and Child Labor

There is a substantial literature on the determinants of child labor.[2] However, studies which deal with the link between technological change and child labor are limited. Even the few existing studies focus mainly on the manufacturing sector and mechanical power. Galbi (1997), for example, points out that one of the most powerful determinants of the decline in the incidence of child labor in industrialized societies was the gradual sophistication of technology. Similarly, a study in Colombia shows that the introduction of wheelbarrows displaced children who had previously carried rocks one at a time (Salazar 1988). Turning to studies dealing with the agricultural sector, Rosenzweig and Evenson (1977) argue that the Green Revolution in India led to a reduction in child labor and promoted school attendance. Similarly, Levy (1985) shows that the mechanization of Egyptian agriculture with tractors and irrigation pumps reduced the demand for child labor in tasks such as picking cotton, hauling freight and driving animals to power water wells. Apart from these few examples, it is hard to find empirical studies which examine the link between the spread of modern agricultural technology and child labor.

Child Labor and Schooling

In contrast, there is a growing body of literature which studies the substitutability between children's schooling and labor and the effectiveness of education-related policy measures in reducing child labor. This literature may be divided into two broad categories. The indirect or reduced-form approach studies the links between child work and schooling by examining the effects of education-related measures such as concentration of schools, distance to schools, school fees (subsidies) and school quality on the incidence of child labor. If schooling and child work are substitutes, then a reduction in school fees or a reduction in the time required to reach school should lead to an increase in school attendance and a reduction in the incidence and duration of work. Studies using this approach report mixed results.

For example, Grootaert (1999) reports that the child labor-force participation in rural Côte d'Ivoire is responsive to distance from school. According to his estimates, a $3 reduction in annual schooling costs (induced by increased school proximity) may lead to a 1 percentage point reduction in the probability of child labor-force participation. However, schooling costs are not found to be statistically significant correlates of child labor in urban Cote d'Ivoire. Cartwright and Patrinos (1999) find a strong positive relationship between schooling costs and child labor-force participation in urban Bolivia. In contrast, Cartwright's (1999) work on Colombia shows that higher school costs are associated with a lower probability of working. Using data from the Tanga region of mainland Tanzania, Akabayashi and Psacharopoulos (1999) report that children work longer hours per day in localities with lower school concentration. Their measure of school quality has no influence on child work.

Grootaert and Patrinos (1999) argue that the empirical ambiguities in the effects of schooling-related policy measures on child labor-force participation are largely due to data limitations. While this argument has its merits, it is possible that households adjust to changes in school prices (quality) along dimensions other than children's work. For instance, Ravallion and Wodon (2000) show that school-enrolment subsidies, specifically monthly food rations to households in rural Bangladesh, reduce the incidence of child labor. However, they emphasize that the decline which may be ascribed to the subsidy accounts for a small proportion of the increase in school enrolment, implying higher school attendance comes mainly at the expense of children's leisure. Thus, child labor-force participation may not be very responsive to reductions in school fees. Hazarika and Bedi (2003) report a similar finding for Pakistan. They find that reductions in costs of schooling increase school enrolment, but the corresponding reduction in labor-force participation is not as large, suggesting that the increase in the probability of attending school comes from a reduction in time allocated to leisure.

The direct or structural approach gauges the links between schooling and child labor by comparing children's educational outcomes across work status. Psacharopoulos (1997) uses data from Bolivia and Venezuela to show that children who work are more likely to fail at school and that child work reduces educational attainment by almost two years. In contrast, Patrinos and Psacharopoulos's (1997) work on Peru shows that child labor is *not* detrimental to schooling. While these studies represent some of the first attempts at directly gauging the effect of child work on schooling, their inclusion of work status, a choice variable, as an exogenous regressor may not be appropriate. Ignoring the endogeneity between school participation and working status may exaggerate the negative effects of work on school attendance if working children are less likely to go to school even if work was not an option. In contrast to these studies, Akabayashi and Psacharopoulos (1999) account for endogeneity and examine the trade-off between hours of work, school participation and children's skills in reading and mathematics. The authors report that for boys an additional hour of work reduces their ability to tackle mathematical problems by 8 per cent. For girls there is no negative effect on mathematical skills; however, working reduces their ability to attend school. Heady (2003) similarly examines the effect of work on the learning achievement of children in Ghana. The study does not control for endogeneity but includes a variable which captures the ability of children. A notable aspect of Heady's work is that he draws a distinction between work outside the household and domestic work and finds that only work done outside the household harms achievement.

Our work in this chapter is a combination and extension of the direct and indirect approaches. We seek to examine the effect of the numbers of hours worked by children on school attendance and their ability to read and write. While the indirect approach is well suited to examining the effect of changes in school prices and quality on child work, it does not allow for a clear assessment of whether this harms attendance or reading and writing ability. Given the main aim of our work, it is natural to adopt the direct approach. A credible implementation of the direct approach requires that we account for the potential endogeneity between school participation and hours of work. In this chapter we adopt a two-stage method to tackle endogeneity. The first-stage requires reduced-form estimates of school attendance and hours of work relationships. Thus, our implementation of the direct approach nests the indirect approach.

Although our chapter shares some of the features of the studies outlined above, it differs in several ways. First, in addition to the usual determinants of child labor we include a set of variables which allow us to explore the immediate, short-run links between the availability of modern agricultural technology and child work. Second, the bulk of the literature uses a discrete indicator – or set of discrete indicators – to measure child work. This measure of work is not very informative, and it is likely that the ambiguities in the existing direct-approach literature arise due to the use of this limited variable. Our chapter uses a more informative measure – the total number of hours worked by a child in a week. This measure allows us to identify whether there is a certain threshold of hours worked beyond which work begins to harm the development of a child. Third, in addition to the total number of hours, we also have detailed information on the type of work and hours devoted to each type of activity. This information allows us to identify whether certain types of work may be more harmful than others.

ANALYTICAL FRAMEWORK AND EMPIRICAL SPECIFICATION

In this section we present a framework which explores the interaction between schooling – whether a child can read and write – and hours of work under two regimes.[3] We first consider a situation where there is a functioning market for child labor, and families can freely hire in or hire out child labor at a market wage rate w. In the second regime we relax this assumption and consider situations where households are not able to hire in or hire out child labor. The framework also highlights the key econometric issues which need to be considered and tackled.

A Complete Market for Child Labor

Consider a household consisting of a child and its adult guardians. Assume the adults maximize a twice-differentiable quasi-concave utility function:

$$U = U(C, l, S; E) \qquad (6.1)$$

where C is a composite consumable representing the household's standard of living, l is the child's leisure, S is the child's school attendance and E is a vector of exogenous child, household and demographic characteristics which parameterize the utility function. The second component of the model is a household production function, $q = f(L, I; K)$, where L signifies total child labor input in household production. L may consist of both household child labor, L^H, and hired child labor. There is no restriction on the composition of the total child labor input, as households are free to hire in or hire out child labor at a market-determined wage rate. I is a vector of intermediate inputs. K is a vector of exogenous variables which includes the elements in E but may also include other exogenous variables such as land quantity, land fertility, number of plots, regional controls and other factors that may influence production.[4]

The adults allocate the child's total endowment of time, T, between school attendance (S), leisure (l), work in the labor market (extra-household child labor), L^M, and work in household production (intra-household child labor), L^H. Utility maximization is subject to the time constraint:

$$T = l + S + L^M + L^H = l + S + L^S \qquad (6.2)$$

where L^S, the total labor supplied by the child, is the sum of extra-household labor, L^M, and intra-household labor, L^H. Let Y denote adult contribution to household income. Since Y and the output of child labor in household production must together suffice to meet the costs of hiring child labor, household consumption and schooling, the household's budget constraint may be written as:

$$Y + f(L, I; K) = C + pS + w(L - L^S) \qquad (6.3)$$

where p represents the price of schooling. The household adults may be assumed to maximize the utility function (6.1) subject to (6.2) and (6.3).

Before dealing with the utility maximization decision, consider the household's demand for child labor input in household production. Optimal labor demand, that which maximizes 'profit', may be obtained by maximizing $f(L, I; K) - wL - rI$, where r represents the prices of the intermediate inputs. The maximization yields the household's demand for child labor as a function only of w, r, and K and may therefore be represented as:

$$L^{D*} = L^D(w, r, K) \qquad (6.4)$$

Having determined the optimal demand for child labor and the maximized value of child output, the consumption choices of the household may be obtained by maximizing the Lagrangian function of the optimization problem:

$$Z = U(C, l, S; E) + \lambda[Y + wT + \{f(L^*, I^*; K) - wL^* - rI^*\} - C - (w + p)S - wl]$$

$$(6.5)$$

where λ denotes the Lagrange multiplier. The first-order conditions (FOC) for an interior utility maximum may be solved for optimal C, S, and l. From the time constraint, (6.2), household child labor supply, L^S, equals T less the sum of S and l. Since optimal S and l are each functions of w, p, E and Y by assuming that Y is a function of the subset of exogenous variables E, optimal S and L^S may be represented as:[5]

$$S^* = S(w, p, E) \qquad (6.6)$$

$$L^{S*} = L^S(w, p, E) \qquad (6.7)$$

The labor supply (6.7) and labor demand (6.4) equations show that changes in the price of schooling affect the supply of labor but does not influence the demand for labor.[6] It is possible to draw sharper implications. Consider first, the case of optimal household child labor supply exceeding optimal demand, i.e., $L^{S*} > L^{D*}$. Child labor input in household production will then consist entirely of household child labor, so that optimal intra-household child labor supply is given by:

$$L^{H*} = L^{D*} = L(w, r, K). \tag{6.8}$$

Since household child labor unused in household production will be supplied to the labor market, optimal extra-household child labor supply may be denoted as:

$$L^{M*} = L^{S*} - L^{D*} = L^S(w, p, E) - L^D(w, r, K) \tag{6.9}$$

According to equation (6.8), changes in the price of schooling, p, will not influence the optimal intra-household labor supply of children engaged in extra-household (market) work. On the other hand, equation (6.9) indicates that optimal extra-household child labor supply may respond to changes in the price of schooling.

Next, consider the case where $L^{S*} < L^{D*}$. Now, $L^{M*} = 0$ and intra-household labor supply will be given by:

$$L^{H*} = L^{S*} = L^S(w, p, E) \tag{6.10}$$

with the difference drawn from the labor market. Equation (6.10) implies that the price of schooling, p, may influence the intra-household labor supply of children unengaged in market work. Thus, the model predicts that while extra-household labor supply may respond to changes in schooling costs, effects of these costs on a child's intra-household labor supply may depend on whether the child is also engaged in market work.

There are three implications of the model: (1) the extra-household labor supply of children may be (positively) associated with schooling costs; (2) the intra-household labor supply of children providing extra-household labor should not respond to changes in schooling costs; (3) the intra-household labor supply of children unengaged in market work may be (positively) associated with schooling costs. These implications may be tested via estimation of child labor-supply functions. For further details on the testing procedure see Hazarika and Bedi (2003).

A Constrained Market for Child Labor

So far we have assumed that it is possible for families to hire in or hire out labor without any hindrance. However, there are several factors which may inhibit the market for child labor. For example, there may be limited work

Attending School, Reading, Writing and Child Work in Rural Ethiopia 193

opportunities for a child outside the confines of a household. Alternatively, during certain periods of the agricultural cycle there may be a shortage of child labor supply.

Consider a situation where a farming household is constrained on the supply side, that is, at the prevailing market wage rate optimal labor supply exceeds optimal labor demand:

$$L^{S*} = L^S(w, p, E) > L^{D*} = L^D(w, r, K) \qquad (6.11)$$

and there are no off-farm employment opportunities. A household rationed in this way can turn to its own farm for further employment until it achieves household equilibrium. In such situations the amount of labor used does depend on household preferences. Instead of the market wage, the equilibrium intra-household hours of work provided by children will now depend on household valuation of child time or on a shadow child wage denoted by w^*. Equilibrium hours of work provided by children may be represented by:

$$L^{H*} = L^S(w^*, p, E) = L^D(w^*, r, K). \qquad (6.12)$$

Now consider the opposite case, i.e., at the prevailing market wage household demand for labor outstrips household supply of child labor and it is not possible to hire in any additional workers.

$$L^{S*} = L^S(w, p, E) < L^D = L^D(w, r, K). \qquad (6.13)$$

Faced by this constraint, household equilibrium will depend on a shadow child wage. Once again, it will be optimal for a child to apply labor to his or her own farm until the shadow wage equilibrium is achieved (as shown in 6.12).

Thus, in situations where there are limited possibilities of hiring in or hiring out labor, the distinction between labor demand and supply cannot be maintained. The observed hours of work provided by a child depends on variables which influence the demand and supply of child labor. Unlike the case of complete markets, where the effect of schooling-related variables depends on whether a child works outside the household or within the household, such distinctions are not relevant in the case of a constrained market. Accordingly, school attendance and hours of work may be expressed in terms of the following functions:

$$S^* = S(w^*, p, E) \qquad (6.14)$$

$$L^{H*} = L^S(w^*, p, r, E, K) \qquad (6.15)$$

The preceding sections considered the link between schooling (prices) and work in the context of a complete and incomplete market for child labor, respectively. As displayed, the links between schooling (costs of schooling) and child work may depend on whether labor is performed within or without the household. Our assessment of the relevant information on Ethiopia shows that while child labor is widespread, there is no well-developed market for child labor with a market-determined wage rate. Almost all children work within the context of the household and distinctions between intra-household and extra-household work, labor demand and labor supply do not appear to be meaningful in the Ethiopian context.[7] Thus, our empirical work is based on the assumption of an incomplete market for child labor.

Empirical Approach

The direct approach that we adopt in this study requires the estimation of a structural schooling equation. For the time being consider a linear specification of schooling:

$$S^* = \beta_{Sw^*} w^* + \beta_{Sp} p + \beta_{SE} E + \beta_{L^{H^*}} L^{H^*} + \varepsilon_S \tag{6.16}$$

where the βs are coefficients to be estimated and ε_S captures the effect of unobservables. Our schooling variable is dichotomous. If we assume that the error term is normally distributed we may employ a probit model to estimate (6.16). However, since an hour of work is a choice variable, it is quite likely that a single-equation estimation of (6.16) will lead to inconsistent estimates. There are several methods which may be used to obtain consistent estimates of the schooling equation. Here we use Rivers and Vuong's (1988) two-stage conditional maximum likelihood (2CML) procedure. Reduced form expressions for the schooling and hours of work may be written as:

$$S^* = \beta_{Sw^*} w^* + \beta_{Sp} p + \beta_{SE} E + \varepsilon_S \tag{6.17}$$

$$L^{H^*} = \beta_{Lw^*} w^* + \beta_{Lp} p + \beta_{Lr} r + \beta_{LE} E + \beta_{LK} K + \varepsilon_L. \tag{6.18}$$

In the first stage we estimate the hours of work equation (6.18) using OLS.[8] In the second stage we include estimates of the residual ($\hat{\varepsilon}_L$) from this first step-regression in (6.17).

This procedure yields:

$$S^* = \beta_{Sw^*} w^* + \beta_{Sp} p + \beta_{SE} E + \beta_{L^{H^*}} L^{H^*} + \lambda \hat{\varepsilon}_L + \varepsilon_S \tag{6.19}$$

As shown by Rivers and Vuong (1988), this augmented probit equation yields consistent estimates. An advantage of this procedure is that estimates of λ may be used to perform an exogeneity test.

If working reduces school attendance and harms the ability of a child to attend school, then the coefficient of hours of work in equation (6.19) should be negative. On the other hand, if working and schooling are not incompatible, then this coefficient may be positive or may not be different from zero.

While the estimation procedure has been discussed, a key issue which still needs to be confronted is the identification of these two-stage models. There are several possibilities to explore. First, since our hours of work equation is estimated using OLS and our schooling equation is a probit equation, we may achieve identification on the basis of differences in functional form. While this approach is feasible, differences in functional form are a weak basis for identification. A look at the framework sketched above shows that there may be variables which influence child labor without a direct influence on schooling. These include variables such as the prices of intermediate inputs, denoted by r, and the vector of exogenous variables, denoted by K. It is possible that these variables influence the hours of work provided by a child but have no direct effect on schooling. Their effect on schooling may be mediated via their influence on the hours of work decision. Thus, a second identification strategy is to exclude the variables denoted by r and K from the schooling equation. While we rely on this identification strategy, it is questionable. In our empirical work we conduct a sensitivity analysis to examine variations in the estimates in response to changes in the identification strategy.

THE DATA

The Department of Economics of Addis Ababa University, in collaboration with Oxford University, the International Food Policy Research Institute, the United States Agency for International Development and the University of Bonn's Center for Development Research, has carried out five rounds of a rural household survey.[9] The data used for this study are drawn from the fifth round of the rural survey, that was conducted during the 1999–2000 crop season in 18 peasant associations. The 18 survey sites are located in four major regional national states, i.e., the Amhara National Regional State, the Tigray National Regional State, the Oromiya National Regional State and the Southern Nations, Nationalities and Peoples Regional State. These regions include more than 90 per cent of the country's population and account for a similar proportion of economic output.

We used pre-tested survey questionnaires designed to assess the living standards of individuals and households to gather information. Data were collected from 1,680 households consisting of 9,844 individuals. A special feature of the fifth edition of the survey was the inclusion of information on the work activities of children. We collected detailed information on the time-use patterns of children in the age group 4–15 in the seven days preceding the survey. Household heads were asked to provide information on the hours spent by children on farming, child care, carrying out domestic chores, fetching wood and water and herding.

In this chapter we restrict our attention to children between four and 15 years of age on whom we have complete information. This yields a sample of 3,043 children. A detailed discussion of the dependent variables in our analysis (patterns of work, school attendance and the ability of children to read and write) is provided in the next section and in Tables 6.1, 6.2 and 6.3. The specification of the equations to be estimated and a description of the dependent variables are provided in Table 6.4.

PATTERNS OF WORK AND SCHOOL ATTENDANCE

With an estimated population of over 60 million, Ethiopia is the second-largest country in Sub-Saharan Africa. It is one of the world's least-developed countries and has a per capita GDP of about $110. Agriculture is the mainstay of the economy and accounts for about 45 per cent of GDP, 90 per cent of foreign exchange earnings and employs about 85 per cent of the population.

In terms of labor laws, a reading of the Ethiopian constitution and current legislative measures on child labor shows that Ethiopia follows international standards and gives consideration to the rights and the welfare of the child as embodied in the UN CRC. Labor laws stipulate a minimum age of 14 years for admission to employment and allow employment between the age of 14 and 18 only as apprentices and even then under a number of restrictions. However, the Ethiopian labor law does not make any reference to child labor in the subsistence agricultural sector, and household employment is exempt from the law. Thus, an estimated 85 per cent of the national economic activity falls outside the protection of the labor code, as it consists of small-scale and subsistence farming.

Patterns of Work

Previous work on Ethiopia report a very high incidence of child labor. Admassie (2000) provides a picture of the work activities of children based on a 1994 rural

Table 6.1   Work Participation Rates and Hours of Work of Children age 4–15 (standard deviation)

	Total (N=3677)	Male (N=1785)	Female (N=1892)	T-statistic[a] (p-value)
Work Participation (%)	74.4	74.4	74.5	0.868
	(43.6)	(43.6)	(43.5)	(0.385)
Total hours worked per week	29.61	29.99	29.21	0.410
	(27.23)	(27.54)	(26.9)	(0.681)
Hours worked on week days:	25.10	25.25	24.93	0.063
	(24.02)	(24.01)	(24.03)	(0.946)
Fetching Wood/Water	4.72	3.70	5.80	8.58
	(7.44)	(6.65)	(8.05)	(0.000)
Domestic Tasks	5.80	3.47	8.27	14.49
	(10.21)	(8.17)	(11.51)	(0.000)
Child Care	2.57	1.55	3.63	8.35
	(7.54)	(6.27)	(8.56)	(0.000)
Farm Work	2.16	2.91	1.36	6.97
	(6.84)	(7.98)	(5.27)	(0.000)
Herding	9.85	13.61	5.86	13.71
	(17.72)	(20.09)	(13.73)	(0.000)

Note: Figures are based on an Ethiopian Rural Household Survey conducted in 1999.
[a]Two-tail t-statistic, absolute value. The null hypothesis is equality of means for males and females.

household survey. But compared to that study, the dataset which we use contains far more detailed information on the primary and secondary occupations of every member of the household, including children above the age of four years. This allows us to construct a detailed portrait of the work activities of children.

Table 6.1 summarizes work participation rates and the time children spend on different types of work. Column 1 provides this information for all children in the age group 4–15, while columns 2 and 3 present gender specific information. The final column tests for any statistically significant differences in participation rates and hours of work across gender. About 75 per cent of all children participate in work activities. On average, a child spends around four hours a day or approximately 30 hours a week on work activities. There are no differences in participation rates or the mean number of hours (total) worked across genders.[10]

While total time spent on work activities does not differ by gender, breaking down our data allows us to decompose the total number of hours worked by children into five different types of work. Table 6.1 presents this breakdown. Boys spend more than 50 per cent of total hours of work on herding and 10–15 per cent on activities such as farm work, fetching water and wood and other

Figure 6.1   Hours of Work by Age and Gender

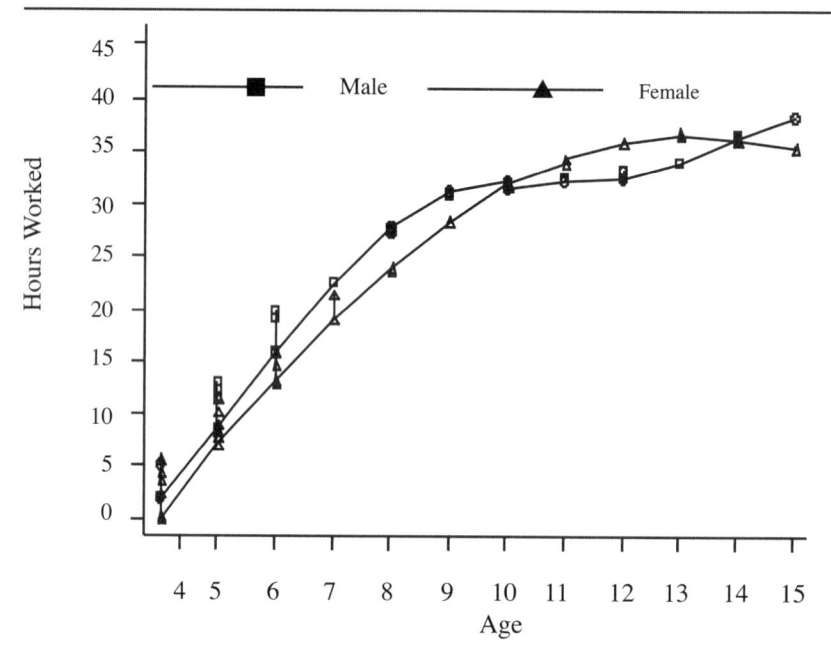

Figure 6.2   Work Participation by Age and Gender

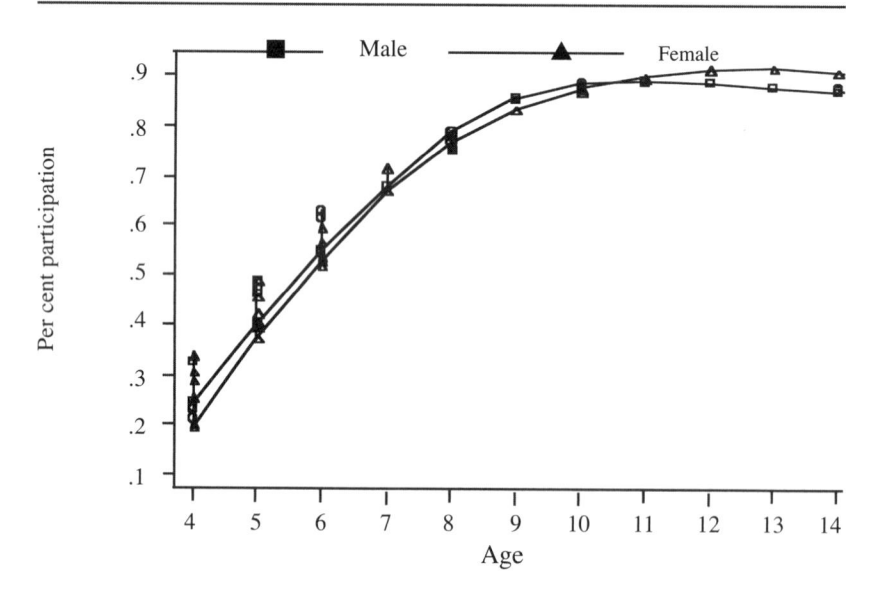

Table 6.2 School Participation and Writing and Reading Ability of Children Age 7–15 (standard deviation)

	Total (N = 2657)	Male (N = 1365)	Female (N = 1292)	T-statistic[a] (p-value)
School participation (%)	43.9 (49.6)	47.0 (49.9)	40.7 (49.1)	3.245 (0.0012)
Writing and reading ability (%)	39.4 (48.8)	43.0 (49.5)	35.6 (47.9)	3.918 (0.0001)

Notes:
Figures are based on an Ethiopian Rural Household Survey conducted in 1999.
[a] Two-tail t-statistic, absolute value. The null hypothesis is equality of means for males and females.

domestic tasks. Girls spend considerable time on domestic tasks (about 33 per cent of total work time) followed by around 23–24 per cent on fetching wood and water and herding, respectively.

To examine the dynamics of work participation and hours of work, Figures 6.1 and 6.2 present graphs which depict the gender-specific relation between age and hours of work and age and work participation.[11] The figures show that children as young as four have a 21 per cent participation rate and spend about five hours a week on work activities. Work activities increase with age and show a concave pattern. By the age of 11 work participation rates reach a peak of 91 per cent, while weekly hours of work reach a peak of about 41 per cent at the age of 14.

A more disaggregated picture of the link between hours of work and age is provided in Figure 6.3 which presents the relationship between hours of work and age for each of the five different work activities. They show that gender-specific work patterns may already be discerned at the age of four, with boys spending more time on herding and girls more time on child care. For the other types of work activities (fetching water, domestic, farm work) differences appear when children are between six and seven years old, with girls spending more time on domestic tasks and fetching water and wood and boys attending to farm work.

Schooling, Reading and Writing

Table 6.2 presents school enrollment rates and information on the proportion of children who are able to read and write in Ethiopia. This information pertains

Figure 6.3   Hours of Work by Activity, Age and Gender

a. Fetching Water and Wood

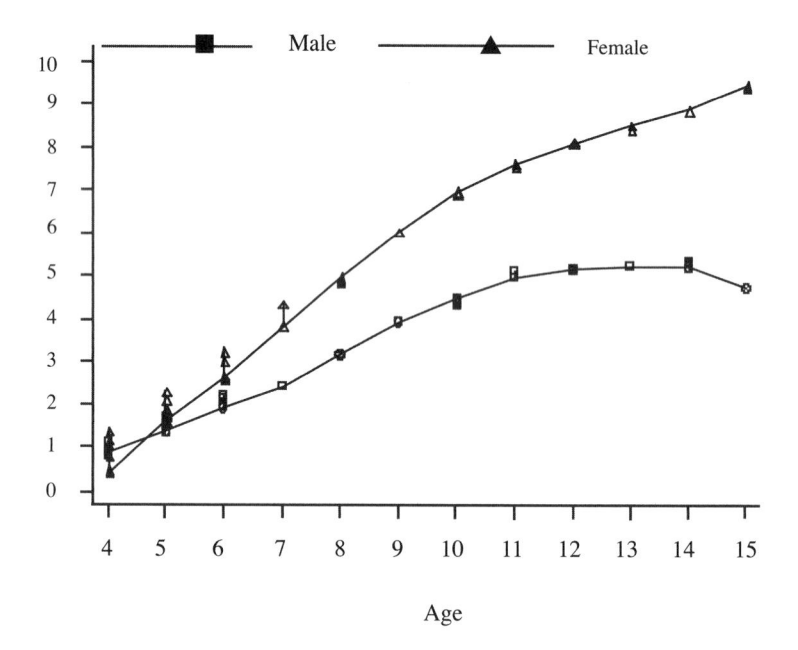

b. Farm Work

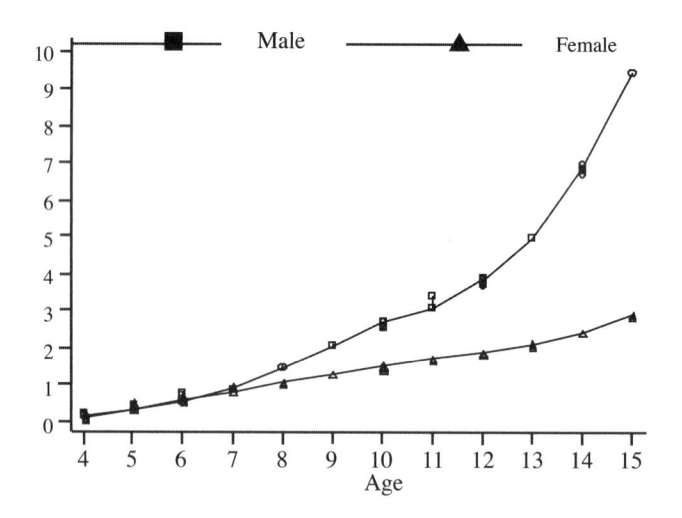

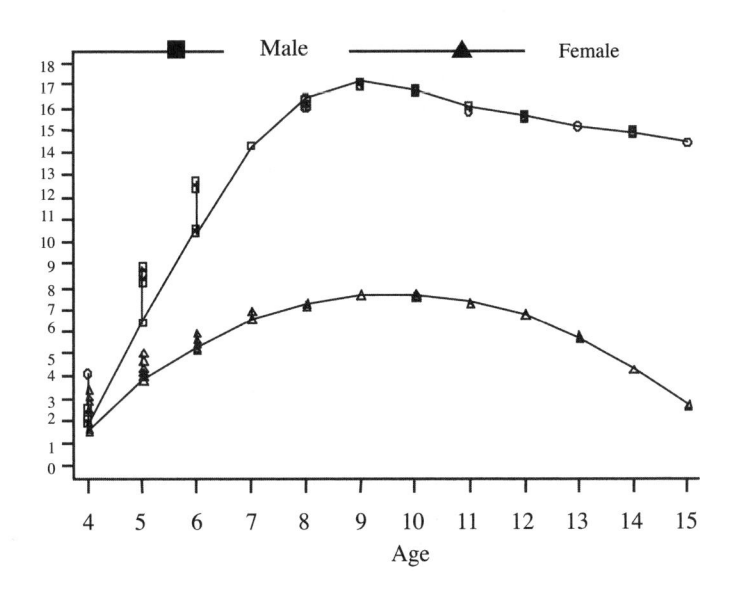

Figure 6.3 (continued)

c. Domestic Tasks

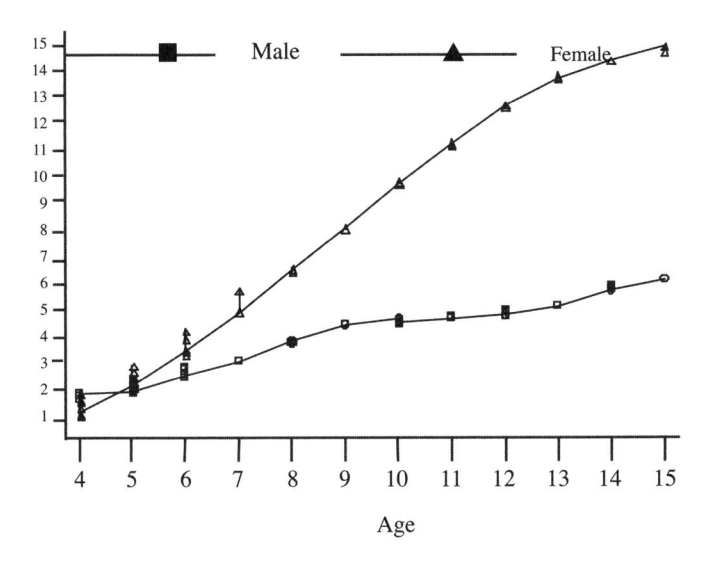

d. Herding

Figure 6.3 (continued)

e. Child Care

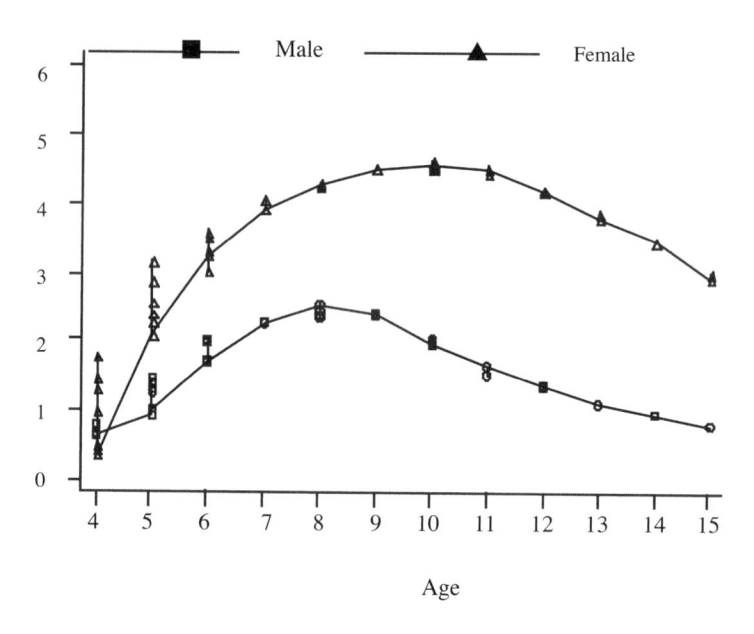

[Figure: Child Care - line graph showing Male and Female values by Age from 4 to 15]

to children above the age of seven, when children are usually expected to enroll in primary school. As Table 6.2 shows, the school participation rate is quite low at about 44 per cent.[12] There are clear differences across gender, with 47 per cent of boys attending while the corresponding level is 41 per cent for girls. To obtain an idea of the dynamic patterns in school participation, Figure 6.4 presents estimates of the probability of attending school as a function of age for the full sample and by gender. The probability of attending school increases with age and reaches a peak of about 60 per cent for boys and about 50 per cent for girls. Gender differences in the probability of attending school emerge between the age of nine and ten and remain steady at about 7–10 percentage points until children reach the age of 15.

Patterns in the reading and writing ability of children are very similar to the patterns of school participation.[13] About 40 per cent of children are able to read and write. While 43 per cent of boys are able to read and write, the corresponding figure for girls is about 36 per cent. The ability to read and write increases with age and reaches a peak (at age 13) of about 58 per cent for boys and 43–44 per cent for girls. There is a gap (4 per cent) between school participation and the ability to read and write which implies that not all those

Figure 6.4 Schooling by Age and Gender

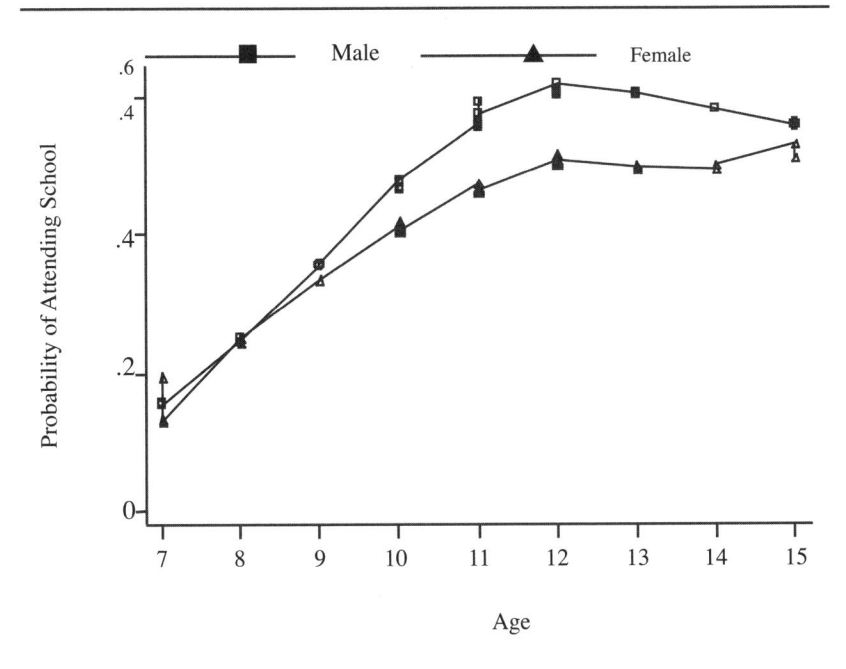

who attend school acquire the ability to read and write. Apart from this gap, age-specific patterns in the two variables are similar and suggest that school attendance and the ability to read and write may be treated synonymously.

Work Participation, Schooling and Human Capital

This chapter seeks to examine whether the work activities of children hinder their ability to go to school and interfere with the development of their reading and writing abilities. To obtain a preliminary idea of the relationship between these variables, we examined successively, the bivariate relationships between work participation and school participation, and the relationship between hours of work and school participation. Table 6.3 presents our estimates. We find that children who attend school are more likely to work. About 92 per cent of the children who go to school work, while the figure is about 87 per cent for those who do not attend school. If we had no additional information we might conclude that work participation does not hinder school participation. However, our information on the duration of work allows us to go beyond participation rates. Children who attend school contribute about 34 hours of work in a week while those who do not attend contribute 38 hours a week. Despite the lower

Table 6.3a   Schooling and Work by Children Age 7–15 (standard deviation)

	School = 0 (N=1488)	School = 1 (N=1169)	T-statistic[a] (p-value)
Work participation (%)	86.6	91.6	4.06
	(34)	(27.7)	(0.000)
Total hours of work in a week	38.44	34.36	4.00
	(28.06)	(23.13)	(0.000)
Hours worked on week days	33.03	28.39	5.12
	(24.93)	(20.7)	(0.000)
Fetching wood and water	5.68	6.26	1.875
	(7.98)	(7.97)	(0.061)
Domestic tasks	7.21	7.94	1.685
	(11.07)	(11.32)	(0.092)
Child care	3.27	2.69	1.5803
	(8.76)	(7.16)	(0.114)
Farm work	2.63	3.11	1.828
	(7.78)	(7.76)	(0.0676)
Herding	14.24	8.38	8.1556
	(21.59)	(13.17)	(0.000)

Table 6.3b   Schooling and Work by Boys Age 7–15 (standard deviation)

	School = 0 (N=723)	School = 1 (N=642)	T-statistic[a] (p-value)
Work participation (%)	86.0	91.2	3.05
	(35)	(28.2)	(0.002)
Total hours of work in a week	40.07	33.68	4.48
	(28.87)	(23.09)	(0.000)
Hours worked on week days	34.28	27.63	5.31
	(25.36)	(20.2)	(0.000)
Fetching wood and water	3.85	5.45	4.081
	(6.59)	(7.87)	(0.000)
Domestic tasks	3.95	4.91	1.942
	(9.01)	(9.23)	(0.052)
Child care	2.23	1.38	2.263
	(8.36)	(4.70)	(0.024)
Farm work	3.53	4.27	1.519
	(9.25)	(8.77)	(0.128)
Herding	20.71	11.63	8.20
	(24.17)	(14.97)	(0.000)

Table 6.3c Schooling and Work by Girls age 7–15 (standard deviation)

	School = 0 (N=765)	School = 1 (N=527)	T-statistic[a] (p-value)
Work participation	0.872	0.920	2.75
	(0.33)	(0.271)	(0.003)
Total hours of work in a week	36.90	35.20	1.165
	(27.21)	(23.18)	(0.244)
Hours worked on week days	31.86	29.31	1.923
	(24.48)	(21.2)	(0.053)
Fetching wood and water	7.41	7.26	0.319
	(8.76)	(7.99)	(0.754)
Domestic tasks	10.28	11.64	1.967
	(11.93)	(12.47)	(0.049)
Child care	4.25	4.28	0.060
	(9.02)	(9.07)	(0.952)
Farm work	1.78	1.70	0.253
	(5.96)	(6.04)	(0.800
Herding	8.12	4.43	4.629
	(16.67)	(9.16)	(0.000)

Note: Figures are based on an Ethiopian Rural Household Survey conducted in 1999.
[a] Two-tail t-statistic, absolute value. The null hypothesis is equality of means conditional on school enrolment status.

number of hours worked by children who do attend school, their work burden – about five hours a day – is substantial. A look at the differences in the type of work activities carried out by the two groups reveals a clear pattern. For four of the five work activities there are no differences in patterns of work by school status. The only difference lies in the time spent on herding. Children who attend school spend far less time on herding (eight hours) than children who do not attend school (14 hours).

Gender-specific patterns are presented in Tables 6.3b and 6.3c. The pattern for boys matches the overall pattern. Work participation rates for school-attending boys are higher than for boys who do not attend school, while average hours of work is higher for those who do not attend school (34 versus 40). The differences in the duration of work stem mainly from the time spent on herding by boys who do not attend school. Similarly, girls who attend school have a higher participation rate but, unlike boys, average hours of work do not differ across schooling states. Regardless of their schooling status, girls provide about

35–36 hours of work effort in a week. There are differences across schooling status in terms of the individual work activities. Girls who attend school spend less time on herding (4.4 versus 8 hours) but more time on domestic tasks.

The numbers presented in Table 6.3 and the discussion so far suggests that there may be a negative relationship between the probability of school attendance and the number of hours worked. To explicitly explore the bivariate relationship between school attendance (reading and writing ability) and hours of work, Figure 6.5 presents estimates from a loess regression of the probability of attending school on the total number of hours of work. The figure shows a non-linear relationship between the probability of attending school and hours of work. School participation and working are positively related until about 30 hours of work, but beyond that peak there is a negative relationship between the two variables. The same pattern prevails for the probability that a child can read and write. These patterns suggest that it is only beyond a certain number of hours of work that the labor contribution of children begins to hinder school attendance and their ability to read and write.

REDUCED FORM AND STRUCTURAL RELATIONSHIPS

Specification

The reduced form schooling and reading-and-writing-ability (RWA) equations are specified as functions of the shadow wage of a child, the price and quality of schooling and a vector of exogenous attributes. We treat the shadow wage as a function of the gender, age, ethnicity and religion of a child and several variables which reflect the demographic composition of the household (family size, number of infants, number of females, female-headed household). The cost of attending school is measured by the time taken to reach school. Regardless of school attendance, parents were asked whether they were satisfied with the quality of available education. This variable is used as a crude measure of the quality of educational inputs.

The exogenous variables corresponding to $E(K)$ in equation (6.18) include a set of two indicators which indicate whether the household head has completed primary or secondary education. Variables which capture household wealth and assets include the materials used to construct the roof and the walls of a household's dwelling, the livestock owned by a household and variables which indicate the quantity and quality of the land available to the household. Two additional variables which reflect institutional arrangements and may have a bearing on school attendance/hours of work are whether a household has a

Table 6.4 Descriptive Statistics (full sample)

Variable	Mean	Std. Dev.
Child characteristics		
Male = 1	0.514	0.499
Age	9.505	3.433
Ethnicity and religion		
Amhara = 1	0.248	0.431
Oromo = 1	0.353	0.478
Tigrawi = 1	0.099	0.298
Orthodox Christian = 1	0.546	0.497
Muslim = 1	0.254	0.436
Educational characteristics		
Distance to the closest school (minutes)	40.09	34.38
Satisfied with the quality of education = 1	0.636	0.480
Household demographic and human capital characteristics		
Family size	9.304	3.527
Female headed household = 1	0.200	0.400
Number of infants (0–4 age group)	1.586	1.243
Number of female members in family	3.780	1.833
Head of household has 1–6 years of education = 1	0.210	0.407
Head of household has 7–12 years of education = 1	0.075	0.263
Household wealth and assets		
Roof of dwelling made of galvanized iron = 1	0.288	0.453
Wall of dwelling made of concrete, brick or cement = 1	0.186	0.389
Number of cattle (in livestock units)	4.279	4.052
Small ruminants (in livestock units)	2.936	5.319
Number of equines (in livestock units)	0.855	1.302
Size of cultivable land in hectares	1.324	1.087
Number of plots	3.376	2.246
Weighted fertility of land (1 = good, 3 = poor)	1.591	0.638
Institutional and regional controls		
Sharecropping = 1	0.295	0.456
Participation in traditional labor-sharing arrangement = 1	0.618	0.485
Family resides in region 1 = 1	0.079	0.269
Family resides in region 2 = 1	0.289	0.453
Family resides in region 3 = 1	0.368	0.482
Family resides in region 4 = 1	0.090	0.286
Family resides in region 5 = 1	0.172	0.377
Intermediate inputs		
Percentage of fertilizer users in PA	59.4	34.4
Percentage of machinery users in PA	2.78	5.68
Percentage of improved seed users in PA	21.6	24.9
Percentage of agricultural chemical users in PA	11.7	17.5
Number of Observations		3677

share-cropping contract and whether a household is involved in a traditional labor-sharing arrangement.[14]

Both the schooling and the hours of work equations include the set of variables discussed above. The hours of work equation also contains an additional set of variables which corresponds to r in equation (6.18). Ideally, this set of variables should be the prices of relevant agricultural inputs. Since we do not have this information, we use peasant association (PA) level averages of the use of four inputs as proxies for household access to modern agricultural technologies. We consider the effects of the availability of land-saving technologies such as inorganic fertilizers and high-yielding seed varieties and the effect of labor-saving technologies such as access to tractors, agricultural machinery and agricultural chemicals (pesticides and herbicides) on hours of work. We expect that access to machinery and chemicals will be associated with a reduction in child labor. On the other hand, the application of fertilizers and improved seeds may call for additional effort from children and, in the short run, may increase the demand for child labor.

Schooling and Reading and Writing

Table 6.5 presents reduced-form estimates of the probability that a child attends school. Estimates are presented for the combined sample of children and then for boys and girls separately. For the most part, the probit estimates of school attendance and RWA (not presented) do not differ, and we confine our discussion to the estimates of school attendance.

Consistent with the gender differences discussed earlier, males are more likely to attend school. Being male is associated with an 8 percentage point increase in the probability of attending school. The probability of attending school increases with age (a marginal effect of close to 10 percentage points) and reaches a peak at about twelve and a half years of age.

The effect of the set of demographic variables is markedly different across genders. The size of the household, the number of infants and the number of female members has no bearing on the school attendance decision for boys. For girls, larger family size – particularly the number of infants in a household – sharply reduces the probability of school attendance, while a larger number of female members in a household encourages school attendance. This suggests that adult and child female labor are substitutes.

The cost of attending school, captured by the distance to the closest school, has the expected sign configuration but is not statistically significant. Although crude, our measure of the quality of school inputs has a positive sign and a large effect (14 percentage points) and shows that school attendance decisions are motivated by the perceived quality of school inputs.

Table 6.5 Probability of Attending School, Children Aged 7–15 (standard error)

Variable	Marginal effects full sample	Marginal effects males	Marginal effects female
Male	0.082		
	(0.024)		
Age	0.413	0.474	0.389
	(0.045)	(0.063)	(0.064)
Age squared	−0.016	−0.018	−0.015
	(0.002)	(0.003)	(0.003)
Distance to closest school	−0.0006	−0.0003	−0.0008
	(0.0035)	(0.0005)	(0.0005)
Quality of education	0.137	0.197	0.092
	(0.024)	(0.036)	(0.034)
Family size	−0.010	−0.008	−0.015
	(0.004)	(0.007)	(0.006)
Number of infants	−0.020	−0.003	−0.037
	(0.011)	(0.015)	(0.016)
Number of female members	0.017	0.011	0.032
	(0.009)	(0.012)	(0.012)
Household head has 1–6 years of education	0.079	0.065	0.093
	(0.029)	(0.042)	(0.043)
Household head has 7–12 years of education	0.220	0.148	0.285
	(0.043)	(0.062)	(0.062)
Roof	0.032	0.072	−0.008
	(0.026)	(0.037)	(0.037)
Wall	0.023	0.099	−0.060
	(0.040)	(0.056)	(0.056)
Cattle	0.016	0.015	0.016
	(0.008)	(0.011)	(0.011)
Cattle squared	−0.0003	−0.0001	−0.0004
	(0.0004)	(0.0006)	(0.0006)
Small ruminants	−0.011	−0.007	−0.014
	(0.003)	(0.004)	(0.004)
Landholding in hectares	−0.023	−0.077	0.029
	(0.041)	(0.059)	(0.059)
Landholding in hectares squared	0.0038	0.012	−0.005
	(0.009)	(0.012)	(0.012)
Share cropping = 1	0.021	0.015	0.029
	(0.029)	(0.041)	(0.041)
Labor-sharing arrangements = 1	−0.035	−0.012	−0.065
	(0.027)	(0.039)	(0.039)
Log likelihood	−1311	−665	−614
Number of observations	2227	1159	1068

Note: Other regressors include indicator variables for ethnicity, religion, presence of biological parents in the household, female-headed household and region. Additional continuous variables in the model control for the fertility of the land, number of plots owned by the family, the number of equines and small ruminants.

Parental education has a strong impact on school attendance decisions. The effect is stronger for parents with secondary education. Children from families where the household head has secondary education are 15–28 percentage points more likely to attend school. There are several variables which capture the wealth and asset position of the household. Of these, only the number of cattle owned by the household appears to have an impact on the attendance decisions. The number of cattle owned by a household may increase the need for child labor and reduce school attendance. On the other hand, this variable reflects household wealth and the ability to access credit, and it may be positively associated with school attendance. A priori, it is difficult to sign the effect of this variable. In our case, there is a clear positive effect. An additional unit of cattle owned by a household increases the probability of attending school by about 1.6 percentage points. The amount of land cultivated by a household may also have ambiguous effects on schooling decisions. In the absence of market for child labor, a larger land endowment may reduce the ability to attend school. In our case, we are unable to detect any direct link between land endowment and school attendance. In the Ethiopian context, all land belongs to the state and households may not consider the amount of land which they cultivate to be part of their asset portfolio. It is possible that the lack of a link is a reflection of the insecurity of land tenure.

Variation in the type of institutional arrangements (share-cropping and labor-sharing) across households does not appear to have a strong bearing on school attendance.

Hours of Work

Table 6.6 presents OLS estimates of the total hours of work equation. The tables present estimates for the full sample and separately for males and females.[15] Consistent with the discussion in the earlier sections, there are no differences in the hours of work across genders. As children age they are more likely to work. Based on our estimates, a one-year increase in age is associated with an additional contribution of about three hours of work per week.

The demographic composition of the household and patterns of work are quite interesting. An increase in the number of infants (age 0–3) in a family elicits extra work effort from older children. As may be expected, the marginal effect is much larger for girls (2.6) than for boys (1.4). Less work effort is required from children living in families with a larger number of adult female household members. The effect is large and statistically significant, suggesting that the work effort provided by girls and that provided by adult female members are strong substitutes.

Table 6.6   Hours Worked Per Week by Children Aged 4–15, OLS Estimates (standard error)

Variable	Full Sample	Males	Female
Male	−0.187		
	(0.916)		
Age	11.89	11.53	12.25
	(0.728)	(1.038)	(1.02)
Age squared	−0.456	−0.454	−0.455
	(0.039)	(0.056)	(0.056)
Distance to closest school	−0.002	−0.017	0.020
	(0.014)	(0.019)	(0.020)
Quality of education	0.934	0.523	1.524
	(0.978)	(1.454)	(1.311)
Family size	−0.501	−0.444	−0.625
	(0.171)	(0.251)	(0.238)
Number of infants	1.921	1.358	2.616
	(0.427)	(0.611)	(0.601)
Number of female members	−0.846	−0.354	−1.258
	(0.327)	(0.463)	(0.475)
Household head has 1–6 years of education	−1.136	−2.399	0.439
	(1.084)	(1.541)	(1.526)
Household head has 7–12 years of education	−4.303	−4.808	−2.990
	(1.647)	(2.182)	(2.526)
Roof	1.309	0.557	1.960
	(1.033)	(1.504)	(1.426)
Wall	−5.584	−5.181	−6.866
	(1.527)	(2.173)	(2.105)
Cattle	0.676	0.481	0.894
	(0.294)	(0.415)	(0.410)
Cattle squared	−0.019	−0.012	−0.029
	(0.014)	(0.021)	(0.019)
Small ruminants	0.037	0.044	−0.041
	(0.120)	(0.169)	(0.163)
Landholding in hectares	1.695	2.572	0.822
	(1.896)	(2.339)	(2.596)
Landholding in hectares squared	−0.273	−0.473	−0.058
	(0.387)	(0.446)	(0.528)
Share cropping = 1	−0.031	2.390	−2.591
	(1.061)	(1.554)	(1.445)
Labor sharing arrangements = 1	0.876	1.182	1.012
	(1.105)	(1.624)	(1.510)
Percentage of fertilizer users in PA	−0.030	−0.002	−0.058
	(0.028)	(0.039)	(0.041)
Percentage of machinery users in PA	−0.934	−0.909	−0.926
	(0.146)	(0.214)	(0.198)
Percentage of improved seed users in PA	0.159	0.068	0.254
	(0.046)	(0.065)	(0.066)
Percentage of agricultural chemical users in PA	0.030	0.044	0.026
	(0.047)	(0.070)	(0.064)
R^2	0.249	0.235	0.295
Number of Observations	3043	1577	1466

Note: Other regressors include indicator variables for ethnicity, religion, presence of biological parents in the household, female-headed household and region. Additional continuous variables in the model control for the fertility of the land, number of plots owned by the family, the number of equines and small ruminants.

The variables which reflect the cost and quality of education have no impact on the number of hours worked by children. The coefficients on the two schooling-related variables are the key coefficients in the indirect approach and combining these results with those obtained from the schooling equation suggests that school attendance and hours of work are *not* substitutes. The pattern of results across the two equations indicates that while improvements in school quality will increase the probability of attending school, the additional time spent in school will not come at the cost of reduced hours of work. Thus, a reduction in leisure – not a reduction in the number of hours of work – may accompany an increase in time spent in school.

Education of the household head has strong effects on hours of work. The marginal impact of a household head with secondary education is a reduction in work effort by about four hours. There are sharp differences across gender. While education is associated with a five-hour reduction in the work week for boys, there is no statistically significant impact on girls. These differences across gender are in sharp contrast to the effect of the education of the household head on schooling decisions. Specifically, while both boys and girls from better-educated households are more likely to attend school, it is only boys who are expected to work less. Regardless of school status, girls are expected to complete their quota of work.

Since the wealth variables capture household assets and also, in some cases, the demand for child work, they need to be interpreted carefully. As with the schooling estimates, we are unable to detect a relationship between hours of work and the amount of land a household cultivates. On the other hand, the relationship between an important household asset – cattle – and hours of work is weakly non-linear. As the cattle holdings of families increase, there is an increase in the number of hours of work provided by children. However, beyond a certain point the work effort declines. While the relationship between assets and hours of work is non-linear, it is weak and operates only beyond a substantial cattle holding. For cattle, the peak is reached at about 17 livestock units. This figure is about 3.5 standard deviations to the right of the mean holdings. Thus, for most households increased asset ownership is associated with increased work effort. Given the absence of a well-functioning labor market, the positive relationship between asset ownership and hours of work is not surprising. Overall, the pattern of results suggests that additional asset ownership (cattle) leads to an increase in the number of hours of work and an increase in the probability of attending school.

The final set of variables included in the specification is those which capture the use of modern agricultural technologies. As mentioned earlier, the government of Ethiopia is currently pushing an extensive and aggressive extension program aimed at introducing farmers to new, modern methods of agricultural production. To examine the links between the availability of these technologies and child work we include a set of four variables. These variables are defined as the percentage of households in a peasant association which use fertilizers, improved seeds, agricultural machinery and agricultural chemicals.[16] Of these four measures, the first two may be termed 'land-saving technologies'. The impact of these innovations on the use of child labor is not clear. While increased application of fertilizer and improved seeds may increase the productivity of land, they may also lead to an increase in demand for harvest labor, including child labor, at least in the short run.[17] On the other hand the introduction of labor-saving technologies such as tractors and other agricultural machinery may reduce labor demand for cultivation and planting. Similarly the use of agricultural chemicals such as herbicides may have a labor-displacing effect. The use of herbicides should reduce labor needs for weeding, an important activity for women and children in rural Ethiopia.

Estimates of the effect of the technology variables on hours of work are presented in Table 6.6. Two of the four measures are statistically significant. The availability of machinery has a large negative impact on hours of work. A percentage point increase in the availability of machinery is associated with almost a one-hour reduction in child labor. At the moment the availability and use of agricultural machinery such as tractors, harvesters, threshers and shellers is extremely low in Ethiopia. The extent to which the adoption of such technologies is possible and/or relevant, given the typical features (e.g. small landholdings) of Ethiopian farming, needs to be examined. However it is quite clear from our estimates that the availability of agricultural machinery has an immediate impact on reducing the demand for male and female child labor.

Of the two land-saving technologies only the availability of improved seeds is associated with an increase in the use of child labor. The estimates indicate that a one standard deviation increase in the availability of improved seeds increases a child's workload by about four hours. While the long-term impact of the adoption of improved seeds and the consequent increases in productivity ought to be a decline in child labor, in the short run the spread of this technology may increase the burden of working children.

Structural Relationships (Direct Links)

We begin our examination of the effect of hours of work on schooling and the reading/writing ability (RWA) of children by including total hours of work as an additional regressor in the schooling/RWA equations. This first set of estimates does not treat hours of work endogenously and is similar to some of the early work in this area (e.g., Patrinos and Psacharopouos 1997). The estimates (Probit-1 in Table 6.7) show that there is a negative and statistically

Table 6.7   Probability of Attending School, Children Aged 7–15, Marginal Effects from Probit and Two-Stage Conditional Maximum Likelihood (2CML) Specifications (standard error)

	Full Sample				Males						Females				
	Probit 1	Probit 2	2CML 1	2CML 2	2CML 3	Probit 1	Probit 2	2CML 1	2CML 2	2CML 3	Probit 1	Probit 2	2CML 1	2CML 2	2CML 3
Hours worked per week	−0.0030 (0.0005)	0.004 (0.002)	0.006 (0.013)	0.008 (0.004)	0.008 (0.004)	−0.004 (0.001)	0.005 (0.002)	−0.0004 (0.013)	0.008 (0.006)	0.006 (0.005)	−0.002 (0.001)	0.005 (0.002)	0.004 (0.022)	0.009 (0.006)	0.005 (0.005)
Hours worked per week squared *100		−0.009 (0.002)	−0.009 (0.002)	−0.009 (0.002)	−0.009 (0.002)		−0.011 (0.003)	−0.010 (0.003)	−0.010 (0.003)	−0.010 (0.003)		−0.008 (0.003)	−0.008 (0.003)	−0.008 (0.002)	−0.007 (0.002)
Lambda			−0.002 (0.013)	−0.004 (0.004)	−0.004 (0.004)			0.005 (0.014)	−0.003 (0.005)	−0.001 (0.004)			0.001 (0.022)	−0.004 (0.005)	−0.0002 (0.005)
Peak		23.9	31.7	47.9	47.9		22.6	0	36.2	26.9		30.9	23.1	56.6	31
N	2227	2227	2227	2227	2227	1159	1159	1159	1159	1159	1068	1068	1068	1068	1068
Log likelihood	−1290	−1277	−1270	−1276	−1279	−648	−639	−636	−639	−641	−611	−605	−601	−605	−613

Figure 6.5   Schooling by Hours of Work

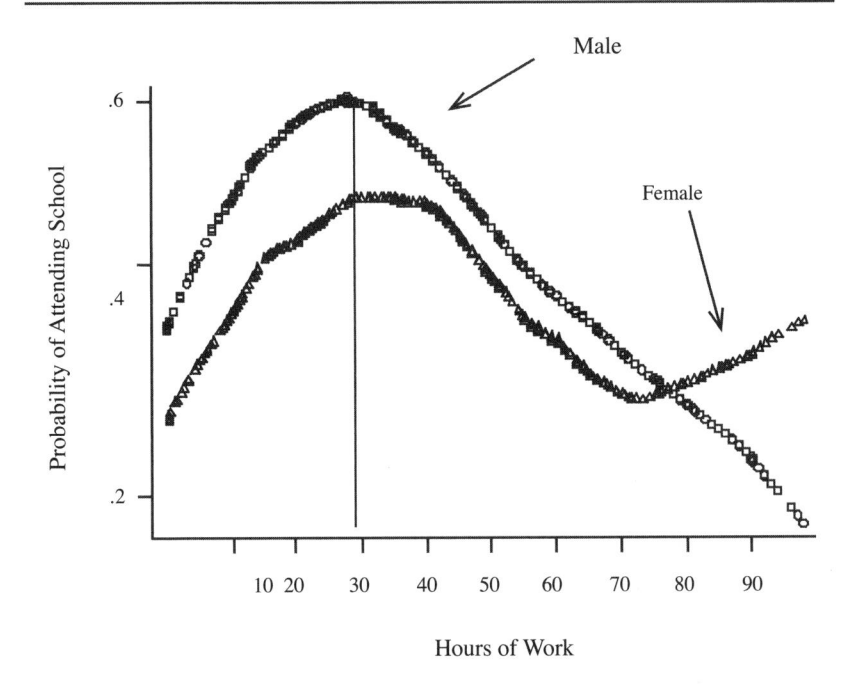

significant relationship between hours of work and schooling/RWA. The magnitude of the variable indicates that a ten-hour increase in work effort is associated with a 2–4 percentage point decline in school attendance and reading and writing ability.[18]

As displayed in Figure 6.5, we detect a non-linear relationship between hours of work and school attendance/RWA. Taking a cue from these estimates we re-estimate a probit model with a quadratic specification of the hours of work variable. The results are consistent with the patterns displayed in the figures. There is a clear non-linear relationship between hours of work and school attendance. According to the probit estimates (Probit-2), initially there is a positive relationship between hours of work and school attendance/RWA. This positive effect declines gradually, and beyond a certain threshold additional work effort is associated with declining school participation/RWA. According to our estimates, the inflexion point occurs between 16–22 hours of work for reading and writing ability and between 24–31 hours of work for school attendance. The non-linear relationship and different thresholds suggests that a work effort of about two hours a day does not interfere with the formal human capital development of a child. Beyond this threshold, and between a daily workload of two-to-three hours a day, a child's school performance will likely suffer. A workload of more than three hours a day may be expected to hinder school performance and attendance. An alternative way of interpreting the threshold effect is to consider the position of the 16-hour threshold in the distribution of the hours of work variable. We find that 60 per cent of the children in our sample provide more than 16 hours of work; thus, working may have a negative impact on the school performance and attendance for at least 60 per cent percent of children in rural Ethiopia.

As discussed earlier, if work and schooling are endogenous, then single-equation probit estimates will be misleading. For example, if unobserved variables which influence schooling are negatively correlated with hours of work, then the probit estimates presented in Table 6.7 will be overestimates of the negative effect of work on schooling. To account for the potential endogeneity we use the two-stage conditional maximum likelihood (2CML) approach sketched above.

Table 6.7 presents three sets of estimates based on the 2CML approach. These estimates rely on different identification strategies.[19] For all three sets of estimates the coefficient λ on the endogeneity correction term is usually negative and statistically insignificant. This pattern of results suggests that schooling and hours of work are not simultaneously determined. Of course, lack of precision and the inability to detect an endogenous relationship may lie in the poor quality of the instruments. Notwithstanding the statistical insignificance, the negative sign on the coefficient supports the idea that probit estimates which do not correct for endogeneity exaggerate the negative effect of work on schooling. Accordingly, the estimates which we present in columns Probit-1 and Probit-2 err on the side of caution and may be thought of as providing estimates of the lowest threshold at which work may begin to interfere with school performance and school attendance.

So far we have been concerned with the effect of the total number of hours of work on school attendance and RWA. It is possible that, among the five broad types of work activities for which we have information, some are more harmful than others. To examine this possibility, one approach is to re-estimate the schooling models with the inclusion of a disaggregated set of five hours-of-work variables. A comprehensive assessment of the differential effect of work-type requires us to examine the endogeneity between each type of work and schooling. While data requirements preclude such a comprehensive approach, we can still provide an idea of the effects of the different types of work. Figure 6.6 presents loess estimates of the bivariate relationship between school attendance and each type of work activity.

The various components of Figure 6.6 reveal some clear-cut patterns. The clearest effect is that for both males and females, herding activities and

Figure 6.6   Probability of Attending School by Work Activity

a. Fetching Water and Wood

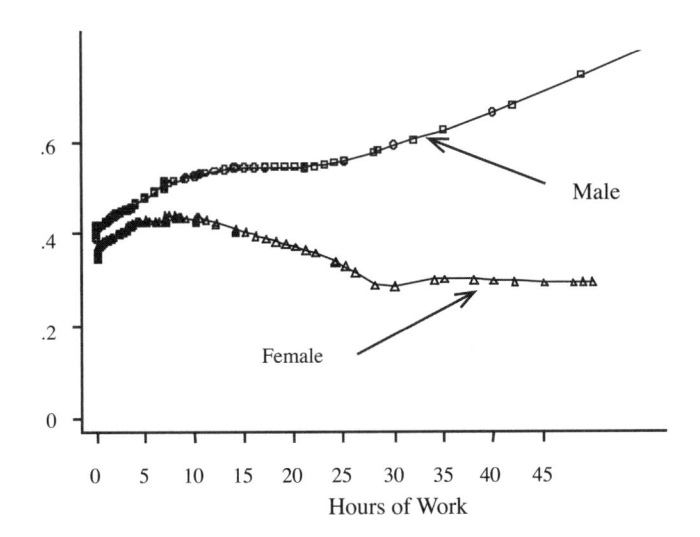

b. Farm Work

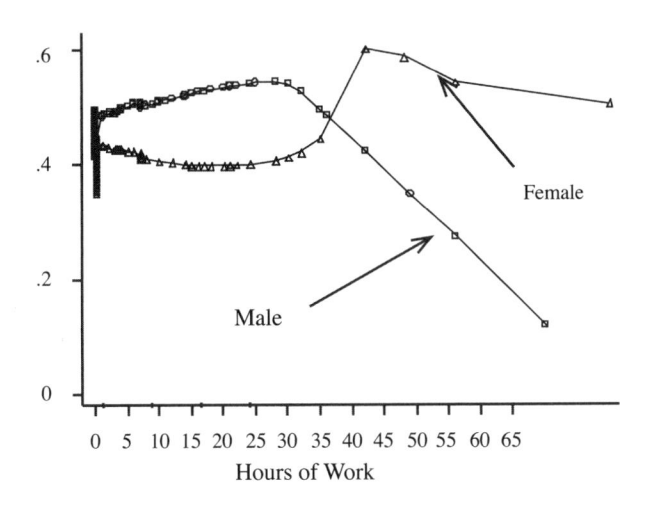

218   *Economic Reform in Developing Countries*

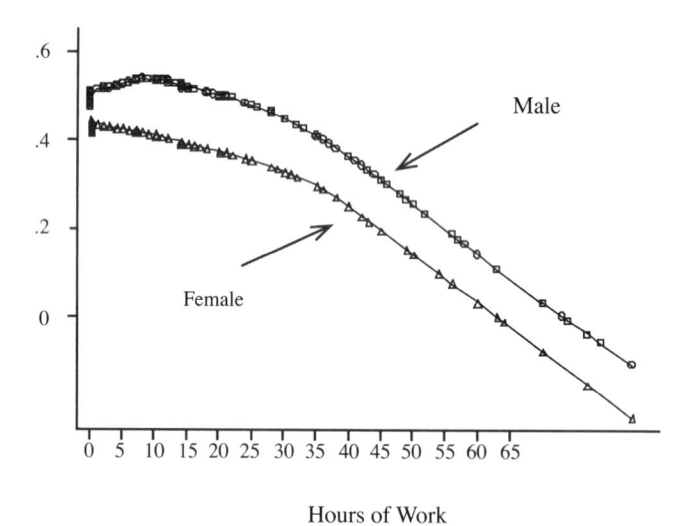

Figure 6.6   (continued)

c. Domestic Tasks

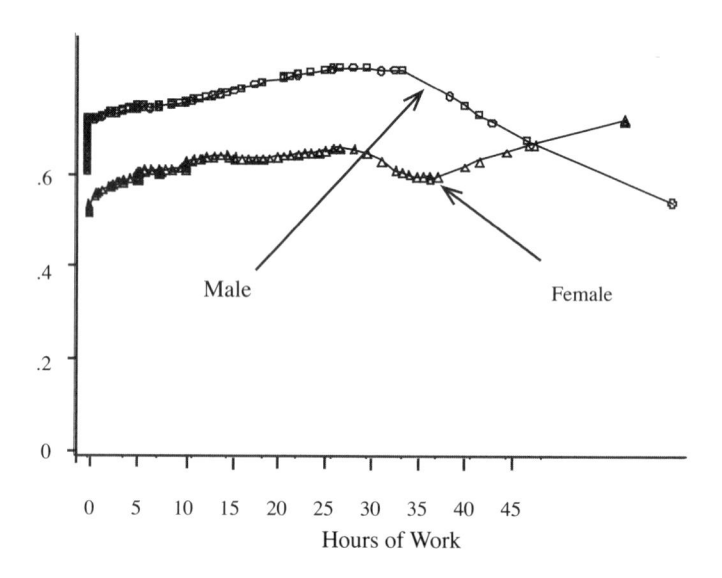

d. Herding

Figure 6.6 (continued)

e. Child Care

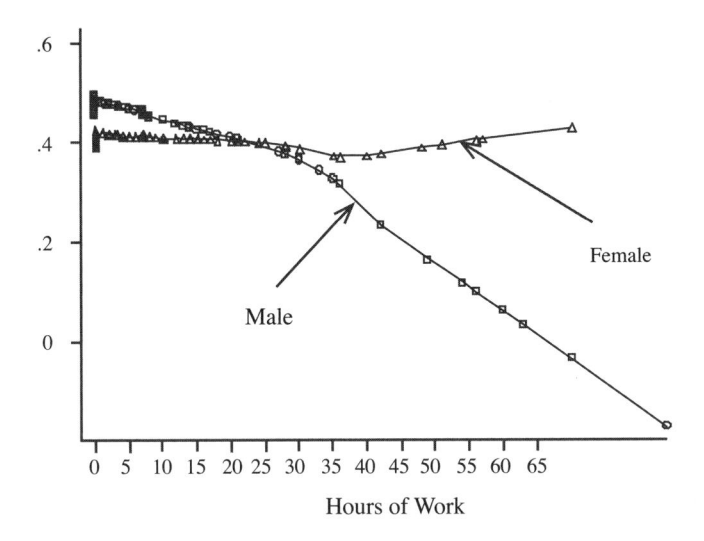

[Chart: Child Care — Hours of Work (x-axis: 0 to 65) vs. values (y-axis: 0 to .6), with Male and Female curves labeled]

Hours of Work

school attendance are unequivocally incompatible. There is a negative and approximately linear relationship between hours of work spent on herding and schooling. Consistent with the overall effect of hours of work, the effect of farm work is non-linear. Up to a certain threshold there is a positive relationship which gradually becomes negative. The effect is far clearer for boys than for girls. The effect of child care on school attendance is negative for the total sample. Once again, the effect is pronounced for boys but unclear for girls. For the other types of work activities the effects on schooling are not very distinct. Domestic work and schooling appear to be uncorrelated, while there appears to be a positive link between schooling and fetching wood and water.[20]

CONCLUSION

Child labor is a sensitive and controversial issue. What constitutes child labor, what is the best way to address it and its consequences are hotly debated topics. Although the highest incidence of child labor is found in Sub-Saharan Africa, studies on child labor on the continent are limited and sketchy. To fill some of the gaps in the literature, this chapter takes advantage of a recently collected dataset which contains a module specially designed to gather information on the work activities of children in the 4–15 age group. This new information allowed us to address several issues of topical concern. First, we used the detailed data on children's time-use patterns to provide an idea of the incidence and intensity of child labor in rural Ethiopia. Second, we assessed the factors responsible for determining the allocation of child time to schooling and work. Third, we examined the consequences of child labor on school attendance and the reading and writing ability of children.

Participation

We began our analysis by establishing the patterns of the child labor force and schooling participation among Ethiopian children. Although not entirely unexpected, labor-force participation in rural Ethiopia is very high. We found that as early as four years of age about 21 per cent of children are involved in work activities and by the age of ten almost all children are involved in some form of work. On average children contribute 29–30 hours of work per week. While there are gender differences in the allocation of time to different types of work activities, with boys spending more time on herding and farm work and girls allocating more time to domestic chores, there are no differences in the total time allocated to work.

While the high intensity of work effort is striking, the low levels of school participation may be of greater concern. We found that only about 44 per cent of children in the age group seven to 15 attend school and about 40 per cent of the same age cohort is able to read and write. While both boys and girls shoulder the same workload, boys are far more likely to attend school than girls (47 per cent versus 40 per cent).

Our assessment of the factors responsible for school and work participation revealed that school-related measures such as school quality and price have a strong effect on schooling but have no impact on the allocation of time to work. Policies leading to improvements in the quality of education are likely to encourage school attendance but may not lead to a reduction in child work. Our analysis supports the idea that household schooling and work decisions should be viewed separately. It is quite likely that any increase in school participation induced by quality increases in education is likely to come from a reduction in leisure but not in work.

Technology

The impact of demand-side characteristics, such as the prevailing production technology, on child work is relatively unexplored in the African context. The government's ongoing extension program in Ethiopia focuses on spreading modern agricultural technology among Ethiopian farmers and may affect both agricultural productivity as well as the allocation of child time to work. In this study we examined the impact of the increasing availability of agricultural machinery, chemicals (pesticides and herbicides), fertilizers and improved seeds on child work. We found that the increased availability of agricultural machinery sharply reduces the demand for child labor. The impact of land-saving technologies such as fertilizers and improved seeds is ambiguous. In the short run, their presence was associated with an increase in the work burden. Whether labor-displacing technology such as machinery and chemicals is the best way to increase agricultural productivity is debatable. However, if the aim is to have an immediate and direct impact on child labor, then policies designed to spread the use of labor-saving technologies are most likely to achieve this goal.

Substitutes

The third issue that we examined in this chapter was whether schooling and work are substitutes. We used an indirect and direct approach to tackle this issue. Since variables which reflect the price or quality of schooling have no impact on child work, the indirect approach supported the idea that schooling and work are *not* substitutes. In contrast the direct approach led to a far more nuanced picture. We detected a non-linear relationship between duration of work and school attendance. Initially, there is a positive relationship between school attendance and RWA. However 16–22 hours of weekly work affects the reading and writing abilities of a child, while school attendance remains unaffected. Beyond this threshold RWA and school attendance suffer. Although data is limited, we were able to examine the links between five different types of work and school attendance. We found that herding, farm work and child care activities were incompatible with school attendance. On the other hand, domestic work and fetching wood and water did not appear to have a detrimental effect on schooling. While this conclusion is still tentative, what is clear is that with 60 per cent of children working more than 16 hours, formal human capital development of a majority of Ethiopian children is hindered.

Finally, the results presented here echo Sen's idea that the range of reforms must be carefully considered in order to bring about social change. Specifically, improving educational outcomes requires changes not only in educational but also agricultural policies which influence the working patterns of children and, through this impact, educational outcomes. An exclusive focus on educational policies as the 'magic bullet' to ensure that all children attend school would have missed the powerful influence of the demands placed on children as sources of productive labor.

The results pertaining to educational outcomes support the idea that a set of reform policies initiated in one area may have multiple positive effects. However, there should be no presumption that all policies and reform packages will have multiple positive effects. Indeed, this chapter shows that while child labor responds to changes in agricultural policies, it is not sensitive to changes in educational policy.[21] These differential effects highlight the idea that conventional wisdom may not always hold and that policymakers need to verify and carefully examine the potential effects of proposed policies and reform packages.

NOTES

1. Our aim is to detect whether the number of hours worked by children has an impact on their formal human capital development. In the rest of the chapter we use the terms child work and child labor to refer to the total number of hours worked by children. Our concept of work includes the time spent by children on five activities, that is, farming, domestic chores, child care, herding and fetching water/wood.
2. For an extensive set of references see Ray (2000).
3. The discussion here refers to school attendance and work. However, in the empirical work we consider the interaction between school attendance and work and the interaction between RWA and work.
4. Land available for cultivation is assumed to be exogenous. This is appropriate because in Ethiopia agricultural land is state property. Households are granted rights to cultivate land on a long-term basis and the market for leasing land is thin.
5. We do not have information on Y and thus treat Y as function of the vector of exogenous variables E. To the extent that the variables in this vector are not exogenous it is possible that the regression estimates are biased. While this is a possibility we have no reason to suspect that this is a potentially large problem.
6. The separation of the household's production decision (optimal child labor input in household production, L^{D*}) from its consumption decisions is a well-known feature of agricultural household models. As long as it is possible to hire in and hire out child labor without hindrance, it is predicted that household demand for child labor will be independent of household child labor supply.
7. The lack of a well-developed market for child labor may be attributed to the patterns of land-use in Ethiopia. Almost all households in rural Ethiopia have access to some agricultural land and there do not appear to be sharp inequalities in land-use rights. Less than half a percent of households in our sample have no access to land. The mean holding is about 1.32 hectares with a standard deviation of 1.08.
8. In the indirect approach the idea is to estimate these two equations and examine the effects of the price of schooling on schooling and hours of work. Schooling and hours of work will be substitutes if β_{L_p} is positive.
9. The University of Bonn's Center for Development Research only participated in the fifth round of the survey.
10. Kernel density estimates of hours of work show that the mode of the distribution occurs between 20–30 hour of work and that gender differences in the distribution of hours worked are minor. Formal statistical tests are unable to reject the null hypothesis of equality of the

distributions. The kernel density estimates are based on the Epanechnikov kernel and a width calculated using the Silverman (1986) optimal bandwidth formula. Deaton (1997) contains further details on kernel density estimation and a discussion on appropriate bandwidth and choice of kernels.

11. These graphs are based on estimating locally weighted sum of squares (lowess) regressions of hours of work on age (Figure 6.2) and participation on age (Figure 6.3). A bandwidth of 0.8 was used for obtaining the locally weighted regression smoother. Further details on lowess estimation are available in Deaton (1997).
12. In 1996 the primary school Gross Enrolment Rate (GER) in Ethiopia was 42.9 percent. This enrolment rate is quite low as compared to other countries in Eastern Africa and is amongst the lowest in the entire continent. For example, in 1996 the GER in Sudan was 50.9 percent, it was 66.1 per cent in Tanzania and 74.3 per cent in Uganda. Admassie (2000) provides educational statistics for other African countries.
13. Reading and writing pertains to the ability of a child to read and write in Amharic. The questionnaire asks respondents, usually the head of the household, to indicate whether a child can read, can write, can read and write or is illiterate. Respondents decide the category in which to place a child on the basis of their personal judgement and not on the basis of objective standards.
14. A traditional labor arrangement is a labor-exchange practice where households share the available household labor resources for farm work in a rotating manner. This practice allows households to fulfil their demand for labor, especially during the peak season.
15. In addition to OLS, we used a Tobit model and Powell's Censored Least Absolute Deviations (CLAD) Estimator to estimate the hours of work equation. Since labor-force participation is very high, differences between the OLS and Tobit estimates were not pronounced. These estimates are available on request.
16. An alternative specification would have been to use dummy variables to indicate whether a household uses a particular technology. However, we avoided this approach as the adoption and use of modern technologies may be endogenously determined with the number of hours of work.
17. In future work we plan to carry out an analysis of the long-run impact of fertilizers and improved seeds on child labor.
18. The estimates presented in Table 6.7 pertain to hours of work and school attendance. Results for hours of work and RWA are not presented as they are not substantially different from the work-school attendance estimates.
19. Identification of 2cml-1 is based on functional form differences. The specification of the schooling and work equations are exactly the same. The 2cml-2 method is based on including the intermediate input variables in the hours of work equation but excluding them from the schooling/RWA equations. 2cml-3 is based on excluding the intermediate input variables and the institutional variables (share cropping and labor sharing arrangements), and variables that reflect the quantity and quality of land (landholding, fertility of land, number of plots) from the schooling equation.
20. Exploratory regression analysis confirms these patterns. Herding, child care and farm work hinder the ability of boys to attend school while it is only time spent on herding that appears to have a negative impact on girls. Domestic work and collecting water and wood do not seem to have a detrimental effect on school attendance.
21. This result may seem unexpected but it is not unique. Ravallion and Wodon (2000) and

Hazarika and Bedi (2003) also find that child labour is 'sticky' and does not respond to changes in educational policies.

BIBLIOGRAPHY

Admassie, Assefa (2000), 'The Incidence of Child Labor in Africa with Empirical Evidence from Rural Ethiopia', University of Bonn, Center for Development Research (ZEF) Discussion Paper No. 32.

Admassie, Assefa (2001), 'Allocation of Children's Time Endowment between Schooling and Work in Rural Ethiopia', University of Bonn, Center for Development Research (ZEF) Discussion Paper No. 44.

Akabayashi, Hideo and George Psacharopoulos (1999), 'The Trade-Off Between Child Labor and Human Capital Formation: A Tanzanian Case Study', *Journal of Development Studies*, **35** (5), 120–40.

Amemiya, Takeshi (1984), 'Tobit Models: A Survey', *Journal of Econometrics*, **24** (1–2), 3–61.

Basu, Kaushik and Pham Hoang Van (1998), 'The Economics of Child Labor', *American Economic Review*, **88** (3), 412–27.

Bedi, Arjun S. and Jeffrey Marshall (2000) 'Primary School Attendance in Honduras', *Journal of Development Economics*, **69** (1), 129–53.

Bequelle, Assefa and Jo Boyden, eds. (1988), *Combating Child Labor*, Geneva: International Labor Organization.

Benjamin, Dwayne (1992), 'Household Composition, Labor Markets and Labor Demand: Testing for Separation in Agricultural Household Models', *Econometrica*, **60** (2), 287–322.

Blanc, Cristina Szanton (1994), *Urban Children in Distress: Global Predicaments and Innovative Strategies*, Langhorne, PA: Gordon and Breach.

Canagarajah, Sudharshan and Helen Skyt Nielsen (2001), 'Child Labor in Africa: A Comparative Study', *Annals of the American Academy of Political and Social Science*, **575** (1), 71–91.

Cartwright, Kimberly (1999), 'Child Labor in Colombia', in Christiaan Grootaert and Harry Anthony Patrinos (eds), *The Policy Analysis of Child Labor: A Comparative Analysis*, New York: St. Martin's, pp. 63–102.

Cartwright, Kimberly and Harry Anthony Patrinos (1999), in Christiaan Grootaert and Harry Anthony Patrinos (eds), *The Policy Analysis of Child Labor: A Comparative Analysis*, New York: St. Martin's, pp. 103–29.

Deaton, Angus (1997), *The Analysis of Household Surveys*, Baltimore: Johns Hopkins University Press.

Galbi, Douglas A. (1997), 'Child Labor and the Division of Labor in the Early English Cotton Mills', *Journal of Population Economics*, **10** (4), 357–75.

Glewwe, Paul and Hanan Jacoby (1994), 'Students' Achievement and Schooling Choice in Low Income Countries: Evidence from Ghana', *Journal of Human Resources*, **29** (3), 843–64.

Gronau, Reuben (1977), 'Leisure, Home Production, and Work: The Theory of the Allocation of Time Revisited', *Journal of Political Economy*, **85** (6), 1099–123.

Grootaert, Christiaan (1999), 'Child Labor in Cote d'Ivoire', in Christiaan Grootaert and Harry Anthony Patrinos (eds), *The Policy Analysis of Child Labor: A Comparative*

Analysis, New York: St. Martin's, pp. 23–62.
Grootaert, Christiaan and Ravi Kanbur (1995), 'Child Labor: An Economic Perspective', *International Labor Review*, **2** (134), 187–203.
Hazarika, Gautam and Arjun S. Bedi (2003), 'Schooling Costs and Child Work in Rural Pakistan', *Journal of Development Studies*, **39** (5), 29–64.
Heady, Christopher (2003), 'The Effect of Child Labor on Learning Achievement', *World Development*, **31** (2), 385–98.
Heckman, James J. (1974), 'Shadow Prices, Market Wages and Labor Supply', *Econometrica*, **42** (4), 679–94.
International Labor Organization (1996), 'Child Labor: What is to be Done? Document for Discussion at the Informal Tripartie Meeting at the Ministerial Level', Geneva, International Labor Organization, ITM/1/1996, 12 June.
—— (1997), *Economically Active Population, 1950–2010*, Geneva: International Labor Organization, Bureau of Statistics.
—— (1998), 'Child Labor: Targeting the Intolerable', 86th Session, International Laborr Conference, Geneva.
Jensen, Peter and Helena Skyt Nielsen (1997), 'Child Labor or School Attendance? Evidence from Zambia', *Journal of Population Economics*, **10** (4), 407–24.
Levy, Victor (1985), 'Cropping Pattern, Mechanization, Child Labor and Fertility Behavior in a Farming Economy: Rural Egypt', *Economic Development and Cultural Change*, **33** (4), 777–91.
Lieten, Kristoffel and Ben White (2001), 'Children, Work and Education', in Kristtoffel Lieten and Ben White (eds), *Child Labor: Policy Options*, Amsterdam: Aksant Academic Publishers.
Nieuwenhuys, Olga (1994), *Children's Lifeworlds*, New York: Routledge.
Patrinos, Harry Anthony and George Psacharopoulos (1997), 'Family Size, Schooling and Child Labor in Peru: An Empirical Analysis', *Journal of Population Economics*, **10** (4), 387–405.
Psacharopoulos, George (1997), 'Child Labor Versus Educational Attainment: Some Evidence from Latin America', *Journal of Population Economics*, **10** (4), 377–86.
Ravallion, Martin and Quentin Wodon (2000), 'Does Child Labor Displace Schooling? Evidence on Behavioral Responses to an Enrollment Subsidy', *Economic Journal*, **110** (462), C158–75.
Ray, Ranjan (2000), 'Analysis of Child Labor in Peru and Pakistan: A Comparative Study', *Journal of Population Economics*, 13 (1), 3–19.
Rivers, Douglas and Quang H. Vuong (1988), 'Limited Information Estimations and Exogeneity Tests for Simultaneous Probit Models', *Journal of Econometrics*, **39** (3), 347–66.
Rodgers, Gerry and Guy Standing (1981), 'The Economic Roles of Children: Issues for Analysis', in Gerry Rodgers and Guy Standing (eds), *Child Work, Poverty and Underdevelopment*, Geneva: International Labor Organization.
Rosenzweig, Mark R. and Robert Evenson (1977), 'Fertility, Schooling, and the Economic Contribution of Children in Rural India: An Economic Analysis', *Econometrica*, **45** (5), 1065–79.
Salazar, Maria Cristina (1988), 'Child Labor in Colombia: Bogota's Quarries and Brickyards', in Assefa Bequele and Jo Boyden (eds), *Combating Child Labor*, Geneva: International Labor Organization, pp. 49–60.
Silverman, B.W. (1986), *Density Estimation for Statistics and Data Analysis*, New York: Chapman and Hall.

PART THREE

Reason: Strategies, Not Slogans

7. Declining Primary School Enrollment in Kenya

Arjun Singh Bedi, Paul K. Kimalu, Damiano Kulundu Manda and Nancy Nafula

Investments in education are widely recognized as a key component of a country's development strategy. Increases in the quantity and quality of educational provision have been associated with a wide range of benefits, including enhanced productivity, reduced poverty, better income inequality, improved health and economic growth. Spurred by such evidence, governments in developing countries continue to devote a substantial fraction of their total expenditure to the education sector.

Kenya is no exception. Since independence, the government of Kenya has devoted a substantial portion of its resources to the education sector. Between 1991 and 2000, public expenditure on education accounted for 28.2 per cent of total government expenditure.[1] These investments have led to a comprehensive network of schools and resulted in an impressive expansion of coverage and access to education at all levels. Adult literacy rates have more than tripled from 20 per cent in 1963 to 76 per cent in 1997, and the average educational attainment of the working-age population (age 15–64) is now around six years (see Kimalu et al. 2001).

Despite these impressive gains, a variety of problems continue to hamper the Kenyan education system. In terms of achievement, mean scores in English and mathematics, as measured by the Kenya Certificate of Primary Education (KCPE), are about 50 per cent. With regard to efficiency, about 5–6 per cent of Kenyan primary school students drop out each year, and 15–16 per cent repeat grades; consequently, school completion rates are below 50 per cent.

While high dropout and repetition rates are causes of concern, a more troublesome trend appears to be the decline in school enrollment. These declines have overturned the gains in educational participation achieved in previous years. In particular, the gross primary school enrollment rate (GER) peaked at 115.2 per cent in 1980 and by 1999 had fallen to 86.9 per cent. Similarly the gross secondary school enrollment rate has declined from 29.4 to 21.5 per cent. As part of its poverty eradication plans the government of Kenya seeks to achieve universal primary education by 2015 and expected a 15 per cent increase in primary school enrollment from 1999 to 2005. Notwithstanding these targets, the declining pattern of primary school enrollment suggests that it may be difficult to achieve these aims.

In this chapter we assess the plausibility of various factors which may be responsible for the decline in primary school enrollment. In particular, we explore the impact of recent reforms in school cost-sharing policies, school inputs and curriculum design. Other factors, including school availability, the expected benefits of education and the spread of HIV/AIDS are also considered. We use macro-level temporal information and detailed household survey datasets to analyze mean enrollment patterns and enrollment rates across five expenditure quintiles.

The chapter illustrates Amatrya Sen's third and most important dimension of reform – reason. While reforms are required to improve access to education and the performance of the education sector, they need to be thought through fully and designed carefully. Reforms in cost-sharing or changes in curriculum need to be sensitive to differences in household wealth, income, geography and other context-specific factors if they are to be successful. As the chapter shows, a reliance on an aggregate, cross-section analysis fails to identify how school costs affect enrollment, whereas the use of pseudo-panel data which control for unobserved fixed effects and the use of data disaggregated by expenditure group reveal that school costs are a significant deterrent to enrollment, especially for the poor.

PRIMARY SCHOOL ENROLLMENT: AN ANALYTICAL FRAMEWORK

Drawing upon other studies, we created an analytical model tailored to our needs.[2] We start with the proposition that parents have to determine whether it is worthwhile to enroll their children in school. While attending school yields benefits, it comes at a cost. Direct and opportunity costs associated with school attendance lower the resources available for household consumption. This household choice may be cast in terms of utility functions. Assume that each household has a utility function defined over b and c, where b denotes the benefits associated with attending school and c is household consumption. Accordingly, household utility conditional on school attendance (denoted by subscript 1) is given as:

Declining Primary School Enrollment in Kenya

$$U_1 = U(b, c_1). \tag{7.1}$$

The associated budget constraint is:

$$y = c_1 + p, \tag{7.2}$$

where y is household income, and p represents the total cost associated with school attendance.

In a similar fashion the utility associated with not attending school may be defined by:

$$U_0 = U(c_0). \tag{7.3}$$

The budget constraint is $y = c_0$. Given the utility associated with both options, households choose the option which yields the highest utility. The solution to the unconditional utility maximizing problem is:

$$U^* = \max(U_1, U_0), \tag{7.4}$$

where U^* is the maximum utility. Alternatively, school attendance may be defined in terms of a dichotomous variable, a, where $a = 1$ if a child attends school and 0 otherwise. A child attends school ($a = 1$) if $U_1 > U_0$.

Empirical Specification

Since our purpose is to determine the factors which influence enrollment, we proceed by specifying linear forms of the conditional utility function.[3] For the schooling option:

$$U_1 = \beta_1 b + \beta_2 c + \varepsilon_1, \tag{7.5}$$

where the βs are coefficients to be estimated and ε_1 is assumed to be a mean zero, normally distributed error term with positive variance. Since $c_1 = y - p$, we may rewrite (7.5) to obtain:

$$U_1 = \beta_1 b + \beta_2 (y - p) + \varepsilon_1. \tag{7.6}$$

The utility function for the non-schooling option is:

$$U_0 + \beta_2 y + \varepsilon_0. \tag{7.7}$$

Thus, an individual attends school, i.e. $a = 1$ if $\beta_1 b - \beta_2 p + \varepsilon_1 - \varepsilon_0 > 0$. Hence, the probability of attending school may be written as:

$$\Pr[a = 1] = \Pr[\beta_1 b - \beta_2 p + \varepsilon_a > 0]. \qquad (7.8)$$

Assuming that the composite error term ε_a is normally distributed, we now have an estimable probit enrollment model.

Costs of Attending School

The total cost of sending a child to school includes direct (monetary) and opportunity costs. The available household survey data allow us to construct a measure of the direct costs of schooling. Detailed costs of sending a child to school are available for those attending school. These data are used to compute a district-wide average of the cost of attending school and is used as our measure of the direct cost of schooling.

Turning to opportunity costs, attending school reduces a child's availability for work inside and outside the home. If a child makes substantial contributions to family income or plays an important role in supporting other working members, then the opportunity cost of attending school is likely to be high, and this may curtail the attractiveness of the schooling option.[4] These opportunity costs and the value of a child's time will depend on personal characteristics (age, sex) and the value which parents place on a child's time. Since we do not directly observe opportunity costs, we allow such costs to depend on a vector of child and family characteristics.

Benefits of Attending School

Parents have to ascertain the total benefits associated with school attendance. The main benefit is likely to be the expected addition to a child's human capital. To capture this effect we need a measure of the human capital gains associated with school attendance. Expected test scores are often used to indicate the benefits derived from education. Since such scores are not available for the individuals in our dataset, we use district-wide average test scores from the KCPE examination as a measure of the expected benefits of attending school. These test scores are directly observable by parents and could provide a signal which parents may use to judge the value of schooling. Bedi and Marshall (1999, 2002) provide empirical evidence on the role played by expected test scores in determining educational choices.[5]

In addition to test scores, the quality of school inputs and curriculum likely play a role in determining the expected payoff from education. School inputs may influence enrollment decisions indirectly by influencing test scores (increasing the payoff associated with education) but may also have a direct impact on enrollment. We consider both possibilities in our empirical work.

In accordance with the discussion above, equation (7.8) may be adjusted and rewritten as:

$$Pr[a = 1] = F[\gamma_{SF}SF + \gamma_X X + \gamma_H H + \gamma_{SI} SI], \qquad (7.9)$$

where F represents the standard normal cumulative distribution function, SF represents school fees, X is a vector of child and family characteristics which influence the opportunity cost of enrollment, H is a measure of expected human capital gains, SI is a vector of school inputs and γ represents coefficients to be estimated.

EDUCATION IN KENYA: ENROLLMENT TRENDS

Since gaining independence in 1963, the Kenyan education system has witnessed several changes in structure and curriculum. In the prevailing system (8–4–4), primary education is supposed to start at the age of six and consists of eight years. This is followed by four years of secondary education, paving the way for higher education at a variety of technical institutes, polytechnics and universities. University education consists of a four-year cycle.

Based on data collected in 1997, the educational pyramid reveals that 44 per cent of the working-age population has not completed primary school, while 21 per cent of the working-age population has attained at least eight years of schooling and completed primary school. About 13.7 per cent has completed lower secondary education while 5 per cent has enrolled beyond lower secondary education and have at least ten years of education (see Kimalu et al. 2001).

Although our work focuses on primary school enrollment in the 1990s, it is illuminating to examine enrollment patterns over a longer time period. In 1970 the gross enrollment ratio (GER) in Kenya was 62 per cent, and there was a gap of 20 percentage points between males and females (see Table 7.1a). Due to a rapid expansion of educational availability and the introduction of free education for grades I to IV in 1974, enrollment grew rapidly. By 1980 the GER had reached a peak of 115 per cent, and the gender enrollment gap had narrowed to 10 percentage points. The first enrollment shock occurred between 1984 and 1985[6] and enrollment rates fell from 107 to 99 per cent. In 1989 there was a second shock, and the GER declined from 98 to 92 per cent. Thereafter, there was a gentler decline until the GER reached around 88 per cent

Table 7.1a Gross Primary School Enrolment Rates, 1970–89 (%)

Year	1970	1975	1980	1982	1984	1985	1986	1987	1988	1989
Total	62.1	103.9	115.2	112	107.1	99	98.1	98.2	96.5	98.2
Male	72.3	111.9	120.2	115.8	110.2	101.8	101	100.9	98.7	99.9
Female	51.8	95.9	110.1	112	103.9	96.1	95	95.4	94.4	96.3

Source: World Bank Africa Database 2001.

in 1993.[7] Since then rates have stabilized between 86 and 88 per cent. Despite variations in the overall GER, the gender gap has narrowed considerably, averaging 3–4 percentage points since 1989. There are substantial regional differences in enrollment rates. In 1990 the Central and Western provinces had the highest enrollment rates of around 104 per cent. The Northeastern province and Nairobi Province had the lowest enrollment rate of around 24 and 66 per cent, respectively. Enrollment there rates fell in nearly all provinces during the 1990s. The sharpest declines seem to have been experienced in Nairobi and the Central province (see Table 7.1b).[8]

EXPLAINING THE TRENDS

As outlined above, household choices concerning school enrollment are influenced by the costs and benefits associated with education. In particular, increases in the expected returns from attending school (directly or through provision of better school inputs) are likely to increase the probability of school enrollment. On the other hand, increases in school fees and increases in the opportunity cost of attending school are likely to reduce the probability of enrollment. In this section we consider various changes which may have altered the cost–benefit calculus and influenced enrollment patterns.

School Fees

The government introduced a formal cost-sharing system in 1988 which contributed to a significant enrollment decline in the 1990s. Under the new system the government only pays for teachers' salaries, while parents are required to pay for school uniforms, stationery, textbooks, instructional materials and other school equipment. They also must contribute to school construction and maintenance costs through *harambees* (fund-raising efforts). Although cost sharing as a formal policy was introduced in 1988, it already existed informally. Parents were already paying for school uniforms, textbooks and school maintenance. The real change was the re-introduction of school levies to meet the costs of school materials and instructional equipment.

The timing of this sudden increase in financial responsibilities is consistent with the sharp decline in enrollment rates between 1989 and 1990 at the national and regional levels. As displayed in Table 7.1b, Nairobi and the Central province witnessed the largest declines in enrollment rates, and they were also the provinces with the highest school fees as a ratio of per capita expenditure.

School Curriculum

Kenya's 8–4–4 education system was introduced in January 1985. Reformers sought to place more emphasis on acquiring vocational education in the last two years of primary schooling and throughout secondary school in order to produce self-reliant school leavers with a sound technical education. This placed a substantial financial burden on parents. Physical facilities for teaching, including workshops and home-science classrooms, had to be constructed to cater to the new curriculum. Financial responsibility for these facilities was placed on parents, school committees and the local community served by the school. The five additional subjects to be taught (an increase from six to 11 subjects) under this new curriculum also increased the financial requirements for textbooks. Furthermore, completion of the extended curriculum required children to spend considerably more time in school and increased the opportunity costs of schooling. The doubling of subjects, the additional time required and the financial requirements for constructing new facilities suggest that between 1984 and 1985, total costs of attending primary school may have increased by more than 100 per cent. This curriculum-induced price shock appears to be the main factor behind the first enrollment shock.

Apart from costs, the new curriculum also increased the burden on teachers and students.[9] A reduction in the expected benefits from attending school may manifest itself in a reduction in school participation. The reduction in learning due to the increased pressure of the new curriculum could have played a role in depressing enrollments in subsequent years. However, prima facie there were no reductions in indicators such as school completion rates or KCPE scores (see Table 7.2).[10]

School Inputs

There were some sharp changes in terms of educational inputs during this

Table 7.1b Gross Primary School Enrolment Rates 1990–99 (%)[a]

Year	1990	1991	1992	1993	1994	1995	1996	1997	1998	1999	Change (1990–99)	Cost (%)[b]
Total	92.19	91.40	91.54	87.84	88.49	86.80	86.44	87.61	88.80	86.91	−5.28	2.8
Male	94.16	93.30	93.07	88.83	89.13	87.35	87.33	88.61	89.36	88.11	−6.05	na
Female	90.21	89.40	90.00	86.84	87.83	86.25	85.54	86.60	88.24	85.71	−4.50	na
By province												
Coast	79.93	78.80	78.85	75.09	71.40	73.30	75.57	75.17	73.25	75.95	−3.98	1.85
Central	103.60	102.60	103.56	102.80	101.04	104.95	100.22	100.44	98.20	93.81	−9.80	5.03
Eastern	96.82	97.40	96.35	92.57	91.76	89.86	90.46	90.75	93.84	94.88	−1.94	1.90
Nairobi	66.32	65.30	64.57	50.46	61.47	60.65	58.91	57.12	56.87	54.07	−12.25	7.70
Rift Valley	91.73	90.90	89.53	82.35	83.93	83.32	84.01	85.35	86.68	86.94	−4.79	2.20
Western	104.08	103.00	103.90	100.53	101.65	100.46	99.88	100.33	103.4	100.31	−3.77	2.81
Nyanza	91.06	89.70	92.47	93.54	95.25	86.99	86.22	90.53	92.92	85.75	−5.31	2.28
Northeastern	23.84	22.70	21.80	16.57	21.64	14.94	20.99	24.57	24.83	26.30	+2.46	3.70

Notes:
[a] Enrolment rates are based on figures from the Ministry of Education, Science and Technology, Statistics Section, 1999.
[b] Cost is defined as the primary school fee as a percentage of per capita expenditure. These computations are based on data from the Welfare Monitoring Survey 1994.

Table 7.2 Primary School: Selected Statistics

Year	1990	1991	1992	1993	1994	1995	1996	1997	1998	1999
KCPE Scores[a]	na	na	na	337.6	330.3	na	340.9	na	na	340.6
English (%)[b]	49.9	50.3	50.0	49.2	48.3	48.0	na	na	na	na
Mathematics (%)	48.4	48.1	48.4	47.5	47.4	47.6	na	na	na	na
School Completion Rates (%)[c]	43.2	44.1	46.4	43.4	43.9	42.6	44.3	46.1	47.2	47.7
Trained–Untrained Teacher Ratio[c]	70.2	74.5	72.7	82.0	87.4	90.1	92.8	94.3	96.6	96.1
Student–Teacher Ratio	31.2	31.5	29.9	31.4	31.2	30.5	30.2	30.9	30.8	32.3
Student–Trained Teacher Ratio	44.4	42.2	41.1	38.3	35.7	33.8	32.6	32.8	31.9	33.6

Notes:
[a] Average KCPE scores out of a maximum of 700. Figures are from the Kenya National Examination Council 2000.
[b] Abagi (1997b)
[c] Figures are from the Ministry of Education, Science and Technology, Statistics Section 1999.

period. The ratio of trained to untrained teachers increased sharply from 70 per cent in 1990 to 96.6 per cent in 1998. Correspondingly, while the student–teacher ratio remained around 31–32 per cent, the student–trained teacher ratio fell from 44.4 to 33.6 per cent (see Table 7.2). The increase in the proportion of skilled teachers may be expected to lead to an increase in educational performance and increased educational participation.

Deolalikar (1998) points out that inadequacies in school equipment are one of the most important factors adversely affecting the quality of primary education in Kenya. Since the introduction of the cost-sharing system, parents have been responsible for supplying textbooks, and it is possible that the pupil–textbook ratio has fallen from the 17:1 reported in 1990 (see Kenya, Government of /UNICEF 1994). In any case, the unchanged educational performance of students, despite improvements in the observed quality of teachers, increases the possibility that the lack of other inputs or factors such as an overloaded curriculum may have reduced the expected benefits of attending school and reduced educational participation.

System Capacity

Another possible explanation for the decline in enrollment may lie in the capacity of the primary school system to absorb students. An increase in the primary school-going population coupled with small or no increases in the capacity of the education system would generate a decline in gross enrollment rates. Between 1990 and 1999 the primary school-age population increased by 15.4 per cent – from 5.85 million to 6.75 million. Over the same duration the number of primary schools grew by 18.5 per cent and the number of primary school classes grew by 17 per cent. These numbers suggest that system capacity is not a factor which inhibits enrollment growth. In fact, over this period, the comparatively lower growth rate of 8.9 per cent in the number of enrolled students led to a decline in average class size from 33 to 31.

Labor Market Conditions

One of the main benefits of acquiring education is the expected role education plays in enhancing employment and wage prospects. While Kenya enjoyed an annual average GDP growth rate of around 4.5 per cent between 1963 and 1989, the average annual growth rate between 1990 and 1999 was substantially lower at around 2.5 per cent. This decline in growth rates has been accompanied by a rapid increase in unemployment rates. Between 1989 and 1997 the unemployment rate rose from 6.5 per cent to 18 per cent. Except for individuals with a university education (8 per cent unemployment

Table 7.3 Labor Markets in Kenya: Selected Statistics

Year	1989[a]		1997[b]	
Unemployment rate (%)				
National	6.5		18	
By Education				
No education	na		21	
Grade 1–4	na		15	
Grade 5–8	na		19	
Secondary	na		19	
University	na		8	
Year	1996	1997	1998	1999
Informal sector (%)	61.1	63.6	65.9	68.3

Notes: Unemployment rates are for the age group 15–64.
[a]Figures are from the National Population Census.
[b]Authors' computations based on the 1997 Welfare Monitoring Survey.
[c]Figures from the 2002 Economic Survey.

in 1997) unemployment among individuals with other levels of education was not substantially different from uneducated individuals (see Table 7.3). The composition of employment has also undergone some changes in recent years. Due to declining growth rates and ongoing public sector reforms there has been a shift in employment from the formal to the informal or *jua kali* sector. In 1999, excluding small-scale farming, the informal sector accounted for around 68 per cent of total employment.

The limited employment prospects are matched by a decline in wage prospects. On the basis of their analysis of wages, Appleton et al. (1999) show that average real wages fell sharply between 1978 and 1995. Furthermore, earnings ratios between individuals who have completed at most primary school and uneducated individuals fell from 1.7 in 1978 to 1.4 in 1995. Private returns to education, especially for secondary education, have also recorded a sharp fall during this period. Overall, the reductions in employment prospects, formal sector employment and wage returns for educated individuals may have played a role in reducing the economic incentive to acquire education.

HIV/AIDS

The decline in educational participation during the 1990s appears to coincide with the increased spread of HIV and AIDS in Kenya. AIDS was first reported in Kenya in 1984 and between 1990 and 1999 the HIV prevalence rate increased

Table 7.4a HIV/AIDS Prevalence in Kenya (%): Per cent of HIV Positive Adults (15–49)

Year	1990	1991	1992	1993	1994	1995	1996	1997	1998	1999	2000
National	4.8	6.1	7.4	8.7	9.9	11.0	11.9	12.8	13.9	13.5	13.5
Urban	8.8	10.5	12.0	13.4	14.5	15.5	16.3	16.9	18.1	17.8	17.5
Rural	4.1	5.3	6.5	7.7	8.7	10.0	11.0	11.9	13.0	13.0	13.0

Source: National AIDS and Sexually Transmitted Diseases Control Program (NASCOP), 1999 and 2001 Economic Survey.

from 4.8 per cent to 13.5 per cent (see Table 7.4a). The prevalence of AIDS is considerably higher in urban areas (which is consistent with the greater decline in educational enrollment in urban areas) and adults, i.e. individuals between 15 and 49, account for around 94 per cent of the total number of HIV-positive individuals.

There are several ways in which the spread of HIV/AIDS may have an impact on the education sector (see Stover and Bollinger 1999). First, increased expenditure on health care or a reduction in household income due to the death of a parent may reduce a household's ability to pay school fees and force children to drop out of school. The death of a parent may also increase the opportunity cost of a child's time and result in reduced enrollment. Second, children may drop out of school if they contract the disease themselves. Third, the disease may reduce the supply of experienced teachers. In the Kenyan case, the most likely channels through which HIV/AIDS affects educational participation are a reduction in household income and the attendant increase in opportunity cost. Given that the disease mainly affects individuals older than 15 years, it is unlikely that the incidence of the disease among primary-school children is a major reason for the decline in educational participation.[11] As discussed above, from 1990 to 1998 there was an increase in the supply of skilled teachers, suggesting that the prevalence of HIV does not appear to affect the availability of skilled teachers.[12]

While it seems most likely that HIV/AIDS would have an impact through its effect on reducing household expenditure, empirical evidence of this effect is rather limited. On the basis of cross-country evidence from six African countries, Ainsworth, Beegle and Koda (2002) report that countries with higher HIV prevalence appear to have higher enrollment rates, suggesting that differences in educational policies probably play a far greater role in determining outcomes than the incidence of disease. From a within-country perspective, the same authors use data from a Demographic and Health Survey conducted

Table 7.4b AIDS Prevalence Rates among Pregnant Women and Gross Primary School Enrolment Rates in Sentinel Sites (%)

District, Province	HIV[a] prevalence 1990	Enrollment[b] rate 1990	HIV prevalence 1999	Enrollment rate 1999
Busia, Western	14.4	100.28	28.3	102.97
Garissa, North Eastern	4.0	26.54	6.3	22.16
Kajiado, Rift Valley	1.6	64.16	9.0	59.39
Kakamega, Western	9.1	102.13	12.3	96.02
Kisii, Nyanza	0.0	92.28	15.7	82.25
Kisumu, Nyanza	15.3	87.75	30.7	73.85
Kitale, Rift Valley	2.4	87.55	16.0	94.65
Kitui, Eastern	0.1	103.39	11.4	102.76
Mbale, Western	2.9	102.13	15.9	96.02
Meru, Eastern	0.0	84.29	30.0	78.56
Mombasa, Coast	12.0	73.52	14.3	62.01
Nairobi, Nairobi	10.5	66.32	16.7	54.07
Nakuru, Rift Valley	10.0	96.54	26.5	84.50
Nyeri, Central	2.8	107.02	13.7	90.34
Thika, Central	6.6	87.06	22.5	86.63
Tiwi, Coast	12.8	74.0	23.4	75.3
Correlation		−0.026		0.328
(p-value)		(0.925)		(0.214)

Sources:
[a]National AIDS and Sexually Transmitted Diseases Control Program (NASCOP).
[b]Ministry of Education, Science and Technology, Statistics Section.

between 1991 and 1994 in the Kagera region of Tanzania to examine the effect of adult mortality on primary school enrollment.[13] Their evidence does not suggest that the decline in enrollment rates in Tanzania is strongly associated with adult mortality. They show that, regardless of wealth, households cope with adult deaths by delaying the enrollment of young children (7–10) while maintaining the enrollment of older children (11–14).

In Kenya information on the prevalence of HIV/AIDS is based on a sentinel surveillance system for pregnant women. Each sentinel site represents a number of districts and a certain percentage of the adult population. Information on HIV prevalence among pregnant women and the percentage of the adult population represented by a particular site is used to make projections for the prevalence of HIV in the country's adult population. Table 7.4b presents information on

HIV prevalence rates across 16 sentinel sites, two of which are in rural areas. Our investigation of the link between enrollment rates and HIV prevalence is restricted by data availability and is limited to correlations between HIV prevalence rates (lagged HIV prevalence rates) and enrollment rates. Overall, we cannot detect any link between HIV/AIDS and enrollment.

Trends Reconsidered

In the preceding section we discussed several factors which may have had a bearing on the decline in school enrollment rates in the mid-1980s and early 1990. These factors may be operating simultaneously, and it is difficult to isolate relative effects of each of the possible factors using only descriptive statistics. However, on the basis of the preceding discussion it does seem that the first enrollment shock between 1984 and 1985 may be attributed to additional educational costs induced by the reform of the educational structure and curriculum. Similarly, the second enrollment shock between 1989 and 1990 also appears to be cost-driven and may be attributed to the re-introduction of school levies. Thereafter, the more gradual decline until 1993 may be driven by the reduction in expected gains (stagnant test scores, reduced employment opportunities). The capacity of the school system does not seem to impact enrollment rates. At the same time, there has been a substantial increase in the skill level of teachers during the 1990s, that should reduce the negative effects of other factors. On the basis of our limited information we were unable to draw any link between the spread of HIV and enrollment rates.

So far our discussion has been temporal in nature and has provided a broad sweep of enrollment patterns based on descriptive statistics. In the remainder of the chapter we use household survey data and regression analysis to provide a more detailed picture of enrollment patterns between 1992 and 1997. We try to pin down the relative importance of some of the factors which influence enrollment and examine their effects across expenditure groups.

APPROACH, DATA AND SPECIFICATION

Estimation Approach

Three Welfare Monitoring Surveys (WMS), conducted in 1992, 1994 and 1997, contain adequate information for estimation of equation (7.9). Following a well-established literature, we use a probit model to estimate equation (7.9) for each of the years which we have data. These cross-sectional estimates rely on spatial variation to identify the effect of the independent variables on enrollment. While such cross-section results provide clues on the temporal effects which changes in school costs and school inputs have on enrollment, they are not very convincing.

A far more convincing analysis of temporal changes in enrollment rates requires the use of panel data. Since panel data are not available, an alternative is to follow Deaton (1985) and use repeated cross-section datasets to construct a pseudo-panel dataset. Essentially, this approach consists of pooling information from the three surveys and constructing a panel dataset of district means.[14] We use the sample information in each of the three surveys to construct district-level means for the independent and dependent variables of interest. These district-level means for each year are stacked together to create a panel dataset at the district level. The relationship of interest, where the individual observations have been replaced by district means, may be represented by a linear equation:

$$E = X_t \beta + \varepsilon_t \qquad (7.10)$$

where E_t is the district sample mean of primary school enrollment, X_t is a vector of explanatory variables which are also measured as district sample means, ε_t is an error term and t is a single index that ranges from 1 to T (114) and is the product of the number of districts (38) and the number of surveys (three). Instead of levels, given that our aim is to establish whether changes in enrollment over time are correlated with changes in the dependent variable, a model in differences is more appropriate. Accordingly, our equation of interest is:

$$\Delta E_t = \Delta X_t \beta + \varepsilon_t \qquad (7.11)$$

In words, this equation relates changes in district primary-school enrollment means between 1992 and 1997 to changes in the district-level means of the independent variables between 1992 and 1997.

The district-level means underlying equations (7.10) and (7.11) are based on the sample of people living in a district and not on the entire population living in a district. Accordingly, the sample-based district means may be error-ridden estimators of the population-based district means. Deaton (1985; 1997) shows that, if techniques which account for measurement errors in the variables are used, the sample district means can be used as panel data for estimating relationships of interest.

The key advantage of supplementing the standard estimation of probit models for each year with estimates based on the differenced pseudo-panel dataset is that we can control for unobservable fixed effects. Differencing the data sweeps out time-invariant fixed effects and allows temporal changes in the independent variables to identify the parameters of interest. While the removal of fixed effects is a crucial advantage and should lead to more convincing estimates of price and input elasticities, it comes at a cost. First, since we are dealing with district means and not individual observations, we are unable to control for individual characteristics. Second, the fall in the number of observations when moving from the individual to the district as the unit of observation supports the estimation of very parsimonious specifications.

Overall, in order to tackle the issues of interest in the most comprehensive manner, we present estimates based on the cross-section data as well as estimates based on the pseudo-panel dataset.

Data

Three Welfare Monitoring Surveys (WMS) have been conducted in Kenya. These were carried out in 1992, 1994 and 1997. The remainder of this study is based on datasets which have been created by combining information from these surveys and district-level information for the same year. The district-level data were obtained from the Kenyan Ministry of Education. The WMS contain information on about 10,000 households and over 50,000 individuals from almost all districts in Kenya. These multipurpose surveys contain information on a variety of dimensions, including consumption, child health, fertility and other individual and family characteristics. The surveys also contain detailed information on the education of all household members, including expenditures on education. These individual and household data were merged with district-level information on school inputs. The combined datasets allow us to explore the role of demand and supply-side variables in determining enrollment.[15]

While combining the three WMS with district datasets permits a more complete analysis, there are some data-related drawbacks which need to be pointed out. First, the school input measures are district-level averages and therefore ignore any variation in school inputs within schools in the same district. The limited variation in the school-input data probably affects the standard error of our estimates and reduces their precision. On the other hand, a potential advantage of using average school-input data is that such variables are less likely to be endogenous. While parents may be able to choose the school that their children attend, it is less likely that they can influence district-wide school inputs.

Second, it may be argued that school inputs are correlated with unobserved differences across districts, in other words, the district-level school input/cost variables may be capturing district fixed effects. While we do include regional fixed effects to partially account for the latter objection, including a full set of district effects and a set of district school inputs is not possible in our cross-section work. However, as discussed below, to tackle the potential problem of biased estimates due to time-invariant fixed effects, we construct a panel dataset of district means and allow differences in school costs and school inputs over time to identify the parameters of interest. This estimation approach based on differenced data allows us to sweep out district fixed effects.

Third, while the availability of three WMS permits a more detailed analysis, differences across these surveys in the questionnaires, the time of the year during which the surveys were conducted and differences in geographical coverage hinders temporal comparisons. For example, the 1992 survey has no information on the gender of children. Furthermore, the limited information on the gender of other household members prevents us from linking parents to their children. The surveys were conducted at different times of the year. The 1992 survey was carried out between November and December, the 1994 survey was carried out in June and July, while the 1997 survey was conducted in August and September.[16] In terms of geographical coverage, the WMS 1994 is comprehensive and nationally representative, while the surveys conducted in 1992 and 1997 exclude the North Eastern province and Turkana, Marsabit and Samburu districts. While these districts are thinly populated, they are among the poorest districts in Kenya, and their exclusion prevents the composition of a national picture.[17]

From the preceding discussion it is clear that the data are subject to errors. Despite these shortcomings, we believe that careful use of the data while acknowledging its drawbacks is the best possible way to proceed. Accordingly, in our analysis we attempt to use the three datasets as fully as possible.

Enrollment – Full Sample and by Expenditure Quintiles

We begin by presenting three measures of enrollment calculated on the basis of the three WMS. We present the gross enrollment rate (GER), the net enrollment rate and enrollment rates based on the variable (ever attended school) which we use as the dependent variable in our regression analysis. Estimates based on the full sample are presented in Table 7.5, while Table 7.6 presents enrollment estimates based on the 'ever attended school' variable by expenditure quintiles. There are several noticeable features about these figures. Gender differences in enrollment are minor across the entire sample. Enrollment figures controlling for expenditure show that while gender differences are higher among poorer households, the gap is not very large and it appears to decline over time. In 1994 gender differences at the lowest quintile were about 3 percentage points in favor of boys. This gap fell to about 1 percentage point in 1997.

In terms of temporal trends, according to the Ministry of Education (MOE) data, GER declined between 1992 and 1994 and remained relatively stable

Table 7.5 Primary Education Participation Rates, 1992–97 (Standard Errors)

	1992	1994 Full sample	1994 Restricted sample[b]	1997
Gross enrollment rates (%)[a]				
Total	102.1	94.9	98.5	106.5
	(0.009)	(0.010)	(0.009)	(0.009)
Male	na	95.7	99.3	107.7
		(0.011)	(0.010)	(0.012)
Female	na	94.0	97.7	105.4
		(0.013)	(0.012)	(0.010)
Net enrollment rates (%)				
Total	82.9	77.7	80.6	86.9
	(0.007)	(0.008)	(0.007)	(0.006)
Male	na	78.8	81.7	86.6
		(0.008)	(0.008)	(0.008)
Female	na	76.5	79.5	87.2
		(0.009)	(0.009)	(0.007)
Ever attended school (%)				
Total	85.1	81.8	84.9	90.3
	(0.006)	(0.007)	(0.006)	(0.005)
Male	na	82.7	85.8	90.4
		(0.008)	(0.006)	(0.006)
Female	na	81.0	84.0	90.2
		(0.008)	(0.007)	(0.006)

Notes:
[a] Authors' computations based on Welfare Monitoring Surveys conducted in 1992, 1994 and 1997.
[b] To enable comparisons across the three years, estimates based on the 1994 restricted sample exclude individuals living in areas where the survey was not conducted in 1992 and 1997.

thereafter. The WMS support a pattern of declining GER between 1992 and 1994 but display a sharp increase thereafter. The net enrollment rate and the ever attended school variable record a similar pattern. Although smaller in magnitude, there is a pattern of decline between 1992 and 1994 and a sharp pickup thereafter. Temporal enrollment patterns by expenditure quintiles show that between 1994 and 1997 enrollment increased across all expenditure quintiles. The increases for the bottom 40 per cent of households were about 3–4 percentage points, while for the top three quintiles the gains ranged between 6–7 percentage points. Thus, despite the overall increase, enrollment

Table 7.6 Ever Attend School by Expenditure Quintiles, 1992, 1994 and 1997 (standard errors)

		1992	1994 Full sample	1994 Restricted sample	1997
Total	Quintile 1	81.6	74.9	80.6	85.0
		(0.013)	(0.015)	(0.011)	(0.011)
	Quintile 2	83.7	79.4	83.7	87.5
		(0.012)	(0.012)	(0.011)	(0.009)
	Quintile 3	85.3	82.5	85.1	91.6
		(0.010)	(0.011)	(0.011)	(0.008)
	Quintile 4	86.4	84.7	86.7	92.5
		(0.013)	(0.009)	(0.009)	(0.007)
	Quintile 5	88.5	87.0	88.7	95.1
		(0.013)	(0.010)	(0.010)	(0.008)
Male	Quintile 1		76.4	82.1	85.5
			(0.017)	(0.013)	(0.014)
	Quintile 2		80.6	84.8	88.0
			(0.014)	(0.013)	(0.011)
	Quintile 3		82.6	85.3	91.3
			(0.013)	(0.012)	(0.010)
	Quintile 4		86.9	88.8	92.4
			(0.011)	(0.010)	(0.009)
	Quintile 5		86.6	88.5	95.2
			(0.013)	(0.014)	(0.008)
Female	Quintile 1		73.2	79.1	84.4
			(0.018)	(0.014)	(0.013)
	Quintile 2		78.3	82.5	87.1
			(0.015)	(0.015)	(0.011)
	Quintile 3		82.4	84.9	91.9
			(0.015)	(0.015)	(0.010)
	Quintile 4		82.5	84.4	92.5
			(0.013)	(0.014)	(0.009)
	Quintile 5		87.4	89.0	94.8
			(0.014)	(0.012)	(0.010)

Note: To enable comparisons across the three years, estimates based on the 1994 restricted sample exclude individuals living in areas where the survey was not conducted in 1992 and 1997.

Table 7.7 Selected Descriptive Statistics, 1992–97

	1992 Mean	1992 (Std. Dev.)	1994 Full sample Mean	1994 Full sample (Std. Dev.)
Child characteristics				
Age	10.27	(2.83)	9.99	(2.85)
Male = 1	na		0.510	(0.499)
Order of birth	3.278	(1.717)	3.373	(1.659)
Family characteristics				
Father's schooling	na		5.83	(4.33)
Mother's schooling	na		4.45	(4.14)
Land per capita (acres)	na		0.823	(9.253)
House owner = 1	0.757	(0.428)	0.882	(0.322)
Number of rooms in house	2.617	(1.509)	2.557	(1.513)
Educational characteristics				
Total expenditure on primary education (Shillings per month, current)	52.51	(27.52)	81.62	(71.34)
Total expenditure on primary education (Shillings per month, 1992 prices)	52.51	(27.52)	43.65	(38.15)
Total expenditure on primary education/ per capita consumption (%)	13.04	(0.334)	9.57	(0.352)
Expenditure on primary education[b]	29.27	(19.3)	52.2	(60.6)
Primary education test scores (Max. = 700)	347.89	(22.34)	338.73	(29.47)
Pupil–teacher ratio	31.90	(3.33)	31.91	(5.64)
Teacher, skill level 1 (%)	4.15	(2.03)	5.00	(2.32)
Teacher, skill level 2 (%)	51.2	(7.95)	58.35	(9.17)
Teacher, skill level 3 (%)	22.7	(3.33)	23.87	(5.73)

Notes:
[a]To enable comparisons across the three years, estimates based on the 1994 restricted sample exclude individuals living in areas where the survey was not conducted in 1992 and 1997.
[b]Measure of educational expenditure used in the regressions.

differences between the poorest 40 per cent of households and the richer households increased. For example, the enrollment gap between the richest and the poorest quintiles increased from 6.9 percentage points in 1992 to 10.1 percentage points in 1997.

Table 7.7   (continued)

	1994 Restricted sample[a]		1997	
Variable	Mean	(Std. Dev.)	Mean	(Std. Dev.)
Child characteristics				
Age	10.00	(2.84)	10.26	(2.86)
Male = 1	0.508	(0.499)	0.508	(0.499)
Order of birth	3.359	(1.645)	2.918	(1.533)
Family characteristics				
Father's schooling	6.14	(4.22)	6.30	(4.22)
Mother's schooling	4.71	(4.11)	4.93	(3.99)
Land per capita (acres)	0.863	(9.532)	0.565	(1.238)
House owner = 1	0.879	(0.325)	0.871	(0.334)
Number of rooms in house	2.628	(1.518)	2.670	(1.318)
Educational characteristics				
Total expenditure on primary education (Shillings per month, current)	82.29	(73.22)	97.60	(118.67)
Total expenditure on primary education (Shillings per month, 1992 prices)	44	(39.15)	42.25	(51.37)
Total expenditure on primary education/ per capita consumption (%)	9.52	(0.365)	7.06	(0.092)
Expenditure on primary education[b]	52.8	(63.8)	70.2	(95.7)
Primary education test scores (Max. = 700)	341.38	(24.89)	345.52	(25.96)
Pupil–teacher ratio	31.65	(4.62)	31.64	(4.83)
Teacher, skill level 1 (%)	5.05	(2.19)	9.54	(3.97)
Teacher, skill level 2 (%)	59.76	(6.32)	65.01	(5.58)
Teacher, skill level 3 (%)	23.00	(3.85)	19.7	(4.54)

While the increase in enrollment after 1994 may seem surprising, it appears to be consistent with temporal patterns in school expenses and school inputs. Descriptive statistics presented in Table 7.7 show that total school expenses (in current prices) increased from about 53 shillings per month in 1992 to 98 shillings a month in 1997. However, in real terms there are no increases in expenditure (see Table 7.7) and educational expenses as a proportion of per capita consumption declined from 13 per cent in 1992 to about 7 per cent in 1997. These numbers display a clear increase in the affordability of primary education. Over the same time period, there is a sharp increase in the skill levels of teachers. Consistent with the patterns in Table 7.1, there is an increase in the proportion of teachers at skill levels 1 and 2 and a decline in the number of teachers at lower skill levels.[18] The numbers suggest a clear government policy of upgrading the skill level of teachers while keeping the total number of teachers fixed. The increase in the skill level of teachers and the increase in the affordability of education are consistent with increasing school enrollment.

A final point which needs to be highlighted is the sharp difference between the level of the GER presented in Table 7.5 and the GER based on the MOE data. The gross enrollment rates presented here are considerably higher than the GER presented in Table 7.1. Calculations based on the WMS 1992 yield a GER of 102 per cent, while the corresponding figure obtained from the MOE is about 10 percentage points lower. For 1994 the WMS yield a GER of 95, while the MOE figure is 7 percentage points lower at 88 per cent.[19] For 1997 the gap is larger. The WMS yield a GER of about 106 while the MOE figure is about 88.

A possible explanation for the differences between the two sets of numbers is school coverage. While the MOE figures are restricted to students enrolled in public schools, the household surveys include students enrolled in all schools – public and private. If there was a shift in enrollment from public to private schools it would show up as a decline in enrollment according to the MOE figures. While this is a possible explanation, the existing information on enrollment in private schools suggests that the gap between the two sets of numbers is too large to be explained by private school enrollment (see footnote 10). Having said that, the existing information on private schools is limited, and further assessment of enrollment in private schools is required before the proposed explanation can be verified.

Specification

Our analysis is restricted to children in the age group 6 to 15 years.[20] Depending on the specification, our regressions are estimated over samples ranging from 10,108 observations to 13,510 observations. The dependent variable in our analysis is whether a child has ever attended school. Children who are currently in school and children who had enrolled in school but have subsequently dropped out provide a positive response to this question.[21] The specification of the independent variables follows equation (7.9).

Vector X corresponds to a set of child and family variables. The child-specific variables include age, sex (except for 1992) and birth order. The average child in our samples is 10 years old and there is an even split between males and females. Family characteristics include maternal and paternal years of schooling (except for 1992), and three indicators of household wealth: whether a family owns its dwelling, the number of rooms in the house and the amount of land per capita which the household possesses. Across the three surveys, average schooling of fathers is about six years and for mothers about five years. The average house has three rooms and home ownership is substantial at 78–88 per cent. A noteworthy feature of these variables is that, except for statistically significant differences in landholding per capita (0.9 acres in 1994 and 0.6 in 1997), the means of all the other variables are stable.[22]

Corresponding to *SF*, our measure of school costs consists of household expenditure on school fees, school uniforms, transport and boarding. We exclude other elements of school expenditure as they may contain a discretionary element (endogenous) and could obscure the relationship between school costs and enrollment. The measure of school costs which we use in the regressions is displayed in Table 7.7. As the table shows, the measure of school costs used in our regressions is considerably smaller than the total school costs, that also include expenditure on textbooks, individual tutorials and *harambee* contributions. In terms of the individual expenditure components, in 1992 and in 1994 school uniforms account for the largest share (28–29 per cent), followed by school fees (26–27 per cent), textbooks (21–23 per cent) and *harambee* contributions (13–21 per cent). In 1997 the breakdown was somewhat different, with school fees accounting for 51 per cent of total expenditure followed by expenditure on books (20 per cent) and uniforms (17 per cent).

The average district score on the KCPE examination is included in an attempt to capture the expected benefits of attending school (*H*). If parental decision making is responsive to the expected benefits of attending school, then this variable should exert a positive influence on enrollment (see Bedi and Marshall 2002). The *SI* vector consists of the pupil–teacher ratio, and three variables which represent different levels of teacher qualifications. The average pupil–teacher ratio is around 32 and remains at the same level across the three years under consideration. In terms of international comparisons this ratio is not high (UNESCO 1999). The composition of skilled teachers shows a substantial increase in the level of skilled teachers over the three years. In 1992, the composition of skilled teachers (defined in terms of educational qualifications) consists of around 4 per cent at the highest level, followed by 51 per cent at level two and 23 per cent at level three. The corresponding numbers in 1997 are 9, 65 and 20 per cent.

In terms of geographical spread, more than 90 per cent of the sample lives in rural areas. Accordingly, we do not estimate separate specifications for rural and urban areas and, given the rural-urban composition, our results should be viewed as applicable mainly to rural areas.

Table 7.8 Marginal Effects based on Probit Estimates of Primary School Enrollment, 1992, 1994 and 1997 (Standard Errors)

Variable	1992 (1)	1994 Full sample (2)	1994 Restricted sample (3)
Child characteristics			
Age	0.202*	0.193*	0.159*
	(0.013)	(0.011)	(0.011)
Age squared	−0.008	−0.007*	−0.006*
	(0.0006)	(0.0005)	(0.0005)
Male	na	0.019*	0.014**
		(0.007)	(0.006)
Order of birth	0.004	−0.005***	−0.005***
	(0.003)	(0.003)	(0.003)
Family characteristics			
Father's schooling	na	0.010*	0.007*
		(0.001)	(0.001)
Mother's schooling	na	0.011*	0.009*
		(0.001)	(0.001)
Land per capita	na	−0.001*	−0.001
		(0.0004)	(0.0008)
Home ownership	−0.006	−0.019	−0.021
	(0.020)	(0.022)	(0.017)
Number of rooms in house	0.021*	0.021*	0.016*
	(0.004)	(0.005)	(0.004)
Educational characteristics			
School costs*100	−0.08	−0.06**	−0.04**
	(0.07)	(0.03)	(0.02)
Time taken to reach school	na	na	na
KCPE Score*100	0.01	0.06**	0.04
	(0.05)	(0.03)	(0.03)
Pupil–teacher ratio*100	0.3	−0.002	−0.004
	(0.2)	(0.12)	(0.1)
Teacher, skill level 1 (S1)*100	1.6 *	0.7	0.5
	(0.6)	(0.5)	(0.5)
Teacher, skill level 2 (P1)*100	−0.05	0.4*	0.4*
	(0.15)	(0.08)	(0.1)
Teacher, skill level 3 (P2 & P3)*100	0.06	0.2	0.4*
	(0.2)	(0.2)	(0.1)
Number of observations	10,108	13,306	10,967
Log likelihood value	−3207.01	−4234.77	−3230.42

Table 7.8 (continued)

Variable	1997 (4)	1997 (5)
Child characteristics		
Age	0.020*	0.020*
	(0.0014)	(0.001)
Age squared	0.0001*	0.0001*
	(0.00003)	(0.00003)
Male	0.002	0.0025
	(0.003)	(0.003)
Order of birth	−0.003***	−0.002***
	(0.002)	(0.0014)
Family characteristics		
Father's schooling	0.005*	0.005*
	(0.001)	(0.001)
Mother's schooling	0.004*	0.004*
	(0.001)	(0.001)
Land per capita	0.004**	0.005***
	(0.002)	(0.0025)
Home ownership	0.036**	0.042**
	(0.021)	(0.023)
Number of rooms in house	0.010*	0.009*
	(0.002)	(0.002)
Educational Characteristics		
School Costs*100	0.01	0.01
	(0.1)	(0.01)
Time taken to reach school	na	−0.8*
		(0.2)
KCPE Score*100	0.04*	0.04*
	(0.01)	(0.01)
Pupil–teacher ratio*100	−0.03	−0.04
	(0.07)	(0.07)
Teacher, skill level 1 (S1)*100	0.01	0.02
	(0.1)	(0.1)
Teacher, skill level 2 (P1)*100	0.16***	0.17***
	(0.1)	(0.09)
Teacher, skill level 3 (P2 & P3)*100	−0.1	−0.09
	(0.1)	(0.13)
Number of observations	11,229	11,229
Log likelihood value	−2675.09	−2653.70

Notes: Dependent Variable = 'Has individual ever attended school?'. All specifications include a set of seven provincial indicators and an urban–rural indicator. The educational characteristics are district averages. Standard errors are heteroscedasticity consistent and corrected for the clustered design of the sample. To enable comparisons, estimates based on the 1994 restricted sample exclude individuals living in areas where the survey was not conducted in 1997. *significant at 1 per cent level; ** significant at 5 per cent level; *** significant at 10 per cent level.

RESULTS

We begin by presenting estimates of school enrollment probit equations based on each of the three WMS. This is followed by estimates of a school enrollment probit equation based on pooled data and estimates of an enrollment equation based on the district-level panel dataset. The year-specific estimates permit an examination of patterns in the effects of the independent variables on the enrollment decision and provide an idea of the robustness of the results. The advantage of estimates using pooled data and the pseudo-panel data are that variations over time and across space are used to identify the effect of the school input and school cost variables on enrollment.

In addition to the probit estimates, we present price and school input elasticities. These elasticity estimates are presented for the full sample and for five per capita expenditure quintiles. The quintile-specific estimates are based only on WMS 1994, as it is the only geographically comprehensive WMS. Estimates based on 1992 and 1997 would exclude families living in some of the poorest regions of the country and not present a complete picture of the manner in which school inputs and school costs affect different expenditure quintiles.

School Enrollment: Cross-Section Estimates

Marginal effects based on several specifications of a probit model of school enrollment are presented in Table 7.8. The first column presents estimates based on WMS 1992. Columns 2 and 3 present estimates based on WMS 1994. Estimates in columns 4 and 5 are based on WMS 1997.

Consider the characteristics of children. Estimates based on WMS 1992 and 1994 imply that there is a non-linear relationship between age and enrollment. Age is positively linked to enrollment until about ages 12–14, beyond which there is a rapid drop in the probability of attending school. This indicates that opportunity costs of attending school become important in reducing school participation only at the age at which a child should be finishing primary school. From a policy perspective, this suggests the importance of ensuring that children start school at the expected age of six. Surprisingly, estimates based on WMS 1997 do not display such a pattern. The marginal effect is much smaller than that for the previous years, implying that the probability of attending school is a linear function of age. Estimates for 1994 show that being male increases the probability of attending school by approximately 2 percentage points. However, this male advantage appears to have dissipated by 1997 and implies that male and females are equally likely to be enrolled in school. The order of birth is not linked to school enrollment.

Turning to the family characteristics, the coefficients on maternal and paternal education reveal a well-known picture. A one-year increase in parental education is associated with a 0.5–1 percentage point increase in the probability of enrolling in school.[23] Of the three remaining family variables, home ownership and number of rooms in a house are intended to capture the wealth status of the household, while land per capita may reflect wealth as well as household demand for labor. Across the three surveys the number of rooms in a house is positively correlated with enrollment and is associated with a marginal effect of about 0.8–2.1 percentage points. The effect of land per capita is statistically significant across surveys, but the sign on the coefficient varies. Estimates for 1994 suggest that the household demand for labor effect dominates and ownership of larger plots is negatively correlated with enrollment. In 1997 the effect is exactly the opposite.[24] The changes in the coefficient may reflect seasonal fluctuations linked to the time of the year when the surveys were conducted.[25] Home ownership and enrollment are not correlated. Home ownership rates at about 77–87 per cent are quite high and may not adequately capture differences in household wealth.

The effect of the cost of attending school varies across the three surveys. For 1992, there is a negative effect which suggests that doubling the costs of schooling (about 30 shillings a month) would reduce the probability of school attendance by 2.4 percentage points. However, the effect is not precisely measured. For 1994 the marginal effect is considerably smaller, about half the magnitude of that in 1992 and is statistically significant at conventional levels. For 1997 there is no discernible direct school–cost effect. However, for this year an alternative dimension of school costs, that is, the time taken to reach school, has a sharp effect on school enrollment. A ten-minute increase in getting to school is associated with a reduction in school enrollment of about 0.8 percentage points. The variation in the effect of costs may be linked to the affordability of education. As shown in Table 7.7, school costs as a proportion of per capita consumption decline over time. This declining pattern is consistent with the decline in the effect of school costs on enrollment. Overall, the estimates suggest that school costs do not play a large role in determining enrollment. This conclusion should be tempered by noting that these cross-section estimates rely only on geographical variation (which may be limited) to identify price effects and that the 1992 and 1997 WMS exclude some of the poorest districts in Kenya. These two features may lead to an underestimation of the price effect.

A relative novelty in our chapter is the use of the KCPE exam score as a determinant of enrollment. We argue that this score provides parents with a signal of whether school enrollment yields sufficient human capital benefits. Our estimates show that, for the most part (although not for 1992), there is a positive link between the KCPE score and school enrollment, indicating that parents living in districts with higher KCPE scores are more likely to send their children to school. The marginal effect suggests that an increase in the mean KCPE score by one standard deviation (36 points) is associated with an increase in enrollment probability by 1.4–2.1 percentage points.[26] While this estimate clearly demonstrates the importance of expected benefits in determining school enrollment decisions, it does not suggest how this may be achieved. Determining the appropriate policy interventions requires an analysis of the factors which lead to higher test scores. While our data do not permit such an analysis, based on an analysis of KCPE scores of students from 50 schools, Appleton (1995) reports that the provision of textbooks and the educational qualifications of teachers (at least for boys), appear to be important determinants of test scores.

The school-input variables in our specification are the student–teacher ratio and the skill (educational) composition of teachers in a district. These variables probably exert an indirect influence on the school enrollment decision through their effect on test scores. If this were the only channel of influence, then it would suggest that once KCPE scores have been included, these variables should be excluded from the enrollment specification. However, allowing only this indirect channel of influence is too restrictive. Accordingly, we allow these school inputs to exert a direct effect on enrollment.[27] With regard to the student–teacher ratio, there does not appear to be a link between this measure and enrollment rates. Given the relatively low student-teacher ratio this is not particularly surprising. Furthermore, as mentioned earlier, the use of district-level as opposed to school-level data should mitigate concerns about the endogeneity between the pupil–teacher ratio and enrollment.

Three variables capturing different levels of teacher skill are included in the regression. This allows teacher skills to exert a non-linear impact on enrollment. Overall, the pattern across the individual estimates suggests that enrollment rates and the skill level of teachers are positively correlated. Consistent with a pattern of increasing investment in the skill level of teachers, over time, there is a decline in the marginal effect of this input. For instance, the marginal effect associated with investments in teachers at skill level 2 declines from 0.004 in 1994 to about 0.0017 in 1997. In terms of magnitude, the estimates imply that an increase in the percentage of skilled teachers at level 2 by about 5 per cent would lead to an increase in the enrollment by between 0.85–2 percentage points. The estimates presented here provide support for the government's policy of upgrading the skill level of teachers.[28] Additional investments in teachers at skill levels 1 and 2 and the gradual phasing out of teachers with lower skill levels should lead to increases in enrollment.

School Enrollment: Pooled and Pseudo-Panel Data Estimates

Table 7.9 presents pooled estimates of a school enrollment probit equation and estimates of the school enrollment equation based on the district-level panel data. The results based on the pooled data are quite similar to those for the individual years. Thus, in this section we focus mainly on the panel data estimates. These estimates are based on differenced data, implying that any time-invariant fixed effects have been removed. These estimates provide an idea of the extent to which changes in primary school enrollment between 1992 and 1997 may be attributed to changes in school costs and changes in the skill level of teachers. The parsimonious specification is dictated by the limited changes in several variables, including the KCPE scores, the pupil–teacher ratio, child characteristics and, for the most part, family characteristics.

We first present OLS estimates of the differenced equation. Despite the frugality of the specification, it is notable that almost 40 per cent of the change in primary school enrollment is explained by the two independent variables. The marginal effect of school costs is statistically significant at the 10 per cent level and, in terms of its magnitude, is similar to those obtained from the pooled estimates and from the 1994 cross-section estimates. The estimates suggest that doubling the cost of schooling (about 30 shillings more a month) from its 1992 level would reduce enrollment by about 1.2 percentage points. The message provided by the coefficients on the skill level of teachers is consistent with the cross-section estimates. The estimates clearly show that reducing the number of skilled-teachers at the lowest levels (P2 and P3) encourages enrollment.[29]

As mentioned earlier, since the district-level means are based on sample information they may be error-ridden estimators based on population information. In such circumstances it is important to account for measurement error, especially in the independent variables. In our case, the district-means of the teacher-skill variables have been computed on the basis of population data. Thus, it is only the school cost variable that is subject to measurement error. To account for measurement error and attenuation bias in the school costs variable we resort to instrumental variable (IV) estimation. These estimates are presented in columns 3 and 4 of Table 7.9.[30] Depending on the instrument set used, the effect of school costs on enrollment is negative, statistically significant at conventional levels and 2–3 times larger than the cross-section estimates. According to the IV estimates, doubling the cost of schooling from its 1992 level would reduce enrollment by about 2.4–3.6 percentage points. The overall impression emerging from the cross-section estimates was that school costs do not play an important role in determining enrollment. On the other hand, the panel data estimates suggest that this conclusion may have

Table 7.9 Estimates of Primary School Enrolment, 1992, 1994 and 1997 (Standard Errors)

Variable	Pooled data 1992, 1994 and 1997 (1)	Pseudo panel differenced data OLS (2)	Pseudo panel differenced data IV-1 (3)	Pseudo panel differenced data IV-2 (4)
Child characteristics				
Age	0.036*			
	(0.011)			
Age squared	−0.0001*			
	(0.00005)			
Order of birth	0.002			
	(0.002)			
Family characteristics				
Father's schooling				
Mother's schooling				
Land per capita				
Home Ownership	−0.009			
	(0.010)			
Number of rooms in house	0.021*			
	(0.002)			
Educational characteristics				
School costs *100	−0.04	−0.04***	−0.08**	−0.13***
	(0.026)	(0.024)	(0.04)	(0.07)
KCPE score*100	0.06*			
	(0.02)			
Pupil–teacher ratio*100	−0.08			
	(0.07)			
Teacher, skill level 1 (S1)*100	0.4	−0.06	0.04	−0.3
	(0.12)	(0.24)	(0.2)	(0.3)
Teacher, skill level 2 (P1)*100	0.14*	0.08	0.12	−0.01
	(0.05)	(0.1)	(0.08)	(0.1)
Teacher, skill level 3 (P2 & P3)*100	−0.16**	−0.7*	−0.6*	−0.9*
	(0.08)	(0.3)	(0.2)	(0.3)
Number of observations	40,443	38	38	38
Log likelihood value	−12,252			
R^2		0.377	0.396	0.235

Notes: In column 1 the dependent variable is a discrete variable indicating whether an individual has ever attended school. This specification includes a set of seven provincial indicators, an urban–rural indicator and controls for year fixed effects. The educational characteristics are district averages. Standard errors are heteroscedasticity consistent and corrected for the clustered design of the sample. In columns 2, 3 and 4 the dependent variable is the change in average district enrollment between 1992 and 1997. The independent variables are changes in average district educational characteristics between 1992 and 1997. Columns 3 and 4 present instrumental variables estimates to account for measurement error in the school costs variable. The estimates in columns 2, 3 and 4 are based on data that have been weighted for differences in the sample size in each district. *significant at 1 per cent level; **significant at 5 per cent level; ***significant at 10 per cent level.

been premature. The precision and size of the effects reveal the importance of changes in school costs in determining enrollment.

Price and Input Elasticities by Expenditure Quintiles

So far the discussion has concentrated on the effect of the various educational characteristics on mean enrollment. Given the sharp income inequalities in Kenya, it is likely that there are sharp differences in the effect of school costs and school inputs across different households. To examine these patterns we estimates separate probit enrollment models for five per capita expenditure groups. Subsequently, these estimates are used to determine price and school input elasticities for each expenditure group. The analysis presented in this section is based only on data from the 1994 survey, the only one which is geographically complete. Given that the 1992 and 1997 surveys exclude the poorest areas, estimates based on these surveys are likely to underestimate the effect of school costs and other educational variables on enrollment decisions. Furthermore, since the marginal effects and the price elasticities based on the panel data are 2–3 times larger than those based on the cross-section data, the magnitude of the price elasticities discussed below should be thought of as a lower bound.

The price and input elasticities are presented in Table 7.10. Looking across the table, there is a discernible decline in price elasticities as income rises. For the richest quintile, price increases have no impact on the school enrollment decision, while at all other quintiles there is a statistically significant effect. The effect is largest at the lowest quintile, where a 10 per cent increase in costs would lead to a reduction in enrollment of 1.2 per cent (computed at the mean). Price elasticities computed at a higher price (mean plus one standard deviation) are considerably higher. Elasticities computed at the higher level of school costs show that a 10 per cent increase in school fees would reduce enrollment at the lowest quintile by 3 per cent.

Elasticities with respect to the KCPE score and the two school inputs are also presented in Table 7.10. For the entire sample an increase in the KCPE score by 1 per cent translates into a 0.3 per cent increase in enrollment. The effect of this quality signal is particularly large at the lower quintiles. At the lowest quintile a 1 per cent increase in this measure may lead to a 1.2 per cent increase in enrollment, while the effect at the highest quintile is more muted and results in a 0.4 per cent increase in enrollment. The differential response across quintiles suggests that households at the lower end require a more convincing demonstration of the gains from education (at least as measured by the KCPE score) to send their children to school as compared to households at the upper end of the distribution.[31] The relatively muted effect of this variable

Table 7.10 Point Elasticities by Expenditure Quintiles, 1994 (standard errors)

Characteristic	Total[a]	Quintile 1[b]	Quintile 2	Quintile 3	Quintile 4	Quintile 5
School costs (mean)[c]	-0.039** (0.020)	-0.123* (0.042)	-0.066* (0.027)	-0.057* (0.019)	-0.039* (0.013)	-0.009 (0.009)
School costs (mean + std. dev.)	-0.079*** (0.047)	-0.311** (0.129)	-0.161** (0.076)	-0.145** (0.059)	-0.085* (0.034)	-0.014 (0.014)
KCPE score	0.304** (0.151)	1.200* (0.327)	0.879* (0.258)	0.423* (0.154)	0.652* (0.143)	0.399* (0.118)
Student–teacher ratio	-0.001 (0.064)	-0.083 (0.185)	0.128 (0.156)	-0.108 (0.087)	0.080 (0.059)	0.071 (0.053)
Teacher, skill level 1 (S1)	0.053 (0.038)	0.210** (0.096)	0.000 (0.067)	0.135* (0.040)	-0.017 (0.031)	-0.024 (0.027)
Teacher, skill level 2 (P1)	0.381* (0.075)	0.661* (0.229)	0.688* (0.145)	0.252* (0.080)	0.456* (0.090)	0.177* (0.074)
Teacher, skill level 3 (P2 & P3)	0.085 (0.073)	0.011 (0.189)	0.050 (0.125)	-0.262* (0.074)	0.026 (0.059)	-0.053 (0.047)
Per Capita Monthly Consumption (Shillings)	853 (828.7)	208 (86.2)	432 (56.9)	636 (61.3)	903 (99.4)	1673 (764.9)

Notes: [a]Calculations are based on estimates reported in Table 7.9, column 2. [b]Calculations are based on quintile-specific estimates. Due to the smaller sample size and limited variation in district-level educational indicators, the quintile specific estimates do not include province fixed effects. [c]Point elasticities calculated at the mean of the relevant characteristic. For school costs these elasticities are calculated at the mean and the mean plus one standard deviation. *significant at 1 per cent level; ** significant at 5 per cent level; *** significant at 10 per cent level.

may also be explained by the greater ability of richer households to compensate for any educational deficiencies and the possibility that they treat education as consumption and an investment good. All these reasons support the idea that richer households will be less responsive to expected benefits when making enrollment decisions compared to poorer households.

Regardless of the expenditure quintile, the student-teacher ratio does not exert an effect on school enrollment decisions. In terms of teacher skills, the clearest impact between enrollment and teacher qualifications emanates from teachers at skill level 2. Across quintiles a marginal increase in this measure is associated with a 0.18–0.66 per cent increase in enrollment. The pattern of elasticities across quintiles is similar to that for test scores. Once again, the relatively higher effects of this measure at the lower quintiles suggests that poorer households are more sensitive to the quality of school inputs and need to be convinced that the sacrifice of household consumption will yield adequate benefits.

CONCLUSION

Motivated by the decline in primary school enrollment and the importance attributed to education as a means of alleviating poverty, we have tried to identify the factors responsible for determining primary school enrollment in Kenya. Although we have tried to pull together several sources and present a comprehensive picture, we are aware that in terms of policy measures our analysis focused mainly on the role of school inputs in determining outcomes. The concentration on school inputs is driven by data considerations. We realize that pedagogical processes, school management practices, teacher motivation, the strength of teachers' unions and their lobbying power may play important roles in determining policies and educational outcomes.[32] Despite these limitations, our analysis is one step toward understanding the factors which motivate enrollment in Kenya. Our work raised several points which need to be emphasized.

First, we considered a variety of explanations for the decline in educational enrollment between the mid-1980s and mid-1990s. Based on the assembled empirical evidence we are led to the conclusion that enrollment decline is largely associated with two reforms: the introduction of a new school curriculum between 1984 and 1985 and the introduction of a cost-sharing policy between 1989 and 1990. Both these changes led to a sudden and sharp increase in the cost of attending school and are the most likely causes for declining enrollment. We were unable to find strong support for other explanations, such as the lack of school availability, lack of employment and earning opportunities for educated individuals, inadequate school inputs and the spread of HIV/AIDS. The last factor is often identified as a key explanation, but based on the (extremely limited) information available, we could not find any link between the spread of the disease and the decline in enrollment.

Second, enrollment rates have remained stable since the mid-1990s, according to MOE data, whereas based on our analysis of the WMS, we detected a sharp increase in enrollment rates between 1992 and 1997. The discrepancy may lie in the coverage of the two sets of data. The MOE data do not cover private schools, while the survey data cover enrollment regardless of school type. With the available information we are unable to investigate whether this is the main source of the discrepancy. If correct, it suggests that there may be a diversion of students from public to private schools. Furthermore, it also indicates that while in the short run households may be forced to withdraw children from schools, in the long run alternative and cheaper service providers may allow children to re-enter school. We also detected an increase in the affordability of education between 1992 and 1997. In real terms school expenditure fell by about 19 per cent between 1992 and 1997. This increase in affordability may reflect the increased availability and use of cheaper private schools by poorer households. Further research on the role of private schools in stemming the decline in enrollment as well as a study of the quality of the education which they provide is clearly required.

Third, while enrollment increased between 1992 and 1997, the gains were different across expenditure quintiles. The increases for the bottom 40 per cent of household were about 3–4 percentage points, while for the top three quintiles the gains ranged between 6–7 percentage points. Thus, despite the overall increase, enrollment differences between the poorest 40 per cent of households and the richer households increased. For instance, the enrollment gap between the richest and the poorest quintiles increased from 6.9 percentage points in 1992 to 10.1 in 1997.

Fourth, our analysis of price and input elasticities displayed sharp differences across expenditure quintiles. Price elasticites are 13 times higher for households in the lowest quintiles as compared to the richest. This sharp difference across quintiles highlights the importance of focusing specifically on the effects of cost-sharing policies on the poor.

Fifth, the skill level of teachers is a clear element in determining enrollment. The estimates showed that the issue is not one of crowded classrooms but the competency of teachers. The quintile-specific input elasticities displayed that the poor are four times more responsive to changes in inputs as compared to the rich. Thus, a policy of upgrading the skill level of teachers and phasing out unskilled teachers should have a larger effect on the poor compared to the rich.

Sixth, a methodological innovation in our chapter was the construction of a pseudo-panel dataset using the three cross-section surveys. Although based on a small set of observations, the pseudo-panel data estimates may be more credible than cross-section estimates, as they are not contaminated by fixed effects and exploit variation over time to identify price and input elasticities. Results based on the pseudo-panel data also supported a policy of upgrading teacher skills. The consistent effect of this variable across the two different approaches lends strong support to a continuation of this policy. With regard to school costs, the effects were quite different compared to those based on cross-section data. Based on the pseudo- panel, the school-cost effects were negative, statistically significant and 2–3 times larger than the cross-section estimates. The estimates highlighted the importance of using panel data and variation over time to estimate price elasticities. It is clear that the justification of cost-sharing policies based on cross-section estimates leads to an underestimate of the negative enrollment effects.

Our chapter has shown that conventionally estimated cross-section price elasticities computed at the mean severely underestimate the impact of pro-market cost-sharing policies on poor households. Ideally, a cost-sharing policy with a progressive system of fee-exemptions for households in different quintiles could generate resources without substantially affecting enrollment. However, such schemes have been difficult to enforce (in the Kenyan context see Nganda 2002). As suggested by this study, an alternative approach to ease the fiscal strain and increase enrollment would be to retain the current system of cost-sharing while at the same time following a policy of hiring skilled teachers (higher salaries), phasing out unskilled teachers and allowing the student–teacher ratio to increase. Moderate increases in the student–teacher ratio should not affect enrollment.

The differences in the effect of educational policy across expenditure quintiles, as well as the seesaw changes in educational policy in Kenya, highlight the idea that the reason, to use Sen's terminology, for reform needs to be carefully thought through before initiation and kept continuously under review once implemented. When the 'reach' of a particular policy is expected to be inclusive, uniform policies without regard to differences in income and wealth and other pre-existing conditions may not be successful. In contrast with the idea that policies need to allow for different circumstances, the new Kenyan government, elected in 2002, committed itself to a policy of delivering free primary education for every child which, by design, is inclusive. Whether such a policy can be sustained, however, is debatable. If it can, then educational enrollment will increase and Kenya will be on its way to ensuring universal access to a key public good. Although we succumb to the temptation of concluding on this optimistic note, we are aware that it may be premature.

NOTES

An expanded version of this study was published in the *Journal of African Economics*, **13** (4), 1–43.

1. This figure corresponds to around 5–7 per cent of GDP spent on education during the period 1991 and 2000. In terms of international comparisons this educational expenditure ratio is among the highest in the world (see UNESCO 1999).
2. The framework used here is similar to those in Gertler and Van Der Gaag (1988), Gertler and Glewwe (1990) and Bedi and Marshall (2002).
3. While a linear utility specification has the advantage of simplicity, it also suffers from several disadvantages. Due to linearity, as is evident from equation (7.8), income/consumption is differenced out of the decision rule and does not directly affect the school enrollment decision. In our empirical work we tried alternative utility function specifications, but we were unable to empirically distinguish between linear, log-linear and quadratic in consumption-utility specifications. An additional justification for not including consumption is that it is potentially endogenous. To counter these problems we control for household resources via inclusion of variables such as home ownership, land per capita and number of rooms in a house. Additionally, we assess the role of household expenditure on enrollment by examining it across different expenditure quintiles.
4. For example, Patrinos and Psacharopoulos (1995) show that child earnings account for 27.8 per cent of total income in urban households in Paraguay, while Patrinos and Psacharopoulos (1997) show that child labor contributes 17.7 per cent of household income in rural Peru.
5. It may be argued that expected earnings or expected employment prospects are better indicators of the expected benefits of education and should be used instead of test scores. However, we do not have district-level information on employment rates by education level, ruling out this measure. While it is possible to create a measure of expected earnings, at least for one of the years for which we have data, it is not clear how this measure can be directly influenced by educational policies. On the other hand, school test scores may be influenced by altering the quality of school inputs and may be influenced to a greater extent by educational policies. A further justification for using this measure lies in the relationship between test scores and earnings. Based on their analysis of Kenyan data, Boissiere, Knight and Sabot (1985) report that cognitive skills, as measured by test scores on literacy and numeracy tests, are highly rewarded in the labor market.
6. The World Bank's Africa database (see Table 7.1a) indicates that school enrollments peaked in 1980, while information from Kenya's Economic Surveys show that enrollments peaked in 1983. There is also disagreement on the level of the GER. According to the World Bank's Africa database enrollments fell from 107.1 in 1984 to 99 in 1985. The Economic Surveys report corresponding figures of 103 and 96.
7. Our discussion of enrollment declines is based on gross enrollment rates. It is possible for this rate to fall due to a reduction in the number of children repeating grades. However, numbers from the Ministry of Education (personal correspondence) show that repetition rates have been increasing over time. In 1979 the repetition rate was 8.92 per cent, while in 1993 it is estimated to be around 15.4 per cent.
8. The enrollment figures which we present pertain to enrollment in public schools. If there has been a shift in enrollment from public to private schools, then part of the decline in the gross enrollment rate may be related to this shift. In recent years there has been an increase in the level of private participation. For example, between 1994 and 1997, the number of private schools as a per cent of all primary schools has increased from 0.67 to 2.2 per cent (Ministry of Education 1999). It is estimated that in 1997 around 2–3 per cent of total enrollment is in private schools. The low private participation and the growth of these schools in a time period when enrollments have been more or less stable (i.e., 1994–98), suggest that the shift from public to private schools is not particularly important in explaining enrollment patterns.
9. Abagi (1997) writes that students in primary school are placed under great pressure. 'They are taught 13 subjects, nine of which are examined at the end of Standard 8, stay in school from 7

a.m. to 5 or 6 p.m. and have short holidays'. He goes on to argue that such a burden reduces the motivation for learning and leads to a deterioration in performance.
10. It is possible that changes (declines) in the KCPE scores and the mean school completion rates are masked. Our conversations with KCPE authorities revealed that raw test scores are standardized to a mean of about 350. This standardization explains the stability of the test scores over time and would influence the school completion rates. We spent considerable time trying to obtain details on the standardization procedure. However, apart from indicating that raw test scores were standardized, no additional details were forthcoming. Since it is unlikely that examination authorities would scale test scores in the downward direction and consequently reduce school completion rates, we adopt the view that there were probably no marked improvements in the KCPE scores and school completion rates during the 1990s.
11. According to the UNDP Kenya Human Development Report (1999), 76,744 full-blown cases of AIDS have been reported. Of these around 1 per cent or 736 cases are in the age group 5–14.
12. After 1998 there does appear to be a decline in the number of skilled teachers. Recent statements by the government of Kenya also indicate that in the last few years there may have been a decline in the availability of skilled teachers.
13. The Kagera region is located close to Lake Victoria. HIV prevalence rates in this region are around 33 per cent higher than the country average.
14. A number of the school input variables which we use are district means, and in the context of the current study creating a pseudo-panel data set at the district level is a natural choice.
15. As pointed out by Moulton (1986), in cases where regressors include variables with repeated values within groups (as in the present context), ignoring intra-group error correlation may lead to incorrect statistical inference. Acknowledging this possibility, our estimates of the enrollment equation are corrected for the effects of intra-group correlation.
16. The 1992 and 1997 surveys correspond to the third term of the school calendar, while the 1994 survey corresponds to the second term. Usually enrollment rates tend to decline as the school year progresses and, ceteris paribus, we expect enrollment rates to be lower in 1992 and 1997 as compared to 1994. However, given that there are changes in several variables over time, it is difficult to discern the effect of the different timings of the surveys on enrollment rates.
17. The Northeastern province and the three excluded districts have the lowest enrollment rates in Kenya. As reported in Table 7.1b, the primary school enrollment rate in the Northeastern province was about 26 per cent in 1999.
18. Teachers in Kenya are placed at different levels (S1, P1, P2, P3 and P4) according to their qualifications. Our classification of skilled teachers is defined as follows. The highest level, skill level 1, consists of graduate teachers or teachers with S1 qualifications. Skill level 2 corresponds to P1 teachers, skill level 3 to P2 and P3 teachers and skill level 4 corresponds to P4 and untrained teachers.
19. Our GER for 1994 is very similar to the numbers presented in the basic report on the WMS 1994, prepared by the Kenyan Central Bureau of Statistics (CBS). The CBS estimates a gross enrollment rate of 94.5 (Kenya, Government of, 1996, p. 71).
20. We consider children in the age group 6 to 15 rather than the age group which should be in primary school, i.e., 6 to 13, in order to allow for the possibility of late enrollment in primary school. Estimates based on the smaller age group (6–13) and for a sample of 8–15 year old children were not substantially different.
21. In our data sets there are two variables which may be used to capture enrollment. We have information on whether a child (in the age group 6–15) has ever attended school (which includes children who are currently attending school) and also whether a child is currently in school. The difference between the two variables indicates children who have dropped out of school. In the WMS 1994 we have a total of 13,306 children, 3,553 of these children have never attended school while the remaining 9,753 have 'ever attended school'. Of these, 9,440 are currently still in school and 313 have dropped out. Thus, on the basis of 'Have you ever attended school', 9,753 have and 3,533 have never attended school. On the basis of 'Are you currently attending school', 9,440 are in school and 3,846 (313 drop outs and 3,533 never attended school) are not in school. These numbers suggest that the main problem appears to

be whether an individual ever enters the school system. To focus on this issue and to avoid mixing the initial enrollment decisions with dropping out we decided to use responses to the query, 'Have you ever attended school', as our dependent variable.

22. It is hard to believe that the large differences in the mean land per capita variable across the two surveys can be attributed entirely to sampling variability. However, we are unable to explain the discrepancy as the questions and the units of measurement across the surveys appear to be similar.

23. In preliminary regressions we included a set of controls for parental occupational and industrial affiliation. However, the inclusion of parental education variables eroded most of the effects associated with these variables. Accordingly, we decided to work with a more parsimonious specification.

24. The change of sign may cast some doubt on the robustness of the relation being estimated. However, a careful look at Table 7.8 shows that, except for a few variables, the signs on the statistically significant coefficients do not change. Where they do change, as in the case of school fees and land per capita, it appears to be linked to changes in the timing of the survey or changes in educational policies.

25. The 1994 survey was carried out in June–July 1994 while the 1997 survey was carried out in August–September 1997. While both the surveys were conducted during Kenya's long dry season (June–October), the 1994 survey was carried out at the start of the dry season or at the end of the long rains (March–May). The rainy season is usually the busiest period of the agricultural calendar and the negative link between land per capita and enrollment may reflect the demand for agricultural labor towards the end of the long rains.

26. We also find a link between KCPE test scores and earnings. Based on data from 1994, we found a positive and statistically significant correlation between KCPE scores and earnings of those who have completed primary school (0.23) and between KCPE scores and returns to primary education (0.18). Thus, high KCPE scores signal higher expected earnings and in turn may be expected to motivate enrollment.

27. We also estimated enrollment specifications which excluded the KCPE score. These specifications reflect the direct and indirect effect of school inputs on enrollment. The exclusion of the KCPE scores did not alter the statistical significance of the estimates and the changes in the magnitude of school input variables were minor. The small changes suggest that KCPE scores and school inputs have independent effects on the enrollment decision.

28. The government of Kenya continues to pursue policies of upgrading the skill levels of teachers. In 2002, for the first time, prospective teachers admitted to primary teacher training colleges must have a minimum average grade of C at the secondary school level rather than a D+ (Nation 26 July 2002).

29. The number of observations used to compute the district means differs considerably. To account for these differences, each of the observations in the pseudo-panel data set has been weighted by the square root of the number of observations in each district.

30. The variables used to instrument the differenced school cost variable are differenced versions of district means of age, order of birth, ownership of household and number of rooms in a house. The two sets of IV estimates rely on different combinations of the instruments. The instrument set explains 46–59 per cent of the variation in school costs and does not have an influence on changes in enrollment.

31. While parents at the lower end of the consumption distribution may be less well-educated there should be no presumption that they are unaware of the benefits of better educational performance for the future of their children. First, the average number of years of schooling of fathers in the lowest quintile is about four years, thus, not so low that they are illiterate or unaware of the potential importance of education. Furthermore, based on our field experience in some of the poorest parts of Kenya in October 2004, we found that soon after the release of KCPE scores parents try to move their children to those schools that have recorded the highest test scores.

32. While these other factors are important, they are difficult to capture. Furthermore, even if we were able to account for them it is unlikely that their inclusion would lead to a change in the

basic story of this chapter, that is, school fees, changes in curriculum, the quality of teachers and expected gains from education have a strong bearing on primary school enrollment.

BIBLIOGRAPHY

Abagi, Okwach (1997a), 'Public and Private Investment in Primary Education in Kenya: An Agenda for Action', Nairobi, Institute of Policy and Advanced Research (IPAR) Discussion Paper No. 5.
—— (1997b), 'Status of Education in Kenya: Indicators for Planning and Policy Formulation', Nairobi, Institute of Policy and Advanced Research (IPAR) Special Report.
—— (1997), 'Efficiency of Primary Education in Kenya: Situational Analysis and Implications for Educational Reforms', Nairobi, Institute of Policy and Advanced Research (IPAR) Discussion Paper No. 4.
Abagi, Okwach and Jacqueline Olweya (1999), 'Educational Reforms in Kenya for the Next Decade: Implementing Policies for Adjustment and Revitalisation', Nairobi, Institute of Policy and Advanced Research (IPAR) Special Paper Series No. 3.
Abagi, Okwach, Jacqueline Olweya and Wycliffe Otieno (2000), 'Counting the Social Impact of Schooling: What Kenyans say about their School System and Gender Relations', Nairobi, Institute of Policy and Advanced Research (IPAR) Discussion Paper No. 24.
Appleton, Simon (1995) 'Exam Determinants in Kenyan Primary School: Determinants and Gender Differences', Washington, DC, World Bank, Robert McNamara Fellowship Program Report.
Appleton, Simon, Arne Bigsten and Damiano Kulundu Manda (1999), 'Educational Expansion and Economic Decline: Returns to Education in Kenya, 1978–1995', Oxford, UK, Centre for the Study of African Economies Working Paper Series No. 99–6.
Ainsworth, Martha, Kathleen Beegle and Godlike Koda (2002), 'The Impact of Adult Mortality on Primary School Enrollment in Northwestern Tanzania', *Journal of Development Studies*, **41** (3), 412–39.
Bedi, Arjun S. and Jeffrey Marshal (1999), 'School Attendance and Student Achievement: Evidence from Rural Honduras', *Economic Development and Cultural Change*, **47** (3), 657–82.
—— (2002) 'Primary School Attendance in Honduras', *Journal of Development Economics*, **69** (1), 129–53.
Behrman, Jere Richard and John C. Knowles (1999), 'Household Income and Child Schooling in Vietnam', *World Bank Economic Review*, **13** (2), 211–52.
Boissiere M., John B. Knight and R.H. Sabot (1985), 'Earnings, Schooling, Ability and Cognitive Skills', *American Economic Review*, **75** (5), 1016–30.
Deaton, Angus (1985), 'Panel Data from Time Series of Cross-sections', *Journal of Economics*, **30** (1–2), 109–26.
—— (1997), *The Analysis of Household Surveys*, Baltimore: Johns Hopkins University Press.
Deolalikar, Anil B. (1998), *Public Spending on Education in Kenya: International Comparisons*, Washington, DC: World Bank.

Family Health International/AIDSCAP (1996), AIDS in Kenya: Socioeconomic Impact and Policy Implications, Nairobi: U.S. Agency for International Development.

Filmer, Deon (1999), *Educational Attainment and Enrollment Profiles: A Resource Book Based on Analysis of Demographic and Health Survey Data*, Washington, DC: World Bank.

Gertler, Paul and Jacques van der Gaag (1988), 'Measuring the Willingness to Pay for Social Services in Developing Countries', LSMS, The World Bank, Washington, DC, World Bank Living Standards Measurement Study Working Paper No. 45.

Gertler, Paul and Paul Glewwe (1990), 'The Willingness to Pay for Education in Developing Countries: Evidence from Rural Peru', *Journal of Public Economics*, **42** (3), 251–75.

—— (1992), 'The Willingness to Pay for Education for Daughters in Contrast to Sons: Evidence from Rural Peru', *World Bank Economic Review*, **6** (1), 171–88.

Glewwe, Paul (2002), 'Schools and Skills in Developing Countries: Education Policies and Socioeconomic Outcomes', *Journal of Economic Literature*, **40** (2), 436–82.

Handa, Sudhanshu and Kenneth Simler (2006), 'Quality or Quantity? The Supply-Side Determinants of Primary Schooling in a Poor Rural Economy', *Journal of African Economies*, **15** (1), 59–90.

Kenya, Government of (1964), *Kenyan Education Commission Report: Part I*, Nairobi: Government Printer.

—— (1965a), *Kenyan Education Commission Report: Part II*, Government Printer, Nairobi.

—— (1965b), *Sessional Paper No. 1 on African Socialism and its Application to Planning in Kenya*, Nairobi: Government Printer.

—— (1976), *Report of the National Committee on Education Objectives and Policies*, Nairobi: Government Printer.

—— (1985), *Report of the 8–4–4 Implementation, Evaluation Committee*, Nairobi: Government Printer.

—— (1988), *Sessional Paper No. 6 on Education and Manpower Training for the Next Decade and Beyond*, Nairobi: Government Printer.

—— (1996), *Welfare Monitoring Survey II: Basic Report*, Nairobi: Government Printer.

—— (1992), *Education for All: Issues and Strategies*, Nairobi: Government Printer.

—— (1999a), *AIDS in Kenya: Background, Projections, Impact and Interventions*, Nairobi: Ministry of Health, National HIV/AIDS and STD Control Program (NASCOP).

—— (1999b), *Education Statistics and Indicators*, Nairobi: Ministry of Education, Science and Technology.

Kenya, Government of /UNICEF (1994), 'Comprehensive Education Sector Analysis: An Analytical Report on Education and Training in Kenya', Nairobi, Comprehensive Education Sector Analysis (CESA) draft report.

Kimalu, Paul K. et al. (2001), 'Education Indicators in Kenya', Nairobi, Kenya Institute for Public Policy Research and Analysis (KIPPRA) Working Paper No. 4.

Knight, John B. and Richard H. Sabot (1990), *Education, Productivity and Inequality: The East African Natural Experience*, New York: Oxford University Press.

Lockheed, Marlaine, Adriaan Verspoor and Deborah Bloch (1991), *Improving Primary Education in Developing Countries*, Washington, DC: World Bank/Oxford University Press.

Maas, Jacob van Lutsenburg and Geert Criel (1982), *Distribution of Primary School Enrollments in Eastern Africa*, Washington DC: World Bank.

Moulton, Brent R. (1986), 'Random Group Effects and the Precision of Regression Estimates', *Journal of Econometrics*, **32** (3), 385–97.

Nganda, Benjamin M. (2002), 'Service Pricing Practices in Public Health Facilities', Nairobi Ministry of Health, unpublished paper.

Patrinos, Harry Anthony and George Psacharopoulos (1995), 'Educational Performance and Child Labor in Paraguay', *International Journal of Educational Development*, **15** (1), 47–60.

—— (1997), 'Family Size, Schooling and Child Labor in Peru: An Empirical Analysis', *Journal of Population Economics*, **10** (4), 387–405.

Stover, John and Lori Bollinger, L. (1999), 'The Economic Impact of AIDS', report for The Policy Project (www.policyproject.com).

United Nations Development Programme (1999), *Kenya Human Development Report*, Nairobi: UNDP.

United Nations Educational, Scientific and Cultural Organization (1999), *Statistical Yearbook*, Paris: UNESCO.

Vos, Rob et al. (2002), 'Budget Implications of Achieving Education Targets', KIPPRA, Nairobi, Nairobi, Kenya Institute for Public Policy Research and Analysis (KIPPRA) Social Sector Division, unpublished paper.

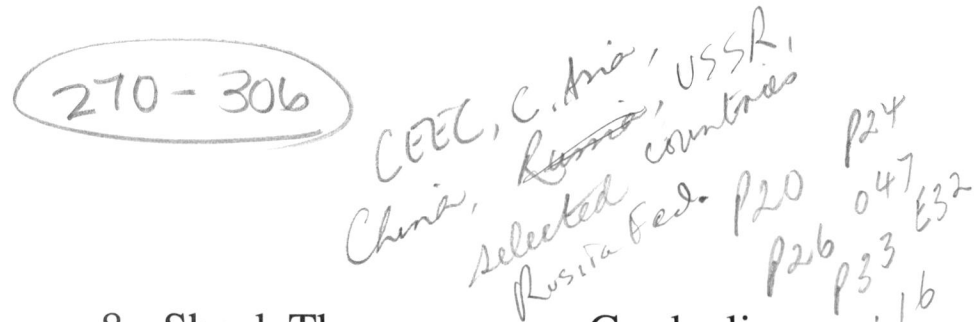

8. Shock Therapy versus Gradualism Reconsidered: Lessons from Transition Economies

Vladimir Popov

After the Berlin Wall collapsed in 1989, market reforms were initiated in the post-communist states of Eastern Europe, the former Soviet republics, China, Mongolia and Vietnam.[1] However, their economic performance was more than disappointing. Nowhere else in the world was the failure of reforms in terms of Amartya Sen's 'three Rs' – reach, range and reason – more spectacular than in Eastern Europe and the countries of the former Soviet Union. Output collapsed, inequalities and crime increased and life expectancy fell. In contrast, reforms introduced in two Asian communist states, China and Vietnam – but not in Mongolia – had more favorable outcomes. In light of these results, it is not surprising that the question of the 'reason' to reform had been at center stage in the policy discussions in the post-reform period. As Sen argues in the foreword to this volume, the basic issue underlying any reform is that some existing arrangements are not right. Therefore, the central question is how can we improve existing institutions and policies and make sure they work better. This chapter analyzes the shock-versus-therapy issue in order to clarify why institutional and policy reforms in transition countries were unable to achieve their goals, and it also contributes to the debate on the reasons to reform.

In Eastern Europe the reduction of output lasted for three or four years and amounted to 20–30 per cent; GDP did not reach pre-recession levels until the late 1990s. This is comparable to the Great Depression (1929–33), when GDP in Western countries fell some 30 per cent and ultimately recovered to pre-recession levels by the end of the 1930s. During World War II national income in the USSR fell 20 per cent in 1940–42, recovered to its 1940 level in 1944, fell again by 20 per cent in 1944–46 as defense industries were converted to civilian use, but exceeded its 1940 level by nearly 20 per cent already in 1948. In the former Soviet republics (FSU) by the end of the 1990s output (GDP) had fallen by about 50 per cent compared with the highest pre-recession level of 1989 (Figures 8.1a and 8.2b). Investment dropped even more, and growing income inequalities meant that real incomes declined dramatically for the majority of the population. On top of that, death rates increased by about 50 per cent, whereas life expectancy declined markedly. In Russia output fell by 45 per cent in 1989–98, death rates increased from 1 per cent in the 1980s to 1.5 per cent in 1994 and stayed at this high level thereafter – meaning over 700,000 additional deaths annually. Over a sustained period of several years, such population losses could be likened to the impact of World War II.

In some of the FSU states which were affected by military conflicts (Armenia, Azerbaijan, Georgia, Moldova and Tajikistan) GDP in 2000 was only 30–50 per cent of its pre-transition levels.

Only in China and Vietnam was there no transformational recession at all, instead, from the very outset of reforms economic growth accelerated. Mongolia had a relatively 'mild' recession – output was falling for four years and fell by about 20 per cent.

In hindsight, the reduction of output which occurred in Eastern Europe and FSU states should be considered an exceptional case in world economic history. There had never been, to the best of my knowledge, such a dramatic, simultaneous decline in output, living standards and life expectancy without extraordinary circumstances, such as wars, epidemics or natural disasters.

Why has the reduction of output and incomes in post-communists countries been so deep and so long? To what extent was this collapse caused by the initial conditions and circumstances – meaning it was predetermined and unavoidable – and to what extent was it 'man made' – the result of poor policy choices? If wrong economic policies are mostly responsible for the collapse, future historians may refer to the transition as the biggest man-made economic disaster in history.

By most accounts, the virtually universal consensus is that 'things went terribly wrong' and that different policies could have avoided most of the misfortunes which struck the former Soviet republics in the 1990s. After all, reforms in China and Vietnam were clearly successful, whereas East European transition economies did better than the FSU states, so it is difficult to accept the idea that the exceptional length and depth of recession in post-Soviet states was predestined and inevitable.

However, when it comes to the discussion of specific policies, there is much less agreement among scholars. The question of why the FSU had to pay a greater price for economic transition is answered differently by those who advocate shock therapy and those who support gradual, piecemeal reforms. Shock therapists argue that much of the costs of the FSU reforms should be attributed to inconsistent policies; namely, to the slow pace of liberalization and the inability of the governments and central banks to fight inflation in the first half of the 1990s. On the contrary, the supporters of gradual transition argue exactly the opposite, blaming all problems on the attempt to introduce a conventional shock-therapy package.

Such conclusions are often based on comparisons of European transition economies or, at best, comparisons of East European countries and former Soviet republics, whereas non-Soviet Asian transition economies (China, Vietnam, Mongolia) are excluded from the analysis. However, even a superficial look at the dynamics of output in these Asian transition economies reveals that it was very different from the patterns which prevailed in Europe. As Figure 8.1a and 8.1b suggest, in Europe the most successful (in terms of output change) economies were those which liberalized faster (the Central European countries). However, in Asia the opposite was true – China and Vietnam, usually considered to be slow liberalizers, did not have any transformational recession. Instead, they experienced accelerated growth right from the start of economic reform. And Uzbekistan and Turkmenistan, that liberalized much more slowly than Kyrgyzstan and Russia, exhibited much better performance.

A number of studies have concluded that fast liberalization and macrostabilization ultimately lead to better performance (Sachs 1996; De Melo, Denizer and Gelb 1996; Fischer, Sahay and Vegh 1996; Åslund, Boone and Johnson 1996; Breton, Gros and Vandille 1997; Fischer and Sahay 2000). To prove their point, authors have tried to regress output changes during transition on liberalization indexes developed by De Melo et al. (1996) and by the European Bank for Reconstruction and Development (published in its annual *Transition Reports*), on inflation and different measures of initial conditions.[2]

The conventional wisdom was probably summarized in the 1996 World Bank's annual development report, *From Plan to Market*, which basically stated that differences in economic performance were associated mostly with 'good and bad' policies, in particular with the progress in liberalization and macroeconomic stabilization. Countries which are more successful at introducing market reforms and decreasing inflation were believed to have better chances to limit the output decline and to quickly recover from the transformational recession. According to the 1996 World Development Report:

> Consistent policies, combining liberalization of markets, trade and new business entry with reasonable price stability, can achieve a great deal even in countries lacking clear property rights and strong market institutions (1996, 142).

The conclusion did not withstand the test of time, since by now most economists would probably agree that because liberalization was carried out without strong market institutions, it led to the extraordinary output collapse in the CIS states.[3]

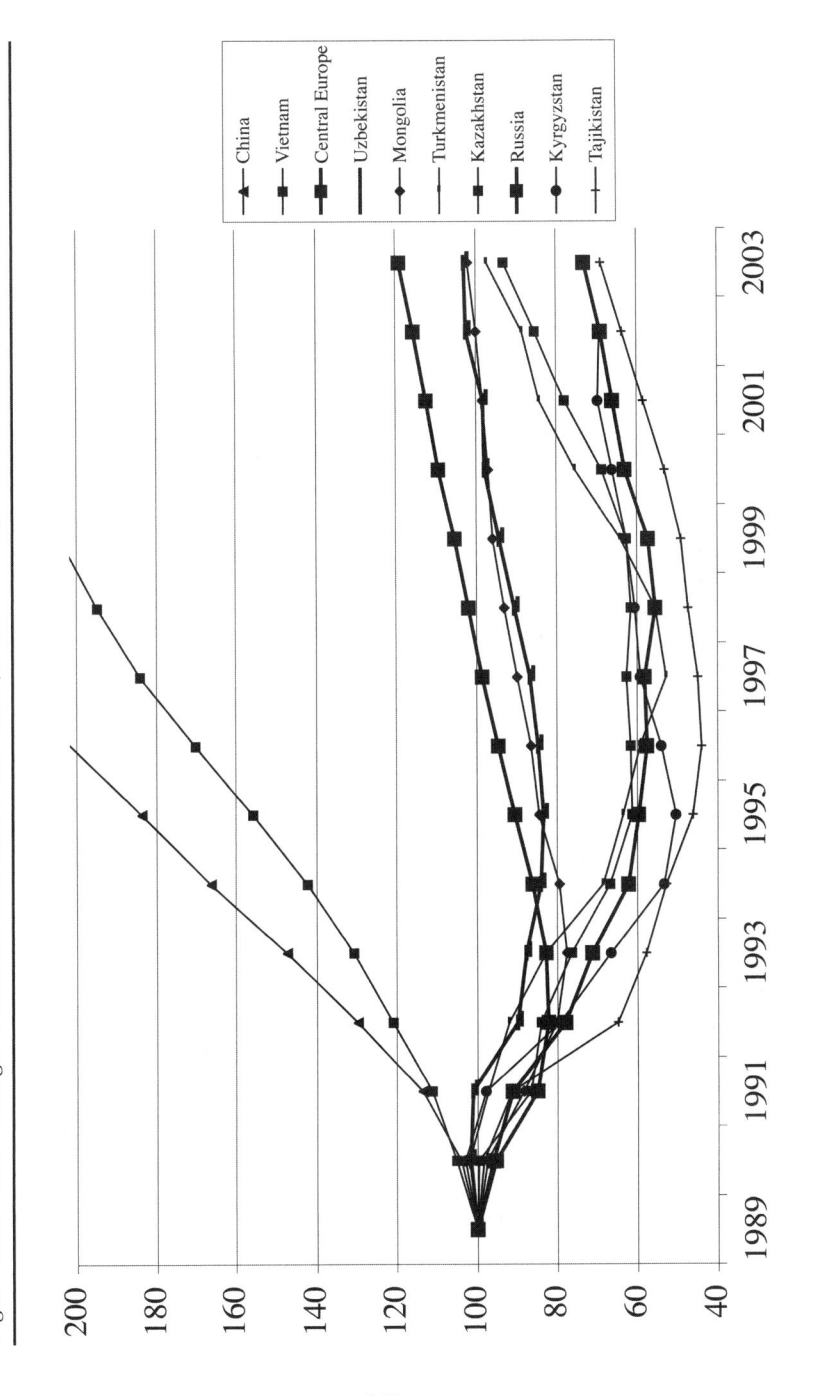

Figure 8.1a GDP Change in Selected Transition Economies (1989 = 100%)

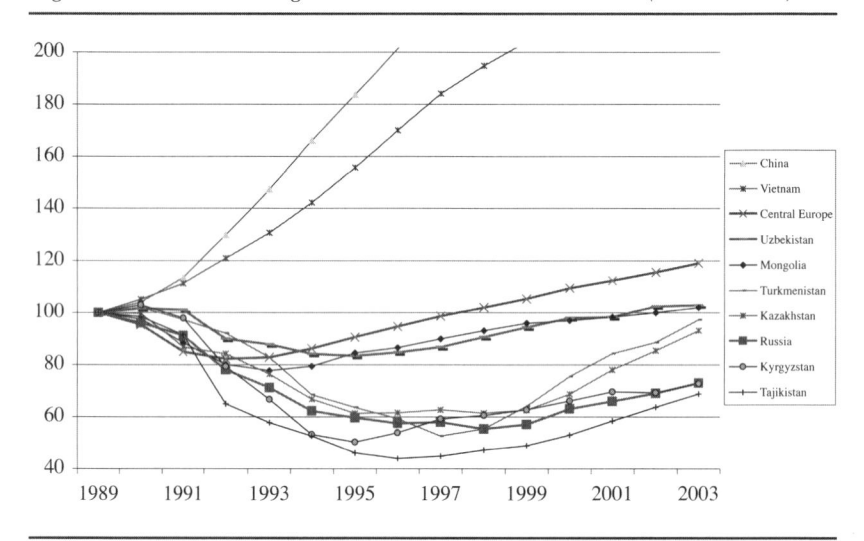

Figure 8.1b GDP Change in Asian Transition Economies (1989=100%)

Source: EBRD, World Bank data.

Liberalization may be important, but the devil is in details, that often do not fit into the generalizations and make straightforward explanations look trivial.

Consider the examples of Vietnam and China – two countries which shared may similarities in initial conditions and achieved basically the same results (immediate growth of output without transformational recession) despite different reform strategies. While Chinese reforms are normally treated as a classic example of gradualism, Vietnamese reformers introduced Polish-style shock therapy (instant deregulation of most prices and convertibility of the dong) even before Poland did in 1989, and they still managed to avoid the reduction of output.[4]

Or, take the example of the differing performance of the (FSU) states. The Baltic States (Estonia, Latvia and Lithuania) are considered the champions of liberalization and stabilization in the region (with a cumulative liberalization index of 2.4–2.9 by 1995), whereas Uzbekistan (with the same index of 1.1 in 1995) is commonly perceived to be one of the worst procrastinators. However, in Uzbekistan the reduction of output from 1990 to 1995 totaled only 18 per cent, and the economy started to grow again in 1996, while in the Baltics output fell in the early 1990s by 36–60 per cent and by 2004, ten years after the nadir of the recession, was still below the pre-recession maximum.

At first glance, there seems to be a positive relationship between liberalization and performance (Figure 8.2). However, a more careful consideration reveals that the link is the result of a sharp difference in the magnitude of the recession in EE countries, as a group, and FSU states, also as a group (Figure 8.2). Within these groups the correlation, if any, is much weaker, not to mention the outliers – China and Vietnam. In recent years the Chinese rank on the Index of Economic Freedom (measured on a scale from 1 to 5 by the Heritage Foundation) was about the same as the Russian one, but the performance of the two countries differed markedly (Figure 8.3).

Overall, attempts to link differences in output changes during transition to the cumulative liberalization index and to macro-stabilization (rates of inflation) have not yielded any impressive results. It turned out that a dummy variable, such as membership in the ruble zone (i.e., FSU) and war destruction, are much more important explanatory variables than either the liberalization index or inflation (Åslund, Boone and Johnson 1996). Other studies which tried to take into account a number of initial conditions (repressed inflation–monetary overhang before deregulation of prices, trade dependence, black market exchange rate premium, number of years under central planning, urbanization, over industrialization and per capita income) found that liberalization also becomes insignificant in some cases (De Melo, Denizer, Gelb and Tenev 1997, 25; Heybey, Murrell 1999; Popov 2000, 2007).

This implies that there is still no good explanation even for the basic stylized facts, such as the ability of China and Vietnam to avoid recession completely or the markedly greater magnitude of the recession in FSU states as compared with East European countries and the differing performance of countries belonging to the same geographical region.

This chapter starts by separating the transformational recession (deviation of actual output from potential) from the process of economic growth (recovery from the transformational recession). The transformational recession (the collapse of output during transition) can be best explained as an adverse supply shock caused by a change in relative prices after their deregulation due to distortions in industrial structure and trade patterns which were accumulated during the period of central planning. Another adverse supply shock was created by the collapse of state institutions during the transition period, while the speed of liberalization had an adverse effect on performance. Recovery should be treated as a normal growth process: it could be modeled by using conventional growth theory and, in the long run, may demonstrate the ability to capitalize on liberalization by increasing factor efficiency (Shmelev and Popov 1989; Popov 1998a, 1999).

This alternative explanation for the collapse of output during a transformational recession suggests the reduction of output was caused primarily by three groups of factors. First, the adverse supply shock resulting from the deregulation of prices and change in relative price ratios created the

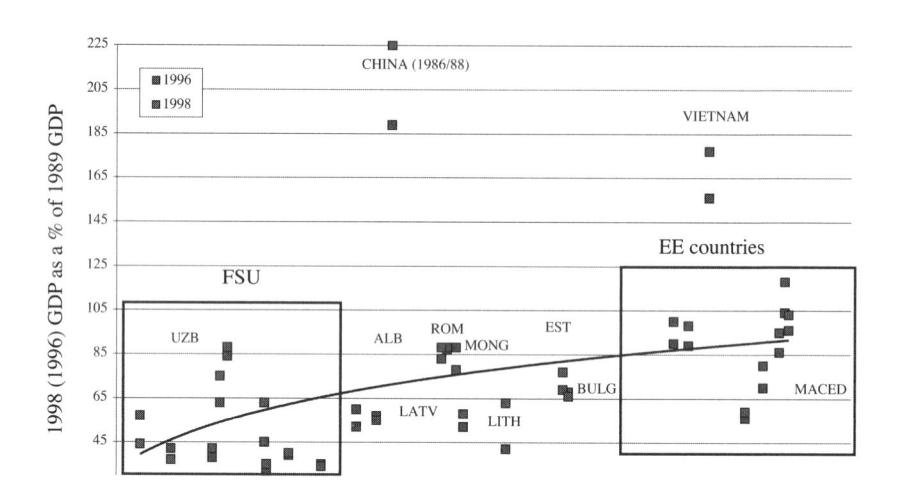

Figure 8.2   Liberalization and Output Change

need to reallocate resources due to distortions in the industrial structure and external trade patterns which existed before transition. Second, another adverse supply shock associated with the collapse of state institutions (understood as the ability of the state to enforce its rules and regulations), occurred in the late 1980s and early 1990s and resulted in chaotic transformation through crisis management instead of an organized and manageable transition. And third, poor economic policies, consisting of macroeconomic mismanagement and import substitution, no matter whether the pursued reforms were gradual or radical. The fast pace of reform per se (shock versus gradual) at the initial stage of transition probably aggravated the reduction of output, because the immediate deregulation of prices created a need for restructuring (reallocation of labor and capital) which exceeded the investment potential of the economy.

Thus, in the first approximation, economic recession during transition was associated with the need to reallocate resources in order to correct the industrial structure inherited from the centrally planned economy. These distortions include over-militarization and over-industrialization, perverted trade flows among former Soviet republics and Comecon[5] countries, excessively large size and poor specialization of industrial enterprises and agricultural farms. In most cases, these distortions were more pronounced in the FSU states than in Eastern Europe, China and Vietnam; the larger the distortions, the greater the reduction of output. The transformational recession was caused by an adverse supply shock similar to the one experienced by Western countries after the oil

Figure 8.3   Indexes of Economic Freedom and GDP Growth in Russia and China

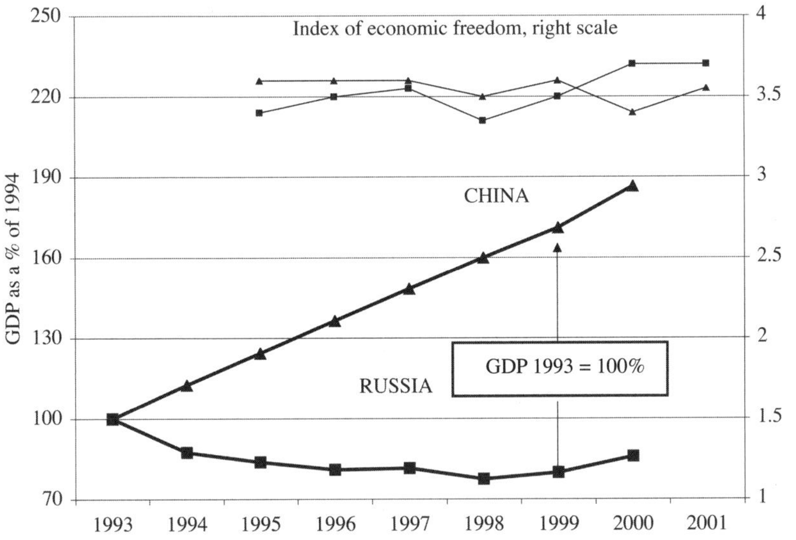

price hikes in 1973 and 1979 and similar to post-war recessions caused by the conversion of defense industries (Kornai 1994).

Institutional collapse provides an additional reason for the extreme depth of the transformational recession. Indeed, the differences between EE countries and FSU on this dimension are striking. The adverse supply shock in this case came from the state's inability to perform its traditional functions – to collect taxes and constrain the shadow economy, to ensure property and contract rights and to maintain law and order. Naturally, an inability to enforce rules and regulations did not create a business climate conducive to growth and resulted in increased costs for companies.

This strong institutional framework explains the success of gradual reforms in China and shock therapy in Vietnam, where strong authoritarian regimes were preserved and institutions from the centrally planned economy were not dismantled before new market institutions were created. The framework also accommodates the relative 'success' of radical reforms in EE countries, especially in Central Europe (Czech Republic, Hungary, Poland, Slovakia, Slovenia), where strong democratic regimes and new market institutions emerged quickly. And it is precisely the collapse of strong state institutions, that started in the USSR in the late 1980s and continued in the successor states in the 1990s, which explains the extreme length and depth of the FSU transformational recession.

To put it differently, Gorbachev's reforms of 1985–91 failed not because they were gradual, but because of the simultaneous weakening of state institutional capacity, leaving the government unable to control the flow of events. Similarly, Yeltsin's reforms in Russia, as well as economic reforms in most other FSU states, were costly not because of shock therapy, but due to the collapse of the institutions needed to enforce law and order and manage the transition.

Finally, economic policy affected performance. Given the weak institutional capacity of the state, i.e. its poor ability to enforce its own regulations, economic policies could hardly be 'good'. Weak state institutions usually imply import substitution and populist macroeconomic policies (subsidies to noncompetitive industries, budget deficits resulting in high indebtedness and/or inflation, overvalued exchange rates), which have a devastating impact on output. However, strong institutional capacity does not lead automatically to responsible economic policies. Examples range from the USSR before it collapsed (strong import substitution and periodic outbursts of open or hidden inflation) to such post-Soviet states as Uzbekistan and Belarus, that had stronger institutional potential than other FSU states, but did not demonstrate substantially better policies (macroeconomic instability, for instance).

Overall, the FSU and Mongolian transition model (with the partial exemption of Belarus, Estonia, Turkmenistan and Uzbekistan) is based on unfortunate combinations of unfavorable initial conditions, institutional degradation and ineffective economic policies, such as macroeconomic populism and import substitution. On the other hand, China, Vietnam – and, to a certain extent, Belarus, Uzbekistan and Turkmenistan – demonstrate how the preservation of strong institutions and a more gradual approach to reforms could counterweigh the negative impacts of initial conditions.

TRANSFORMATIONAL RECESSIONS

Non-Policy Factors: Distortions in Industrial Structure and Trade Patterns

In the first approximation, the transformational recession is basically a supply-side phenomenon, a structural adjustment process resulting from the need to overcome disproportions inherited from the centrally planned economy – high militarization, over-industrialization and underdevelopment of the service sector, the 'under-openness' of the economy and the perverse structure of trade among former Soviet republics and socialist countries. The greater the magnitude of these inherited distortions, the more pronounced the reduction of GDP during the transformational recession.

The supply-side explanation implies that the reallocation of resources (restructuring) due to market imperfections is associated with the temporary loss of output. Thus, declines in the production of non-competitive enterprises and industries is not offset immediately by an increase in the production of competitive industries and enterprises. The problems result from barriers to capital and labor flows, such as poorly developed banking systems and securities markets, uncertain property rights, a lack of easily enforceable and commonly accepted bankruptcy and liquidation procedures, the underdevelopment of land market, housing market and labor market infrastructure and so on.

Attempts to separate non-policy from policy factors by running multiple regressions produce some statistically satisfactory and economically meaningful results.[6] Although there is a relationship between the magnitude of output decline and the liberalization index and inflation (R^2 = 65 per cent), it weakens greatly or even disappears completely once variables which characterize objective conditions are factored in. For example, nearly 70 per cent of the variations in the magnitude of the decline of output can be explained by only two dummy variables (both significant at the 1 per cent level) which account for membership in the FSU and for wars. It is even more remarkable that the addition of a liberalization variable into the equation does not seem to make any difference: the correlation coefficient does not increase when liberalization is taken into consideration. To make matters worse, the coefficient of the liberalization index is not statistically significant and has an unexpected sign: the greater the liberalization, the larger the decline of output. The inflation variable is always significant and has the predicted (negative) sign, but this cannot be considered an important finding because the link between macroeconomic stabilization and economic growth has been demonstrated more than once for a much larger group of countries (e.g., Bruno 1995; Bruno and Easterly 1995).

These results suggest that the usual argument linking Eastern Europe's, especially the Central Europe's, better performance (as compared with the FSU) to better economic policies (greater liberalization) does not necessarily hold. Indeed, the identification and decomposition of the 'FSU effect' may be carried out more effectively by accounting for not just policy variables, but non-policy factors such as the relative magnitude of the distortions in trade and industrial structure.

To avoid the multicolinearity problem, an aggregate indicator of distortions was constructed (summing up all the distortions mentioned above, since they are expressed as a per cent of GDP[7]). There is a fairly strong correlation between aggregate distortions in industrial and trade structure before transition and the subsequent performance during transition, as measured by the GDP change (Figure 8.4). Among countries with minor aggregate distortions (less

280   *Economic Reform in Developing Countries*

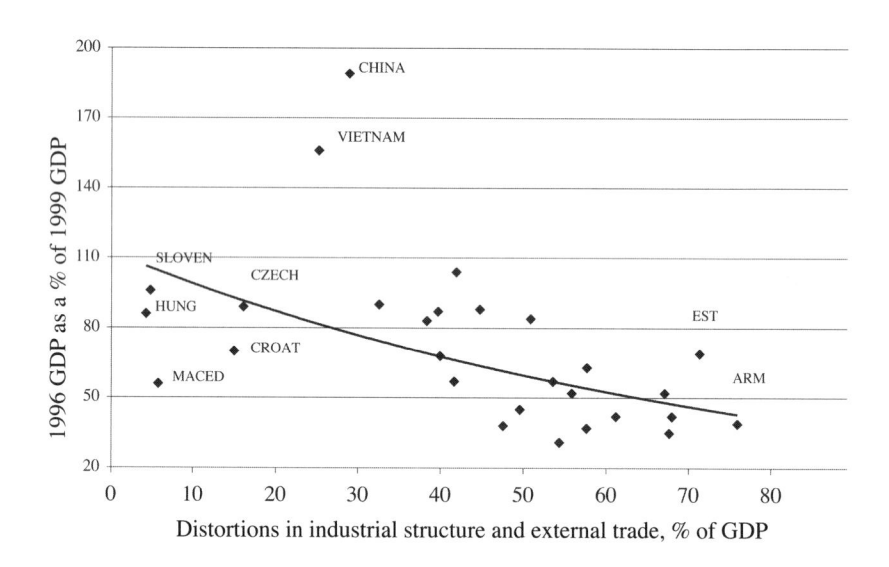

Figure 8.4   Aggregate Distortions in Industrial Structure and External Trade before Transition and GDP Change during Transition

[Scatter plot: x-axis "Distortions in industrial structure and external trade, % of GDP" (0 to 80); y-axis "1996 GDP as a % of 1999 GDP" (20 to 200). Labeled points include CHINA, VIETNAM, SLOVEN, CZECH, HUNG, CROAT, MACED, EST, ARM.]

than 30 per cent of GDP) are three former Yugoslav republics (Slovenia, Croatia and Macedonia), the Czech and Slovak Republics, Hungary, China and Vietnam. All these countries, except war-affected Macedonia, are doing better than most other transition economies. Yet the list of countries with the most distorted economies (aggregate distortions of over 50 per cent of GDP) includes all of the former Soviet republics, except Russia (where aggregate distortions amounted to only 39 per cent of GDP). In fact, aggregate distortions alone may explain 32 per cent of output variations during transition and about 50 per cent of variations if the economies affected by war are excluded. Taking into account the other two non-policy factors characterizing the initial conditions provides statistically sound and robust results: over 60 per cent of the variations in performance may be explained by (1) the initial GDP per capita,[8] (2) aggregate distortions and (3) the war dummy variable.

The addition of the FSU dummy into the equation leads to the absorption of the aggregate distortions variable (the FSU dummy thus plays the role of a proxy for distortions), while the impact of the initial level of GDP per capita and war remains statistically significant. Adding inflation as an explanatory variable improves the results, but including the liberalization index only deteriorates the t-statistics and does not increase the explanatory power of the regression. To put it differently, the observed differences in performance may be explained *mostly* by the unequal initial conditions, while the role of traditional 'good policy' factors appears to be quite limited.

Such an interpretation suggests that recent research aimed at providing some empirical evidence for the conventional wisdom (greater liberalization and stabilization lead to better performance) may not be able to show that countries more advanced in liberalization and fighting inflation are doing better than others. Once the pre-transition initial conditions are taken into account, it turns out that conventionally monitored policy factors, such as the degree of liberalization and rates of inflation, do not explain much. Differences in economic performance in post-communist countries during transition appear to be associated predominantly not with chosen reform paths, but with the magnitude of initial distortions in industrial structures and trade patterns and with the initial GDP per capita.

This is not to say that government policy does not affect performance, but rather to admit that the conventional understanding of policy factors (liberalization and macroeconomic stabilization) is not enough to account for all of them. It may well be that the most important policy factors which affect performance are not associated, despite popular beliefs, with the speed of liberalization and macro-stabilization. Rather, these are the policy measures aimed at preserving and/or creating strong, efficient institutions.

Institutions, Rule of Law and Democracy

The decline of institutional capabilities contributed a great deal to the poor economic performance of Russia and the other CIS states. If regression equations which account only for initial conditions are used to predict economic performance (GDP change), it turns out that China and Vietnam did much better than expected, the Eastern European and Baltic states on average did not do so well, but still better than expected, whereas most CIS states did much worse than expected. It may be hypothesized that these discrepancies are explained by the institutional factor – the ability to preserve strong institutions in China and Vietnam, as well as in East European countries, and the collapse of state institutions in the CIS. The exceptions within the CIS prove the rule: Uzbekistan and Belarus are known not only for proceeding with slow reforms but are also believed to have the strongest state institutions among all CIS members.[9] The Ukrainian example, on the other hand, proves that it is not the speed of reforms *per se* which really matters: being a procrastinator, Ukraine performed worse than expected, arguably due to its poor institutional capabilities (trust in political institutions in Ukraine is markedly lower than in Belarus).

The efficiency of state institutions, understood as the state's ability to enforce its own regulations, is not easily measurable. In most FSU and Balkan countries institutional collapse is observable on several levels, including:

- in the dramatic increase of the share of the shadow economy,
- in the decline of government revenues as a proportion of GDP;
- in the state's inability to deliver basic public goods and appropriate regulatory framework;
- in the accumulation of tax, trade, wage and bank arrears;
- in the demonetization, 'dollarization' and 'barterization' of the economy, as measured by high and growing money velocity;
- in the decline of bank financing as a proportion of GDP;
- in poor enforcement of property rights, bankruptcies, contracts and law and order in general;
- in increased crime rates.

Most these mentioned phenomena may be defined quantitatively with the remarkable result that China and Vietnam are closer in this respect to Eastern Europe than to CIS members. However, the construction of the aggregate index of the efficiency of institutions is problematic, because the rationale for choosing weights is not clear.

One possible general measure is the trust businesses and individuals have in various institutions; on this count FSU states rank much lower than East European countries in all available surveys. In a global survey of firms in 69 countries on the credibility of the state institutions, CIS members had the lowest credibility, below that of Sub-Saharan Africa (World Bank 1997, 5, 35). Especially striking was the gap between Eastern European and CIS countries: differences in the credibility index between South and Southeast Asia and Eastern Europe were less pronounced than differences between Sub-Sahara Africa and the CIS.

Another good proxy for measuring the institutional capacity of the state is the financial strength of the government – the share of state revenues in GDP. Although much has been said about 'big government' and too high taxes in former socialist countries, the downsizing of the government which occurred in most CIS states during the transition went too far. This argument has nothing to do with the long-term considerations of the optimal size of the government in transition economies – it is true that in most of them government revenues and expenditure as a share of GDP are still higher than in countries with comparable GDP per capita. But whatever the long-term optimal level of government spending should be, a drastic reduction of such spending (by 50 per cent and more in real terms) cannot lead to anything else but institutional collapse.

Before the transition, government regulations were pervasive in the socialist states, and the financial power of the state was roughly the same as in West European countries (government revenues and expenditure amounted to about 50 per cent of GDP). This allowed the state to provide the bulk of public goods and extensive social transfers. During the transition, tax revenues as a proportion of GDP decreased markedly in most countries. However, Central European countries and Estonia managed to arrest the decline, while Russia (together with Lithuania, Latvia and several Southeast European and Central Asian states) experienced the greatest reduction. In Vietnam the share of government revenues in GDP grew by 1.5 times in 1989–93. Chinese government revenues as a percentage of GDP have fallen by more than 50 per cent since the late 1970s, but mostly due to cuts in subsidies to enterprises, not due to cuts on spending on goods and services. Besides, it looks more like a conscious policy choice rather than a spontaneous process. Authoritarian regimes have always had better powers to collect tax revenues, if they choose to do so, as did all governments in the centrally planned economies before the transition.

In contrast, in most CIS states the reduction of the government expenditure occurred in the worst possible way – without any coherent plan or reassessment of government commitments. Instead of shutting down some government programs and concentrating limited resources on others to raise their efficiency, the government kept all programs half-alive, half-financed and barely functioning.

This led to the slow decay of public education, health care, infrastructure, law and order institutions, fundamental research and development, etc. Virtually all services provided by the government – from collecting customs duties to regulating traffic – have become symbols of notorious economic inefficiency. There were numerous cases of government failure which further undermined the credibility of the state, since many government-provided public goods were disappearing and only partly replaced by private and semi-private businesses (Popov 1998b).

There are three major patterns of change in the share of government expenditure in GDP,[10] that generally coincide with the three major archetypes of institutional developments. On a broader scale, there are three typical distinct 'models' of transition (see Figure 8.5). Under strong authoritarian regimes (China) cuts in government expenditure occurred at the expense of defense, subsidies and budgetary financed investment, while expenditure for 'ordinary government' as a percentage of GDP remained largely unchanged (Naughton 1997). Under strong democratic regimes (Poland) budgetary expenditure, including those for 'ordinary government', declined only in the pre-transition period but increased during the transition itself. Finally, under weak democratic regimes (Russia) the reduction of the general level of government expenditure led not only to a decline in the financing of defense, investment and subsidies,

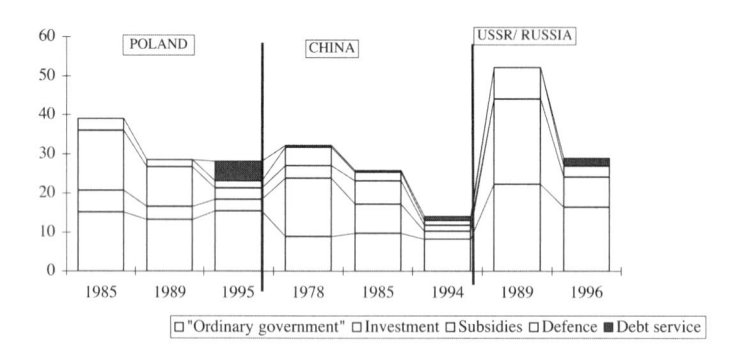

Figure 8.5   Government Expenditure as Percentage of GDP

```
   60 ┬   ┌──────┐           ┌─────┐           ┌──────────┐
      │   │POLAND│           │CHINA│           │USSR/RUSSIA│
   50 ┤   └──────┘           └─────┘           └──────────┘
   40 ┤
   30 ┤
   20 ┤
   10 ┤
    0 ┴────┬─────┬─────┬─────┬─────┬─────┬─────┬──
         1985  1989  1995  1978  1985  1994  1989  1996
```

□ "Ordinary government"   □ Investment   □ Subsidies   □ Defence   ■ Debt service

but also to the downsizing of 'ordinary government', undermining or even destroying the institutional capacities of the state.

While in China total budgetary expenditure and 'ordinary government' are much lower than in Russia and Poland, they were sufficient to keep institutions functioning, since the financing of social security from the government budget was traditionally low. In Russia, however, although expenditure for ordinary government did not seem to be that much lower than in Poland, the pace of its reduction during transition exceeded that of GDP. That is, given the various patterns of GDP dynamics, while in Poland 'ordinary government' financing grew by about one-third in real terms between 1989 and 1995–96 (and it nearly doubled in China), in Russia it fell by about two-thirds. The Russian pattern of institutional decay proved to be extremely detrimental for investment and general economic performance.

After adding the decline in government revenues variable to the ones which characterize initial conditions (level of development and distortions) and external environment (war dummy variable), the explanatory power of the regression increases to 80 per cent along with excellent t-statistics (28 observations). It is quite remarkable that the inclusion of liberalization variables at this point does not improve the quality of regression statistics. Factoring in inflation improves the explanatory power to 88 per cent. The correlation coefficient rises further up to 93 per cent, if other indicators of institutional capacities, such as the share of the shadow economy, are added, although the number of observations in this case is only 17 due to the lack of data (Table 8.1).

Only the Central European economies saw the share of state revenues in GDP remain relatively stable during transition. Outside Central Europe there were only four countries where the share of government revenues in GDP did not fall markedly – Belarus, Estonia, Uzbekistan and Vietnam. The first three are also the top three performers in the FSU region, whereas Vietnam's performance is second to only that of China. Belarus and Uzbekistan, commonly perceived as procrastinators, nevertheless show better results than the more advanced reformers. On the other hand, this is the alternative explanation for Estonia's successful economic transformation as compared with most CIS states and even to other Baltic states; the usual interpretation focuses on progress in liberalization and may overlook the impact of strong institutions.

To sum up, there is enough evidence that differing performance levels during transition, after factoring in initial conditions and external environment, depend mostly on the strength of institutions and not so much on the progress in liberalization per se.

What leads to the institutional collapse and can it be prevented? Using the terminology of political science, it is appropriate to distinguish among strong authoritarian regimes (China, Vietnam and Uzbekistan), strong democratic regimes (Central European countries) and weak democratic regimes (most FSU and Balkan states) (see Figure 8.6). The former two are politically liberal or liberalizing – they protect individual rights, including those of property and contracts, and create a framework of law and administration – while the latter regimes, though democratic, are politically not as liberal, since they lack strong institutions and the ability to enforce law and order (Zakaria 1997).

These regimes constitute the phenomenon of 'illiberal democracies', countries, where competitive elections are introduced before the rule of law has been established. While European countries in the nineteenth century and East Asian countries recently moved from first establishing the rule of law to gradually introducing democratic elections (Hong Kong is the most obvious example of the rule of law without democracy), in Africa, parts of Latin America and India, and now in CIS countries, democratic political systems were introduced in societies without the firm rule of law.

Authoritarian regimes (including communist regimes), while gradually building property rights and institutions, were filling the vacuum in the rule of law via authoritarian means. After democratization occurred and illiberal democracies emerged, they found themselves deprived of old authoritarian instruments to ensure law and order but without the newly developed democratic mechanisms needed to guarantee property rights, contracts and law and order (upper left quadrant in Figure 8.6). It is not surprising that this had a devastating impact on investment climate and output.[11]

As Figure 8.7 suggests, there is a clear relationship between the ratio of the Rule of Law Index on the eve of the transition to the Democratization Index, on the one hand, and economic performance during the transition on the

Table 8.1   Regression of Change in GDP on Non-policy and Policy-Related Factors, Robust Estimates (for China all indicators are for the period of 1979–86 or similar)

Equations	1	2	3	4[c]	5	6
Observations/Variables						
Constant	N=28	N=28	N=28	N=28	N=17	N=17
	5.2***	5.0***	5.5***	5.7***	5.9***	6.1***
Distortions, % of GDP[a]	-.01***	-.01***	-.01***	-.01***	-.01****	-.01****
1987 PPP GDP per capita, % of the US level	-.01***	-.02***	-.01***	-.01***	-.02***	-.01***
War dummy[b]	-.63***	-.58***	-.40***	-.40***		
Decline in government revenues as a % of GDP from 1989–91 to 1993–96	-.01***	-.01***	-.01***	-.01***		
Liberalization index		.06		-.04		-.04
Log (Inflation, % a year, 1990–95, Geometric average)			-.12***	-.14***	-.12***	-.14***
Shadow economy as a % of GDP in 1994					-.02***	-.02***
Adjusted R², %	80	81	88	89	93	93

Notes: Dependent variable = log (1996 GDP as a % of 1989 GDP).

[a] Cumulative measure of distortions as a % of GDP equal to the sum of defense expenditure (minus 3% regarded as the 'normal' level), deviations in industrial structure and trade openness from the 'normal' level (the latter defined as the average indicator for 10 market economies with roughly the same GDP and GDP per capita), the share of heavily distorted trade (among the FSU republics) and lightly distorted trade (with socialist countries) taken with 33% weight.

[a] See Popov 2000 for details.

[b] Equals 1 for Armenia, Azerbaijan, Croatia, Georgia, Macedonia and Tajikistan and 0 for all other countries.

[c] Significant at 12 per cent.

*Significant at 10 per cent; **significant at 5 per cent; ***significant at 1 per cent.

other, although the positive correlation for authoritarian countries is different from that for democracies. That is, democratization without a strong rule of law usually leads to the collapse of output. There is a price to pay for early democratization, i.e. the introduction of competitive elections of government under the conditions where key liberal rights (personal freedom and safety, property, contracts, fair trial in court, etc.) are not well established.

If the Rule of Law and Democracy indexes are included in the basic regression equation, they have predicted signs (positive impact of the rule of law and negative impact of democracy), and they are statistically significant (Table 8.2, equation 8.1). This is consistent with the results obtained for a larger sample of countries. The best explanatory power, however, is exhibited by the index computed as the ratio of the Rule of Law Index to the Democracy Index: 83 per cent of all variations in output can be explained by only three factors – pre-transition distortions, inflation and Rule of Law-to-Democracy Index (Table 8.2, equation 8.2).[12] If the liberalization variable is added, it turns out to be not statistically significant and does not improve the goodness of fit (equation 8.3). At the same time, the ratio of the Rule of Law-to-Democracy Index and the decline in government revenues are not substitutes, but rather complement each other in characterizing the process of institutional decay. These two variables are not correlated, and they improve the goodness of fit, when included together in the same regression, to 91 per cent (equation 8.5), a better result than in regressions with either variable alone. The liberalization index, when added to the same equation, only deteriorates the goodness of fit, is not statistically significant and has the 'wrong' sign.

POST-RECESSION RECOVERY

Factors which determine performance in the recovery period, i.e. after the transformational recession is over, are somewhat different from the factors affecting performance during a transformational recession. First, the cumulative levels of liberalization achieved by 1995 appear to play a positive role at the initial stage of recovery (Figure 8.8). At the subsequent stages, the level of cumulative liberalization achieved by the mid-1990s does not seem to be important (Figure 8.9), but the progress in liberalization (increase in its level during recovery) appears to affect performance positively (Figure 8.10). This result is confirmed by regression analysis (Table 8.3). In most specifications the increase of liberalization during the recovery has a positive and significant effect on economic growth, although the level of liberalization by the mid-1990s is mostly insignificant, except for one specification, where it affects growth negatively.

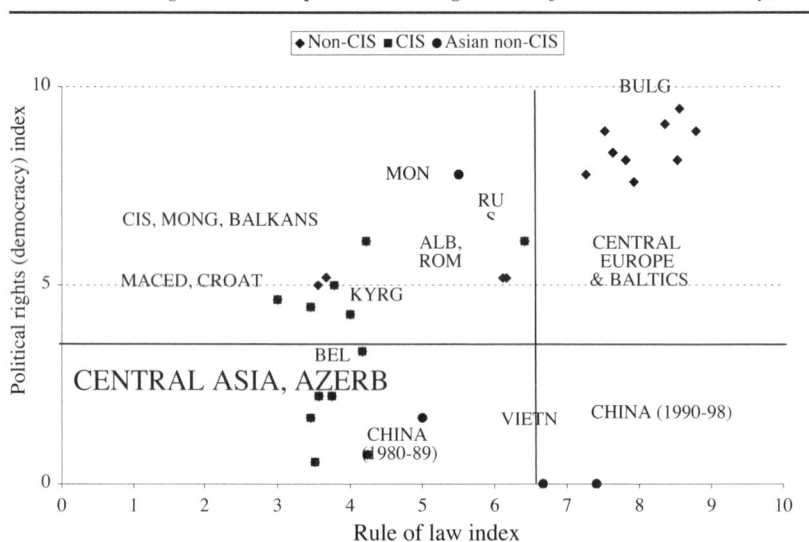

Figure 8.6 Indexes of the Rule of Law and Political Rights (0–10 scale, higher value represents stronger rule of law and democracy)

[Scatter plot showing Political rights (democracy) index on the y-axis (0–10) vs. Rule of law index on the x-axis (0–10), with three series: Non-CIS, CIS, and Asian non-CIS. Labeled points/groups include: BULG (upper right), MON, RU, ALB/ROM, CIS/MONG/BALKANS, MACED/CROAT, KYRG, CENTRAL EUROPE & BALTICS, BEL, CENTRAL ASIA, AZERB, CHINA (1980-89), VIETN, CHINA (1990-98).]

Second, pre-transition distortions do not play any significant role in the recovery period; the coefficient of distortions indicator is not statistically significant in any of the specifications.[13] The war dummy variable is always significant, but acquires a positive sign (it was negative for the recession period) suggesting that countries which suffered from wars in the first part of the 1990s recovered faster in the second half of the decade, likely benefiting from the effects of post-war reconstruction.

Finally, indicators which determine institutional capacity, such as the Rule of Law index (positively), the decline in the ratio of government revenues in GDP and democratization (negatively), continue to affect performance during recovery the same way performance was affected during the transformational recession.

These results are consistent with intuition and previous explanations. During the transformational recession the reduction of output was determined by the magnitude of the pre-transition distortions and by the collapse of institutions, whereas the speed of liberalization did not have any significant impact on performance. In fact (as Appendix 8A shows), the impact of the speed of liberalization was very likely negative, if there even is any effect. The rapid deregulation of prices caused an adverse supply shock which was beyond the economy's ability to reallocate resources. This negative impact of immediate

Figure 8.7   Ratio of the Rule of Law Index to Democracy Index and Output Change

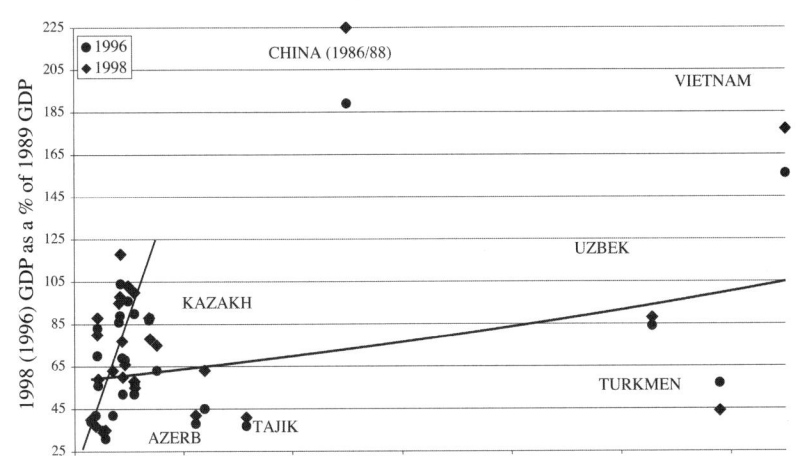

deregulation of prices does not show up in regressions because indexes of liberalization only partially reflect the speed of price deregulation. Of course another reason is that only China carried out price deregulation gradually via the dual-track price system. The other possible reason is the endogeneity of liberalization, that is dealt with below.

During the recovery stage, after inefficient enterprises were shut down in the course of the transformational recession, the pre-transition distortions did not affect performance any longer, but increased liberalization started to pay off. Controlling for the country effects via introducing an indicator of previous performance (GDP change in 1989–96), I obtain a positive correlation between increases in liberalization and performance in 1995–2003. This result is fully consistent with theory (a marketization dividend), but it is observed only in the recovery period, when inefficient sectors of the economy bottom out.

In addition, the impact of the state's institutional capacity on performance is the same – during the transformational recession and during the post-recession recovery. Democratization without the rule of law undermines institutional capacity and has a devastating impact on output (Polterovich and Popov 2007). This mechanism of weakening the institutional capacity in illiberal democracies is only partly associated with downsizing the state. The other part of the process is the decrease in the efficiency of the provision of public

Table 8.2 Regression of Change in GDP in 1989–96 on Initial Condtions, Policy Factors and Rule of Law and Democracy Indexes, Robust Estimates (for China all indicators are for the period of 1979–86 or similar)

Equations	1	2	3	4	5	6	7
Observations/Variables	N = 28	N = 28	N = 28	N = 28	N = 28	N = 28	N = 28
Constant	5.3***	5.4***	5.2***	5.4***	5.4***	5.5***	5.7***
Distortions, % of GDP[a]	−.005**	−.005**	−.003	−.006**	−.007***	−.007***	−.007***
1987 PPP GDP per capita, % of the US level	−.009**	−.006*	−.007**	−.007**	−.009***	−.008***	−.008***
War dummy[b]				−.19***	−.36***	−.37***	−.45***
Decline in government revenues as a % of GDP from 1989–91 to 1993–96					−.011***	−.011***	−.011***
Liberalization index			.05			−.02	.03
Log (Inflation, % a year, 1990–95, geometric average)	−.16***	−.20***	−.18***	−.17***	−.13***	−.13***	−.14***
Rule of law index, average for 1989–97, %	.008***						
Democracy index, average for 1990–98, %	−.005***						
Ratio of the rule of law to democracy index		.07***	.07***	.06***	.05***	.05***	−.003**
Adjusted R², %	82	83	83	85	91	91	90

Notes: Dependent variable = log (1996 GDP as a % of 1989 GDP).
[a] Cumulative measure of distortions as a % of GDP equal to the sum of defense expenditure (minus 3% regarded as the 'normal' level), deviations in industrial structure and trade openness from the 'normal' level (the latter defined as the average indicator for 10 market economies with roughly the same GDP and GDP per capita), the share of heavily distorted trade (among the FSU republics) and lightly distorted trade (with socialist countries) taken with 33% weight.
[a] See Popov 2000 for details.
[b] Equals 1 for Armenia, Azerbaijan, Croatia, Georgia, Macedonia and Tajikistan and 0 for all other countries.
*Significant at 10 per cent; **significant at 5 per cent; ***significant at 1 per cent.

goods. Even controlling for the decline in the ratio of state revenues to GDP, the positive impact of the rule of law on growth and the negative impact of democratization persist.

DEALING WITH ENDOGENEITY

Many authors have pointed to the 'endogeneity of liberalization' variable. Not only is performance explained by the speed of liberalization, but liberalization is also a function of performance (if performance is poor, it is more difficult for the government to push market reforms further). By constructing an instrumental variable (linking liberalization to initial conditions specified only as the pre-transition share of exports in GDP) Krueger and Ciolko (1998) demonstrate that the hypothesis regarding the endogeneity of the liberalization variable cannot be rejected. The worse the initial conditions for transformation, the greater the probability of a deep transformational recession, and delays in liberalization become more likely. Godoy and Stiglitz (2006) examined the impact of the speed of the privatization on performance. Specifically, they instrumented the speed of privatization, using the variables of pre-transition distortions from Popov (2000) and other measures of initial conditions, and concluded that, after controlling for the *level* of privatization, the *speed* (increment) of privatization adversely affected growth in the 1990s.

If there is endogeneity in the regressions presented in previous sections, the estimates cannot be considered correct, so it is necessary to resort to 2SLS estimation. First, the impact of liberalization on performance during recession (1989–96) is examined, and later the impact of the level and change in liberalization indexes on performance during recovery (1995–2003) is analyzed. The Liberalization index in 1995[14] is strongly correlated with the level of democracy in 1990–98 (R=60 per cent), while the level of democracy itself is not correlated with GDP growth in 1989–96 (R=5 per cent), so liberalization can be instrumented with the democracy level variable. The economic meaning of this correlation is rather obvious – it is well established that economic-market-type reforms went hand-in-hand with democratic reforms in post-communist countries (EBRD 1999, chapter 5). The results are presented in Table 8.4.

The surprising result here is that the coefficient for liberalization level in 1995 is negative and statistically significant in most specifications. In other words, the more liberalized the economy by 1995, the larger the reduction of GDP, during the transformational recession. This result is different from the previous regressions; when the liberalization variable was not instrumented, it turned out to be insignificant.

292   *Economic Reform in Developing Countries*

Figure 8.8   Liberalization Index by 1995 and Performance, 1994–98

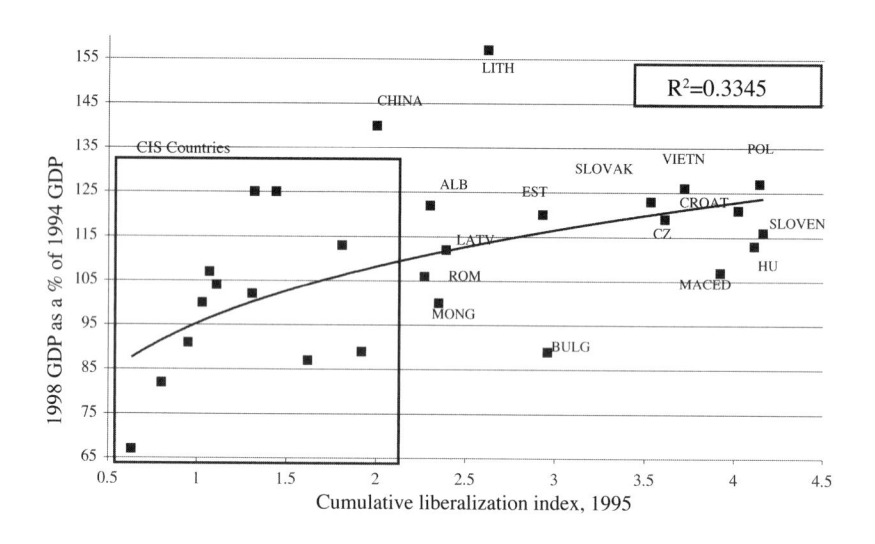

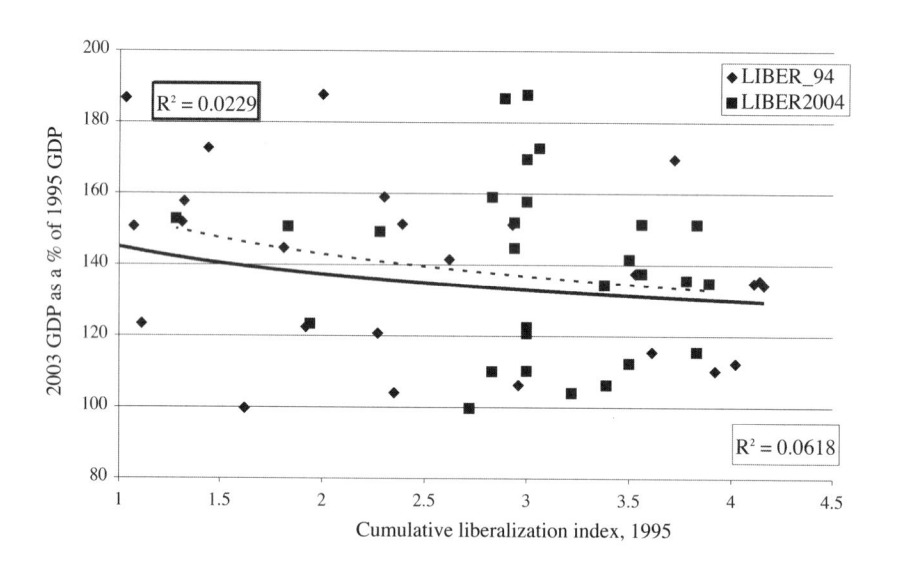

Figure 8.9   Liberalization and Output Growth in Transition Economies, 1995–2003

Figure 8.10   Liberalization Index and Output Growth in Transition Economies, 1995–2003

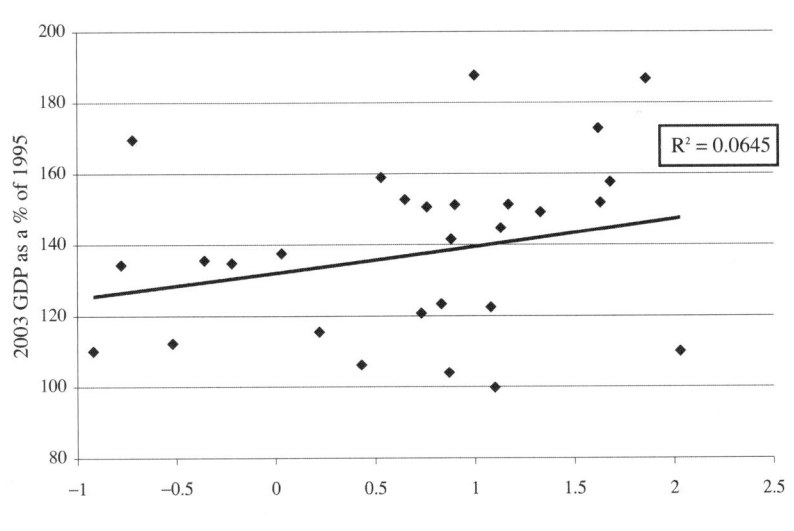

[Scatter plot: 2003 GDP as a % of 1995 (y-axis) vs. Increase in liberalization index in 1995–2003 (x-axis); $R^2 = 0.0645$]

Increase in liberalization index in 1995–2003

On the contrary, for the recovery period, instrumentation of the liberalization variable does not lead to different conclusions, but strengthens previously obtained results. Here it is the *increase* in liberalization during the recovery which needs to be instrumented, because the *level* of liberalization in 1995, before recovery, becomes just one of the initial conditions. Two variables are good candidates for the instruments – the FSU dummy (former Soviet republic) and the preceding (1995) level of liberalization. Both variables are strongly correlated with the increase in liberalization in 1995–2003 (R = 0.76 and R = –0.86, respectively), but not correlated with the GDP change in 1995–2003 (R = 0.24 and R = –0.28), so they could be used as instruments for the change in the Liberalization index in 1995–2003. The economic interpretation of this correlation is that former Soviet republics generally liberalized more slowly than other (East European) transition economies, so that the liberalization index by 1995 was rather low and the bulk of liberalization occurred later than in the East European countries, i.e. in 1995–2003. Besides, the more liberalized the transition economies were by 1995, the closer they were to achieving full liberalization, so the relationship between liberalization stock by 1995 and the subsequent liberalization increment is, as expected, negative. The results in Table 8.5 are no different from those reported in Table 8.3, describing

Table 8.3 Regression of Change in GDP in 1995–2003 on Initial Conditions, Institutional Capacity, Liberalization and Rule of Law and Democracy Indexes, Robust Estimates (for China all indicators are for the period of 1979–86 or similar)

Equations	1	2	3	4	5
Observations/Variables	N=28	N=28	N=28	N=28	N=28
Constant	105***	91***	99***	78***	99***
1996 GDP as a % of 1989 GDP	.33***	.45***	.46***	.24**	
1987 PPP GDP per capita, % of the US level					
War dummy[a]		22.9**	42.3***	32.0***	19.4*
Liberalization index in 1995			−19.9***		
Increase in the liberalization index in 1995–2003	15.3***	16.7***		17.6***	17.6***
Decline in government revenues as a % of GDP from 1989–91 to 1993–96				−.8***	
Rule of law index, average for 1989–97, %			.8**	1.0***	1.2***
Democracy index, average for 1990–98, %				−.6***	−.8***
Adjusted R^2, %	25	38	45	52	55

Notes: Dependent variable = 2003 GDP as a % of 1995 GDP.
[a]Equals 1 for Armenia, Azerbaijan, Croatia, Georgia, Macedonia and Tajikistan and 0 for all other countries.
*Significant at 10 per cent; **significant at 5 per cent; ***significant at 1 per cent.

regressions without the instrumentation of the liberalization–change variable. In fact, the coefficient of the instrumented liberalization–change variable is higher and no less significant than without instrumentation.

Why does the level of 'liberalization stock' accumulated by 1995 have a negative effect on economic performance in 1989–96? This relationship becomes visible only when liberalization is instrumented via a democracy-level indicator, whereas without instrumentation this impact is insignificant. The interpretation of this result is straightforward. Liberalization is best explained by the democratization process (it pushes liberalization forward) and pre-transition distortions (large distortions force policymakers to slow liberalization because they are afraid output will collapse). Democratization pushes liberalization forward too much, even when accounting for other factors such as the negative impact of pre-transition distortions, so liberalization, when determined endogenously, has a negative impact on performance. The impact of residual liberalization (i.e. it is not determined within the specified model) is positive, but insignificant. Including the residual liberalization into the right-hand side of the regression equation is equivalent to including actual liberalization together with the democracy variable (see Table 8.2, equation 8.7) – liberalization impact is positive, but insignificant.

The negative impact of fast liberalization is associated with the rapid decline of non-competitive industries, that is not counterweighed by the rise of competitive sectors. The speed of the transfer of resources from non-competitive to competitive sectors is not infinite and depends on a flow of new investment. Hence, when fast liberalization creates a need for restructuring which exceeds the investment potential of the economy, there is a general reduction of output – a typical supply-side recession which could have been avoided with slower paced liberalization. Figure 8.11 demonstrates that the reduction of output in Russia during the transformational recession was largely structural. Industries with the greatest adverse supply shock (deteriorating terms of trade–relative price ratios), such as light industry, experienced the largest reduction of output. Such a reduction was by no means inevitable, if the deregulation of prices has been gradual (or had losses from deteriorating terms-of-trade for most affected industries been compensated by subsidies). The pace of liberalization had to be no faster than the ability of the economy to move resources from non-competitive (under the new market price ratios) to competitive industries (see Appendix 8A).

Does this mean that liberalization was proceeding faster than necessary, spurred onward by rapid democratization? Certainly. But although it is tempting to think that the democracy variable nicely explains economic liberalization, it cannot be the only reason, because there are options and choices in carrying out government policy. After all, finding an instrument is not the same as

Table 8.4 Regression of Change in GDP in 1989–96 on Initial Conditions, Institutional Capacity, Liberalization and Rule of Law and Democracy Indexes, 2SLS Robust Estimates (for China all indicators are for the period of 1979–86 or similar)

Equations	1	2	3	4
Observations/Variables	N = 28	N = 28	N = 17	N = 17
Constant	6.4***	6.3***	6.0***	6.0***
Pre–transition distortions, % of GDP	–.01***	–.02***		–.004
1987 PPP GDP per capita, % of the US level	–.007**	–.01***		
War dummy[a]	–.45***	–.29[b]		
Liberalization index in 1995	–.18**	–.39*	–.19***	–.19***
Decline in government revenues as a % of GDP from 1989–91 to 1993–96	–.02***	–.02***		
Log (Inflation, % a year, 1990–95, geometric average)	–1.7***	–.22***	–.22***	–.19***
Rule of law index, average for 1989–97, %		–.01[c]		
Increase in the share of shadow economy in GDP in 1989–94, p.p.			–.02***	–.015***
R^2, %	86	77	88	90

Notes: Dependent variable = log (1996 GDP as a % of 1989 GDP).
[a]Equals 1 for Armenia, Azerbaijan, Croatia, Georgia, Macedonia and Tajikistan and 0 for all other countries.
[b]Significant at 12 per cent.
[c] Significant at 16 per cent.
*Significant at 10 per cent; **significant at 5 per cent; ***significant at 1 per cent.

finding the explanation. Unfortunately, there are no examples to the contrary in the post-communist world: only authoritarian regimes were able to choose between shock therapy and gradualism. Most of the authoritarian regimes proceeded with slow reforms, but Vietnam carried out shock therapy; in 1994 Vietnam's liberalization index was 3.92, higher than in most East European countries, even though there was no democracy whatsoever. But among democratic states there are no examples of countries which proceeded with slow economic liberalization. Political-economy factors play a powerful role in shaping economic strategy and there is definitely a grain of truth in the popular saying that there is nothing more endogenous than government policy.

Table 8.5 Regression of Change in GDP in 1995–2003 on Initial Condtions, Institutional Capacity, Liberalization and Rule of Law and Democracy Indexes, 2SLS Robust Estimates (for China the indicator is for the period ten years earlier)

Equations	1	2	3	4
Observations/Variables	N = 28	N = 28	N = 28	N = 28
Instruments for liberalization change in 1995–2003 variable	LIBER95	FSU	LIBER95 FSU	LIBER95 FSU
Constant	97.8***	95.8***	97.7***	79.5***
1996 GDP as a % of 1989 GDP				.18*
War dummy[a]	19.5*	19.8**	19.5*	25.0**
Increase in liberalization index in 1995–2003	18.2***	19.2**	18.3***	22.9***
Decline in government revenues as a % of GDP from 1989–91 to 1993–96	−.76***	−.78**	−.76***	−.65***
Rule of law index, average for 1989–97, %	1.24***	1.28***	1.25***	1.13***
Democracy index, average for 1990–98, %	−.76***	−.76***	−.76***	−.62***
R^2, %	55	54	55	56

Notes: Dependent variable = 2003 GDP as a % of 1995 GDP.
[a] Equals 1 for Armenia, Azerbaijan, Croatia, Georgia, Macedonia and Tajikistan and 0 for all other countries.
*Significant at 10 per cent; **significant at 5 per cent; ***significant at 1 per cent.

CONCLUSION

Differences in performance during the initial stage transformational recession depend strongly on initial conditions such as pre-transition levels of GDP per capita, distortions in industrial structure and external trade patterns. The higher the distortions, the worse the performance, as measured by the GDP change. Furthermore, the higher the GDP per capita before transition, the greater the distortions embodied in fixed capital stock and the more difficult it was to overcome these distortions (because more investment was needed for restructuring) to achieve growth.

Sen suggests that nothing is as important for reformers as the willingness to question why they are doing what they are doing; catchy mottos should not displace consistent reform strategies. The findings in this chapter indicate that this suggestion is especially relevant to the relationship between the institutional capability of the state and liberalization. By focusing on liberalization and macroeconomic stabilization as key policy variables in transition economies, conventional wisdom overlooked the impact of strong institutions. Accounting

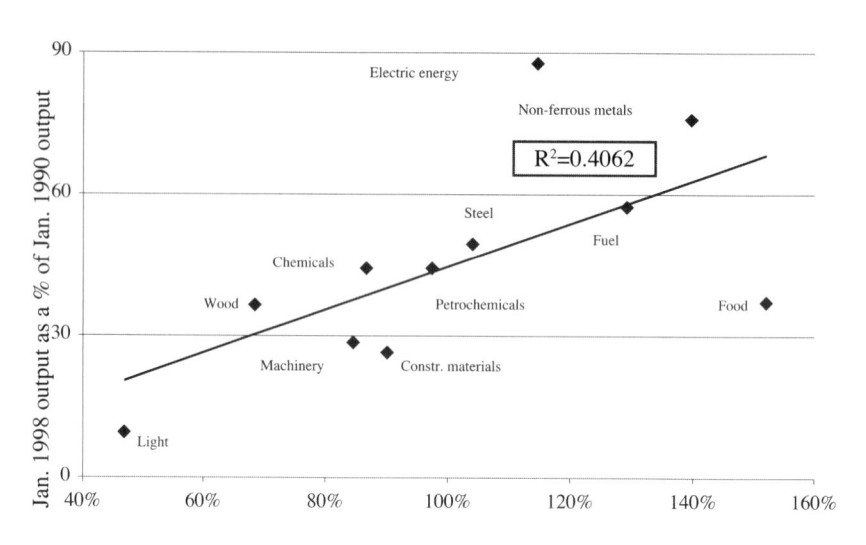

Figure 8.11   Change in Relative Prices and Output in 1990–98 in Russian Industry

[Scatter plot: Jan. 1998 output as a % of Jan. 1990 output (y-axis) vs. Ratio of 1998 prices to 1990 prices as a % of industrial average (x-axis). Data points labeled: Electric energy, Non-ferrous metals, Steel, Fuel, Chemicals, Wood, Petrochemicals, Food, Machinery, Constr. materials, Light. $R^2=0.4062$]

for uneven initial conditions sheds new light on the relative importance of various policy factors. Macroeconomic stability continues to matter a great deal – the inclusion of the inflation variable improves goodness of fit, but the liberalization index in the initial period of transition appears to have a negative impact. It was not statistically significant without controlling for endogeneity, and statistically significant when endogeneity (dependence of liberalization on the magnitude of distortions and, hence, on performance) is accounted for. On the contrary, changes in the institutional capabilities of the state always have a dramatic impact on performance. It follows that the debate about the speed of the liberalization was to a large extent mis-focused, whereas the crucial importance of strong institutions for good performance was overlooked.

In a sense, the importance of preserving the state's institutional capacity to ensure good performance may be considered the main finding of this study, raising strong policy implications. After allowing for differing initial conditions, it turns out that the fall in output in transition economies was associated mostly with a poor business environment, resulting from institutional collapse. Liberalization, when it is not complemented with strong institutions, cannot ensure good performance.

Institutional capacities, in turn, depend to a large extent on the combination of the rule of law and democracy. The data seem to suggest that both authoritarian and democratic regimes can have strong rule of law and deliver efficient institutions, whereas under weak rule of law authoritarian regimes do a better job of maintaining efficient institutions than do democracies. In short, the record of illiberal democracies in ensuring institutional capacities is the worst, that predictably has a devastating impact on output.

Moreover, the impact of the speed of liberalization at the initial stage of transition, i.e., during the transformational recession, appears to be negative, if any. If the speed of liberalization is considered to be endogenous, i.e., determined by political economy forces pushing it forward or holding it back, it turns out that the impact of liberalization was negative, rather than positive. The reason for the negative impact is probably associated with the economy's limited ability to adjust to new price ratios that emerge after rapid liberalization: but investment constraints do not allow the rapid transfer of capital stock from inefficient to efficient industries, so the economy may be unable to compensate for the fall in output in non-competitive sectors by a rise in competitive sectors (see Appendix 8A).

In either case, the process of output collapse in transition economies is best described by the supply-side recession model, where the key determinants are initial conditions and the strength of institutions, whereas the speed of liberalization had an adverse effect on performance.

In the recovery stage liberalization starts to affect growth positively and the impact of pre-transition distortions disappears. Institutional capacity and macroeconomic policy continue to be important prerequisites for successful performance. Liberalization, that proceeds much more slowly at the recovery stage (and for some countries is even negative – see Figure 8.10) influences performance positively, because it creates market stimuli without causing the rapid collapse of inefficient industries, which cannot be compensated fully by the rise of efficient industries due to investment constraints.

To be sure, these factors are not sufficient to explain an China's 'economic miracle' – China remains an outlier in all regressions. Very rapid growth is virtually always associated with the increase in the export-to-GDP ratio, i.e. it is an export-led growth, and requires respective industrial strategy. The key and most efficient instrument of this export-oriented industrial strategy appears to be an undervalued exchange rate, maintained through the accumulation of foreign exchange reserves (Polterovich and Popov 2004; 2005).

NOTES

This chapter is partly based on two articles published in *Comparative Economic Studies*: 'Shock Therapy versus Gradualism: The End of the Debate (Explaining the Magnitude of the Transformational Recession)', **42** (1), 1–57 and 'Shock Therapy versus Gradualism Reconsidered: Lessons from Transition Economies after 15 Years of Reforms', **49** (1), 1–31.

1. Gradual reforms started in China in 1979. Vietnam, after experimenting with gradual reforms in 1986–89, launched a more radical reform program in 1989.
2. Liberalization indexes are estimated by experts' measures of progress in three areas: (1) price liberalization and abolition of state trading monopolies, (2) deregulation of foreign trade and currency convertibility regimes and (3) privatization of enterprises and banking reform. Liberalization indexes are computed as the sum of liberalization flows for six years (1989 to 1994) by De Melo, Denizer and Gelb (1996) and are consistent with European Bank for Reform and Development (EBRD) liberalization indexes published annually in the EBRD *Transition Report*, so they characterize the increase in liberalization over the six initial years of reforms. For China, Mongolia and Vietnam there are estimates only for 1989–94, so I use my own estimates for the year 2003 for these three countries and for 1979 –84 period for China, because market reforms started in China in 1979.
3. Founded on December 8, 1991, the Commonwealth of Independent States is a loose alliance of 12 former Soviet republics: Armenia, Azerbaijan, Belarus, Georgia, Kazakhstan, Kyrgyzstan, Moldova, Russia, Tajikistan, Turkmenistan Ukraine and Uzbekistan. (Due to a civil war, Georgia did not join until 1993). The Baltic republics, Estonia, Latvia and Lithuania refused to attend the meeting that created the organization. The CIS was founded to coordinate economic, foreign, and security policy in the Soviet successor states.
4. While Vietnamese industry, excluding constantly and rapidly growing oil production, experienced some downturn in 1989–90 (-6 per cent in 1989 and 0 per cent in 1990) agricultural growth remained strong, so that GDP growth rates virtually did not fall (5–6 per cent a year).
5. Council for Mutual Economic Assistance, a Soviet-bloc trade zone.
6. More detailed description of the data and regressions is in Popov (2000, 2007).
7. For explanations of distortions indicator see sources for Table 8.1 and (Popov, 2000).
8. Following Gerschenkron (1962), this factor is sometimes referred to as an 'advantage of backwardness'. With respect to transition economies, this general argument has an additional dimension. Because of distortions in infrastructure and other fixed capital stock created by decades of central planning, the magnitude of the needed restructuring was greater in the socialist economies with higher capital/output ratios, i.e. a higher level of GDP per capita. It may be argued that in poor agricultural economies distortions were not 'cast in stone', since the relatively primitive fixed capital stock was less susceptible to distortions and, even if distorted, was not so large in comparison with GDP as it was in more advanced industrialized transition economies. Hence, restructuring in more backward countries did not require as much investment (as a per cent of GDP) as in more advanced transition economies.
9. The decline in government revenues as a per cent of GDP in these countries was less pronounced than elsewhere in CIS.
10. Data for China (World Bank, 1996), Russia (Goskomstat) and Poland (Rocznik Statystyczny 1990, Warszawa; and data from the Polish Institute of Finance provided by Grzegorz W. Kolodko) do not include off-budget funds, that are very substantial in all three countries and are used mostly for social security purposes. Defense expenditure are from official statistics, i.e. lower than Western estimates, which is likely to lead to overstatement of spending for investment and subsidies at the expense of defense outlays. For USSR/Russia investment and subsidies are shown together.
11. The Democracy Index is the average of political rights index for 1990–98, taken from Freedom House (http://www.freedomhouse.org/rankings.pdf), but inverted and calibrated, so that complete democracy coincides with 100 per cent, whereas complete authoritarianism with 0 per cent. The Rule of Law Index is taken from (Campos 1999). For China, Vietnam and

Mongolia data from the International Country Risk Guide, 1984 to 1998, are calibrated so that 100 per cent corresponds to the highest possible rule of law.
12. For a larger sample of countries (all developing and developed countries, not only transition economies), the result is that there is a threshold level of the Rule of Law Index: if it is higher than a certain level, democratization affects growth positively, if lower, then democratization impedes growth (Polterovich and Popov 2007).
13. This is consistent with the result obtained in (Popov 2000, 2007) and Godoy and Stiglitz (2004).
14. This Liberalization Index is constructed as explained earlier by De Melo et al. (1996) as the sum of liberalization 'flows' for six years (1989–94 for all countries, except China, for which the period is 1979–84). Assuming that before transition the level of liberalization in communist economies was negligible, the 1995 Liberalization Index can be interpreted as the cumulative 'stock' of liberalization by 1995 or as the total 'flow' of liberalization in the first six years of reforms.

BIBLIOGRAPHY

Åslund, Anders, Peter Boone and Simon Johnson (1996), 'How to Stabilize: Lessons from Post-Communist Countries', *Brookings Papers on Economic Activity*, **1**, 217–313.

Breton, Paul, Daniel Gros and Guy Vandille (1997), 'Output Decline and Recovery in the Transition Economies: Causes and Social Consequences', *Economics of Transition*, **5** (1), 113–30.

Bruno, Michael (1995), 'Does Inflation Really Lower Growth?', *Finance and Development*, **32** (3), 35–38.

Bruno, Michael and William Easterly (1995), 'Inflation Crisis and Long-Run Growth', Cambridge, MA, National Bureau of Economic Research (NBER) Working Paper No. 5209.

Campos, Nauro F. (1999), 'Context is Everything: Measuring Institutional Change in Transition Economies', Washington, DC, World Bank Policy Research Working Paper No. 2269.

De Melo, Martha, Cevdet Denizer, Alan Gelb and Stoyan Tenev (1997), 'Circumstance and Choice: The Role of Initial Conditions and Policies in Transitions Economies', Washington, DC, World Bank Policy Research Working Paper No. 1866.

De Melo, Martha, Cevdet Denizer and Alan Gelb (1996), 'Patterns of Transition from Plan to Market', *World Bank Economic Review*, **10** (3), 397–424.

European Bank for Reconstruction and Development (1999), *Transition Report*, London: EBRD, 1999.

—— (2001), *Transition Report*, London: EBRD, 2001.

Fischer, Stanley, Ratna Sahay and Carlos, A. Vegh (1996), 'Stabilization and Growth in the Transition Economies: The Early Experience', *Journal of Economic Perspectives*, **10** (2), 45–66.

Fischer, Stanley and Ratna Sahay (2000), 'The Transition Economies after Ten Years', Cambridge, MA, National Bureau of Economic Research (NBER) Working Paper No. 7664.

Gerschenkron, Alexander (1962), *Economic Backwardness in Historical Perspective*, Cambridge, MA: Belknap Press.

Godoy, Sergio and Joseph Stiglitz (2006), 'Growth, Initial Conditions, Law and Speed

of Privatization in Transition Countries: 11 Years Later', Cambridge, MA, National Bureau of Economic Research (NBER) Working Paper No. 11992.
Heybey, Berta and Peter Murrell (1999), 'The Relationship between Economic Growth and the Speed of Liberalization During Transition', *Journal of Policy Reform*, **3** (2), 121–37.
Kornai, Janos (1994), 'Transformational Recession: The Main Causes', *Journal of Comparative Economics*, **19** (2), 39–63.
Krueger, Gary and Marek Ciolko (1998), 'A Note on Initial Conditions and Liberalization during Transition', *Journal of Comparative Economics*, **26** (4), 618–34.
Naughton, Barry (1997), 'Economic Reform in China. Macroeconomic and Overall Performance', in Doowon Lee (ed.), *The System Transformation of the Transition Economies: Europe, Asia and North Korea*, Seoul: Yonsei University Press, chapter 2.
Polterovich, Victor and Vladimir Popov (2004), 'Accumulation of Foreign Exchange Reserves and Long Term Economic Growth', in S. Tabata and A. Iwashita (eds) *Slavic Eurasia's Integration into the World Economy*, Sapporo: Slavic Research Center, Hokkaido University, pp. 161–98.
—— (2005), 'Appropriate Economic Policies at Different Stages of Development', Moscow, New Economic School Working Paper.
—— (2007), 'Democratization, Quality of Institutions and Economic Growth', in Natalia Dinello and Vladimir Popov (eds) Political Institutions and Development: Failed Expectations and Renewed Hopes, Cheltenham: Edward Elgar, 2007, pp. 72–100.
Popov, Vladimir (1998a), 'Investment in Transition Economies: Factors of Change and Implications for Performance', *Journal of East-West Business*, **4** (1/2), 47–98.
—— (1998b), 'Will Russia Achieve Fast Economic Growth?', *Communist Economies and Economic Transformation*, **10** (4), 421–49.
—— (1999), 'Investment, Restructuring and Performance in Transition Economies', *Post-Communist Economies*, **11** (4), 445–62.
—— (2000), 'Shock Therapy versus Gradualism: The End of the Debate (Explaining the Magnitude of the Transformational Recession)', *Comparative Economic Studies*, **42** (1), 1–57.
—— (2007), 'Shock Therapy versus Gradualism Reconsidered: Lessons from Transition Economies after 15 Years of Reforms', *Comparative Economic Studies*, **49** (1), 1–31.
Sachs, Jeffrey D. (1996), 'The Transition at Mid-Decade', *American Economic Review*, **86** (2), 128–33.
Shmelev, Nikolai and Vladimir Popov (1989), *The Turning Point: Revitalizing the Soviet Economy*, New York: Doubleday.
World Bank (1996), *From Plan to Market*, New York: Oxford University Press.
World Bank (1997), *The State in A Changing World*, New York: Oxford University Press.
Zakaria, Fareed (1997), 'The Rise of Illiberal Democracies', *Foreign Affairs*, **76** (6), 22–43.

APPENDIX 8A: ADVANTAGES OF GRADUAL REFORMS

Assume for a moment that market-oriented reforms lead to increased long-term welfare in all countries, no matter how far from the technological frontier. Should governments proceed with fast (or even instantaneous) reforms or with gradual, incremental reforms? In the 1990s scholars and policymakers alike widely debated this issue regarding the post-communist economies. Shock therapists advocated rapid changes, while gradualists favored a slower pace, such as China's dual-track system to deregulate prices. Based on the experiences of transition economies, it is safe to conclude that if reforms create a need to reallocate resources, the speed of reforms should not overstretch the investment potential of the economy.

To illustrate this conclusion, consider a country where the deregulation of prices (or the elimination of trade tariffs and subsidies) leads to a change in relative price ratios and thus produces an adverse supply shock for at least some industries. Capital should be reallocated from industries facing declining relative prices and profitability to industries with rising relative prices. If 20 per cent of total output is concentrated in non-competitive industries, then this entire sector should disappear either gradually or immediately, depending on how fast relative prices change. Capital is not homogeneous and cannot be moved to the competitive sector, although labor can be reallocated to the competitive sector without costs. Marginal capital productivity in the competitive sector in this example is higher than in the non-competitive and is equal to one-third. Assume further that all investments go into the competitive sector and that net investment is equal to 10 per cent of GDP. These simple assumptions produce the output trajectories shown at Figure 8A.1.[1]

If reforms are carried out instantly, then output in the unprofitable sector, again accounting for 20 per cent of total output, falls immediately, and savings for investment are generated only by the competitive sector, so that it takes seven years to reach the pre-recession level of output. Alternatively, reforms could be carried out slowly (gradual price deregulation or elimination of tariffs/subsidies), so that every year output in the non-competitive sector falls by 30 per cent. In this case the transformational recession is milder, and total output recovers by the fifth year.

The best trajectory, of course, is the one with a deregulation speed which leads to output reduction in the non-competitive sector at a natural rate, i.e. as its fixed capital stock retires in the absence of new investment. If the retirement rate of fixed assets in the non-competitive sector is 10 per cent, and deregulation proceeds at such a pace that only 10 per cent of the total non-competitive sector is phased out annually, there would be no reduction of total output (in both sectors) at all. On the contrary, growth rates would increase constantly,

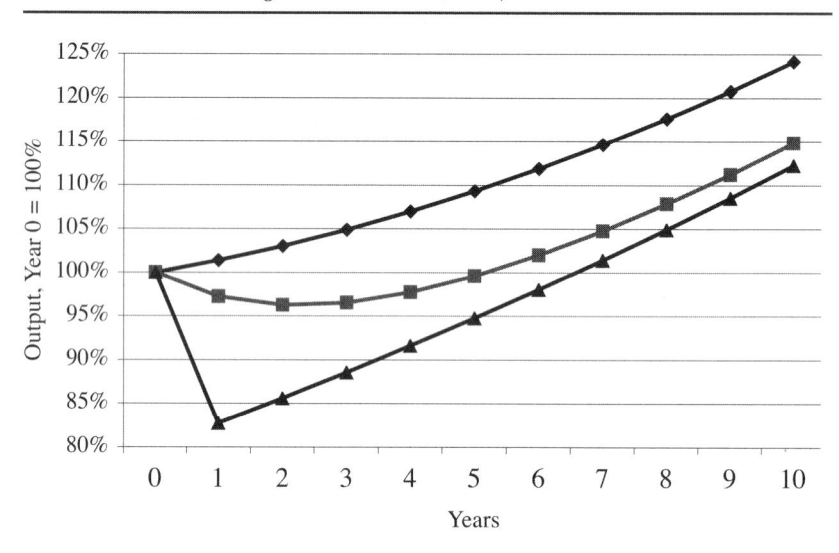

Figure 8A.1 Hypothetical Trajectories of Output (Year zero = 100%, assuming instant liberalization)

Notes: Size of non-competitive sector (NC) in the initial year = 20 per cent of total output; net investment (s) = 10 per cent of total output; marginal capital productivity, output increase per unit of net investment (a) = 1/3.

approaching the steady state 3.4 per cent annually by year 25. The slower rate of deregulation, implying a more gradual output reduction in the non-competitive industries, would require some investment into supporting capital stock and output in the non-competitive sector. This is clearly a sub-optimal option, since the productivity of investment in this sector is by definition lower than elsewhere.

This example illustrates a limit to the speed of reallocating capital from non-competitive to competitive industries. This pace is determined by the net investment/GDP ratio (gross investment minus retirement of capital stock in the competitive industries, since in non-competitive industries the retiring capital stock should not be replaced anyway). It is not reasonable to wipe away output in non-competitive industries faster than capital is being transferred to more efficient industries. If there are other factors of production which can be transferred faster than capital, such as labor, there is a trade-off between using labor in non-competitive industries, but with high capital/labor ratios, and transferring this same labor to competitive industries, but without much capital (low capital/labor ratios) for the time being. Also, the logic which applies to physical capital could be applied to the human capital as well.

Market-type reforms in many post-communist economies created exactly this kind of bottleneck. Countries which adopted shock therapy found themselves in a supply-side recession: the excessive speed of change in relative prices required a magnitude of restructuring which was simply non-achievable with the limited pool of investment. Up to half of their economies was made non-competitive overnight. Output in these non-competitive industries fell for about a decade and fell in some cases to virtually zero, whereas the growth of output in competitive industries was constrained by the limited investment potential and was not enough to compensate for the output loss in the inefficient sectors (Popov 2000).

The problem is still there for many transition economies, since many domestic price ratios are quite different from those of the world market. Fuel and energy prices, for example, in most cases are still way below the world market prices. In Russia electricity tariffs are several US cent per kwh, whereas in Western and even in Central European countries they are about 10 cents (European Bank for Reconstruction and Development 2001). Meanwhile, the third most important Russian export commodity (after oil and gas) is extremely energy intensive aluminum, produced out of largely imported bauxite. If Russian electricity prices are increased to the world level instantly, the investment required to create jobs just for the workers of aluminum smelters going out of business may exceed the meager investment potential of the whole national economy.

In short, the speed of adjustment and restructuring in every economy is limited, if only due to the limited investment potential needed to reallocate capital stock. This is the main rationale for the *gradual* phasing out of tariff and non-tariff barriers, of subsidies and other forms of government support of particular sectors (it took nearly ten years for the European Economic Community and NAFTA to abolish tariffs). This is a powerful argument against shock therapy, especially when the reforms involved result in a sizeable reallocation of resources. For Western countries with low trade barriers, low subsidies, few price controls, etc. even fast, radical reforms are not likely to require restructuring which would exceed the limit of investment potential. But for less developed countries with many distortions in their economies supported by explicit and implicit subsidies, the fast removal of these subsidies could easily result in a need for restructuring which is beyond the economy's ability due to investment and other constraints.

NOTE

1. Total output consists of output of competitive and non-competitive sectors: $Y_n = (Y_n^C + Y_n^{NC})$ and is equal to 1 or 100 per cent in the initial year. Output in the non-competitive sector in the year n, Y_n^{NC}, is equal to the share of the non-competitive sector in total output in the initial year, NC, multiplied by $(1-\alpha)^n$, where α is the rate of reduction of output in the non-competitive sector determined by the speed of deregulation: $Y_n^{NC} = (1-\alpha)^n * NC$. Output in the competitive sector in the year n is equal to the output of the preceding year, Y_{n-1}^C, plus the increase in output equal to marginal capital productivity, a, multiplied by the share of net investment in GDP, s, multiplied by total output: $Y_n^C = Y_{n-1}^C + a*s*(Y_n^C + Y_n^{NC})$. Solving for total output, we get: $$Y_n = \frac{Y_{n-1}^C + (1-\alpha)^n * NC}{1 - as}.$$

9. Enhancing Income Opportunities for the Rural Poor: The Benefits of Rural Roads

Javier Escobal and Carmen Ponce

This chapter analyzes the welfare effects triggered by connecting rural villages to rural and urban centers through road rehabilitation and maintenance, important elements of Peru's Rural Roads Program. Although both Peruvian public officials and academics typically consider such programs to be successful, there is a need to document the impacts and understand the processes they trigger. What features of the program can be improved? What complementary interventions could foster more sustainable income generating opportunities and in general more inclusive social and political processes? Answering these questions requires a more thorough understanding of the causal connections underlying the welfare effects of such interventions, rather than a narrow focus on the one-dimensional outcomes typically measured in surveys. Amartya Sen refers to this broad perspective as 'reason', the third and most important of his dimensions of successful reform. Sen calls on researchers and policymakers to continually ask: Why we are doing this? How can we improve the actions we implement in order to achieve the goals we pursue? What should we prioritize and how can implemented actions complement each other to achieve goals more efficiently? We believe this chapter contributes to this line of analysis.

A country's rural road network is typically made up of tracks, trails, footpaths and dirt roads which link rural villages and towns and often connect to secondary roads, allowing residents to access markets and social services which their own communities do not provide. Tracks, trails and footpaths, defined here as 'non-motorized roads', ease the movement of people and animals over typically steep terrain and are characterized by low quality standards and limited distance. 'Motorized roads' – also known as country roads – are engineered earth roads which connect small towns and villages by means of public transport or cargo trucks. Ideally, motorized roads generate a fluid connection to secondary roads and connect rural populations to urban areas.

In most developing countries this rural road network is vital, typically accounting for more than half of the national transport network, but only a marginal part of the national budget is allocated to road construction, rehabilitation and maintenance. Peru's rugged topography and great ecological and climatic diversity have led local policymakers to acknowledge the importance of investing in rural transportation infrastructure. However, such recognition does not necessarily translate into an appropriate allocation of public funds. This type of infrastructure is expensive to construct and maintain, due to frequent landslides and avalanches, and the beneficiary population tends to have marginal political representation. Consequently, politicians tend to overlook rural roads infrastructure and put funding into other projects which will be more profitable in terms of votes. Therefore, there is an urgent need to document the benefits which this kind of public investment brings to the population it serves. Not only do policymakers need to see the results, but the national population, typically concentrated in a few urban areas, needs to be convinced of the positive results of investment in rural roads.

While academics largely agree about the need to invest in rural infrastructure, especially roads, as an effective component of rural poverty eradication efforts, they tend to emphasize the increased access to social services and markets, without establishing the changes individual households might experience in aggregate welfare measures like consumption and income. Although better access to health and education services has an undoubtedly positive impact on household welfare, greater access to product and factor markets does not necessarily entail higher levels of welfare, because the household capacity to generate income could be threatened by increasing levels of competition in local markets. Therefore, an analysis of the effects of road rehabilitation on the level and composition of household income is essential to understanding the welfare impacts of this type of public intervention. Identifying how interventions work and what can be improved, as Sen demands, requires a better understanding of the causal connections underlying the enhanced opportunities brought about by road rehabilitation.

Multiple studies have documented how rural road infrastructure investment affects access to product and factor markets and key public services without controlling for other covariate effects which could either strengthen or attenuate positive results. One way to overcome this problem is propensity score matching techniques, which facilitate the construction of counterfactual scenarios which are sufficiently robust to enable researchers to claim causal relations. Developed by Rosenbaum and Rubin (1983) and extended by Heckman, Ichimura and Todd (1998), this methodological framework has not been used to evaluate rural road construction, rehabilitation and maintenance projects.

This chapter explores some methodological modifications which are necessary to adapt propensity score matching to assess the benefits which investment in rural road rehabilitation may generate. Since many of the samples used in these studies lack a households sample size sufficient to guarantee minimum statistical representativeness at the town level, it is not generally possible – using available information – to balance the two household samples (access to rehabilitated or to non-rehabilitated rural roads) in terms of observable characteristics. However, both samples can be balanced in two stages: First, by ensuring that towns are comparable in terms of certain basic characteristics (community organizational capacity, economic activity indicators, access to public services, length of road section or size of town, etc.). Second, by simulating welfare indicators which would correspond to observed households, if all have the same assets endowments (human, organizational or physical capital), so that the assessment of rehabilitation effects will account only for the differences in returns and non-observables which differentiate an intervention scenario from a non-intervention one.

THE BENEFITS OF RURAL ROADS

Even though the focus of infrastructure investment in developing countries has shifted away from large-scale projects (highways, railways and big irrigation schemes) to smaller-scale but more locally important investments, such as rural roads or micro-hydroelectric power plants, relevant impact assessments of the effects on local poverty or living standards are still scarce.

The relationship between poverty reduction and rural infrastructure provision has been discussed from a macro perspective by various authors. Ahmed and Donovan (1992), Lipton and Ravallion (1995) and Booth, Hanmer and Lovell (2000), among others, point out the existence of strong linkages among rural infrastructure investment, agricultural growth and poverty reduction. These studies draw evidence from Southeast Asian countries like Indonesia or Malaysia, where massive growth in rural infrastructure was followed by a long period of economic growth and a dramatic reduction in rural poverty. Although the causal connection is not clearly established, they suggest that growth is a result of rising agricultural productivity and new job opportunities created by infrastructure improvements.

More recently, authors like Jalan and Ravallion (2002) have highlighted the importance of rural infrastructure facilities and the complementarities among them as an essential requirement for rural income growth and poverty reduction. These authors find that overcoming poverty traps is crucial to assure not only access to key public facilities, like roads or electricity, but also to the adoption of a critical mass of complementary key public infrastructure facilities.

As Gannon and Liu (1997) point out, other studies have recognized the microeconomic mechanisms by which road infrastructure investment facilitates economic growth and poverty reduction. According to these authors, rural infrastructure investment reduces production and transaction costs, fosters trade and promotes the division of labor and specialization, key elements for sustainable economic growth. Similarly, Block and Webb (2001) find that higher road density promotes specialization, enabling farmers to develop more intensive agriculture based on modern inputs. However, Gannon and Liu also note that rural infrastructure improvements foster increases in the profitability of public and private assets belonging to households which have access to such infrastructure.[1]

Although the literature identifies many areas where positive impacts of such investments are expected, only a few studies have made progress in establishing a clear causal link between infrastructure provision and any welfare indicator. Most studies are limited to documenting in more or less detail how access to infrastructure facilities by the rural poor reduce the time and costs involved in accessing product and factor markets or accessing social services like health and education.[2] These studies have often been criticized for their methodological designs, that prevent them from assessing clear causal links among road construction, rehabilitation and maintenance and the different impact indicators. Frequently, these studies just show associations between a greater provision of transport infrastructure and reduced transport costs, increased access to markets and public services or even greater economic growth and lower poverty rates, without controlling for other potential covariates. If control variables are incorporated, it typically is not done systematically enough to allow the construction of the counterfactual scenario needed to make such causal claims.

Only a few studies have moved forward in the direction of constructing counterfactual scenarios. Ahmed and Hossain (1990) carried out the first study which sought to systematically control for the most important covariates in order to estimate the impact of rehabilitated rural infrastructure. With a sample of 129 villages in Bangladesh, this study finds that villages with better road access have greater agricultural output, greater total incomes and better access to health services, particularly for women. The findings also suggests that roads would have increased wage income opportunities, especially for residents without farmland.

Binswanger, Khandker and Rosenzweig (1993) pioneered a method to construct counterfactual scenarios to study the welfare impact of rural infrastructure. Using time series information in a random sample of 85 districts from 13 states in India, they show that road infrastructure investment fostered agricultural output growth, higher usage of fertilizers and a larger credit supply. The conceptual framework helps overcome simultaneity problems created when assessing causal relations between infrastructure investment and other variables of interest. To avoid the correlation of non-observable variables with each district's infrastructure endowment – which would bias impact estimates – these authors implicitly construct a counterfactual scenario based on a random selection of districts.

Levy (1996) carried out a similar study on the socioeconomic impacts of road rehabilitation by comparing pre-existing and post-rehabilitation conditions using a sample of four rural roads in Morocco. To control for context covariates, other than rehabilitation itself, which could have affected the outcome, Levy compares the data on the performance of these four rehabilitated rural roads with that of two non-rehabilitated roads. From this 'before–after' and 'with–without' comparison, the study finds that the impacts from rural road rehabilitation were more important than the expected reduction in transport costs, showing significant increases in agricultural output as well as important changes in the crop portfolio and usage of inputs and technologies. In addition, the study identifies clear causal linkages between rehabilitated road infrastructure and access to education, particularly for girls, as well as a substantial increase in the use of public health services. Although this case study does not intend to be representative of a wider area, in methodological terms it does manage to construct solid counterfactual scenarios to establish causal relations between rural road investment and key variables associated with rural household welfare.

Bakht (2000) compared rehabilitated roads in Bangladesh to 'controls' and found considerable expansion in passenger and freight traffic and reductions in transport costs. However, Bakht falls short in assessing the effects on the welfare of beneficiary households, as he does not construct a counterfactual scenario in which households located along non-rehabilitated roads possess characteristics comparable to those located near rehabilitated roads.

DATA AND METHODOLOGY

This chapter measures the impact of rural road rehabilitation on household welfare, focusing on two key indicators: consumption and income.[3] This is done by comparing welfare levels of households living near rehabilitated roads (treated households) with an estimate of the welfare level these same households would have experienced had the rehabilitation not taken place. Since this estimate is constructed based on the information provided by households living near non-rehabilitated roads (potential control households), the accuracy of the impact assessment depends on how comparable both types of households are in terms of their characteristics other than the quality of the road.

This section describes the source and characteristics of the information used, as well as the methodology applied to estimate the impact of road rehabilitation on average welfare of *treated* households. As previously mentioned, this impact measurement focuses on: (1) per capita household income level; (2) composition of per capita household income (considering four possible sources of income: agricultural self-employment, agricultural wage labor, non-agricultural self-employment and non-agricultural wage labor); and (3) per capita household consumption level.

The data used in this study comes from household and town-level surveys carried out during March 2000 as part of the impact evaluation of the first phase of the Peruvian Rural Roads Rehabilitation and Maintenance Program – PCR (Cuánto 2000). Household surveys focused on household socioeconomic characteristics, whereas town-level surveys gathered information from local authorities, police stations, magistrate courts and businesses on public services and town socioeconomic characteristics.

Begun in 1996, PCR is part of a national program to rehabilitate road infrastructure and reduce rural poverty in Peru. Although PCR activities essentially involve the rehabilitation of rural roads (both motorized and non-motorized), complementary activities include strengthening organizational and management capacities of local micro-scale enterprises responsible for the maintenance of the rehabilitated motorized roads. The program includes rural areas of 314 districts with high poverty rates, located in 12 of Peru's 24 departments (Cajamarca, Ancash, Huancavelica, Huánuco, Junín, Pasco, Apurímac, Ayacucho, Cusco, Puno, Madre de Dios and San Martín). The program seeks to ensure the institutional and financial sustainability of maintenance activities, as they are gradually transferred to local governments.

The surveys gathered information from 2,038 households, distributed among 384 towns; 1,150 surveyed households live along road segments rehabilitated by PCR and 888 live in segments not rehabilitated by PCR. The samples were designed as follows.[4] Selection of households living near rehabilitated road segments was random and three-staged, with systematic selection for the first stage, probability proportional to town size for the second stage and random selection for the third stage. In addition, for households living near motorized roads, the selection process was stratified by geographic domain. In relation to the sample units, rehabilitated road sections were selected in the first stage (74 motorized road sections and 16 non-motorized road sections), towns in the second stage (two, or in some cases three, towns per road section), and households in the third stage (between four and six households per town). Information from households and towns located in road sections which did not benefit from PCR activities was also collected; these households were used as a control group during program evaluation. Consequently, the selection process of this second group of households was not random. In particular, the evaluators sought to have each control road section (non-rehabilitated by PCR) be similar to one treated road section (rehabilitated by PCR) in agro-climatic conditions (like altitude), hierarchy of the towns connected by the road (province or district capitals), road function (connection to the same secondary road), distance to commercial circuits and type of road (motorized or non-motorized).

Despite the existence of these road-section matching criteria, the control group inadvertently included households which had access to roads which had been rehabilitated but not by PCR. Obviously, these households could bias the assessment of the PCR impact. In particular, 34 per cent of control households located in non-motorized road sections and 38 per cent of control households located in motorized road sections reported benefiting from road rehabilitation activities carried out by NGOs working in the area, their municipalities or other public institutions. To overcome this problem, we reclassified households as follows: treated households are those located in rehabilitated road sections (whether by PCR or another institution), whereas the group of potential controls is formed by households located in road sections which did not benefit from any rehabilitation work. However, while maintenance activities are undertaken for motorized roads rehabilitated by PCR, it was not possible to establish if similar actions took place on the roads rehabilitated by other institutions.[5] Table 9.1 shows the distribution of households and towns according to type of road (motorized or non-motorized) they access and the adjusted treatment status (rehabilitated or non-rehabilitated).

Concerning comparability, we found systematic differences in key socioeconomic variables between the group of potential control households (towns) and the group of treated households (towns). Consequently, an important part of the methodological design concerned the construction of a suitable counterfactual scenario which would yield estimates free of bias otherwise introduced by welfare effects derived from better access to private and public assets other than rehabilitated roads.[6]

Below we detail the methodological framework devised for this study. First, however, a few notes are in order on the broad idea and the key issues to be addressed by the methodological design. The estimate we ultimately look for is:

Rehabilitation effect on treated households $= E(Y_{1i} \mid d_i = 1) - E(Y_{0i} \mid d_i = 1)$ (9.1)

Table 9.1   Distribution of the Sample (for households and towns)

Type of Road	State of the Road Non-rehabilitated	rehabilitated	Total
Non-motorized rural road			
Households	106	214	320
Towns	21	43	64
Motorized rural road			
Households	307	1,411	1,718
Towns	62	258	320
Total–households	413	1,625	2,038
Total–towns	83	301	384

where $d_i = 1$ indicates that household i belongs to the treated group in the actual scenario, and Y_{ji} represents household i's per capita income (or consumption) in scenario j (with j = 0 if referring to the hypothetical scenario, and j = 1 if referring to the actual one). Evidently, the first addend in (9.1) is known while the second one is not and must be estimated. Thus, the key issue in this study lies in constructing the counterfactual scenario; that is, answering the question: What would treated household welfare be if road rehabilitation had not taken place $[E(Y_{0i} | d_i = 1)]$?

The methodological framework proposed by the literature on matching is widely used for non-experimental studies like this one. In particular, we use the propensity score matching technique, that fosters an efficient use of information from households which access non-rehabilitated roads, to construct a counterfactual scenario. The methodology is based on studies by Rosenbaum and Rubin (1983) and Heckman, Ichimura and Todd (1998), as well as on Heckman, Lalonde and Smith's (1999) comprehensive review of evaluation methodologies for public projects. Nevertheless, adjustments were made in order to address two issues:

1. Household information is not representative at the town level. Therefore: (1) the average welfare effect of road rehabilitation cannot be assessed at the town level (the level at which the probability of accessing a rehabilitated road is defined); and (2) matching households according to the probability of accessing a rehabilitated road cannot be based on characteristics of surveyed households, but rather on the town in which they live.

2. There is no longitudinal household data to construct baselines for both groups. The lack of information about household characteristics prior to rehabilitation rules out the possibility of performing more accurate estimations than those feasible from cross sectional information, particularly the possibility of getting the difference-in-difference estimator.[7]

Following the methodology proposed by Heckman, Ichimura and Todd (1998), we can perform ex-post adjustments over a set of household characteristics (vector X_i) in order to ensure comparability between potential controls and treated households. Such adjustment should ensure that the distribution of the indicator Y_0 (per capita income of any household if road rehabilitation does not take place) within a subgroup of households – defined by their closeness in X – is the same for the group of households living near non-rehabilitated roads as the distribution which would be observed for the treated households group if rehabilitation had not taken place. That is:

$$E(Y_{0i} \mid d_i = 1, X) = E(Y_{0i} \mid d_i = 0, X) \qquad (9.2)$$

To ensure that both sides of this expression are well defined simultaneously, we need to condition these expected values on a support region, over the set of characteristics X, common to both groups (treated and potential controls). In this way, the outcomes obtained by those households (from both groups) which belong to this common support will be comparable. Once we control over the set of characteristics X, which defines the support region common to both groups, it is possible to estimate the average outcome of the treated group – had it not obtained access to a rehabilitated road – by calculating the average outcome of the group of potential controls (weighting each control household according to its closeness in X to each treated household).

Following Rosenbaum and Rubin (1983), it is possible to reduce the dimensionality of the common support's definition problem by estimating a propensity score which reflects the conditional probability of accessing a rehabilitated road, given the vector of characteristics X:

$$Pr(d = 1 \mid X) = Pr(X) \qquad (9.3)$$

By incorporating the contribution of these authors and following the conceptual framework proposed by Heckman, Ichimura and Todd (1998), it is possible to establish that if the distribution of Y_0 is independent of the conditional distribution of d on X, within the common support defined on the set of characteristics X, the distribution of Y_0 is also independent of the conditional distribution of d on $Pr(X)$ (within the referred common support).

Following this methodological framework, one of the main tasks consists of defining the set of characteristics X to be used to establish the common support within which both groups are comparable. Typically, these characteristics are chosen due to their influence on a household's probability to access a rehabilitated road, so that it is possible to find households with similar probabilities and replicate the randomness associated with experimental designs. In the context of this study however, these characteristics are defined at the town level. That is, the probability of accessing a rehabilitated road is the same for all households which belong to a town located in a rehabilitated road section. In this sense, town characteristics (and not household variables) are relevant to construct the propensity scores. If a representative number of households at the town level were available, it would be possible to define household welfare indicators at that aggregate level, and the mean effect of rehabilitation could be adequately assessed at the town level. However, given that the survey's sample design only considered an average of four-to-six households per town, it is not possible to expect statistical representativeness at that level. Therefore, it is necessary to establish two levels of analysis: first, the town level, at which the common support is defined and the sampled households' probability of accessing a rehabilitated road section is estimated; and second, the household level, where the average welfare effect is measured.

The empirical specification followed three stages: (1) construction of the common support; (2) construction of the outcome variables to be assessed (per capita household income or consumption, controlling for assets possession) and (3) households matching (based on the common support) and calculation of the means difference between the treated and control groups. Next, we describe each of these stages.

Stage One

This stage defines what constitutes 'common support'. Specifically, it estimates the probability of a town accessing a rehabilitated road (propensity score) and restricts the number of observations to be incorporated in the evaluation depending on the intersection of the access probability range of both treated and control groups. The probability of accessing a rehabilitated road is the common support's summary indicator, a one-dimensional figure which reflects the multidimensional space of those characteristics which influence whether or not the relevant road has been rehabilitated. In that sense, this probability estimate (propensity score) incorporates different kinds of variables which could have influenced the decision of a third-party (or the community itself) to rehabilitate the road section reaching the town. These variables include the community's organizational capacity, economic activity, provision of public education and health services, size, length of road section and geographical domain, among others.

Stage Two

One of the study's distinctive features lies in the fact that its unit of analysis is the household, not the town. This is an important feature, because the probability of accessing a rehabilitated road is determined at the town level, not at the household level. Here the differences in household characteristics between the treated group and the potential control group are statistically significant, implying that the critical variables which ensure comparability between households, regarding the welfare indicator, are not related solely to the probability of a household accessing a rehabilitated road. In fact, this probability depends on the town's characteristics, and – given the lack of household representativeness at a town level – it is independent of observed differences between households within towns. Therefore, it is obvious that the household matching methodology – which works under the propensity score closeness criterion – is not sufficient to construct a counterfactual scenario for treated households, as this indicator is not sensitive to differences among household characteristics (characteristics which influence the assessed welfare level). Since it is not possible to overcome this problem by incorporating individual household characteristics in the propensity score estimate, it was necessary to construct a welfare indicator which could isolate the differences in individual household characteristics between treated and potential control groups. This welfare indicator, controlled by household individual characteristics, will be evaluated in stage three.

Before turning to stage three, we present the procedure used to construct this welfare indicator. In particular, the estimated equation (semi-logarithmic regression) we used to control for individual characteristics or assets possession has the following form:

$$Y = \sum_j b_j dX_j + \sum_j b_j (1-d)X_j + \mu \qquad (9.4)$$

where Y is the logarithm of the household welfare indicator (for example household per capita income), X is the set of j household assets, b_j is the return from each of those assets, d indicates the group the household belongs to (one if it is a treated household and zero if it is a potential control), and μ is the error term. This equation is useful as long as there is no correlation between the non-observables (μ) and those assets included as covariates (X), implying that the estimated parameters are unbiased. If these parameter estimates were biased, we could not guarantee that the assessed variable adequately isolates the welfare differences derived from differences in asset endowment between households from both road sections. To ensure this condition was fulfilled, separate equations were estimated for each type of road (motorized and non-motorized) and the X set of variables was carefully selected. The variables included in equation (9.4) to control for the differences between both groups due to assets possession included variables related to human, organizational, physical, financial and public capital. As far as this study measures the short-term impact of road rehabilitation, it is reasonable to consider these variables as exogenous.

In addition, it is important to note that the first two elements on the right side of equation (9.4) are orthogonal. If a household lives along a rehabilitated road section, $d = 1$, the second element of the equation is null. This specification allows us to capture the difference in returns to each type of asset estimated for rehabilitated and non-rehabilitated road sections. Even though these parameter estimates are the same as those obtained if two separate equations are estimated (one for treated and the other for potential controls), standard errors are different. Thus, the specification in (9.4) maximizes efficiency of b_j estimators. Importantly, the econometric specification incorporates a heteroskedasticity correction and acknowledges possible sources of correlation between non-observable characteristics of households located within the same road section.

Regarding which observations to use at this stage, it is important to restrict the household sample used in (9.4) to the subgroup of households (treated and potential controls) which make up the common support group calculated in stage one. By doing so, the process of controlling for differences in asset possession is done only for those households which will be considered as possible matches in the stage three.

After estimating (9.4) it is possible to establish the following identity:

$$\left[\bar{Y}^R - \bar{Y}^{NR}\right] - \sum_j \left[(\bar{X}_j^R - \bar{X}_j^{NR}) * \hat{b}_j^{NR}\right] = \sum_j \left[(\hat{b}_j^R - \hat{b}_j^{NR}) * \bar{X}_j^R\right] + \left[\bar{e}^R - \bar{e}^{NR}\right] \quad (9.5)$$

The left side of (9.5) represents the means difference between the group of households which has access to rehabilitated roads (R) and the group which has access to non-rehabilitated roads (NR), controlling for the difference in asset possession between both groups. The right side of this identity reflects the two components of the rehabilitation effect: measuring the rehabilitation effect due to the difference in assets returns and measuring the rehabilitation effect due to the differences in non-observables. These two components will be estimated in stage three, after matching households under the propensity score's closeness criterion.

To construct the welfare indicator for each household (controlled by differences in assets) which allows for calculation of (9.5) in stage three, the following specification is used:

$$Y_i^R - \sum_j \hat{b}_j^{NR} X_{ij}^R = \sum_j (\hat{b}_j^R - \hat{b}_j^{NR}) * X_{ij}^R + e_i^R \qquad (9.6)$$

for household i living along a rehabilitated road section; and

$$Y_i^{NR} - \sum_j \hat{b}_j^{NR} X_{ij}^{NR} = e_i^{NR} \qquad (9.7)$$

for household i living along a non-rehabilitated road section.

Finally, to obtain an estimate of the logarithm of per capita income (consumption), the predicted average of the log income (consumption) for the household group living in a non-rehabilitated section is added to (9.6) and (9.7): $\hat{b}_{NR}\overline{X}^{NR}$. This is equivalent to simulating the logarithm of per capita income (consumption) for each household, assuming that all households have an identical level of assets, that equals the average level of the group which has no access to road rehabilitation. This variable is transformed from logarithms to income (consumption) levels before proceeding to stage three. This transformation facilitates the interpretation of the average effect estimator.

Stage Three

The final stage matches households living near rehabilitated road sections to those in non-rehabilitated sections, according to their closeness within the common support. After that we calculate the difference between average outcomes – controlled by differences in asset possession – of both groups. Matching the welfare outcomes of both groups allows us to adequately balance both household samples with regard to observable characteristics which, as indicated by Heckman, Ichimura and Todd (1997) in the context of job training programs, constitute the main concern in estimating the average effect of a program. These authors point out the relatively small importance of differences in non-observables in biasing the average effect estimator, when compared to the differences in observables between both samples.

Regarding the matching process, there are basically two options available: one-to-one matching and smoothed matching.[8] In both cases, the role of each observation of the potential controls in the construction of the counterfactual scenario is defined according to the propensity score obtained in the first stage. The practical difference is that one-to-one matching uses only one control observation for each treatment (the observation showing the propensity score closest to the treatment observation), while smoothed matching constructs a counterfactual observation for each treated individual, according to all control observations belonging to the common support, weighting each control observation according to its closeness to the treated household. In econometric terms, the first option minimizes bias, while the second privileges efficiency.

Given the data characteristics, we chose smoothed matching. We had expected the scarce number of controls for each treated household to be the main problem, while potential bias problems would be less important, since control road sections sampled were chosen due to their similarities to the treated ones.

Finally, we used bootstrapping techniques to construct the confidence intervals of the average effect estimates, since this permitted us to incorporate the propensity score estimation errors into the standard errors of the estimated outcome effects (Sianesi 2001).

RESULTS

As mentioned above, estimating average welfare effects of road rehabilitation requires a high level of comparability between control and treated groups regarding household and town characteristics (other than rehabilitation) which could have influenced the observed outcome (income or consumption). Table 9.2 presents summary statistics which shed light on comparability issues for both types of roads. This table shows a statistically significant imbalance between treated and control households in some of the characteristics influencing household welfare. Here, we present some examples of household characteristics which, if not adequately controlled, might distort the estimation of average welfare effects.

First, Table 9.2 shows that surveyed households living in towns articulated to non-rehabilitated roads have greater access to basic public services. For example, households in the potential control group have more access to drinking water and electricity, whether they are connected through motorized or non-motorized roads. Furthermore, potential controls articulated to non-motorized roads report a greater access to sanitation. Human capital indicators show statistically significant differences favoring households near non-rehabilitated rural roads. In particular, along non-motorized roads, households articulated to non-rehabilitated sections have greater access to secondary schooling, while for the non-motorized case, residents from non-rehabilitated road sections report higher than average years of education for household members – excluding the household head – than those reported for treated households.

These results highlight the importance of establishing controls in stage two in order to isolate the welfare effects which differential endowments of public assets and human capital have on treated and non-treated households. The intuition here is that if we agree that greater accessibility to public goods and services raises complementary public investment profitability (road rehabilitation in this case), or that a higher education level fosters more profitable income generation opportunities, then a direct comparison of treated and non-treated welfare levels would underestimate the benefits of road rehabilitation activities.

Nevertheless, there is a set of productive assets (like farmland, livestock and transport goods) which are significantly larger in households located near rehabilitated rural roads. In this case, the potential bias would counter that described above, as households with greater productive resources could accrue additional benefits as a result of rehabilitation. Finally, there are asset categories where results are mixed, like in human capital demographics (household size and age of the household head) and organizational capital (at both household and town level).

To address this lack of comparability between households from rehabilitated rural roads and non-rehabilitated rural roads, we used the three stages of analysis detailed above. In particular, the propensity score estimate was constructed according to town-level variables before rehabilitation, like organizational capacity variables (if the town had a community assembly, associations for water management, local government offices), economic activity indicators (number of commercial or productive businesses per 100 residents, average income of these businesses, credit availability), access to public services, primary and secondary schools, road length, town size and geographical location.

Table 9.3 reports results of probit regressions used to model the town's probability of having its road section rehabilitated, with the binary outcome taking value one if the town has access to a rehabilitated road and zero otherwise. The selection of variables to be incorporated in each estimation (for both non-motorized and motorized roads) privileged the modeling criterion versus the statistical significance criterion. Based on the propensity score estimates, it was possible to construct the common support region for both types of households (treated and potential controls). In this process, 96 households from non-motorized roads and 44 households from motorized roads were dropped from the sample, because they fell outside the common support range. These observations represent 30 per cent and 3 per cent of the originally available sample of households from non-motorized and motorized sections, respectively.

Finally, constructing the welfare indicators to be evaluated required establishing several controls over the welfare indicators originally reported by households. Those controls were based on parameters estimated by semi-

Table 9.2 *Summary Statistics of Main Variables (mean values and statistical significance of their differences)*

	Non-motorized rural road[1]		
Variable	Non-rehabilitated	Rehabilitated	
Number of households	106	214	
Number of towns	21	43	
Human capital (household level)			
Household size	5.1	4.9	
Gender of head-of-household (% male)	84.9%	92.1%	**
Age of head-of-household	47.0	44.0	**
Mother tongue of head-of-household (% native)	56.6%	65.9%	*
Years of education of head-of-household	6.3	6.5	
Average years of education of other members	4.7	4.1	*
Organizational capital (household level)			
Sent or received remittences (last 12 months)	39.6%	32.7%	
Monthly occurrences of social and community activities (average per member)	0.5	0.8	*
Physical capital (household level)[2]			
Privately owned house	81.1%	85.5%	
House's wall: wood	0.9%	0.6%	
House's roof: tile, thatched or bamboo	43.4%	35.0%	*
Value of durable goods (US$)	128.9	81.3	***
Value of transport goods (US$)	109.4	202.6	**
Hectares of farmland (irrigated land equivalent)	1.6	3.6	***
Value of the cattle (US$dollars at baseline prices)	562.3	907.7	***
Public capital (household level)			
Access to electricity	44.3%	29.4%	***
Acces to water: connected to public network	52.8%	40.7%	**
Sanitation services: connected to public network	11.3%	8.6%	
Sanitation services: septic or cess tank	47.2%	33.5%	***
Number of public programs accessed by the household	4.4	4.9	***
Infrastructure & socioeconomic indicators (town level)			
Public telephone	23.8%	11.6%	
Community premise or club	66.7%	39.5%	***
Irrigation canal	42.9%	20.9%	**
Community assembly	71.4%	72.1%	
Local government premise	52.4%	48.8%	
Primary school	90.5%	81.4%	
Secondary school	33.3%	37.2%	
Business premises (per 100 inhabitants)	0.9	0.9	
Credit institution	19.0%	20.9%	
Police station	14.3%	16.3%	
Population	1,271.0	653.2	*
Length of the relevant road sections (km)	9.7	11.3	
Altitude (miles)	3,263.8	3,193.8	
Road accessibility indicators (town level)			
Percent variation of freight rates (US$/Kg)			
Percent variation of travel time along the road section	–3.8%	–11.5%	**

Table 9.2   (continued)

	Motorized rural road[1]	
Variable	Non-rehabilitated	Rehabilitated
Number of households	307	1411
Number of towns	62	258
Human capital (household level)		
Household size	5.1	5.0
Gender of head-of-household (% male)	89.5%	89.7%
Age of head-of-household	45.6	43.8 **
Mother tongue of head-of-household (% native)	38.4%	45.7% ***
Years of education of head-of-household	7.3	7.2
Average years of education of other members	4.8	4.7
Organizational capital (household level)		
Sent or received remittances (last 12 months)	37.8%	33.4% *
Monthly occurrences of social and community activities (average per member)	0.8	0.8
Physical capital (household level)[2]		
Privately owned house	83.4%	81.3%
House's wall: wood	1.0%	6.1% ***
House's roof: tile, thatched or bamboo	43.0%	37.8% **
Value of durable goods (US$)	147.4	138.3
Value of transport goods (US$)	188.8	189.0
Hectares of farmland (irrigated land equivalent)	4.3	5.7 **
Value of the cattle (US$dollars at baseline prices)	664.1	839.3 **
Public capital (household level)		
Access to electricity	55.0%	48.3% *
Acces to water: connected to public network	62.9%	56.3% *
Sanitation services: connected to public network	18.4%	16.4%
Sanitation services: septic or cess tank	46.8%	47.9%
Number of public programs accessed by the household	4.9	4.9
Infrastructure & socioeconomic indicators (town level)		
Public telephone	33.9%	27.1%
Community premise or club	50.0%	47.3%
Irrigation canal	53.2%	47.3%
Community assembly	74.2%	82.9% *
Local government premise	71.0%	67.1%
Primary school	93.5%	93.8%
Secondary school	69.4%	54.7% **
Business premises (per 100 inhabitants)	0.9	1.6 **
Credit institution	25.8%	29.1%
Police station	43.5%	46.0%
Population	2,198.9	1,683.9
Length of the relevant road sections (km)	12.6	21.3 ***
Altitude (miles)	2,613.4	2,662.5
Road accessibility indicators (town level)		
Percent variation of freight rates (US$/Kg)	−2.8%	−9.0% **
Percent variation of travel time along the road section	−11.5%	−35.8% ***

Notes:
1. The asterisks indicate whether the difference (positive or negative) between the mean value of rehabilitated roads and the mean value of non-rehabilitated roads is statistically significant at: *10 per cent level; **5 per cent level; ***1 per cent level.
2. Exchange rate: 3.456 Soles per US$.

Table 9.3 *Probit Regression for Access to a Rehabilitated Rural Road (town-level estimates)*

Variable	Motorized road		Non-motorized road	
Length of the road (km)	0.052	***	0.044	*
	(0.012)		(0.025)	
Town has a tourist attraction	−0.139		−1.241	**
	(0.207)		(0.630)	
Population (inhabitants)	0.000		−0.001	**
	(0.000)		(0.000)	
Town has a police station	−0.025		1.229	**
	(0.223)		(0.624)	
Number of business units (per 100 residents)[a]	0.175	**	−0.932	***
	(0.071)		(0.301)	
Town has communal facilities	−0.238		−1.428	***
	(0.174)		(0.509)	
Towns has some irrigation infrastructure	−0.207		−1.660	***
	(0.216)		(0.542)	
Town has a community assembly	0.312		0.989	*
	(0.240)		(0.529)	
Town has a municipal government	0.306			
	(0.236)			
Town has a primary school	0.312			
	(0.361)			
Town has a secondary school	−0.572	**	0.993	**
	(0.243)		(0.408)	
Town has a credit institution	−0.126		1.254	*
	(0.224)		(0.680)	
Town has a titling and registry office	−0.090			
	(0.208)			
Town located in the central highlands	−0.393		−1.254	**
	(0.257)		(0.552)	
Constant	−0.279		2.208	***
	(0.479)		(0.638)	
Number of towns	320		64	
Number of households	1718		320	
Wald chi^2(14)	31.840		0.044	
Prob > chi^2	0.004		−1.241	
Pseudo R^2	0.211		−0.001	
Log likelihood	−124.1292		−25.8968	

Note: Numbers in parentheses are the robust standard errors. ***Significant at 1 per cent level; **significant at 5 per cent level; *significant at 10 per cent level.

[a] These business units include manufacturing units or business that may provide transport communication, trade, personal or community services.

logarithmic regressions of income and consumption levels. In the case of income composition, a tobit estimation was used for each income source indicator (agricultural self-employment, agricultural wage employment, non-agricultural self-employment and non-agricultural wage employment), each of which was expressed in logarithms. In this case, the same set of variables was used in the regressions estimated for each income source.

The variables used to control for the differences in assets possession reflect each household's endowment in terms of five types of capital:

- human: household size, age, gender, mother tongue and years of education of the head-of-household, average years of education of the household members;
- organizational: money remittances, received or sent by the household, monthly average household participation in social or communal activities;
- physical: house property status, characteristics of the walls, roof and floor of the house, value of durable goods and transport goods, farmland size and value of livestock;
- financial: presence of credit institutions in the town where the household lives; and
- public: connection mode and access to public services like electricity, water and sanitation services.

Since this study evaluates the short-term impact of rural road rehabilitation, it seems reasonable to consider these variables as exogenous.

The selection criteria for variables incorporated in each regression were economic relevance to identify the initial set and statistical significance to establish controls which allowed us to make both samples – treated households and potential controls – compatible. This helped verify that the signs of the relations between individual characteristics and welfare indicators were intuitively reasonable.[9]

RURAL ROAD REHABILITATION AND HOUSEHOLD INCOME

Rural road rehabilitation may affect the income of the beneficiary population through different mechanisms. First, reductions in transport and marketing costs may increase the supply of agricultural products which are brought into the market or the effective price paid to the farmer, either of which would increase agricultural income. However, as income-generation opportunities may also increase, the benefited economic agents could substitute agricultural self-employment for other income sources which have greater profitability or only become available after road rehabilitation. For example, rural households could increase their non-agricultural self-employment income by producing handicrafts or increase their participation in agricultural or non-agricultural labor markets. Since road rehabilitation may bring in cheaper products to compete with local agricultural production, this substitution of income sources could be even greater. As shown by the various authors reviewed above, the recomposition of agricultural income resulting from greater and better access to any infrastructure will depend on the structure of private assets like education, available farmland and access to credit, as well as on the presence (or absence) of complementary public infrastructure (i.e. electricity, telecommunications) which might change the expected impacts. At an aggregate level, changes in labor supply and demand might also affect the local salary structure, especially if the road affects a labor market which was much less dynamic before the rehabilitation took place.

In conclusion, the effects of road rehabilitation on income structure cannot be known a priori, as it remains an essentially empirical issue. By using the propensity score matching technique, we have constructed a counterfactual scenario which made it possible to compare the income level and composition of households which benefited from road rehabilitation with the expected income they would have had in the hypothetical scenario; namely, without rehabilitation. The results presented in Table 9.4 show that, for the motorized road case, the rehabilitation allowed beneficiaries to gain over $120 in annual per capita income. This increase is statistically significant and amounts to more than 35 per cent of the control households' average income. In the case of non-motorized roads, the increase is smaller and not statistically significant. This difference in welfare impact between households articulated to product and factor markets through motorized roads and households articulated through non-motorized roads is consistent with what was posed by Jalan and Ravallion (2002). Although comparability between households located near rehabilitated roads and households located near non-rehabilitated roads is ensured by the methodology applied here, households which access markets through motorized roads generally have average higher education, more farmland and greater access to complementary public infrastructure – like telephone, electricity, drinking water and sanitation – than households living near non-motorized roads. The complementarities between these assets and the rehabilitated road explain the greater welfare increases observed in the group of households articulated through motorized roads.

The breakdown of the estimated difference in outcomes between rehabilitated and non-rehabilitated motorized rural roads, following equation

Table 9.4 *Mean Effect of Road Rehabilitation on Household's Per Capita Income (US$ per year)*

	Non-motorized rural road		Motorized rural road	
Outcome variable	Estimated effect	Standard error	Estimated effect	Standard error
Per capita income				
Total effect	66.90	73.29	121.77***	40.81
differences in returns	57.3%		88.5%	
differencies in non-observables	42.7%		11.5%	
Per capita income composition				
Agricultural self-employment income	73.33[a]	54.03	24.64	15.13
Agricultural wage income	21.17	21.30	11.86[b]	6.41
Non-agricultural self-employment income	−97.81***	58.11	6.31	27.24
Non-agricultural wage income	60.75*	40.42	114.78***	20.86

Notes: Bootstrapped standard errors based on 200 replications of the data with 100 per cent sampling. ***Significant at 1 per cent level; **significant at 5 per cent level; *significant at 10 per cent level; [a]significant at 12 per cent level; [b]significant at 15 per cent level.

(9.5), suggests that the impact of rehabilitation is due mainly to differences in returns to the assets which those households possess, rather than to differences in non-observable characteristics. Table 9.4 shows that 88.5 per cent of the difference in outcomes can be accounted for by the difference in returns to assets. The fact that non-observables account for a small share of the differences in outcomes can be viewed as a complementary indicator of a reasonable econometric specification of the simulation model used to control for differences in asset holdings between those living near rehabilitated and non-rehabilitated motorized roads.

The results also suggest that road rehabilitation would have allowed for important increases in non-agricultural wage incomes. This evidence is consistent with that reported by Corral and Reardon (2001) for Nicaragua and by de Janvry and Sadoulet (2001) for Mexico. In the case of Peru, areas with poor road access have a very restricted labor market; consequently, wage income represents a very small fraction of total income. Starting from such a small base, road rehabilitation would have accounted for only a moderate increase in wage income, but this increase would be substantial if compared to wage income which existed before rehabilitation: non-agricultural wage income would have more that doubled both in motorized roads as in non-motorized

Table 9.5 *Effect of Road Rehabilitation on Probability of Accessing Labor Markets (per cent)*

Outcome variable	Non-motorized rural road Estimated effect	Non-motorized rural road Standard error	Motorized rural road Estimated effect	Motorized rural road Standard error
Agricultural self-employment	−1.8	5.2	−7.8[a]	4.1
Agricultural wage employment	4.4	6.9	−0.6	4.4
Non-agricultural self-employment	−9.6	14.3	−5.8	6.4
Non-agricultural wage employment	9.1	9.4	8.8*	4.1

Notes: Bootstrapped standard errors based on 200 replications of the data with 100 per cent sampling. ***Significant at 1 per cent level; **significant at 5 per cent level; *significant at 10 per cent level; [a]significant at 11 per cent level.

roads. Data from Table 9.4 also shows that increases in non-agricultural wage income for those households articulated to markets through non-motorized rural roads would have occurred at the expense of non-agricultural self-employment (mainly associated with handicraft manufacture and retail commerce). However, in the case of motorized roads, the increase of non-agricultural wage income is achieved without a decrease in the other income sources; moreover, a marginal increase of agricultural wage income was observed. The fact that we observe a 'trade-off' between income sources in non-motorized roads, but not in motorized roads, could be attributed to either higher prices or lower costs in self-employment or, in the case of wage income, to greater access to higher-valued job opportunities after rehabilitation.

These income increases resulting from road rehabilitation could be due to greater access to labor markets (new job opportunities appear) or alternatively to increased wage income among those who were already carrying out activities in the labor market. Table 9.5 shows an estimate of the increase in the probability of accessing the labor market because of rehabilitation. Since the unit of analysis is the household, estimated increases refer to households which did not have access to such markets before rehabilitation. Results seem to indicate that the appearance of new job opportunities would only occur for non-agricultural wage-employment in those areas articulated to markets through rehabilitated motorized roads. A comparison between these results and the estimated income increases shown in Table 9.4 suggests that for the case of non-motorized roads, larger incomes from non-agricultural wage-employment and non-agricultural self-employment would be associated with increases in the time allocated to such activities, rather than to the appearance of new job opportunities for households which were not previously linked to the labor markets. In the case of the increase registered for non-agricultural wage income, for those households articulated to markets through motorized roads, the fact that the change in the probability of accessing the labor market is statistically significant suggests that this market would have become much more dynamic because of rehabilitation. Thus, not only would wage income opportunities among those who were already articulated to the labor market have increased, but also road rehabilitation would have increased the probability of new individuals accessing the labor market.

In addition, complementary evidence in the data suggests that agricultural and non-agricultural wages in markets around rehabilitated areas are not higher than what they would be had rehabilitation not taken place. This evidence is consistent with findings by Jacoby (2000), who identifies a significant but very weak correlation between agricultural wages and market distance. Thus, the benefits from a greater labor market insertion would come from a change in time allocated to wage employment and self-employment than from an increase in wages resulting from an improvement in road infrastructure.

CONSUMPTION AND SAVINGS

How much does the estimated income expansion translate into an increase in consumption? The results reported in Table 9.6 may seem a bit disconcerting. By comparing the annual per capita consumption from those households connected to product and factor markets through rehabilitated roads against the per capita consumption they would have had if rehabilitation had not happened, we observe an annual per capita increase of $48 in the case of non-motorized roads and $12 for non-motorized roads. These figures are quite small and are not statistically significant.

Why did the significant increase in income estimated for households along motorized roads not translate into an increase in consumption? Table 9.7 shows the estimated changes resulting from rehabilitation, reflected in the main saving mechanism of Latin American rural economies – livestock.[10] In rural Peru, and especially in the area under study, the limited development of the financial market makes livestock and food stocks – and to some extent durable goods – the main saving mechanisms for rural households. These households purchase, breed and sell livestock to face inflation, family emergencies or unfavorable climatic shocks. In order to analyze livestock changes (quantum changes), an aggregate indicator of all kinds of animals was constructed, valuing them with the same set of prices, obtained from secondary sources.[11] Moreover, to ensure comparability, controls over the differentiated possession of other assets were

Table 9.6 Mean Effect of Road Rehabilitation on Households' Per Capita Consumption (US$ per year)

	Non-motorized rural road		Motorized rural road	
Outcome variable	Estimated effect	Standard error	Estimated effect	Standard error
Per capita consumption				
Total effect	47.62	55.01	12.29	31.74
differences in returns	40%		92%	
differencies in non-observables	60%		8%	

Notes: Bootstrapped standard errors based on 200 replications of the data with 100 per cent sampling. ***Significant at 1 per cent level; **significant at 5 per cent level; *significant at 10 per cent level.

included in the estimation, following an analogous procedure to that used while constructing welfare indicators.

When livestock owned by households located along rehabilitated roads is compared with the stock these same households would have had if road rehabilitation had not taken place, there is an increase of $259 observed in the case of motorized roads. This change is statistically significant and represents a 65 per cent increase over the livestock which those household would have had if the relevant roads had not been rehabilitated. This change in assets is equivalent to 56 per cent of the average annual per capita income of a treated household. In the case of non-motorized roads, although the average increase between treated and controls appears somewhat larger ($271), the within-variance is such that statistically the outcome is not different from zero.

When the impacts of rural rehabilitation on income, consumption and savings are examined jointly, a rather consistent outcome appears. For non-motorized roads, the only short-term changes which can be clearly identified after rehabilitation are an increase in non-agricultural wage income and a marginal increase in agricultural income. These increments take place at the expense of a reduction in the income associated with self-employed non-agricultural activities like retail trade, handicrafts or machinery repair. What could explain this? We hypothesis that the market expansion derived from road rehabilitation could have triggered a reduction in consumption of local products, that would be substituted by products coming from out-of-region sources, with the subsequent displacement of local small industry and a change of income generation strategies towards wage activities.

In the case of motorized rural roads, where households have a larger set of public assets which could complement the benefits of road rehabilitation,

Table 9.7 Mean Effect of Rural Rehabilitation on Household Livestock (US$ at Baseline Prices)

Type of road	Estimated effect	Standard error
Motorized rural road	259.42***	96.60
Non-motorized rural road	271.05	224.57

Notes:
Bootstrapped standard errors based on 200 replications of the data with 100 per cent sampling.
***Significant at 1 per cent level.

a significant increase in total income takes place, mainly associated with a greater dynamism of the labor market. However, the higher incomes generated by rehabilitation have not been allocated to consumption but rather to savings. This suggests that income increase derived from road rehabilitation is not being perceived as a change in their permanent income. Although the Rural Roads Rehabilitation Program analyzed here takes into account road maintenance, beneficiary rural households could perceive such effects as temporary. In the case of roads rehabilitated by other institutions, permanent maintenance activities may not have been planned or may have been deficiently implemented. Under this perception, roads would eventually go back to their previous state, and transit would be seriously affected by the landslides and avalanches common to these areas, that could cause the road to be closed during several months of the year. In effect, if maintenance is not perceived as permanent, the optimal strategy for these households would be to take advantage of new income generation opportunities and channel them to savings rather than to increased consumption.

Is income gain being perceived as transitory the most plausible explanation? The best alternative explanation for this savings strategy – accumulating livestock – is that an increase in the profitability of investments due to improved roads has triggered livestock acquisitions. According to this argument, under imperfect financial markets this savings strategy would be the only way to accumulate resources until a critical mass is achieved. This is a sensible explanation, as far as the scale of the aimed investment is larger than the observed livestock acquisitions. Given that this investment is not likely to be related to agriculture activities, since the profitability in this sector has not risen, we would expect it to be related to non-agricultural investments. However, the scale of non-agricultural investments, typically made in the regions under analysis, tends to be small compared to livestock investment. Thus, we reaffirm our belief that the sustainability of road maintenance is a key issue behind the estimated differences in welfare outcomes derived from road rehabilitation.

CONCLUSION

This chapter has uncovered several processes triggered by road rehabilitation and maintenance programs which help explain their impact on rural welfare in the specific case of Peru. It has also contributed to a better understanding of how control groups can be constructed to evaluate the impact of reform programs more generally. Sen has rightly emphasized the importance of constantly reviewing and evaluating reform programs. Comparing a target group with a control group provides perhaps the most effective tool for investigating the rationale or 'reason' for continuing with a program. Careful construction of a control group allows a more complete understanding of why such programs affect rural welfare the way they do and can suggest 'reasons' why some effects may not be fully realized under certain restrictions. This knowledge enhances opportunities for more sharply focused interventions.

This study shows that short-term impacts from rural road rehabilitation could be linked to changes in income-generation sources, as road improvement enhances off-farm employment opportunities, especially in non-agricultural wage activities. This information could be used in a cost–benefit analysis of rural road rehabilitation projects. In addition, the study finds that the income expansion generated after rural roads rehabilitation, especially in areas articulated to product and factor markets through motorized roads, did not induce similar increases in consumption. This apparent contradiction could be reconciled by verifying that additional income was allocated to savings, in the form of livestock accumulation. Such behavior is consistent with an economic rationale whereby road improvement would not be perceived as permanent by the beneficiaries, who then would face incentives to save the transitory gains of road rehabilitation. This could happen because some of those rehabilitated roads are not maintained or to the fact that those permanent maintenance activities contemplated in the programs are not perceived by the beneficiaries as sustainable in the long term.

Even though this study recognizes, due to limitations of the available data, that the results obtained for the group of households articulated by motorized roads are more robust than those obtained for the case of non-motorized roads, it is important to note that there is some evidence that households near motorized roads tend to benefit more from rehabilitation than do those in non-motorized roads. In the case under study, households along rehabilitated motorized roads had, on average, higher education, more farmland and greater access to public infrastructure than those located along non-motorized rehabilitated roads, so the greater gains from rehabilitation obtained by households who live near motorized rehabilitated roads are probably due to the complementarities between the larger endowment of assets and road rehabilitation. Given the limitations of the data used for this study, it was not possible to carry out a comparative analysis of the benefits obtained by households living near rehabilitated roads (motorized and non-motorized). However, this is a crucial research area which could improve the understanding of the complementarities between public and private assets and contribute to the design of public programs in rural areas.

This study also presented evidence of how road rehabilitation affects the importance of wage employment in rural household's income-generation strategy. Furthermore, it recognizes non-agricultural wage income as the main source of positive effects of both motorized and non-motorized roads rehabilitation in the short-term. It is worth to note that the available information only allowed for evaluating changes at a household level; hence, the impact on household accessibility to new sources of income generation could be established, but it was not possible to analyze in depth the impact on job opportunities and its returns at the individual (household-member) level. In this sense, it seems important to complement this analysis with another which could look at the changes this type of public intervention generates in time allocation strategies within the household.

In addition to the study of short-term impacts of road rehabilitation, it is necessary to highlight the importance of other impacts, such as those related to changes in crop portfolios, technological changes at both agricultural and non-agricultural level and changing consumption patterns, all of which require longer periods of observation. This type of longer-term analysis should become an essential research area in order to contribute to the formulation of public policies focused on sustainable strategies of poverty reduction in rural areas.

Finally, it is worth emphasizing that although this study was not designed to establish policy recommendations, it presents clear evidence of the strong impact which rural road improvement has on the beneficiary population. In addition, it alerts us to the importance of ensuring that rehabilitation activities are not transitory, by guaranteeing maintenance so that rural households can make long-term decisions about investment and consumption which maximize the positive impact of road rehabilitation. Sustaining the benefits evidenced here will require ensuring the creation and strengthening of local institutional arrangements responsible for maintaining the rural roads network.

We believe the conclusions and hypothesis for future research raised in this study contribute to a better understanding of what can be achieved in terms of improving accessibility of rural households to national economic, political and social processes. In particular, our research points to the complementarities, the 'range' of policies and programs, that can be exploited in order to foster development in rural societies like those in Peru.

NOTES

We are grateful to the Peruvian Economic and Social Research Consortium (CIES), funded by CIDA and IDRC of Canada, who supported the initial stage of this research and to the World Bank who supported its completion. Substantial progress and writing of this study was done while Javier Escobal was appointed as a Guggenheim fellow to work on the links between rural producers and markets between 2001 and 2002. We are also grateful to the authorization provided by the World Bank and the Rural Roads Program (PCR) of the Ministry of Transport of Peru for the usage of the survey on which this study is based. We would also like to acknowledge the comments to earlier drafts of this study provided by Arie Kuyvenhoven, Ruerd Ruben and Nico Heerink, from the Development Economics Group, University of Wageningen and Dominque van de Walle and Peter Lanjouw from the World Bank. Finally, we appreciate the comments provided by Lyn Squire from GDN and Jose María Fanelli from CEDES. Of course, we are responsible for any remaining errors and for the analysis contained in this study.

1. Although another potential impact of rural road infrastructure investments could be a change in attitudes toward risk, we have not found any empirical studies on this subject.
2. For a more thorough literature review on this subject, see Escobal and Ponce (2002).
3. Differences between income and expenditure in rural areas of developing countries are associated with whether households consider resulting income flows to be transitory or permanent rather than related to taxe structure, the explanation usually raised for urban settings.
4. This process was followed separately for both types of roads motorized and non-motorized.
5. This, of course, is not the only source of potential bias. Nevertheless, overcoming other potential sources of bias such as systematic differences in the ability to organize collective action across towns is the main concern of the methodological design, which will be explained in the next subsection.
6. Concerning the quality of the data available for this study, we identified outliers and omitted observation problems among household and town reports. Details of how we dealt with these problems are available in Escobal and Ponce (2002).
7. Smith and Todd (2000) assess the performance of cross-section and longitudinal matching estimators and conclude that the most robust estimator is the difference-in-difference estimator, as it eliminates bias sources that are invariable along time. However, this estimator requires longitudinal information not available for this study.
8. See Heckman, Ichimura and Todd (1998), Heckman, LaLonde and Smith (1999), Dehejia and Wahba (1998) and Sianesi (2001).
9. Estimated equations used to construct the simulated income and consumption outcome variables are available upon request.
10. See Townsend (1995) or, more recently, Wenner (2001).
11. The prices of each type of animal where obtained from Peru's 2000 Living Standard Measurement Survey.

BIBLIOGRAPHY

Ahmed, Raisuddin and Cynthia Donovan (1992), *Issues of Infrastructural Development: A Synthesis of the Literature*, Washington, DC: International Food Policy Research Institute.

Ahmed, Raisuddin and Mahabub Hossain (1990), *Developmental Impact of Rural Infrastructure in Bangladesh*, Washington, DC: International Food Policy Research Institute.

Bakht, Zaid (2000), 'Poverty Impact of Rural Roads and Markets Improvement and Maintenance Project of Bangladesh', paper presented at the World Bank South Asia Poverty Monitoring and Evaluation Workshop, India Habitat Centre, New Delhi, 8–10 June.

Binswanger, Hans P., Shahidur R. Khandker and Mark R. Rosenzweig (1993), 'How Infrastructure and Financial Institutions Affect Agricultural Output and Investment in India', *Journal of Development Economics*, **41** (2), 337–66.

Block, Steven A. and P. Webb (2001), 'The Dynamics of Livelihood Diversification in Post-Famine Ethiopia', *Food Policy*, **26** (4), 333–50.

Booth, David, Lucia Hanmer and Elizabeth Lovell (2000), *Poverty and Transport: A Report Prepared for the World Bank in Collaboration with DFID*, London: Overseas Development Institute.

van Buuren, Stef and Karin Oudshoorn (2000), 'Multivariate Imputation by Chained Equations: MICE V1.0 User's manual', Leiden, TNO Prevention and Health, Report PG/VGZ/00.038.

Corral, Leonardo and Thomas Reardon (2001), 'Rural Nonfarm Incomes in Nicaragua', *World Development*, **29** (3), 427–42.

Cuánto, I. (2000), *Perú: Informe Final de Evaluación del Proyecto de Caminos Rurales* [Peru: Final Report of an Evaluation of the Project for Rural Roads] Lima: Ministry of Transportation and Communcations.

Dehejia, Rajeev H. and Sadek Wahba (1998), 'Propensity Score Matching Methods for Non-Experimental Causal Studies', Cambridge, MA, National Bureau of Economic Research (NBER) Working Paper No. 6829.

Escobal, Javier and Carmen Ponce (2002), 'The Benefits of Rural Roads: Enhancing Income Opportunities for the Rural Poor', Lima, Group of Analysts for Development (GRADE) Working Paper No. 40-I.

Gannon, Colin A. and Zhi Liu (1997), 'Poverty and Transport', Washington, DC, World Bank Discussion Paper TWU-30.

Heckman, James J., Robert LaLonde and Jeffrey A. Smith (1999), 'The Economics and Econometrics of Active Labor Market Programs', in Orley Ashenfelter and David Card (eds), *Handbook of Labor Economics, Volume 3A*, Amsterdam: North-Holland, pp. 1865–2097.

Heckman, James J., Hidehiko Ichimura and Petra Todd (1997), 'Matching as an Econometric Evaluation Estimator: Evidence from Evaluating a Job Training Program', *Review of Economic Studies*, **64** (4), 605–54.

—— (1998), 'Matching as an Econometric Evaluation Estimator', *Review of Economic Studies*, **65** (2), 261–94.

Jacoby, Hanan C. (2000), 'Access to markets and the benefits of rural roads', *Economic Journal*, **110** (465), 713–37.

Jalan, Jyotsna and Martin Ravallion (2002), 'Geographic Poverty Traps? A Microeconometric Model of Consumption Growth in Rural China', *Journal of Applied Econometrics*, **17** (4), 329–46.

de Janvry, Alain and Elisabeth Sadoulet (2001), 'Income Strategies among Rural Households in Mexico: The Role of Off-farm Activities in Poverty Reduction', *World Development*, **29** (3), 1043–56.

Khan, Qaiser M. (1989), 'Transaction Costs Approach for Estimating Development Benefits of Rural Feeder Roads', paper presented at the Transportation and Economic Development conference 'Transportation Research Record No. 1274', Williamsburg, Virginia, 5–8 November.

Levy, Hernan (1996), 'Morocco-Socioeconomic Influence of Rural Roads: Fourth Highway Project', Washington, DC, World Bank, Operations Evaluation Department Impact Evaluation Report. Report No. 15808.

Lipton, Michael and Martin Ravallion (1995), 'Poverty and Policy', in Jere Behrman T. N. Srinivasan (eds), *Handbook of Development Economics, Volume 3B*, New York: Elsevier Science, pp. 2551–2657.

Rosenbaum, Paul R. and Donald B. Rubin (1983), 'The Central Role of the Propensity Score in Observational Studies for Causal Effects', *Biométrica*, **70** (1), 41–55.

Sianesi, Barbara (2001), 'An Evaluation of the Swedish System of Active Labour Market Programmes in the 1990s', London, Institute for Fiscal Studies Working Paper No. WP02/01.

Smith, Jeffrey and Petra Todd (2000), 'Does Matching Overcome Lalonde's Critique of Nonexperimental Estimators?', London, Ontario, University of Western Ontario, unpublished paper, available at: http://www.bsos.umd.edu/econ/jsmith/nsw112200.pdf.

Townsend, Robert M. (1995), 'Consumption Insurance: An Evaluation of Risk-Bearing Systems in Low-Income Economies', *Journal of Economic Perspectives*, **9** (3), 83–102.

Wenner, Mark (2001), 'Rural Finance Strategy', Washington, DC, Inter-American Development Bank Working Paper RUR-104.

World Bank, (1994), *World Development Report: Infrastructure for Development*, Washington, DC: World Bank Group.

10. The Performance of State-Owned Enterprises and Newly Privatized Firms: Does Privatization Really Matter?
Mohammed Omran

Privatization has become a major political and economic phenomenon, and scholars continue to explore the theoretical and empirical dimensions of the subject. In particular, analysts are asking a fundamental question: Why privatize? Reducing the size of the public sector has been one important motive for reform, particularly in the former socialist and communist economies. But a motive expressed in such general terms can hardly be a convincing reason to justify privatization, especially given the distributive effects usually induced by state divestiture. As Amartya Sen argues, reformers must have a reason to seek a reform. That is, there must be a motive to modify unsatisfactory institutional arrangements and policies and a reason for choosing the priorities to pursue. The goal of this chapter is to analyze this problem using the Egyptian privatization experience.

Between 1960 and 1990, state-owned enterprises (SOEs) handled most of Egypt's economic activity under the direction of various ministries. Poor management and weak capitalization inevitably had a negative effect on SOE efficiency and financial viability (Road 1997). Egypt launched a privatization program in 1991 to improve its economy. The first step in Egypt's privatization program was to cut off subsidies to SOEs (Field 1995). In 1991 Egypt's 314 SOEs were grouped under 27 holding companies (reduced to 14 by 2001) responsible for all the affiliates in various sectors. The government initially used three approaches to divest the SOEs: selling shares through the domestic stock market, selling strategic stakes of shares to anchor investors through public auction and selling firms to employee shareholder associations (McKinney 1996). In addition, some firms were liquidated because they were deemed not economically viable due to enormous debt burdens. The number of the Egyptian privatized firms, classified by industry and method of sale, is given in Table 10.1.

As seen from Table 10.1a, Egypt's privatization program had a slow beginning. However, in 1996 the new cabinet accelerated the privatization process and began a push to publicize its privatization program. To increase the stock supply on Egypt's capital market, the government concentrated on full rather than partial privatization.[1] As a result, the value of privatized firms accelerated significantly until mid-1998, when a liquidity shortage, a foreign currency crisis and the overall negative performance of the Egyptian stock market delayed the program.

Most empirical studies of privatization examine the financial and operating performance of privatized firms or compare the performance of SOEs to private firms without directly testing the performance of privatized firms relative to SOEs. This study tests the performance changes of privatized Egyptian firms after matching them to control firms (SOEs) according to size and industry. This chapter contributes to the existing literature in two ways. It looks at a country in the Middle East and North Africa, a region which has been neglected in the literature, and it evaluates the performance changes of newly privatized Egyptian firms versus the performance changes of existing SOEs of similar industry and size.[2]

As Barber and Lyon (1996) indicate, matching sample firms to control firms based on industry, size and past performance will lead to well-specified test statistics. Following their lead, 54 SOEs were chosen to serve as a control group for the privatized firms, based on industry[3] and size.[4] However, because of data limitations I could not consider basing the matching of firms on past performance. An advantage of using SOEs is that their pre-privatization conditions are identical to privatized firm conditions, as both samples operated under the same polices and regulations.

Sample firms are categorized as either 'fully privatized firms' or 'partially privatized firms'. Since government control continues in cases of partial privatization, firms do not realize the full benefits of privatization, This allows for an investigation of whether the performance changes of these firms differ from SOEs according to the type of privatization.[5] Moreover, I consider intra-industry comparisons between privatized firms and SOEs to capture the effect of market structure on the performance changes of these firms.

By using 54 privatized firms with a matching number of SOEs, I show that after privatization, both types of firms experience significant improvements in profitability and operating efficiency coupled with significant declines in leverage and employment, while showing no significant change in output. However, using adjusted data and considering the performance changes of SOEs, the results demonstrate that in all measures – apart from sales efficiency and employment – there are no significant differences in performance between privatized firms and SOEs. These results should be treated with caution, as

Table 10.1 Number of Privatized Firms in Egypt

10.1a Total Number of Privatized Firms Classified by Method of Sale

| | Full Privatization ||| Partial Privatization ||| Yearly Total ||
Year	Anchor Investor	IPO*	ESA**	Liquid-ation	IPO*	Asset Sales	Leases	Number	Value***
1990	–	–	–	1	–	–	-	1	n.a.
1991	–	–	–	3	–	–	–	3	n.a.
1992	–	–	–	1	–	–	–	1	n.a.
1993	–	–	–	6	–	–	–	6	n.a.
1994	3	-	7	2	2	–	–	14	664
1995	1	1	3	2	7	–	–	14	1215
1996	3	13	–	1	6	1	-	24	2791
1997	3	14	3	3	2	1	2	28	3396
1998	2	8	12	6	1	3	-	32	2361
1999	8	-	5	7	–	2	6	28	2784
2000	5	1	-	3	-	6	10	25	2476
Until Feb.2001	1	-	-	2	–	3	2	8	n.a.
Total	26	37	30	37	18	16	20	184	15687

10.1b Classification of Privatized Firms by Industry****

Sector	Number of firms
Pharmaceutical	5
Mining	4
Construction	8
Food	11
Housing and tourism	5
Electricity generation and distribution	4
Metallurgy	2
Cotton and international trade	2
Weaving and trade	1
Chemical industries	7
Industrial engineering	3
Maritime and inland transport	2
Total	54

Notes: *Initial public offering; **Employees shareholders association; ***Millions of Egyptian pounds; ****Based on holding companies classifications by the Ministry of Public Enterprises.
Source: Egyptian Ministry of Public Enterprise Sector (2001).

the findings of no significant differences between privatized firms and SOEs might be attributed to other reasons, such as the SOEs' specific characteristics, the power of non-parametric tests, the small sample size, the change in the economic system in Egypt or the SOE restructuring process.

Accepting the results at face value, the evidence provided by this study could mean that privatization improved the performance of privatized firms, which, in turn, could have had important spillover effects on SOEs in terms of competition, demonstration and anticipation effects. Competition effects mean that the better performance of privatized firms forced SOEs to improve as well; demonstration effects mean that privatized firms showed other firms how to operate more efficiently; and anticipation effects refer to the perceived effectiveness of privatization which forced SOE managers to improve their performance because they realized that their firms might be privatized next. Indeed, a study over a longer period is needed before these results could be considered conclusive. However, this chapter provides an important first step.

PRIVATIZATION AND FIRM PERFORMANCE

Theoretically, privatization might cause firms to operate more productively, because managers are subjected to the pressures of the financial markets and to the monitoring and discipline of profit-oriented investors. Additionally, the change in ownership structure of privatized firms shifts the firm's objectives and incentives away from those that are imposed by politicians toward those which aim to maximize efficiency, profitability and shareholder wealth. By going public, firms would have increased entrepreneurial opportunities because they would be free of government control (D'Souza, Megginson and Nash 2004). Furthermore, when Hartley and Parker (1991) developed a conceptual framework based on property rights and public choice approaches, they showed that privatized firms are more efficient than SOEs because public firms put social objectives ahead of profit.[6]

However, the reduction in government ownership is not the only factor, as a competitive environment and capital-market discipline also increase the efficiency of these firms (de Castro and Uhlenbruck 1997). In this context, Vickers and Yarrow (1991) suggest that competition can greatly improve monitoring possibilities and hence increase incentives for production efficiency. Thus, it follows that private firms are more efficient than SOEs in competitive environments. On the other hand, in noncompetitive industries or in industries with natural monopoly elements, the performance of privatized firms is ambiguous and results from empirical studies are inconclusive (Boubakri and Cosset 1998). Vining and Boardman (1992) argue that at low levels of competition, differences between public and private ownership would be insignificant, as both types of firms would adopt similar rent-seeking behaviors. However, when competition increases, private ownership offers incentives and motivation for managers to proactively adopt profit-maximizing behavior (Stano 1975; Alchian 1977). In addition, D'Souza and Megginson (1999) indicate that privatized firms working in competitive industries are likely to yield solid and rapid economic benefits as long as there are no distortionary measures that hinder competition.

While these authors conclude that ownership does matter under competitive environments, other researchers pay more attention to the role of competition rather than ownership per se. Parker and Hartley (1991) point out that the source of efficiency gains might lie less in ownership status than in competition and that the greatest efficiency gains are produced where competition replaces monopoly. When both private and public firms are exposed to the same competitive pressures and market signals, they are expected to yield similar levels of allocative efficiency, regardless of their ownership structure (Färe, Grosskopf and Logan 1985). In the same vein, Forsyth (1984, 61) states, 'Selling a government firm makes no difference to the competitive environment in which it operates; ownership and competitive structure are separate issues'.

Empirically, many previous studies focus on comparing the pre- and post-privatization financial and operating performance of former SOEs, and they confirm that privatization in general leads to a significant increase in profitability, efficiency, capital investment spending, output and dividend payout. In addition, a significant decrease in leverage is documented, although there is no consensus as to the impact of privatization on employment levels (Megginson, Nash and Randenborgh 1994; Boubakri and Cosset 1998; D'Souza and Megginson 1999). What is even more interesting is that the 1994 and 1998 studies generally find insignificant differences between competitive and noncompetitive firms – although when differences are found, competitive firms are generally seen to improve more; yet, the 1999 study found that firms in noncompetitive industries have significantly better performance than do competitive-industry firms.

However, these studies and other related empirical works are unable to determine whether these results are due to the privatization process itself or to other factors, since they do not consider a benchmark of control firms matched to their sample firms. Boubakri and Cosset (1998) tried to test whether some of the performance might be attributed to economy-wide effects by using market-adjusted accounting performance measures, but industry performance benchmarks were not explored because of data limitations.

According to Megginson and Netter (2001), it is hard to compare SOEs to privately owned firms due to two methodological difficulties. First it is difficult to determine the appropriate set of benchmarks, especially in developing economies with a limited private sector. Second, there are fundamental reasons why certain industries are government-owned and others are privately owned. Despite this, some researchers have successfully compared the performance of SOEs with privately owned firms. Boardman and Vining (1989) and Vining and Boardman (1992) find that private firms are significantly more profitable and efficient than SOEs and mixed-ownership enterprises. Majumdar (1996) confirms the same findings, and Tian (2000) notes that Chinese private firms perform at a significantly superior level to that of mixed enterprises. Also, LaPorta and López-de-Silanes (1999) document significant improvements in privatized firms with respect to output and sales efficiency, concluding that the performance of privatized firms narrows when compared with privately controlled firms. Moreover, Dewenter and Malatesta (2001) find that private firms are significantly more profitable, have less debt and are less labor-intensive than SOEs. On the other hand, Pinto, Belka and Krajewski (1993) suggest that the significant improvement registered in Polish SOEs was due to a macroeconomic stabilization package, even without privatization. Additionally, Kole and Mulherin (1997) document that SOE performance is not significantly different from that of privately owned firms. Unlike most of the previously cited studies, which do not directly test the performance of privatized firms relative to SOEs, I consider this issue by comparing the performance of 54 Egyptian privatized firms to those of their SOE counterparts.

THE DATA

Data for this study were obtained from Egyptian firms which had been privatized and have at least two years of both pre- and post-privatization data. To allow time for the program to stabilize – and because Egyptian privatization was initiated in 1991 but did not actually fully start until 1994 – the timeframe for this study is 1994–98. As seen in Table 10.1a, the total number of privatized firms reached 184 in February 2001. However, excluding some types of privatization – liquidations, asset sales and leases – this left a population of only 111 firms. Excluding firms with less than two years of post-privatization data further reduced the sample to 76 firms. Also, I was only able to find 54 comparable SOEs, based on industry and size, to serve as the control group for the privatized firms. The final sample thus consists of 108 firms: 54 privatized firms, of which 38 experienced full privatization and 16 underwent partial privatization, and 54 SOEs, comprising the control group.

Table 10.1b shows the distribution of firms according to the type of industry. The sample is well-diversified, since it exhibits a wide dispersion across different types of industries. The Public Sector Information Center provided firm pre-privatization dataas well as figures for the SOE matching control group. The Egyptian Capital Market Authority provided data for the privatized firms, as they are listed on the stock exchange.

METHODOLOGY AND EMPIRICAL MODEL

The methodology used in this chapter incorporates many accounting performance measures to allow for comparison between pre- and post-privatization performance. I expect privatization to increase profitability, operating efficiency, output, level of employment and leverage. Profitability is measured by four proxies. The first is real earnings before interest and tax (EBIT), that refers to deflating EBIT using the appropriate consumer price index (CPI) values, then normalizing them to equal 1.00 in year zero so that other year figures are expressed as a fraction of the net income of the year of privatization.[7] The three other measures of profitability are return on sales (ROS), return on assets (ROA) and return on equity (ROE), referring to earnings before interest and tax divided by sales, assets and equity, respectively.[8] Operating efficiency is determined by two variables: sales efficiency (SALEFF) and income efficiency (INEFF), that refer to sales per employee and EBIT per employee, respectively. Output is proxied by real sales which are computed using the normalization method after adjusting sales for inflation. Employment is measured as the total number of employees (EMPL). Leverage is computed as total debt to total assets (TDTA).[9]

Employing the methodology of Megginson et al. (1994), I calculate the mean value of each performance variable prior to and after the date of privatization for each individual privatized firm and its matched SOE, excluding the year of privatization (year zero).[10] Therefore, the minimum time-interval data for each firm is five years (from at least year -2 to year $+2$). Before I test for significant changes in performance, several tests are employed to determine whether the accounting performance measures of privatized firms and SOEs can be adequately modeled by a normal distribution.

I employ four different tests: (1) standardized skewness, (2) standardized kurtosis, (3) Shapiro-Wilk and (4) chi-squared goodness-of-fit to determine whether the accounting performance measures could be adequately modeled by normal distribution. The results (not reported here) indicate that these variables, for both privatized firms and SOEs, are significant departures from normality. Consequently, the non-parametric Wilcoxon signed-rank test is adopted to test for significant differences in performance based on median values.[11] Also, I use a proportion test to determine whether the proportion (P) of firms experiencing changes in a given direction is greater than what would be expected by chance, typically testing whether $P = 0.5$.

As argued earlier, it is important to understand what would have been the performance of SOEs following privatization had they not been divested and to determine whether all changes in privatized firms are attributed to privatization or to other exogenous variables. To overcome the problem of different past performance between privatized firms and SOEs, I specify the following methods to measure the variables.[12]

Absolute Performance Change

To test for significant differences in performance changes between privatized firms and SOEs, I adjust the data to ensure that such comparisons are valid. The method used calculates the absolute change in mean performance for each firm, privatized or SOE, as follows:[13]

$$APC = P_{i,t} - P_{i,t-1} \qquad (10.1)$$

Since absolute changes are problematic as a measure of performance when the measure of performance itself is an absolute measure, I also calculate the post-privatization performance relative to the pre-privatization for each firm, privatized and SOEs, as follows:

$$APC = (P_{i,t} - P_{i,t-1}) / P_{i,t-1} \qquad (10.2)$$

where *RPC* is the relative performance change.

Having computed the *APC* and the *RPC* for each variable and each individual firm, I again tested for the normality of the new data set. The results from normality tests (not reported here) indicate clearly that the data do not follow a normal distribution. As a result, non-parametric tests are, again, adopted.[14] Since privatized firms and SOEs tend to be two independent samples, I employ the Mann-Whitney test for the significant difference in medians.[15]

EMPIRICAL FINDINGS AND ANALYSIS

In this section, I report the empirical findings of the statistical analysis for the changes in the performance variables described above. The analysis considers both privatized firms and SOEs (Tables 10.2 and 10.3). The year zero of a given control firm (SOE) would be the year of privatization of its sample firm (privatized). I also utilize the Mann-Whitney test to find out whether the performance change in privatized firms differs from those of SOEs. This comparison is undertaken based on both absolute and relative performance change methods (Table 10.4). An important point here is that in case of partial privatization, the government still has a significant influence on firms, so it might consider social objectives over business objectives. Hence, the logic suggests that full privatization which allows the sale of voting shares – possibly giving control to outside investors – is most conducive to efficiency improvements (D'Souza and Megginson 1999). Therefore, I test for the proposition that the performance changes of privatized firms might differ according to whether these firms experience full or partial privatization and report the results in Tables 10.5 and 10.6.

Profitability

Theoretical and empirical studies confirm that transferring ownership from the public to the private sector should lead to an increase in profitability, as private management would show a greater concern for profits compared to governments. I measure profitability by four proxies: (1) EBIT, (2) ROS, (3) ROA and (4) ROE.[16] Results from Table 10.2 reveal that all profitability ratios, apart from ROE, increase significantly after the divestiture of privatized firms. For example, the mean (median) ROS increases from 0.15 (0.09) to 0.18 (0.12). All statistical tests pass the critical values of significance at the 1 per cent level for most profitability ratios. The increase in the profitability measures is equally significant at as low as 67 per cent and as high as 73 per cent of the sample firms. Such findings are consistent with what Megginson et al. (1994), Boubakri and Cosset (1998) and D'Souza and Megginson (1999) have documented. However, the results for SOEs presented in Table 10.3 are similar to those of privatized firms. EBIT, ROS and ROA exhibit significant increases in medians at the 10 per cent level for EBIT and ROS and at the 1 per cent level for ROA. Such increases in these ratios are achieved by 60, 61, and 67 per cent of the sample firms, respectively.

Although it appears at first that privatized firms perform better than SOEs, because the levels of significance are higher, I could not confirm whether such differences in performance changes are significant or not. Hence, I adjusted the data to test for this proposition.

I report equality of performance change results for privatized firms and SOEs in Table 10.4 using the absolute and the relative performance change methods. Using the non-parametric Mann-Whitney test,[17] I find insignificant differences in performance changes between privatized firms and SOEs for all profitability ratios. To check the robustness of these findings, I further test for significant differences in performance changes between fully privatized

Table 10.2   Test for Significance Changes in Performance of Privatized Firms

Variables	No. firms 'Increased' (Decreased)	Mean before (Median)	Mean after (Median)	Mean change (Median)
Profitability				
Earnings before interest and tax (EBIT)	40 '29' (11)	0.727 (0.645)	1.07 (1.06)	0.343 (0.40)
Earnings before interest and tax to sales (ROS)	54 '36' (18)	0.149 (0.09)	0.183 (0.117)	0.034 (0.028)
Earnings before interest and tax to assets (ROA)	54 '36' (18)	0.07 (0.06)	0.10 (0.092)	0.03 (0.025)
Earnings before interest and tax-to-equity (ROE)	34 '19' (15)	0.305 (0.303)	0.33 (0.317)	0.025 (0.031)
Operating Efficiency				
Sales efficiency (SALEFF)	54 '29' (25)	0.927 (0.97)	1.06 (1.01)	0.133 (0.016)
Income efficiency 'before interest and tax' (INEFF)	40 '29' (11)	0.71 (0.59)	1.16 (1.1)	0.45 (0.505)
Output				
Real sales (SAL)	54 '23' (31)	0.962 (0.998)	0.94 (0.95)	−0.022 (−0.05)
Employment				
Total employment (EMPL)	54 '13' (41)	3337 (2632)	3136 (2226)	−201 (−166)
Leverage				
Total debt to total assets (TDTA)	54 '19' (33)	0.235 (0.208)	0.195 (0.138)	−0.04 (−0.03)

Table 10.2 (continued)

Variables	Z-statistic for difference in median (P-value)	Percentage of firms that changes as predicted	Z-statistic for significance of proportion (P-value)
Profitability			
Earnings before interest and tax (EBIT)	2.57 (0.005)	0.73	2.69 (0.004)
Earnings before interest and tax to sales (ROS)	1.71 (0.04)	0.67	2.31 (0.01)
Earnings before interest and tax to assets (ROA)	3.13 (0.0009)	0.67	2.31 (0.01)
Earnings before interest and tax-to-equity (ROE)	0.60 (0.25)	0.56	0.51 (0.30)
Operating Efficiency			
Sales efficiency (SALEFF)	0.66 (0.25)	0.54	0.41 (0.66)
Income efficiency 'before interest and tax (INEFF)	3.00 (0.001)	0.73	2.69 (0.004)
Output			
Real sales (SAL)	−0.67 (0.75)	0.43	0.95 (0.83)
Employment			
Total employment (EMPL)	−3.80 (0.0001)	0.76	3.85 (0.0001)
Leverage			
Total debt to total assets (TDTA)	−1.33 (0.09)	0.61	1.80 (0.036)

Table 10.3 Test for Significance Changes in Performance of State-Owned Enterprises (SOEs)

Variables	No. firms 'Increased' (Decreased)	Mean before (Median)	Mean after (Median)	Mean change (Median)
Profitability				
Earnings before interest and tax (EBIT)	40 '24' (16)	−0.68 (0.78)	0.97 (0.96)	1.65 (0.19)
Earnings before interest and tax to sales (ROS)	54 '33' (21)	−0.06 (0.02)	−0.024 (0.032)	0.036 (0.014)
Earnings before interest and tax to assets (ROA)	54 '36' (18)	−0.033 (0.012)	0.014 (0.028)	0.047 (0.017)
Earnings before interest and tax to equity (ROE)	34 '15' (19)	0.12 (0.141)	0.06 (0.154)	−0.06 (−0.006)
Operating Efficiency				
Sales efficiency (SALEFF)	54 '35' (19)	1.04 (0.97)	1.46 (1.12)	0.42 (0.11)
Income efficiency 'before interest and tax' (INEFF)	40 '26' (14)	−0.60 (0.80)	0.26 (1.06)	0.86 (0.53)
Output				
Real sales (SAL)	54 '25' (29)	1.06 (1.03)	1.11 (0.96)	0.05 (−0.06)
Employment				
Total employment (EMPL)	54 '7' (47)	3486 (2616)	2798 (2152)	−688 (−461)
Leverage				
Total debt to total assets (TDTA)	54 '19' (35)	0.44 (0.41)	0.37 (0.20)	−0.07 (−0.08)

Table 10.3 (continued)

Variables	Z-statistic for difference in median (P-value)	Percentage of firms that changes as predicted	Z-statistic for significance of proportion (P-value)
Profitability			
Earnings before interest and tax (EBIT)	1.46 (0.07)	0.60	1.31 (0.096)
Earnings before interest and tax to sales (ROS)	1.61 (0.06)	0.61	1.80 (0.036)
Earnings before interest and tax to assets (ROA)	2.4 (0.008)	0.67	2.31 (0.01)
Earnings before interest and tax to equity (ROE)	−0.51 (0.70)	0.44	0.51 (0.70)
Operating Efficiency			
Sales efficiency (SALEFF)	2.87 (0.002)	0.65	2.04 (0.021)
Income efficiency 'before interest and tax' (INEFF)	1.76 (0.046)	0.65	1.65 (0.052)
Output			
Real sales (SAL)	−0.46 (0.62)	0.46	0.68 (0.75)
Employment			
Total employment (EMPL)	−6.11 (0.0000)	0.87	5.31 (0.0000)
Leverage			
Total debt to total assets (TDTA)	−2.69 (0.00)	0.65	2.04 (0.021)

Table 10.4 Comparison of Performance Changes Between Privatized Firms and SOEs (Absolute and Relative Performance Change Methods)

Categories	Proxies	Absolute Performance Change Method					Relative Performance Change Method				
			Median					Median			
		Number of firms	Privatized firms	SOEs	Av–Rank (P–value)	Number of firms	Privatized firms	SOEs	Av–Rank (P–value)
Profitability	Earnings before interest and tax (EBIT)	40	0.40	0.15	41–40 (0.81)	33	0.29	−0.13	36–31 (0.24)
	Earnings before interest and tax to sales (ROS)	54	0.03	0.014	55–54 (0.97)	33	0.19	−0.002	35–32 (0.47)
	Earnings before interest and tax to assets (ROA)	54	0.025	0.016	55–53 (0.78)	33	0.25	0.13	35–31 (0.43)
	Earnings before interest and tax to equity (ROE)	34	0.03	−0.006	35–33 (0.47)	32	0.10	−0.25	34–31 (0.65)
Operating Efficiency	Sales efficiency (SALEFF)	54	−0.016	0.11	49–60 (0.09)	54	−0.014	0.11	49–60 (0.09)
	Income efficiency 'before interest and tax' (INEFF)	40	0.51	−0.51	40–41 (0.85)	33	0.32	0.16	35–32 (0.58)
Output	Real sales (SAL)	54	−0.05	−0.11	55–54 (0.92)	54	−0.055	−0.10	56–53 (0.65)
Employment	Employment (EMPL)	54	−166	−459	65–44 (0.00)	54	−0.076	−0.16	63–45 (0.003)
Leverage	Total debt to total assets (TDTA)	54	−0.033	−0.068	58–51 (0.23)	49	−0.25	−0.24	50–49 (0.94)

Table 10.5 Comparison of Performance Changes Between Fully Privatized Firms and SOEs (Absolute and Relative Performance Change Methods)

		Absolute performance change method				Relative performance change method			
			Median				Median		
Categories	Proxies	Number of firms	Full privatization	SOEs	Av-Rank (P-value)	Number of firms	Full privatization	SOEs	Av-Rank (P-value)
Profitability	Earnings before interest and tax (EBIT)	30	0.41	0.08	31–29 (0.63)	23	0.28	−0.14	24–22 (0.25)
	Earnings before interest and tax to sales (ROS)	38	0.03	0.002	40–36 (0.45)	23	0.05	−0.04	25–21 (0.38)
	Earnings before interest and tax to assets (ROA)	38	0.02	0.01	39–37 (0.70)	23	0.25	0.11	25–21 (0.35)
	Earnings before interest and tax to equity (ROE)	24	0.03	−0.006	25–24 (0.72)	22	0.025	−0.12	24–22 (0.79)
Operating Efficiency	Sales efficiency (SALEFF)	38	−0.04	0.24	32–44 (0.092)	38	−0.08	0.26	33–43 (0.086)
	Income efficiency 'before interest and tax' (INEFF)	30	0.53	0.56	31–30 (0.89)	23	0.32	0.06	25–21 (0.34)
Output	Real sales (SAL)	38	−0.05	−0.14	40–36 (0.57)	38	−0.055	−0.13	40–36 (0.45)
Employment	Employment (EMPL)	38	−214	−532	45–31 (0.002)	38	−0.11	−0.19	45–31 (0.004)
Leverage	Total debt to total assets (TDTA)	38	−0.033	−0.068	41–36 (0.36)	34	−0.21	−0.20	36–33 (0.52)

Table 10.6 Comparison of Performance Changes Between Partially Privatized Firms and SOEs (Absolute and Relative Performance Change Methods)

		Absolute performance change method				Relative performance change method			
			Median				Median		
Categories	Proxies	Number of firms	Partial privatization	SOEs	Av–Rank (P-value)	Number of firms	Partial privatization	SOEs	Av–Rank (P-value)
Profitability	Earnings before interest and tax (EBIT)	10	0.40	0.36	10–11 (0.79) 15–17 (0.32)	10	0.41	0.16	10–10 (0.97) 10–11 (0.62)
	Earnings before interest and tax to sales (ROS)	16	0.03	0.07	16–17 (0.90)	10	0.30	0.78	10–11 (0.91)
	Earnings before interest and tax to assets (ROA)	16	0.03	0.04	11–10 (0.52)	10	0.41	0.35	11–10 (0.73)
	Earnings before interest and tax to equity (ROE)	10	0.04	−0.008	15–17 (0.56)	10	0.20	−0.38	14–18 (0.36)
Operating efficiency	Sales efficiency (SALEFF)	16	0.08	0.18	10–11 (0.62)	16	0.07	0.23	10–11 (0.68)
	Income efficiency 'before interest and tax' (INEFF)	10	0.49	0.40	14–18 (0.22)	10	0.49	0.87	14–18 (0.27)
Output	Real sales (SAL)	16	−0.05	0.12	19–12 (0.086)	16	−0.05	0.12	19–13 (0.091)
Employment	Employment (EMPL)	16	−123	−285	17–15 (0.40)	16	−0.02	−0.06	13–17 (0.23)
Leverage	Total debt to total assets (TDTA)	16	−0.077	−0.18		15	−0.21	−0.20	

firms and their SOE counterparts (Table 10.5) and partially privatized firms and their SOE counterparts (Table 10.6). The results from both tables confirm that there are no significant differences in performance changes between these subsamples at any level. The results also show that privatized firms, whether they experience full or partial privatization, tend to perform similarly to SOEs, which makes the effect of privatization on firm performance hard to identify.

Operating Efficiency

Since it is expected that privatization will provide a better allocation of resources – whether financial, human or technological – divestiture should yield an improvement in operating efficiency. To test this prediction, two ratios are used: SALEFF and INEFF.[18]

With regard to privatized firms, results in Table 10.2 show that there is no statistically significant difference in SALEFF performance. However, the mean (median) of INEFF increases from 0.71 (0.59) of the year-zero level during the pre-privatization period to 1.16 (1.1) of the year-zero level during the post-privatization period, a change which is significant at the 1 per cent level. This improvement is achieved by 73 per cent of the sample firms. The results tend to be partially consistent with the literature, as Megginson et al. (1994), Boubakri and Cosset (1998) and D'Souza and Megginson (1999) document significant increases not only in INEFF, but also in SALEFF.

As far as SOEs are concerned, results given in Table 10.3 indicate that both SALEFF and INEFF increase significantly at different levels, and such increases are achieved by 65 per cent of sample firms for both ratios. Such results raise two issues. First, the performance changes in SOEs seem to be equal to or better than privatized firms, given the fact that the denominator for SALEFF and INEFF ratios is the same (number of employees). Second, the performance change in SALEFF of privatized firms is not statistically significant, while it is highly significant for INEFF. The differences between the performance changes in both ratios could actually be due to the success of new management in controlling and reducing expenses more than increasing sales, as INEFF grows more compared to SALEFF.

Extending the analysis to show whether there is any significant difference between the performance changes of privatized firms and SOEs, the findings given in Tables 10.4, 10.5 and 10.6 seem to be consistent with the just-stated results. For both absolute and relative performance change methods, significant differences in performance change are documented for SALEFF. More precisely, the results suggest that SOEs' performance change is better than privatized firms as a whole and better than fully privatized firms at the 10 and 5 per cent levels, respectively. However, no significant difference in performance change is observed between SOEs and partially privatized firms. In addition, no significant differences in performance changes between the subsamples have been found for INEFF. These results, in fact, tend to be consistent with Hutchinson's (1991) findings, in which public ownership in the United Kingdom corresponds with higher labor productivity, while private ownership relates to a higher level of profits.

Output

Many studies have argued that privatized firms should increase their output due to competition pressures, better incentives and more financing opportunities (Megginson et al. 1994; Boubakri and Cosset 1998). I test this proposition by computing the average inflation-adjusted sales level for the pre- and post-privatization period as a proxy for output. The results show no significant difference in changes in output for either privatized firms or SOEs. Surprisingly, just 43 per cent of privatized firms exhibit an increase in output while the remainder shows a decrease. Such results tend to contradict the expected increase in output following privatization. Yet these findings seem to be consistent with Boycko, Shleifer and Vishny's (1996) argument: that effective privatization will lead to a reduction in output, since the government can no longer entice management (through subsidies) to maintain inefficiently high output levels. Since a statistically insignificant change in SALEFF for privatized firms is documented, the insignificant change in output might be understandable. However, for SOEs, previous results indicate a significant increase in SALEFF and an insignificant change in output, so it is especially interesting that the significant increase in SALEFF would be entirely due to the reduction in levels of employment rather than to an increase in output. Extending the analysis to compare the performance changes of privatized firms and SOEs, I find insignificant differences for the full sample and subsamples.

Employment

One crucial issue in privatization is how employment levels change after firms move from government control to the private sector. There is neither a theoretical nor an empirical consensus on how privatization affects employment levels. On one hand, privatization might lead to an increase in the level of employment since firms probably would target growth and expand investment spending. Most SOEs tend to be overstaffed for social reasons, thus extensive layoffs would be expected. I test for this variable by computing the average level of employment before and after privatization. For both privatized firms and SOEs, the results document significant decreases in the level of employment at the 1 per cent level, and this is achieved by 72 per cent and 87 per cent of the sample privatized firms and SOEs, respectively. The results for privatized firms contrast with Megginson et al. (1994) and Boubakri and Cosset (1998), but they are consistent with Ramamurti (1997) as well as LaPorta and López-de-Silanes (1999), who document a significant decrease in the level of employment.

To confirm whether such a significant decrease in the employment level is identical for subsamples, the results show that there is a significantly larger decline in the number of employees in SOEs compared to privatized firms. Again, these results would add further proof to the previous findings that the significant difference in performance change between privatized firms and SOEs in terms of SALEFF is – mainly – that SOEs cut the level of employment more than privatized firms do. However, it is quite interesting and unexpected to find that the SOEs' drop in level of employment is significantly greater than that of privatized firms. An explanation here is that there might be some waves of downsizing in SOEs preceding privatization, as an effort to restructure these firms before selling them. Further, the Egyptian government offers a generous early-retirement program to employees who take the opportunity to retire from the civil service and establish their own small businesses.

Leverage

A firm's capital structure might change significantly in response to moving from the public to private sector. After privatization, firms will no longer have the advantage of borrowing funds at a lower rate, but they will have the opportunity to access the equity markets, domestically and internationally (Bradley, Jarrell and Kim 1984). In light of that, the debt ratio is expected to decline following privatization. To test for this proposition, I measure changes in leverage by total debt to total assets (TDTA). For both privatized firms and SOEs, the results document a significant decline at the 10 per cent level for the first sample and at the 1 per cent level for the latter one.

I also find no significant difference in leverage changes between privatized firms and SOEs for the full sample as well as for subsamples. The results are understandable for privatized firms, but the question here is how to explain the significant decline in the leverage ratio for SOEs. One possibility is that the government would like to prepare its SOEs for sale to investors. Hence, improving some accounting measures, such as leverage, would make firms more attractive for investors and bring higher selling prices to the government.

For Further Investigation

At this stage, the results do not seem different from previous studies. Boardman and Vining (1989) find that mixed enterprises are no more profitable than SOEs, suggesting that full private control could be essential to achieving performance improvements. Conceivably, the insignificant change in performance between privatized firms and SOEs might be because the Egyptian government retains a stake in privatized firms, and total private ownership does not exist. On further analysis I found that 16 of the fully privatized firms experienced a 100 per cent transfer of ownership from the state to the private sector. I then followed the same methodology previously given to determine whether those firms (100 per cent privatized) perform significantly better than their control group (SOEs).

The results reported in Table 10.7 are similar to those reported in Table 10.5. They contradict those documented in the literature in which private firms perform significantly better than SOEs. However, the findings are consistent with Pinto et al. (1993), who argue that the significant improvement in privatized firms is due to a macroeconomic stabilization package, even without privatization, and Kole and Mulherin (1997), who find a similar performance for SOEs and private firms.

Since it seems that ownership structure does not matter, I shift the investigation to the impact of market structure, since the source of performance might be due to competition. It is then more appropriate to partition the sample into competitive and noncompetitive industries. Unfortunately, I was not able to accurately determine the degree of competitiveness across these different types of industries. However, I rely on Ott's (1991) illustrative guide to the competitive environment in which Egyptian industrial firms operate, given that most of the sample firms here are industrial in nature, as shown in Table 10.1b. The results (not reported here) tend to be similar to those shown in the previous analysis; i.e., there are no significant differences between privatized firms and their SOE counterparts in either competitive or noncompetitive industries. It is hard to believe that both ownership and market structure do not matter in determining the firm performance. However, it could be argued that Ott's picture regarding competition status in Egypt has changed over time. Indeed, prior to the economic reform program, privatization process and World Trade Organization membership requirements, SOEs enjoyed privileges not offered to the private sector. Nevertheless, with privatization, competition is enhanced and the private sector is allowed to participate in most economic activities.

Also, according to Boubakri and Cosset (1998) and D'Souza and Megginson (1999), noncompetitive firms are those operating in a regulated market and/or are relatively free of market products (such as firms in telecommunications, utilities and banking industries). All other firms operate in a competitive

Table 10.7 Comparison of Performance Changes Between 100% Privatized Firms and SOEs (Absolute and Relative Performance Change Methods)

		Absolute performance change method					Relative performance change method				
			Median					Median		
Categories	Proxies	Number of firms	100% privatization	SOEs	Av-Rank (P-value)	Number of firms	100% privatization	SOEs	Av-Rank (P-value)
Profitability	Earnings before interest and tax (EBIT)	12	0.96	0.84	12–11 (0.84)	12	0.26	−0.36	14–10 (0.25)
	Earnings before interest and tax to sales (ROS)	16	0.05	0.007	18–14 (0.19)	12	0.18	−0.12	14–11 (0.21)
	Earnings before interest and tax to assets (ROA)	16	0.04	0.02	19–14 (0.52)	12	0.14	−0.06	14–10 (0.25)
	Earnings before interest and tax to equity (ROE)	10	0.26	0.09	12–8 (0.36)	9	0.02	−0.23	11–8 (0.28)
Operating efficiency	Sales efficiency (SALEFF)	16	0.005	0.09	12–18 (0.26)	16	−0.06	−0.01	14–18 (0.64)
	Income efficiency 'before interest and tax' (INEFF)	12	1.47	1.27	13–12 (0.87)	12	0.29	−0.04	14–10 (0.24)
Output	Real sales (SAL)	16	0.025	0.16	18–14 (0.18)	16	−0.10	−0.09	15–17 (0.60)
Employment	Employment (EMPL)	16	−175	−600	20–12 (0.02)	16	−0.12	−0.19	19–13 (0.09)
Leverage	Total debt to total assets (TDTA)	16	−0.028	−0.033	17–15 (0.68)	14	−0.01	−0.06	15–13 (0.60)

357

environment. Looking at the sample firms, it is clear that none of them operates in a noncompetitive environment. Furthermore, to privatize noncompetitive firms, governments need to build and develop regulatory capabilities prior to privatization. In view of the lack of regulations, the time needed to build institutions and the regulatory authorities necessary for markets to function (especially in developing countries), competitive firms are usually the first ones to be privatized. If such propositions hold true, then the sample firms should operate in a relatively competitive environment. Consequently, it is not surprising that the performance change of privatized firms is similar to that of SOEs, since in competitive environments SOEs perform just as well as private firms. These results tend to be consistent with the findings of Caves and Christensen (1980), Hutchinson (1991) and Parker and Hartley (1991).

Furthermore, I also try to capture industry effects by comparing the performance changes of privatized firms with their SOE counterparts in the 12 different industries given in Table 10.1b. Although sample sizes are too small in many industries for significance tests, the results (not reported here) for larger samples document similar findings.

However, the results of this chapter should be treated with caution for several reasons. First, SOEs (the control group) are usually less profitable and less efficient than privatized firms, because better firms are usually privatized first. As a result, SOEs can improve profitability and efficiency more rapidly, so the deck might be stacked against privatized firms. Second, the power of the non-parametric test used is less than the power of the parametric one; thus, the findings of no significant difference in performance changes between privatized firms and SOEs could simply be due to the power of the test and/or the small sample size. Third, Egypt adopted a successful economic reform program in late 1990. Improved performance changes in privatized firms and SOEs might have resulted because credible reform can improve, to some extent, the performance of SOEs by narrowing the gap between private and public firms' performance. Finally, the evidence presented by this study could be attributed to the fact that the Egyptian government restructures its SOEs before selling them; consequently, these firms show the same performance changes as privatized firms. If this is the case, longer study periods could prove whether such improvement in SOEs would be sustainable and match the performance of privatized firms.

Alternatively, accepting the results at face value, the evidence of this study could mean that privatization improved the performance of privatized firms, which in turn, had important spillover effects on SOEs in terms of competition, demonstration and anticipation.

CONCLUSION

This study documented the critical performance changes of Egyptian firms which experienced full or partial privatization between 1994 and 1998. Because Egypt had adopted a program of economic reform by late 1991, structural breaks in the economic environment did indeed exist between the pre- and the post-privatization period. Rather then relying only on unadjusted accounting performance measures, this study goes further to match each sample firm (privatized) to a control firm (SOEs) with similar pre-privatization situations.

For privatized firms, it documents significant increases in profitability and operating efficiency and significant declines in leverage and employment, although no significant change in output is observed. For the same study period, SOEs show similar trends in most performance measures. To a lesser extent, there are significant increases in profitability, but largely, the results show significant increases in operating efficiency.

Most of these findings for privatized firms seem to be consistent with benchmark studies in terms of changes in profitability, operating efficiency and leverage. However, some other results tend to contradict some previous empirical findings, as significant decreases for employment and insignificant changes in output were uncovered. The study extends the analysis by matching privatized firms to control firms (SOEs) based on industry and size. The results show no significant differences in performance changes between privatized firms and SOEs in most accounting performance measures.

To gauge the robustness of the results, I classified privatized firms into two groups: fully privatized and partially privatized. The fully privatized firms are then divided into those with a nonzero government stake and those with a zero government stake. The results indicate that there is no difference in performance changes between fully privatized firms and their SOE control group, partially privatized firms and their matching group of SOEs and 100 per cent privatized firms and their matching SOEs for most accounting performance measures. Such consistency of results across subsamples illustrates that the performance changes of privatized firms are similar to SOEs, regardless of full or partial privatization.

The results also indicate that the sample firms tend to operate in a competitive environment, and thus it is not surprising that SOEs perform just as well as privatized firms. Such results support previous findings which suggest that both public and private ownership will yield similar performance under competitive environments.

The findings reported in this chapter have several policy implications. First, governments need to pay more attention toward building and developing regulatory capabilities prior to privatization in order for the market to function and to help privatized firms and SOEs perform efficiently. Second, policymakers should realize that changing ownership structure per se has no instant 'magical' effect on firm performance, but in time would yield greater rewards when competition replaces monopoly. Finally, should governments for any particular policy reason like to retain control over specific industries, they should nevertheless allow the private sector to compete with their SOEs, which would encourage these SOEs to shift their management style toward maximizing efficiency and profitability in order to survive. This will produce solid and rapid financial benefits for the economy as long as there are no economy-wide distortions which hinder competition.

Summing up, although a study over a longer period is needed before these results could be considered conclusive, the findings of this study should not prevent policymakers from considering privatization as a vehicle for economic development. Privatization as a policy could motivate private and public firms to better face future changes in the economic system. Thus there can be good reasons to privatize. In analyzing the reason for reform, this study illustrates the importance of careful comparison with a control group before any conclusions can be drawn. The approach points to a number of other dimensions which must be considered. Reformers might need to shift their focus from just ownership and consider the effects of market structure or the power of competition as well. This conclusion is in line with Sen's view that it is important to bear in mind the interdependencies created by a reform process.

NOTES

An earlier version of this chapter was published by *World Development* in 2004. See 'The Performance of State-Owned Enterprises and Newly Privatized Firms: Does Privatization Really Matter?', *World Development*, **323** (6), 1019–41.

1. In this chapter 'full privatization' means selling 51 per cent or more of an SOE's shares to the private sector, while 'partial privatization' refers to selling less than 50 per cent.
2. Since privatization took place as a response to Egypt's new economic climate (the country had adopted a program of economic reform by late 1991), comparing pre- versus post-privatization performance without considering changes in economic policies would generate misleading results.
3. The industry-matched method is based on all SOEs prior to privatization being grouped into 14 holding companies according to sector. In turn, each individual privatized firm is matched with a SOE from the same holding company.
4. As for the size-matching method, size is measured as the book value of total assets. For each privatized firm, I selected an SOE with total assets in the 70–130 per cent range, based on Barber and Lyon's (1996) argument that the 70–130 per cent size filter yields test statistics which are well specified. Each privatized firm is matched first to an SOE within the same industry and then with book value of total assets within 70–130 per cent of the privatized firm. However, over 85 per cent of firms are matched within the range of 90–115 per cent.
5. Later in the empirical analysis, I divide 'fully privatized' firms into two categories: those for

which the government retains a nonzero fraction of the firm (16 firms) and those which are 100 per cent privately owned firms – i.e., the government does not retain any nonzero fraction of the firm (22 firms).
6. For more details, see Hartley and Parker (1991).
7. Sales efficiency, net income efficiency and real sales are computed similarly.
8. I use nominal values of earnings before interest and tax; they are not adjusted for inflation or normalized as in the computation of the first ratio, EBIT.
9. I use another proxy for leverage – long-term debt to equity – and find a similar result. However, since equity figures in some firms are negative, meaning the number of valid observations will be less, I list the results of total debt to total assets instead. The results using long-term debt to equity are available from the author upon request.
10. I exclude year zero because it includes both the public and private ownership phases of privatized firms.
11. I also employ the parametric t test for the significant changes in mean, but since the test for normality is rejected for most variables, this would violate one of the important assumptions underlying the t-test. I report only the non-parametric results, given that Barber and Lyon (1996), among others, show that the non-parametric Wilcoxon test statistics are uniformly more powerful than parametric t-statistics when data are not normally distributed. Results from the parametric test are available from the author upon request, but they should be treated with caution.
12. As a check on the robustness of these methods, I employ two rigorous methods to further adjust the data and find similar results. Details about these methods are given in the Appendix. For the sake of space, I did not present the statistical tests and the findings from these methods, but they are available from the author upon request.
13. The same equation is applied to calculate the absolute performance change for SOEs by considering year zero for each SOE as the year of privatization of the sample matched privatized firm, so I have mean performance prior to the date of this year and mean performance after the date of the same year.
14. I also test for normality of subsamples, partially privatized SOEs, fully privatized SOEs, and 100 per cent privatized SOEs. Further, I document that data are not normally distributed.
15. As a check on the robustness of the Mann-Whitney test, I also utilize the Wilcoxon signed-rank test and find that results are qualitatively similar. I did not report the findings from the Wilcoxon signed-rank test here for the sake of space, but they are available from the author upon request.
16. Net income might be affected by several variables, for example, taking tax credits or carry forwards which do not relate to the current year's performance; selling some assets prior to privatization and then reporting capital gains in income statements, thus artificially reflecting an increase in net income; and effects of levels of debt in the post-privatization period. For these reasons, I calculated the profitability ratios using profit before interest, taxes and extraordinary items in order to reflect the operating income of the firm, instead of using net income. However, results using net income are found similar to results that use earnings before interest, tax and extraordinary items. I do not report the statistical results here for the sake of space, but they are available from the author upon request.
17. Results reported for the Mann-Whitney test are corrected for ties.
18. I use EBIT to refer to income for the reasons mentioned in note 16.

BIBLIOGRAPHY

Alchian, Armen Albert (1977), *Economic Forces at Work*, Indianapolis, IN: Liberty Press.

Barber, Brad and John D. Lyon (1996), 'Detecting Abnormal Operating Performance: The Empirical Power and Specification of Test Statistics', *Journal of Financial Economics*, **41** (3), 359–99.

Boardman, Anthony E. and Aidan R. Vining (1989), 'Ownership and Performance in Competitive Environments: A Comparison of the Performance of Private, Mixed and State-Owned Enterprises', *Journal of Law and Economics*, **32** (1), 1–33.

Boubakri, Narjess and Jean-Claude Cosset (1998), 'The Financial and Operating Performance of Newly Privatized Firms: Evidence from Developing Countries', *Journal of Finance*, **53** (3), 1081–110.

Boycko, Maxim, Andrei Shleifer and Robert W. Vishny (1996), 'A Theory of Privatization', *Economic Journal*, **106** (435), 309–19.

Bradley, Michael, Greg A. Jarrell and E. Han Kim (1984), 'On the Existence of Optimal Capital Structure: Theory and Evidence', *Journal of Finance*, **39** (3), 857–78.

Caves, Douglas W. and Laurits R. Christensen (1980), 'The Relative Efficiency of Public and Private Firms in a Competitive Environment: The Case of Canadian Railroads', *Journal of Political Economy*, **88** (5), 958–76.

de Castro, Julio O. and Klaus Uhlenbruck (1997), 'Characteristics of Privatization: Evidence from Developed, Less-Developed and Former Communist Countries', *Journal of International Business Studies*, **28** (1), 123–43.

Dewenter, Kathryn L. and Paul H. Malatesta (2001), 'State-Owned and Privately Owned Firms: An Empirical Analysis of Profitability, Leverage, and Labor Intensity', *American Economic Review*, **91** (1), 320–34.

D'Souza, Juliet and William Megginson (1999), 'The Financial and Operating Performance of Privatized Firms During the 1990s', *Journal of Finance*, **54** (4), 1397–438.

D'Souza, Juliet, William L. Megginson and Robert C. Nash (2004), 'Effect of Institutional and Firm-Specific Characteristics on Post-Privatization Performance: Evidence from Developed Countries' (17 November). Available at SSRN: http://ssrn.com/abstract=621762.

Egyptian Ministry of Public Enterprise Sector (2001), *Privatization Program Performance from the Start to February 2001*, Cairo: Ministry of Public Enterprise Sector.

Färe, Rolf, Shawna Grosskopf and James Logan (1985), 'The Relative Performance of Publicly Owned and Privately Owned Electric Utilities', *Journal of Public Economics*, **26** (1), 89–106.

Field, M. (1995), 'The Slow Road to Privatization', *Euromoney: Middle East, Markets Supplement*, 12–13 November .

Forsyth, Peter (1984), 'Airlines and Airports: Privatization, Competition and Regulation', *Fiscal Studies*, **5** (1), 61–75.

Hartley, Keith and David Parker (1991), 'Privatization: A Conceptual Framework', in Attiat Ott and Keith Hartley (eds), *Privatization and Economic Efficiency: A Comparative Analysis of Developed and Developing Countries*, Camberley, UK and Brookfield, VT: Edward Elgar, pp. 11–25.

Hutchinson, Gladstone (1991), 'Efficiency Gains through Privatization of UK Industries', in Attiat Ott and Keith Hartley (eds), *Privatization and Economic Efficiency: A Comparative Analysis of Developed and Developing Countries*, Camberley, UK and Brookfield, VT: Edward Elgar, pp. 87–101.

Kole, Stacey R. and J. Harold Mulherin (1997), 'The Government as a Shareholder: A Case from the United States', *Journal of Law and Economics*, **40** (1), 1–22.

LaPorta, Rafael and Florencio López-de-Silanes (1999), 'The Benefits of Privatization: Evidence from Mexico', *Quarterly Journal of Economics*, **114** (4), 1193–1242.

Majumdar, Sumit K. (1996), 'Assessing Comparative Efficiency of the State-Owned, Mixed, and Private Sector in Indian Industry', *Public Choice*, **96** (1–2), 1–24.

McKinney, Bridget M. (1996), 'Recent Development in Egyptian Investment Policies and Programs, and Pending Reform Legislation', *Middle East Executive Reports*, **19** (7), 9–12.

Megginson, William L., Robert C. Nash and Matthias van Randenborgh (1994), 'The Financial and Operating Performance of Newly Privatized Firms: An International Empirical Analysis', *Journal of Finance*, **49** (2), 403–52.

Megginson, William L. and Jeffrey Netter (2001), 'From State to Market: A Survey on Empirical Studies on Privatization', *Journal of Economics Literature*, **39** (2), 321–89.

Ott, Attiat (1991), 'Privatization in Egypt: Reassessing the Role and Size of the Public Sector', in Attiat Ott and Keith Hartley (eds), *Privatization and Economic Efficiency: A Comparative Analysis of Developed and Developing Countries*, Camberley, UK and Brookfield, VT: Edward Elgar, pp. 184–222.

Parker, David and Keith Hartley (1991), 'Status Change and Performance: Economic Policy and Evidence', in Attiat Ott and Keith Hartley (eds), *Privatization and Economic Efficiency: A Comparative Analysis of Developed and Developing Countries*, Camberley, UK and Brookfield, VT: Edward Elgar, pp. 108–25.

Pinto, Brian, Marek Belka and Stefan Krajewski (1993), 'Transforming State Enterprises in Poland: Evidence on Adjustment by Manufacturing Firms', *Brookings Papers on Economic Activity*, **1993** (1), 213–70.

Road, S. (1997), *Investing in Egypt*, London: Committee for Middle East Trade, June.

Ramamurti, Ravi (1997), 'Testing the Limits of Privatization: Argentine Railroads', *World Development*, 25 (12), 1973–93.

Stano, Miron (1975), 'Executive Ownership Interests and Corporate Performance', *Southern Economic Journal*, **42** (2), 272–78.

Tian, George Lihui (2000), 'State Shareholding and Corporate Performance: A Study of a Unique Chinese Data Set', Working Paper, London Business School.

Vickers, John and George Yarrow (1991), 'Economic Perspective on Privatization', *Journal of Economic Perspective*, **5** (2), 111–32.

Vining, Aidan R. and Anthony E. Boardman (1992), 'Ownership Versus Competition: Efficiency in Public Enterprise', *Public Choice*, **73** (2), 205–39.

N/A →

Index

Acea, C. 173
Acemoglu, D. 41, 151, 170
Ades, A. 36
Admassie, A. 196
Aghion, P. 36, 80, 82
Agmon, T. 129
agriculture
  technological change
    effect on child labor 187
  see also Ethiopia
Aguilar, C. 155, 160
Ahmed, A. 126
Ahmed, R. 309, 310
Ainsworth, M. 240
Aizenman, J. 40, 42, 43
Akabayashi, H. 188
Alchian, A. 341
Alesina, A. 41, 44
Alwang, J. 38, 39
Amin, S. 39
Amsden, A. 36
Antall, J. 6
Appleton, S. 239, 256
Arora, S. 79
Asian Development Bank 132, 145
Åslund, A. 272, 275
Atkins, J. 37
Atkinson, A. 8, 9

Bakht, Z. 311
Banco de Mexico 171
Banerjee, A. 36
Barber, B. 338
Barker, D. 80
Barreix, A. 118, 135
Barro, R. 148
Bedi, A. 188, 192, 232, 251

Beegle, K. 240
Belka, M. 342
Ben-David, D. 36
Bende-Nabende, A. 125, 126
Bertola, G. 41
Bhagwati, J. 35
Bhattacharya, A. 126
Binswanger, H. 310
Blanchard, O. 38
Block, S. 310
Blomström, M. 118, 154
Blumenthal, M. 151
Blyde, J. 173
Boardman, A. 340, 342, 356
Boisvert, R. 39
Bokros, L. 6
Bollinger, L. 240
Boone, P. 272, 275
Booth, D. 309
Borensztein, E. 152
Boubakri, N. 340, 341, 345, 353, 354, 355, 356
Bouillon, C. 85
Boycko, M. 354
Bracho, T. 89
Bradley, M. 355
Breton, P. 272
Brewer, T. 118
Bruno, M. 279
Bureau of Economic and Business Affairs (US) 132

Caballero, R. 41
Cabral, C. 151
Calvo, C. 39
Canagarajah, R. 39
Cartwright, K. 188

365

Case, A. 78, 81
Castelar, A. 151
Caves, D. 358
Caves, R. 118, 135
Cervellati, M. 79
Chakrabarti, A. 129, 134
Chaudhuri, S. 39
Chen, Z. 124, 126
child labor 219
   definition of 185
   education, effects on
      complete market for child labor 190–92
      constrained market for child labor 192–3
      educational outcomes and work status 188–9
      schooling-related policies' effects on incidence of child labor 187–8
   technological change 187
   see also Ethiopia
Christensen, L. 358
Christiaensen, L. 39
Ciolko, M. 291
Cirera, X. 36
Contractor, F. 118
control groups
   evaluation of impact of reform programs 332, 360
   see also Egypt; rural roads rehabilitation and maintenance
Coricelli, F. 11
Corral, L. 327
Cosset, J.-C. 340, 341, 345, 353, 354, 355, 356
Coury, T. 36
Cowell, F. 28
Cristini, M. 151
Cuánto, I. 312

Daude, C. 155, 160
de Castro, J. 340
De Ferranti, D. 44, 50, 104
De Gregorio, J. 152
de Janvry, A. 327

De Melo, M. 272, 275
Deaton, A. 243
Dehn, J. 59
Delgado, C. 36
Denizer, C. 272, 275
Deolalikar, A. 238
Dercon, S. 38, 39, 40, 41
Dethier, J.-J. 6
Dewenter, K. 342
Di Tella, R. 36
Djankov, S. 136
Dollar, D. 35, 44
Donovan, C. 309
D'Souza, J. 340, 341, 345, 353, 356
Dunning, J. 122, 123

early child development
   crucial component of human capital formation 81, 84
   ECD programs 81
   effect on education 77, 78, 97, 104, 105
   intergenerational transmission of poverty 81
   investment in 97, 98
   links to adult ailments 80–81
   stature 81, 92
   see also Mexico
Easterly, W. 37, 40, 41, 279
EBRD 272, 274, 291, 305
economic growth
   pro-market reforms
      need also for policies to overcome market failures 80
economic transition *see* transition economies
education
   benefits of investments in 229
   impact of nutrition and health 79, 81, 84
   link with stature 93, 94, 95, 96, 97
   see also child labor; early child development; Ethiopia; Kenya; Mexico
Egypt
   comparison of privatized firms with

SOEs 358, 359
100 per cent transfer of ownership 356, 357, 359
anticipation effects 358
competition effects 358
competitive and non-competitive industries 356, 358, 359
data 342–3
demonstration effects 358
employment 346, 347, 348, 349, 350, 351, 352, 354–5, 357
fully privatized firms 351, 359
industry sectors 358
leverage 346, 347, 348, 349, 350, 351, 352, 355, 357
methodology 338, 340, 342, 343, 344, 345, 359
operating efficiency 346, 347, 348, 349, 350, 351, 352, 353–4, 355, 357
output 346, 347, 348, 349, 350, 351, 352, 354, 357
partially privatized firms 352, 359
profitability 345, 346, 347, 348, 349, 350, 351, 352, 353, 357
privatization program 337, 338
privatized firms
 industry sectors 339
 method of sale 337, 339
 numbers of 339
Egyptian Ministry of Public Enterprise Sector 339
ENIGH 86, 98, 101, 102, 103
ENSA 86, 90, 91, 93, 98, 99
Esquivel, G. 171
Ethiopia
 agricultural extension program 186, 212–13, 220–21
 agriculture sector 196
 child labor laws 196
 market for child labor 194
 market-oriented reforms 186
 reading and writing ability of children 199, 202, 203, 220
  need for range of policies to improve educational outcomes 221, 222
  relationship with hours of work 206, 213–16, 221
 school participation 199, 202, 220
  factors determining 202, 203, 208–10, 220
  need for range of policies 220
  relationship with hours of work 203, 204, 205, 206, 213–16, 221
  relationship with types of work 204, 205, 206, 216–19, 221
  relationship with work participation 203, 204, 205, 221
 structural-adjustment program 186
 study of schooling and child labor
  data 195–6
  descriptive statistics 207
  empirical approach 194–5
 work activities of children 196, 197
  factors determining hours worked 210–12, 220
  participation rates 197, 198, 199, 220
  technological change effects 208, 211, 212–13, 220–21
  types of work 197, 199, 200–202, 220
  weekly hours 197, 198, 199, 220
European Bank for Reconstruction and Development (EBRD) 272, 274, 291, 305
Evenson, R. 187

Färe, R. 341
FDI *see* foreign direct investment
Fernandez, R. 101
Fertig, A. 78, 81
Field, M. 337
Fischer, S. 272
Flemming, J. 11
Fogel, R. 78, 79, 80
Forbes, K. 37
foreign direct investment (FDI)
 advantages of inflows 152
 Asia

Asian economic crisis 119
distribution of FDI amongst
    countries 119, 120, 121
FDI from developed and developing
    countries 121–2
share of global FDI flows 119
determinants of 122–3, 152, 153,
    172–3
developed and developing
    countries, from, 117, 136, 137,
    138, 139
market-related determinants 118
model of 123–4, 133–44, 145, 146
emergence of 122
emerging countries 148, 150
global FDI flows
    growth of 148, 149
    share of Asian countries 119
    share of developed and developing
        countries 119, 120
    share of FDI in total investment
        flows 148, 149
international policies 123, 132, 137–8,
    139
    ASEAN Investment Area (AIA)
        133, 135, 137
    non-binding investment principles
        (NBIP) (APEC) 132–3, 135
Mexico 170, 171
    dispute settlement in international
        panels 172, 183–4
    effect of NAFTA 170, 171
national FDI policies 118, 123, 128–9,
    133, 134, 139
    fiscal and financial incentives
        130–31, 135
    removal of restrictions 131–2, 135,
        136, 139
    tariff policies and openness to trade
        129–30, 134, 135
overall economic policies 123, 124,
    126, 127, 133, 134
    availability of skilled labor 124,
        126, 133, 134
    cost of capital 124–5, 126, 133, 134
    cost of labor 124, 126, 133, 134

economic stability 127, 128, 133,
    134
exchange rates 125, 126, 127, 133,
    134
inflation rate 127, 128, 133, 134
infrastructure costs and availability
    125, 126, 133, 134
market potential 124, 126, 126, 133,
    134
market size 124, 133, 134
privatization 119
range of policies needed to attract FDI
    139
see also property rights protection
Förster, M. 5
Forsyth, P. 341
Frankel, J. 36
free trade agreements 153
effect on foreign direct investment
    154, 155
see also property rights protection
Freire, W. 86, 92
Frey, B. 126, 127, 128
Friedman, E. 136
Froot, K. 127

Gable, J. 41
Galbi, D. 187
Galor, O. 82, 83
Gannon, C. 310
Gavian, S. 36
Gavin, M. 41
Gelb, A. 272, 275
Glewwe, P. 39, 40, 86, 92, 93, 94
Glick, R. 37
Globerman, S. 128
Godoy, S. 291
Goldberg, L. 126
Gorbachev, M. 278
gradual reform *see* shock therapy versus
    gradual pace of reform
Grootaert, C. 187, 188
Gros, D. 272
Grosskopf, S. 341
Grubert, H. 118
Guisinger, S. 118, 128

Guner, N. 101

Hall, G. 39, 40
Hanmer, L. 309
Hart, O. 136, 153
Hartley, K. 340, 341, 358
Hausmann, R. 41
Hazarika, G. 188, 192
Heady, C. 189
health
   HIV / AIDS
      school enrolment in Kenya 239–42
   impact of nutrition and health
      on education 79, 81, 84
      long-term income and economic
         growth 77, 78, 79, 80
   stature
      as health indicator 81, 92
      link to education 93, 94, 95, 96, 97
   see also early child development;
      human development; Mexico
Heckman, J. 308, 314, 315, 319
Heitzmann, K. 39
Hellman, J. 155
Helpman, E. 152
Hertel, T. 36
Heybey, B. 275
Hines, J. 118
Hnatkovska, V. 41, 42, 44
Hoddinott, J. 39, 43
Hoekman, B. 118
Hölscher, J. 11
Holzman, F. 38
Holzmann, R. 39, 40
Hossain, M. 310
Howitt, P. 80, 82
human development
   emergence from poverty 78
   intergenerational cycle of investment
      in nutrition, health and education
      79–80
   market failures 84, 105
   pro-market reforms 80, 85
   technophysio evolution 79
   see also early child development;
      education; health; Mexico

Hungary
   austerity package 6, 10
   economic growth 6
   economic transition 3, 4
   employment rates 7
   income distribution 8, 22–3, 30–34
      age and education combined effects
         18, 19, 20, 21, 22
      age of household head 15, 17, 19,
         31, 32, 34
      between-group inequalities 12, 16,
         17, 18, 19, 20, 32, 33, 34
      changes driven by relative position
         of those at extreme income
         deciles 7, 8, 9
      communist system, effect of 7
      economic liberalisation 7
      education of household head 15, 16,
         18, 19, 30, 32, 33
      employment composition of
         households 15, 16, 18, 19, 22,
         30, 32, 33
      ethnicity 15, 18, 31, 32, 34
      family size 15, 18, 19, 31, 32, 34
      gender of household head 15, 17,
         31, 32, 34
      personal distribution of equivalent
         incomes 12, 13
      range of policies, need to consider
         23
      reach of reforms, importance of 23
      relative decline in position of the
         poorest 11
      settlement types 13, 14, 15, 17, 18,
         19, 30, 32, 33
      shares of selected income deciles 8,
         9
      structural dimensions 13, 15–19,
         20, 33, 34
      study data and methods 4–6, 27–9
      technological development and skill
         upgrades 22
      trends in income inequality 7, 9, 10,
         11, 12, 22
      within-group inequalities 12, 13,
         14, 16, 17, 18, 20, 30, 31, 32,

33, 34
post-transition regime 4
radical economic strategies and gradual social policy reforms 6
recession 6
social policies 6, 7
socialist regime 4
see also trade liberalization; transition economies
Hutchinson, G. 354, 358
Hymer, S. 122, 152

Ichimura, H. 308, 314, 315, 319
ILO 145
IMF 145, 149
income distribution
　Mexico 85
　see also Hungary
International Labour Office (ILO) 145
International Monetary Fund (IMF) 145, 149
Islam, R. 41

Jacoby, H. 86, 92, 93, 94, 329
Jalan, J. 39, 309, 326
Jarrell, G. 355
Jenkins, S. 28, 29
Johnson, S. 151, 170, 272, 275
Jørgensen, S. 38, 39, 40
Judson, R. 41, 44

Kenya
　benefits of attending school 232–3
　costs of attending school
　　direct costs 232
　　opportunity costs 232
　education reforms
　　careful thought and continuous review 230, 263
　education system 233
　　problems of 229
　free primary education for every child 263
　public expenditure on education 229
　school completion rates 235, 237
　school enrollment 229–30, 233–4, 236, 242, 261, 262
　analytical model 230–33
　capacity of primary school system 238, 242
　child characteristics 250, 252, 253, 254, 258
　costs 234–5, 238, 242, 249, 250, 251, 252, 253, 255, 257, 258, 259, 261, 263
　cross-section estimates 254–6, 263
　curriculum changes 235, 242, 261
　data for study of 244–5
　descriptive statistics for study of 248, 249
　estimation approach for study of 242–4
　'ever attended school' variable 245, 246, 247
　expenditure quintiles 245, 246, 247, 248, 262, 263
　family characteristics 250–51, 252, 253, 255, 258
　gender gap 233, 234, 236, 245
　geographical spread 251
　gross enrolment rate 245, 246, 250
　HIV / AIDS 239–42
　labour market conditions 238–9, 242
　net enrolment rate 245, 246
　pooled and pseudo-panel data estimates 254, 257–9, 263
　private schools, availability and use of 262
　regional distribution 234, 236
　school costs and inputs' elasticities by expenditure quintiles 259–61, 262, 263
　school test scores 242, 251, 252, 253, 255, 256, 258, 259, 260, 261
　student–teacher ratios 251, 252, 253, 256, 258, 259, 260, 261, 263
　teachers' skill levels 238, 242, 249–50, 251, 252, 253, 256,

257, 258, 259, 260, 261, 262, 263
school test scores 235, 237
student–teacher ratios 237, 238
teachers' skill levels 237, 238
years of schooling 233
Kenya, Government of / UNICEF 238
Kertesi, G. 19
Kézdi, G. 18
Khan, M. 124, 126
Khandker, S. 310
Kim, E. 355
Kimalu, P. 229, 233
King, E. 92, 93
Klein, M. 126, 155
Knowles, J. 101
Koda, G. 240
Kokko, A. 154
Kole, S. 342, 356
Köllő, J. 18, 19
Kornai, J. 3, 6, 277
Kose, M. 37, 41, 42, 50
Kraay, A. 35, 40, 44
Krajewski, S. 342
Krishnan, P. 39
Krueger, A. 36
Krueger, G. 291
Kumar, N. 118, 128

La Porta, R. 151, 170, 342, 355
Lahiri, A. 36
Lall, S. 36
Lalonde, R. 314
Larrea, C. 86, 92
Lee, J.-W. 152
legal institutions *see* property rights protection
Legovini, A. 85
Levinger, B. 81
Levy, H. 311
Levy, V. 187
Levy-Yeyati, E. 155, 160
Ligon, E. 39, 44
Lindert, K. 39
Lipton, M. 309
Liu, Z. 310

Lizondo, J. 152
Loayza, N. 41, 42, 44
Logan, J. 341
López-de-Silanes, F. 342, 355
Loree, D. 118, 128
Love, J. 136
Lovell, E. 309
Lubotsky, D. 78, 81
Lundberg, M. 40, 42
Lustig, N. 40, 42, 85
Lutter, C. 86, 92
Lyon, J. 338

Maddison, A. 80
Majumdar, S. 342
Malatesta, P. 342
Marshall, J. 232, 251
Martin, P. 41
Mayer-Foulkes, D. 80, 82, 89, 90
Mazzi, S. 37
Mbekeani, K. 124
McCulloch, N. 36
McKinney, B. 337
Megginson, W. 340, 341, 343, 345, 353, 354, 355, 356
Mellor, J. 36
Mendoza, E. 36
Meng, Q. 36
Mexico
    barriers to education 104, 106
    early child development 84, 106
    education and health study
        adolescent schooling decisions 90–97
        data 86
        distribution of schooling 98–105, 106
        methodology 86–7
        returns to education and health in adult income 87–90
    failures in health and education investment 98, 105, 106
    foreign direct investment 170, 171
        dispute settlement in international panels 172, 183–4
        effect of NAFTA 170, 171

human capital development 84
poverty trap 77, 78, 84
  human capital accumulation 105
  prolonged transition 82
  study of 83–4
  pro-market reforms 85
    income inequality 85
    increased returns to education 85
    reach and range of reforms 78, 106, 107
Micklewright, J. 8, 9, 11
Milanovic, B. 11, 36
Montalbano, P. 39
Mookherjee, D. 28
Moya, R. 151
Mulherin, J. 342, 356
Mundell, R. 38, 129
Murrell, P. 275
Mutti, J. 118

NAFTA 170
  dispute resolution 171
  effect of FDI in Mexico 170, 171
Nash, R. 340, 341
Naughton, B. 283
Nenova, T. 136
Netter, J. 341
Nganda, B. 263
North, D. 148
Nunnenkamp, P. 118

OECD 155, 171
Olivei, G. 155
Organisation for Economic Cooperation and Development (OECD) 155, 171
Orphanides, A. 41, 44
Ott, A. 356

Pallage, S. 41
Parker, D. 340, 341, 358
Patrinos, H. 87, 188, 213
Paxson, C. 78, 81
Perry, G. 44, 50
Peru
  rural roads *see* rural roads rehabilitation and maintenance

Pietrobelli, C. 36
Piketty, T. 36
Pinto, B. 40, 42, 43, 342, 356
Polterovich, V. 289, 299
Popov, V. 275, 283, 289, 291, 299, 305
poverty trap
  concept of 81–2
  data difficulties 82–3
  dynamic poverty trap 82
  human development 78
  prolonged transition 82
  see also Mexico
Powell, A. 151
Prasad, E. 37, 41, 42
Pritchett, L. 39, 80
privatization 337
  allowing private companies to compete with retained SOEs 360
  anticipation effects 340
  competition and ownership structure 360
  competition effects 340
  demonstration effects 340
  determinant of FDI 119
  interdependencies, need to consider 360
  motives 337, 360
  performance of firms 340, 341, 342
    comparison with SOEs 341, 342
    competitive industries 340, 341
    non-competitive industries 340–41
  regulatory capabilities 359–60
  speed of
    impact on performance 291
  see also Egypt
propensity score matching techniques 308
  see also rural roads rehabilitation and maintenance
property rights protection
  foreign direct investment
    dependent on level of protection 153, 173
  free trade agreements
    arbitration panels 154, 181, 182
    improvement of domestic

institutions 154, 155, 173
impact of free trade agreements on FDI 147, 148, 172, 173
   empirical analysis and data 155–60, 177, 178–80, 181–2
   illustration of range of reforms 173
   results of analysis 160–67, 167–70
   importance of 148, 151
   institutional quality of emerging countries 148, 150
   licensing, effect on 173
   Mexico
      dispute settlement in international panels 172, 183–4
      effects of NAFTA 170, 171
Psacharopoulos, G. 188, 213

Quah, D. 80
Quisumbing, A. 39, 43

Rai, A. 39
Ramamurti, R. 355
Ramey, G. 41
Ramey, V. 41
Randenborgh, M. van 341
range
   definition of 147
   interdependencies 117, 186
   pro-market reforms 80
   rural roads rehabilitation and maintenance 333
   see also Ethiopia; foreign direct investment; Hungary; Mexico; property rights protection
Ravallion, M. 188, 309, 326
Ravelli, A. 80
Razin, A. 36
reach 35
   economic growth policies 80
   economic reach 3
   identification of contributors and beneficiaries 3–4
   political reach 3
   social reach 3
   see also Hungary; Mexico; socioeconomic vulnerability

analysis; trade liberalization
Reardon, T. 327
reason
   continual assessment of reforms 297, 307, 308, 332
   control groups 332, 360
   interdependencies, need to consider 360
   motive for reform 337
   need to verify the potential effects of proposed policies 222
   see also Egypt; Kenya; rural roads rehabilitation and maintenance; shock therapy versus gradual pace of reform; transition economies
Rivers, D. 194, 195
Road, S. 337
Robe, M. 41
Robinson, J. 151, 170
Rodriguez, F. 35
Rodrik, D. 35, 36, 41, 44
Rogers, C. 41
Rolfe, R. 126
Root, F. 126
Rose, A. 37
Rosenbaum, P. 308, 314, 315
Rosenzweig, M. 187, 310
Roubini, N. 41, 44
Rubin, D. 308, 314, 315
Rugman, A. 122
rural roads rehabilitation and maintenance
   motorized roads 307
   non-motorized roads 307
   permanence of road maintenance 331, 332, 333
   propensity score matching techniques 308, 309, 314, 315, 316, 318, 319, 320, 321, 326
   range of policies and programs 333
   research requirements
      longer-term analysis 333
   road network 307, 308
   town's probability of having road rehabilitated 321, 324

welfare effects 308, 310, 332, 333
  comparability between control and treated groups 320, 321, 322, 323
  consumption 329, 330, 331, 332
  controls over welfare indicators 321, 325
  counterfactual scenarios 310–11
  data and methodology 311–20
  economic growth and poverty reduction 309, 310
  income 325–9, 332, 333
  motorized roads 330, 331, 332–3
  non-motorized roads 330, 332, 333
  savings 329, 330, 331, 332

Sachs, J. 272
Sadka, E. 36
Sadoulet, E. 327
Saggi, K. 118
Sahay, R. 272
Sala-i-Martin, X. 148
Salazar, M. 187
Sarkar, R. 151
Savedoff, W. 87, 89, 92
Schechter, L. 39, 44
Schneider, F. 126, 127, 128
Schultz, T. 87, 89, 92
Schürch, B. 80, 92
Scott, J. 85, 105
Scrimshaw, N. 80, 92
Scully, G. 148
Sen, A. 3, 35, 37, 77, 79, 117, 147, 173, 186, 221, 230, 263, 270, 297, 307, 308, 332, 337
Servén, L. 41
Shapiro, D. 128
Shleifer, A. 354
Shmelev, N. 275
shock therapy versus gradual pace of reform 303–5
  China and Vietnam 271, 274
  Hungary
    radical economic strategies and gradual social policy reforms 6
  see also transition economies

Shorrocks, A. 28
Sianesi, B. 320
Siegel, P. 38, 39
Smith, J. 314
social inequalities
  determinants of 4–5
  see also income distribution
socioeconomic vulnerability analysis 37, 38, 39
  definition of vulnerability 38
  macro approach 39–41
    limits of 41–2
  micro approach 39
  reach of reforms 38, 66
  see also trade liberalization; volatility
speed of reform *see* shock therapy versus gradual pace of reform
Squire, L. 40, 42
Srinivasan, T. 35
Stabridis-Arana, O. 89, 90
Stano, M. 341
stature
  as health indicator 81, 92
  link to education 93, 94, 95, 96, 97
Steckel, R. 80, 86
Stein, E. 155, 160
Stein, J. 127
Stiglitz, J. 41, 291
Stover, J. 240
Sumarto, S. 39
Sunde, U. 79
Suryahadi, A. 39
Svejnar, J. 38, 53
Swagel, P. 41, 44

Talvi, E. 41
Taylor, C. 118
technological change
  effect on child labor 187
    Ethiopia 208, 211, 212–13, 220–21
  effect on income distribution
    Hungary 22
technophysio evolution 79
Tenev, S. 275
Terrones, M. 42
Tesliuc, E. 39

Thomas, R. 148
Thomas, T. 39, 44
Tian, G. 342
Timmer, C. 36
Tinbergen, J. 153
Todd, P. 308, 314, 315, 319
Topa, G. 39
Tornell, A. 171
Tóth, I. 5, 19
trade liberalization
  benefits of 35
  CEECs
    EU trade policy 45
    level of trade openness 45, 46–7
    volatility of per capita consumption 45, 50, 51, 52, 53, 54, 55, 56, 57
    volatility of per capita GDP 45, 50, 52, 53
    volatility of terms-of-trade 45, 48–9
    volatility of trade openness 45, 47
  effects of shocks 37
  instability 36
  international crises 37
  socioeconomic vulnerability 36, 37, 53, 56, 58–9, 66
    CEECs after EU accession 62, 63, 64, 65
    international policy coordination 65
    methodology for assessment of 42–5
    policies to mitigate the impact of shocks 66
    reach of policy reforms 65–6
    volatility effects 50–52, 53, 54, 55, 56, 57, 58, 59, 60–61, 62, 65, 66
  terms-of-trade volatility 36
  see also socioeconomic vulnerability analysis; transition economies; volatility
transition economies
  decline in output, living standards and life expectancy 270, 271
  domestic price ratios 305
  economic growth in China and Vietnam 271
  similar results with shock therapy and gradualism 274
  institutional quality
    impact of 297, 298, 299
  liberalization
    as a function of performance 291
  macroeconomic stability
    impact of policies on economy 272, 275
  membership in the ruble zone
    explanatory variable 275, 279, 280
  output change
    Asia 274
    Europe 273
  post-recession recovery
    cumulative levels of liberalization 287, 289, 292–3, 294, 295, 297, 299
    institutional capacity 288, 289, 291, 294, 297, 299
    post-war reconstruction 288, 294, 297
  shock therapy versus gradual pace of reform
    theories on impact of 271–2, 276, 278, 296, 299, 305
  transformational recession
    distortions in industrial structure and trade patterns 275, 276, 277, 278, 279–81, 286, 290, 297, 299
    institutional capabilities 272, 276, 277, 278, 281–7, 288, 289, 290, 299
    liberalization 274, 275, 288, 289, 291, 295, 299
    poor economic policies 276, 278
  war economies
    explanatory variable 275, 279, 280, 290
  see also Hungary; trade liberalization
Trevino, L. 125, 126, 127

Uhlenbruck, K. 340

UNCTAD 118, 119, 120, 121, 124, 130, 145
UNESCO 145, 251
United Nations 132, 145

Vallejo, H. 155, 160
Van Der Gaag, J. 81, 97
Vandille, G. 272
Vegh, C. 41, 272
Velasco, A. 36
Vickers, J. 340
Villela, L. 118, 135
Vining, A. 340, 342, 356
Vishny, R. 354
volatility
  determinants of 41, 73–5
  effects of 40–41
  measurement 42–3
  see also trade liberalization
Vuong, Q. 194, 195

Wade, R. 36

Webb, P. 310
Wimmer, L. 79
Winters, L. 36, 37
Wodon, Q. 188
Wolf, H. 41, 44, 50
Woodward, D. 126
World Bank 40, 46, 48, 50, 51, 81, 145, 149, 234, 272, 274, 282
World Investment Directory 122
World Trade Organization (WTO) 130, 137
Worth, T. 137
WTO 130, 137

Yarrow, G. 340
Yeltsin, B. 278
Yi, K.-M. 41, 50

Zakaria, F. 285
Zamudio, A. 89
Zeira, J. 82, 83